Mapping COVID-19

Mapping COVID-19: A Multidisciplinary Approach

Edited by

Tejinder Kaur Dhaliwal
Bali Bahadur

GYAN

Published, 2021

Published by

Gyan Publishing House
5, Ansari Road
Daryaganj, New Delhi-110002
Phone: 011-47034999, 9811692060
www.gyanbooks.com
E-mail: books@gyanbooks.com

Printed at: Gyan Press, Delhi.

Cataloging in Publication Data—DK
Courtesy: D.K. Agencies (P) Ltd. <docinfo@dkagencies.com>

Mapping COVID-19 : a multidisciplinary approach / edited by Tejinder Kaur Dhaliwal, Bali Bahadur.
pages cm
Contributed articles.
ISBN 9788121220460

1. COVID-19 Pandemic, 2020- —India. 2. COVID-19 Pandemic, 2020- 3. COVID-19 Pandemic, 2020- —Social aspects—India. 4. COVID-19 Pandemic, 2020- —Economic aspects—India. I. Dhaliwal, Tejinder Kaur (College principal), editor. II. Bahadur, Bali, 1981- editor.

LCC RA644.C67M37 2021 | DDC 362.196241400954 23

Dedicated

To

Corona Warriors of Our Society

Contents

Economic Effects COVID-19

Migrant Workers and COVID-19 Pandemic

Role of Political Institutions & Media during COVID-19 Pandemics

Environment and Ecological Impact of COVID-19

Acknowledgements

It is really difficult to express a deep sense of gratitude adequately by just using words. However we wish to express our sincere gratitude to Bibi Jagir Kaur ji honourable President of Shiromani Gurdwara Parbandhak Committee, Sri Amritsar and S. Harjinder Singh Dhami honourable Chief Secretary, SGPC Amritsar and Sr. Manjit Singh Barkandi, Additional Secretary, Local Managing Committee (LMC) of Guru Nanak College, Sri Muktsar Sahib for their blessings, valuable guidance and constant encouragement.

We are very thankful to Prof. Paramjit Singh Judge, President Indian Sociological Society, for his encouragement and intellectual inputs during different stages of compilation of this volume.

We are also very thankful to Prof. Kuldip Chand Agnihotri, Vice-Chancellor, Central University of Himachal Pradesh, Dharamshala for his valuable guidance and writing forewords of this book.

We value the contribution of all the people who have taken out time to become part of the project by providing us with informative articles on the important subject of COVID-19 pandemics.

We owe special thanks to our family members for their support during the busy hours of work. Lastly, we are well aware of the fact that this book would not have this decent look without the efforts of Gyan Publishing House for that our thanks go out to them as well.

Tejinder Kaur Dhaliwal &
Bali Bahadur

Foreword

The Corona epidemic has affected many aspects of human life. A world-wide epidemic of such magnitude has been beheld after a long interval of time. Encouraged by the pace at which many mysteries of nature were being discovered by humans for the last few decades, many people started clamouring about how humans have successfully conquered nature. However, numerous other scholars have cogently emphasised that the welfare of man is possible only by keeping pace with nature and not by waging war against it. In the medieval north-western India, sprouted the spiritual lineage of "*Dash Guru Prampra*" (दशगुरुपरम्परा) and all of them beginning with first Guru Shri Nanak Devji to the tenth Guru Shri Guru Gobind Singhji, reinforced the significance of maintaining harmony with nature through their teachings. In the modern times, Mahatma Gandhi recommended maneuvering of nature only to the extent of fulfilling the essential needs of all. Indian culture is attributed with the quality of being an environment-oriented culture.

Nevertheless, industrialisation and urbanisation have vastly and significantlystruck nature. Also, man under the sway of his animal instincts has widely tried to modify the internal framework of nature. It is also being said that the birth of a virus named Corona is the result of this tampering with nature. In the olden times, when there was no widespread and quick network of transport, an epidemic of any kind would remain confined only around the area of its origin.The resistance of human body might also have been high during those times and therefore the human body could fight and kill the deadly virus. But the changing lifestyles around the world have reduced man's God-given immunity and the advancement in the means of movement and travel has given wings to the rapidity of such epidemics. It is due to this reason that the entire world came under the grip of this micro virus and it took away the lives of millions of people.

Consequently, studies were initiated to analyse the effects of this virus in various fields of life and the changes that could occur due to its impact. Experts in the field of medicine and science are investigating the impact and damage caused by this virus and also trying to find ways to eradicate it, but it needs to be mentioned here that many scholars have already started studying its repercussions in social and cultural realms and have also presented the findings of their research.

The ***Mapping COVID-19: Multi-disciplinary Approach*** is one such work, which accomplishes the academic investigation of the effects and outcomes of Covid-19 on various fields of human concern. This book is an anthology of about three dozen scholarly research papers. It discusses various important themes like the past history of epidemics, the consequences and impact of the Corona virus around the world including the changes caused due to it. It simultaneously analyses its implications on the human rights of people during this period. The book manifests a detailed study of the impact of this epidemic in the fields of health, education and economics. It also describes how the epidemic has affected the lives of Indians living overseas. It conclusively studies the influence of this epidemic on the media and the prevailing political institutions. This research work would be a remarkable accomplishment, dealing with the influence of this epidemic on various turfs of human apprehension in one single volume. It is immensely remarkable to note that the research scientists who have contributed for this work are young and have innovatively examined exclusive case studies making it absolutely authentic.

This volume has been edited by Dr Tejinder Kaur Dhaliwal, the Principal of Guru Nanak Dev College in Muktsar, Punjab. Dr Bali Bahadur, who is the Head of the Sociology Department in the same college, has ably assisted her in this initiative. Each of them can be lauded for their efforts in bringing out this scholarly output. Dr Tejinder Kaur Dhaliwal is basically a science student, but she has long and momentous experience in educational management. She has been the Chairperson of the Punjab School Education Board and I have had the honour to serve as the Vice Chairman at the same time. So I am personally familiar with her scholarship, her interest in exploring knowledge and research. Her proficiency in administration is self-evident. The Guru Nanak Dev College of Muktsar with its high academic standards and significant developmental achievements is a testimony of her stature and calibre. But it is generally found that a person who ventures into administrative activities often distances himself from his subject of academic study and inclination. I would like to congratulate Dr Dhaliwal because she is not only active in the field of academics and research but she has always qualitatively excelled in it.

Dr Bali Bahadur is a resident of my native region; he completed his graduation from my village Mukundpur. In the field of sociology, there has been a constant need for such social scientists, who do not glorify the half-baked theories of western thinkers about the Indian social system but rather present authentic theories and conclusions based on case studies. Dr Bhim Rao Ambedkar expressed this desire indirectly while presenting his research paper on India's caste system at Columbia University many years ago. Looking at the research work of Dr. Bali Bahadur, I am hopeful that such young social scientists would be able to study the Indian society more authentically. I think that the social scientists today should also consider the causes of different mind-sets and reactions prevalent in the Sapt Sindhu region with reference to the challenges created by the Corona epidemic. The epidemic will be over, but the sociologists will continue to study its effects for a long time. This voluminous work will then definitely cater as a great work of reference.

Prof. Kuldip Chand Agnihotri
Vice-Chancellor,
Central University of Himachal Pradesh,
Dharamshala, HP

List of Contributors

Aarti Sharma: Assistant Professor & Head, Department of Biotechnology, Guru Nanak College Sri Muktsar Sahib. (Pb)

Akwinder Kaur Aulakh: Research Scholar, Department of Sociology, Panjab University, Chandigarh

Amandeep Singh: Assistant Professor, Department of Mechanical Engineering. Baba Banda Singh Bahadur Engineering College, Fatehgarh Sahib, Punjab, India

Amanpreet Kaur: Assistant Professor in Computer Science, Department of Computer Science and Applications, Guru Nanak College, Sri Muktsar Sahib, Punjab

Harpreet Kaur: Assistant Professor, Department of Computer Science and Engineering, Punjabi University, Patiala, India

Harpreet Kaur: Assistant Professor in Botany Department of Basic Sciences, Guru Nanak College, Sri Muktsar Sahib (Punjab)

Harveen Kaur: Assistant Professor, P.G. Department of Computer Science, G S S D G S Khalsa College, Patiala, India

Jagmeet Kaur: Assistant Professor & Head, P.G. Department of Commerce, Guru Nanak College, Sri Muktsar Sahib, Punjab

Jagsir Singh: Assistant Professsor & Head Department of Sociology, Bebe Nanki Guru Nanak Dev University College, Mithra Kapurthala, Punjab, India

Jaspal Kaur: Assistant Professor, Departments of Laws, Guru Nanak Dev University Regional Campus, Jalandhar, Punjab

Meenu Sharma: Research Scholar, Department of Sociology, Panjab University, Chandigarh, India

Monika Garg: Assistant Professor & Head Department of Business Administration, Guru Nanak College, Sri Muktsar Sahib, Punjab

Navjot Kaur: Assistant Professor of English, Guru Nanak Prem Karamsar College, Nadala, Kapurthala, Punjab

Navneet Kaur: Assistant Professor in Commerce, Sant Mohan Singh Khalsa Labana Girls College, Barara, Ambala, Haryana

Navpreet Kaur: Assistant Profeesor, Department of Food Processiong, Guru Nanak College, Sri Muktsar Sahib (Pb)

Navneet Saini: Assistant Professor, P.G. Department of Sociology, Guru Nanak College, Sri Muktsar Sahib, Punjab

Neha Gupta: Assistant Professor, Education Department, Doaba College, Jalandhar, Punjab

Nelofar Ara: Research Scholar, Department of Sociology, Lovely Professional University, Phagwara, Punjab

Rachana Sharma: Assistant Professor, Department of Sociology, Guru Nanak Dev University, Amritsar

Raja Adnan Razzaq: Chairman, Society for Migration Studies, Islamabad, Pakistan. Former, Assistant Professor, Faculty of Contemporary Studies, NDU, Pakistan.

Rajveer Kaur: Assistant Professor, Department of Basic Sciences, Guru Nanak College, Sri Muktsar Sahib, Punjab

Raj Kumar: Assistant Professor, Department of History, DAV College, Jalandhar, Punjab, India

Rekha: Assistant Professor, Department of Sociology, Trinity College, Jalandhar, Punjab

Renu Bala: Assistant Professor, Majha College for Women, Tarn Taran, Punjab

Roohi Sharma: Assistant Professor in Teaching of Computer Science, Swami Sarvanand College of Education, Dinanagar, Punjab

Rupinder Kaur: Assistant Professor, P.G. Department of Fashion Designing, Guru Nanak College, Sri Muktsar Sahib, Punjab

Rupinderpal Kaur: Assistant Professor, Department of Computer Science and Applications, Guru Nanak College, Sri Muktsar Sahib, Punjab

Sandeep Kaur Brar: Assistant Professor, P.G. Department of English, Guru Nanak College for Girls, Sri Muktsar Sahib, Punjab

Seema Kapoor: Assistant Professor and Head Department of English, Guru Nanak College, Sukhchainana Sahib, Phagwara, Punjab

Sharnjeet Kaur: Assistant Professor in Chemistry, Department of Basic Sciences, Guru Nanak College, Sri Muktsar Sahib, Punjab

Shamika Kumar: Assistant Professor, Department of Economics Guru Nanak College, Sukhchainana Sahib, Phagwara, Punjab

Sukanya Das: Assistant Professor, Department of Sociology, Lovely Professional University, Phagwara, Punjab

Sukhvinder Kaur: Assistant Professor in Zoology, Department of Basic Sciences, Guru Nanak College for Girls, Sri Muktsar Sahib, Punjab

Sunil Kumar: Assistant Professor & Head, P.G. Department of Computer Sciences, Guru Nanak College, Sri Muktsar Sahib, Punjab

Prologue

Globalisation envisages a borderless world. It may be attributed by an accelerated flow of goods, people, capital, information, and energy across borders, often enabled by technological developments. Over the past three decades, globalisation has dominated the world's economic order. However, on the negative side, globalisation has been criticised on account of exacerbating global disparities, spread of international terrorism and cross-border organised crime, and allow for the rapid spread of disease. Recently novel coronavirus has become a global disease as World Health Organisation has declared it a pandemic in March 2020. A pandemic is the worldwide spread of a disease. The history's worst known infectious disease outbreak of the Spanish flu occurred in 1918. The influenza virus H1N1 killed more than 50 million people and infected over 500 million people across the world (WHO, 2020). Starting from the Spanish flu of 20th century, the world has witnessed several disease outbreaks. Some of the major pandemics since the 20th century are Spanish flu, Asian flu, Hong Kong flu, HIV, SARS, Swine flu, MERS, Ebola and now most dangerous novel coronavirus. The coronavirus outbreak came to light on December 31, 2019 when the World Health Organisation (WHO) was informed by the Chinese government about the numerous cases of pneumonia with unfamiliar etiology. The outbreak was initiated from the Hunan seafood market in the Wuhan city and quickly infected more than 50 people. The Hunan seafood market was the selling point of live animals such as frogs, bats, birds, rabbits and marmots. On January 10, 2010, the National Health Commission of China suggested it was a viral pneumonia, but further this virus was identified as novel corona virus. Initially, it was assumed that the seafood market had infected animals so people were infected from this virus if they visited the market. Further investigation showed that some individuals were infected with the virus with no record of visiting the market. Thus, later observations revealed that the effect of the virus varied from human-to-human. Spreading of virus occurs due to the close contacts with an infected person, exposure to virus-containing aerosols during sneezing, coughing, respiration. These aerosols can penetrate to the lungs via inhalation through the nose or through the mouth. Subsequently the disease spread to more Provinces in China, and to the rest of the world. After that the World Health Organisation declared the COVID-19 outbreak as Sixth Public Health of Emergency Services (SPHEC) on January 30, 2020.

The coronavirus COVID-19 pandemic is the defining global health crisis of our time and the greatest challenge we have faced since World War-II. Since its emergence in Asia late last year, the virus has spread to every continent except Antarctica. But the pandemic is much more than a health crisis. It is also an unprecedented socio-economic crisis. It has not only harmed the health of people but has posed serious threats to the economy and marginalised communities of worldwide. It has the potential to create devastating social, economic and political effects that will leave deep scars. The current pandemic has greatly impacted the world economy, every day, people are losing jobs and income, with no way of knowing when normality will return. Small island nations, heavily dependent on tourism, have empty hotels and deserted beaches. The International Labour Organisation estimates that 195 million jobs could be lost. The World Bank projects a US$110 billion decline in remittances this year, which could mean 800 million people will not be able to meet their basic needs.

The coronavirus pandemic has brought science back to the center of discussion, including in countries where populist leaders used to delegitimise the scientific approach to the virus. Epidemiologists, medical doctors and biologists bring us hard facts: the pandemic progresses every day, it is far worse than a "strong flu" and takes thousands of lives on all continents. Social scientists have come up with facts that are as hard and as unquestionable while the virus itself is a biological agent that may infect each of us. Public health policies and social inequalities matter at least as much as the way our bodies react to it when it comes to the virus' deadly consequences. They have shown that the COVID-19 pandemic is not only a sanitary crisis, it is also a social and political crisis, and should be treated as a moment of rupture that will bring major change in our lives, our societies and our world. While often sidelined by policy-makers, social sciences contributions in dealing with the coronavirus pandemic have been as important as, and in many ways complementary to, hard sciences.

Along with the economic and political institutions the pandemic also has affected academic institutions as teaching and assessment activities have hampered since the beginning of this pandemic. In addition, there was an imminent disruption in academic and research activities including class room teaching, face to face conferences and conventions. Among many challenges, academics have to strive hard to remain engaged professionally and socially with students and colleagues.

In case of India,the first case of COVID-19 in India was reported on January 30, 2020. The index patient was a student who had returned from Wuhan. Thereafter, only 2 more cases were reported in February. Subsequently, more cases came to the forefront in the month of March and there has been a surge in the number of cases since the latter half of April 2020. India has promptly responded to the novel threat. International borders have been shut and nationwide lockdown has been imposed since March 25. The Government of India has taken a number of measures, including the implementation of hygienic awareness, isolation and quarantining the patients, closure of important entry points on international borders, closure of educational institutions, parks, business centers, and postponement of national and international flights, the launch of clinical trials, and epidemiological surveillance, with the aim of protecting the population. Together with these efforts an optimal allocation of prevention measures, medical resources, organisation of production activities, and, eventually, maintenance of national economic development throughout the country. But the biggest challenge in India's fight against COVID-19 was the population, with a population density that is almost 3 times that of China. The scenario is potentially worse in urban slums where the population density may exceed more than 250,000/km, making social distancing impossible. As many as 140 million people in India are migrant daily-wage labourers. With imposition of nationwide lockdown, they are being forced to flock back to their villages without being able to abide by government advisories of social distancing. Unfortunately, another major hurdle in India's struggle against COVID-19 has been the attitude and action of some of the citizens; there have been occasional reports of civilians hiding travel history in an attempt to escape quarantine and people participating in otherwise forbidden massive religious gatherings. Apart from this low literacy rate and general lack of awareness leading to non-seriousness of people towards the adoption of social distancing and hand hygiene. The high population density in major cities of India has facilitated the spread of virus.

In light of the above discussion we can say the COVID-19 pandemics is not only affected the health of the people it has badly affected the economy, politics, religion, education and every social aspect of the human beings. Recently former governor of Reserve Bank of India Raghuram Rajan said that there are no real estimates now on how devastating impact of coronavirus will be on the global economy as well as the Indian economy.

In brief, the situation is worse than that during a war, since demand has collapsed. Businesses and finance companies are likely to fail and employment severely impacted. To deal with the health and economic crisis, governments have announced emergency and set up special task forces on the economy. Therefore, the coronavirus pandemics is such a complex phenomenon which can not be understood with any single approach so to understand the effects of this pandemics, we need a multidisciplinary approach which is the aim of this book.

There are several contemporary issues and approaches which needs to be discussed and are being debated also the present volume containing the reflections of academicians from diverse fields and working in different parts of the country. The spirit behind the attempt is to reach an understanding of the effects of COVID-19 on different facets of life as well as on the various parts of the society. The research papers included in the book seek to assess the scenario in the wake of the pandemic at both local and global level. Hence, beginning with historicising pandemics in general, it proceeds with conceptualisation of COVID-19 and carries on the deliberations with the topics like world scenario; the pandemic and human rights; health challenges in the period; effects on education, economy, environment, and migrant workers; and the role of political institutions in these hard times. Further, there is also a discussion on the mechanisms to minimise the negative consequences of the calamity. The book is going to be a real help for the students and academicians working on the pandemic across the disciplines social sciences, commerce and computer.

Raja Adnan Razzaq in his paper "Hazardous Journey into Economic Uncertainty in Developing Nations: An insight into Pakistan's fight against COVID-19" tried to explore history of the pandemics. According to him, from the beginning of mankind, epidemics and pandemics did play a vital role in reshaping the economic map of the world. Novel diseases have always threatened the world and often had pushed the human race to the wall. The pandemics like Circa, Plagues, The Black Death, Yellow Fever, Flu, Polio, AIDS, Dengue, Swine Flu etc had devastating impacts on human race in the past. He further argues that COVID-19 pandemic has unprecedented economic impacts on world's biggest economies. The under developed and developing countries has suffered the most as the resultant lockdown broke the economic backbone of these unfortunate countries. The developed countries somehow managed to afford the impacts of global lockdown by providing bare necessities to their people at their doorsteps, whereas the poor countries not only failed to protect their people against this pandemic, their economies collapsed, industries paralyzed causing serious unemployment which invited and elevated the domestic crime rate. In light of the history of pandemics he highlight the initial outbreak, spread and impact of the corona virus on Pakistan's socio-economic life as Pakistan lost one-third of its revenue and its exports dropped by 50 percent, the response from people and the government, conspiracy theories denying the actual threat, economic nosedive due to nationwide lockdown, closure of educational and other business oriented institutions, governmental response with the help of the army and other national and international organisations, loss of lives, curfews and measures taken to contribute in the international efforts to provide relief and ensuring full support in finding a cure/vaccine.

Raj Kumar in his paper "The Pandemics in India: Past and Present" discussed the history of pandemics in India. He correlated COVID-19 pandemics with Spanish Influenza and presents a comparative study of death toll due to Spanish Influenza is performed with pandemic COVID-19 of major developed countries of the world with India (second largest populated countries of the world). The comparisons and results express that developing countries like India has performed much better in handling COVID-19 pandemic, whereas the developed nations are badly hit by COVID-19. By exploring the history of pandemics, he further argues that Spanish Influenza pandemic which occurred about approximately, hundred years ago in 1918 caused a great number of deaths worldwide. He further argue that during Spanish Influenza India suffered badly as maximum deaths were seen in India. On the basis of that experts predicted that in case of any future pandemic, the developing countries will be great sufferer as compared to developed countries of the world. After the origin of present Pandemic COVID-19 from China, all countries of the world were hit hard but developed countries suffered more as compared to the developing countries.

Navpreet Kaur in her paper "Genetic Comparison of Novel Coronavirus to SARS and MERS: A Review" has made an attempt to highlight the genetic composition of novel corona virus. According to her coronaviruses are known to cause illness that varies between a common cold to more severe diseases like severe acute respiratory syndrome (SARS) and the Middle East respiratory syndrome (MERS). The fresh surfacing of a novel corona-virus epidemic (Covid-19) in December, 2019 swamped the entire world by March, 2020. There are several co-morbidities associated with Covid-19 infections such as cardiovascular diseases, diabetes, cerebro-vascular diseases and abnormalities like coagulation activation, myocardial injuries, cellular immune deficiency, secondary bacterial infections, and hepatic and kidney injuries. At present, Covid-19 associated pathologies have no medicine or anti-virus vaccine and it can be managed by infection prevention, control measures and supportive care. The existing antivirals for HIV and other viral infections such as Remdesvir, Favilavir, Chloroquine and hydroxychloroquine etc., are being prescribed that weaken the virus entry to the cell and thus prevent them from multiplying. COVID-19 is also genetically similar to SARS-CoV and MERS, hence better structural details of surface proteins and the basis of replication, structure and pathogenesis may provide a novel way to the development of drugs and/or vaccine.

Harveen Kaur, Harpreet Kaur and Amandeep Singh in their paper "To Fight Covid-19 Using Machine Learning Approach: A Challenge" tried to provides an overview of the specified Machine Learning Prediction Algorithms to make it easy for the researcher to choose a predictive technique depending on criteria matched so that COVID-19 can be tackled ahead of time. They talked about major machine learning algorithms to predict COVID-19. Four state- of- the- art of the Machine Learning algorithms i.e. Decision tree, Naïve Bayes, Random Forest Tree and K-Means Algorithm have been discussed and compared by them in their paper making it easeful for researcher to choose the best one according to environment of research. They advocated that besides this, it will also help researcher to know the pitfalls of existing ones so that they can figure out what is lagging behind as there exist no predicting algorithm till date that can predict COVID-19 with 100 percent of accuracy.

Jagsir Singh in his paper "COVID-19 and Cities in Punjab" examine the pattern of urbanisation in Punjab by which the concentration of population confines to the big city centers becomes venerable during the Coronavirus pandemics. He explores the effects of this 'big city oriented urbanisation' on the health of the people. He found that unplanned urbanisation is a big threat to sustainability because if we see the patterns of COVID-19 pandemics, the big urban centers are on high risks due to so many reasons. India has no exception, the cases of COVID-19 are increasing day by day and the main concentration of the virus is in cities. Although big urban centers suffering more but it does not mean small cities are safe; they also are facing multiple challenges because they are already lag behind on account of economy and services because the process of urbanisation in India is big city oriented. The flow of population, finance, infrastructure and services stick toward big urban centers. On the other hand insufficient infrastructure in the small cities is incapable for combat the present pandemic situation. Public health system is struggling to fulfill the expectations of the masses.

Sandeep Kaur Brar in her paper "COVID-19: The Deglobalisation Virus" advocates that globalisation is responsible for the spread of COVID–19 pandemics all over the world. As this fact cannot be denied that globalisation, which is characterised by unparalleled levels of human interaction and mobility, has facilitated the fast spread of highly contagious diseases. She believes that the spread of the novel coronavirus (Covid-19) is accelerating due to human hypcr-interconnection. She tries to highlight that this Covid-19 virus has forced us to rethink about globalisation. It is argued that the world needs to redefine the definition of globalisation in order to make it more human-centric instead of market and profit oriented. In the concluding remarks she argues that the present pandemic has taught us a lesson that to harvest the benefits of globalisation, we need to manage the risks.

Rupinder Kaur in her article "Covid-19 Pandemics a Global Disaster" discussed the COVID-19 pandemics as global disaster she highlighted the role of internet, media, print media and means of transportations and communication for making the world as global village. Proving it as disaster she highlighted the effects of this pandemic on the economy, society and educational institutions of the society that how this pandemic created a big economic crisis in the world which will be responsible for upcoming financial recession in the world. She further stressed upon the fact that how this unparalleled crisis puts healthcare systems, people's safety and the economy under strain, it is imperative that transparency and accountability remain at the heart of the global response. This is to fight against Corona virus together not be corrupted. COVID-19 is a Global disaster so whole world are in this grip. At this time we can say that "Prevention is better than cure".

Navjot Kaur in her article on "Effect of COVID-19 on India" feels that the world is facing humanity's biggest crisis since World War II. Almost every country has been affected by the devastating Coronavirus disease (COVID-19). Further she believe that the world is passing through a great uncertainty. She predicted that, the Coronavirus has put the world economy at a major risk especially the developing countries like India. The immediate and future impact of Covid-19 on India is devastating, especially from economic and social perspective. Hopefully in other aspects, for instance; technology and environment, this virus strengthen the India's infrastructure. Hospitality, aviation and travel & tourism industries is severely impacted. As everyone is embracing the latest technical innovations so as to save on rising costs as well as human labour, which currently is difficult to handle. Covid-19 pandemic compelled India to loosen various policies and laws so that the economy that is standstill at this moment can again be put in path of growth. She is worried about the shrinking GDP growth which is projected to -5 percent, latest estimates by World Bank. This means that our country's income will decrease in FY2021. This is worrisome as external debt and India's international investment position is not strong. This will hit very hardly to all the sectors and Job market in India. In order to revive the economy again India has to give stimulus in the form of various funds to the lagged sectors, while containing the impact of Covid-19 on health and safety of the country's people.

Seema Kapoor in her article "The World After 2020" tries to access the effects of Coronavirus pandemics in the world society. She argues that the post-pandemic world would not be same. It will be different in many ways i.e. economically, socially and health-wise. She highlighted that as the necessity is the mother of invention and it will made us realise the real value of ICT tools in teaching learning, governance and different aspects of economy. We learn through this crisis that digital transformation has been accelerated. People have become and will be more health conscious in the future. They have started realising the value of life over livelihood. The nations will need to increase the budget for health, science, education and technology and increase focus on sustainable development. Tourism will continue but visa regimes will be tightened.

Jaspal Kaur in her article "COVID -19 in India: An Analysis of Human Rights Perspective" analyses the COVID -19 pandemic from the human rights perspectives. She tried to examine how the preventive measures on part of the GOI notwithstanding the good intentions, led to the human rights violations apropos COVID-19. She highlighted that hardships and sufferings faced by the people especially the weaker sections of the society during public curfew, lockdown, social distancing period. She argues that during this phase, the people had faced several problems like inadequacy of medical care, high handedness on the part of the police, and migration of people without any transport facility, consequently resulting in violation of human rights particularly right to life. According to her pandemic and human right violation more or less seems to be interwoven.

Navneet Saini in her paper "Human Rights amid the COVID-19 Outbreak" also tries to assess the effects of Covid-19 pandemics by using human right perspective. She tries to throws light on some of the key issues of human rights which are at stake when the country enforced preventive measures to look after the collective health, such as quarantines, travel bans and other such restrictions, access to information along with the responsibility of states to make sure the access to preventive care, goods and services for the public. She further argues that the lockdown has unduly harmed the marginalised communities because of loss of livelihood and shortage of foodstuff, shelter, wellbeing and other indispensable needs.

Arti Sharma in her paper on "COVID-19: Public Health Emergency in India during Pandemic" argues that the current pandemic is a health emergency for the world and the situation is even worse for the third world countries that lack infrastructure and resources. Even the situation is deadly for India which the most densely populated country of the world. She further highlighted that it is not only the health issue related to COVID -19 is matter of public health concern for India. Mental health and well-being of all age groups especially of elderly people and children and psychosocial issues among migrants in community are also burning issue in health sector. She believe that microorganisms because of their ingenuity affected humankind in past and present. It is undeniable that they will continue to cause pandemics in future also. So she suggested to strengthen the biomedical research and healthcare system in India to meet health emergencies in the future. The COVID-19 pandemic has created opportunities to build an improved response mechanism in health sector for future health crises

Akwinder Kaur Aulakh in her paper "Harsh Impacts of COVID-19 on Sex Worker's Health and Socio-Economic Conditions" argues that also though the COVID-19 pandemic, primarily related to the health crisis, is exposing existing inequalities and disproportionately affecting people already criminalised, marginalised and living in precarious health and economic situations. She highlighted that how the Corona-virus pandemic has worstly affected the sex work industry in India. Sex workers who are already stigmatised and marginalised victims of morality are outside from the social protection mechanisms and suffering to find alternative source for livelihood in the pandemic. The COVID-19 protocols make the trade difficult to practice. The pandemic represents the grim reality of sex workers in India. Sex workers are vulnerable to hunger and poverty, violence, brutality of police and lack of access to proper medical care amidst the pandemic due to denial of human rights and exclusion from the government schemes. Her paper captures the challenges posed by daily curfews and lost economic income coupled with changes to sex work that increase potential exposure to infection, stigmatisation, violence and various health concerns.

Roohi Sharma in her article "Changing Role of ICT Practices in Teaching and Learning" tries to identify the changing roles of ICT practices in teaching-learning correlating it with Covid-19 pandemic and also discuss the challenges, advantages and limitations that are imposed by the increasing use of ICT in the time of crisis. According to her, ICT has played a very important role in the sudden outbreak of a deadly disease called Covid-19 caused by a Corona Virus which shocked the entire world because all schools, workplaces have been shutdown to contain the spread of this novel virus. ICT has reduced the barrier of social distancing and lockdown with the help of so many digital and online initiatives and tools. She also suggested that the education system should not only be equipped with ICT tools but the teachers, students should be trained and made competent in ICT skills.

Nelofar Ara and Sukanya Das in their paper "Impact of COVID-19 on Mental Health of Students in Kashmir: A Sociological Reminder during COVID-19 Pandemic Lockdown" tries to examines the effects of COVID-19 on educational institutions as well on the mental health of students in Kashmir. They have also given some important suggestions that can prepare education institutions and health professionals for addressing the mental health needs and challenges posed by COVID-19 Pandemic. They argues that even before the pandemic started, most of the students have experienced one or more diagnosable mental disorders in Kashmir valley because of not ending political disturbance in the valley and now the psychological effects of COVID-19 can increase this number and can exacerbate student's mental health issue. In Kashmir, female literacy rate is already quite low and stands at 65.48 percent according to the census of 2011 and it has been expected that these serious conditions will make it poorer.

Rupinder Kaur in her paper "A Study on Supply Shortage of Critical Primary Needs during COVID-19 Pandemic in India" tries to highlights the shortage of supply of necessary prinerry commodities during the lockdown period. She argues that like other governments worldwide, Indian government also declared the lockdown throughout the country to stop Corona virus from spreading. No doubts, the goal of lockdown is to flatten the curve of new infections but it also carries other problems along with, for instance, it results in severe shortage in the supply of very basic equipment required to fight the disease like PPE kits, grocery items, vegetables and fruits etc. According to her, the major reason being break in the supply chain of basic raw material. Pandemic crisis could quickly put a strain on the food supply chains and medical healthcare system. In her paper she tries to present a study on prevailing needs and their supply chain for common people as well as people involved in healthcare system.

Amanpreet Kaur in her article on "Covid-19: A Pedagogical Development" discusses a topology undertaken to assess the education during COVID-19 pandemic. She also discusses the background; technological resources beneficial for students during this pandemic. She further advocate that there are significant opportunities to learn from the pedagogical developments by other universities for strengthening the students with online learning. Further she explore how the education is supported at international level with new concepts introduced.

Harpreet Kaur in her article "Impact of COVID-19 on Education System", highlights the potential impact of terrible COVID-19 outbreak on the education system and some prompted new examples of educational innovation during this period and several effective measures to meet the upcoming challenges in the post-COVID future of education. She argues that global education system faced the digital divide at great level which put the future of millions of students at risk. COVID-19 has become a catalyst to innovate new resources for educational institutions, nevertheless, unpreparedness and rapid transition of in-person teaching to online teaching dramatically affected the education system of all the underdeveloped as well as prosperous nations. The outbreak of corona virus bring into light several innovations in the education system, however, level and quality of digital access is not accessible in some remote areas. Therefore, she feels that it is the need of the hour to design the plan of action to deal with the problem of global recession of education.

Sharnjeet Kaur in her paper "Impact of COVID -19 on Psychology of Students and their Experience in Lockdown" deals with the detailed study of mental behaviours of students during COVID-19 about their classroom study loss, experiences of online study for the first time in this critical pandemic situation and their future plans in the post-COVID period. She has used online survey method for collecting data by using a self-administered questionnaire. She found that most students have great experience of online examination. However, a considerable extent of students have various viewpoints about their tentative arrangements in the post-COVID-19 period and their classroom study loss. Student's understanding status was positively related with their age category. She argues that students are not content with their online classes and need to do their further classes just at college. It will at that point impact on their self-motivation to accomplish work and furthermore on mental status of students.

Rajveer Kaur in her article "Staggering Impact of COVID-19 on Global Education" tries to assess the effect of novel coronavirus pandemic on the education all over the world. She feels that this pandemic has breakdown the conventional mode of teaching and learning by introducing

ICT use for this purpose. Although online teaching has been started by many institutions which have not successfully considered to be the most appropriate one. Moreover, it has caused various types of disruptions in the internal assessment. So, COVID-19 has not only exaggerated global education but it has also imposed an impact on the mental health of children and academic staff.

Rekha in her article "Education in COVID-19: Challenges and Opportunities" discussed the challenges and opportunities in online education system. She argues that due to COVID -19 pandemic the online teaching-learning process has become more prevalent in India. She discussed the role of various government bodies such as Ministry of Human Resource Development (MHRD), the National Council of Educational Research and Training (NCERT) and the Department of Technical Education for providing various platforms such as DIKSHA, E-PATHSHALA, SWAYAM, SWAYAM PRABHA and MOOCs created to online system for education in India. Apart from this many institution are using conferencing apps like Google Meet, Google Classroom, Zoom and WebEx for conducting interactive classes. But apart from this online education also faces many challenges too. The lack of face to face interaction with the instructor, absence of traditional classroom and socialisation is among some other issues highlighted by the students.

Monika Garg in her article "COVID-19 Pandemic: A Tough Break to Indian Trade and Industry" tries to investigates hit and brunt of corona pandemic on Indian business, trade and industry. She specifically talked about the pandemic effects on the pharmaceutical industry, tourism industry, aviation industry, automobile industry, electronic industry, oil industry, textile industry and micro, small and medium enterprise sector, hospitality industry, entertainment and sports industry, poultry industry agriculture industry, education industry etc. According to her reduction in the consumption due to lockdown leads to decrease in demand which ultimately reduces revenue and profits of almost all the traders and industrialists. All the players in the economy such as producers, consumers, debtors, creditors, government, entrepreneurs, banks, financial institutions will bear great loss due to this pandemic.

Jagmeet Kaur in her paper "Impact of Corona Pandemic on Banking and Financial Sector in India" tries to analyzed the negative impact of Corona pandemic on the Indian economy, its banking and financial sector, measures taken by Reserve Bank of India and government of India to counter this pandemic and as well as post-corona challenges that India may face in the future. She argues that the extent of the impact of novel corona virus is big unknown at the moment but it will be definitely severe. However, the Reserve Bank of India is assuring that in comparison to the rest of the world, India will be the least affected country. But the situation is worse than that during a war, since demand has collapsed. Businesses and finance companies are likely to fail and employment severely impacted. She further suggested that if a social breakdown is to be avoided the budget will have to be revamped with resources focused to mitigate the crisis confronting the marginalised sections of society.

Shamika Kumar in her article "COVID-19 and Its Impact on Global Economy" tries to assess the effects of Coronavirus pandemics on the world economy. According to her, the spread of the coronavirus bring the global economy to its knees because policy-makers in many countries were under pressure to respond to the coronavirus outbreak. As a result, many governments made fast policy decisions that had far-reaching positive and negative effects on their respective economy many countries plunged into a recession. The spread of the virus encouraged social distancing which led to the shutdown of financial markets, corporate offices, businesses and events and the exponential rate at which the virus was spreading, and the heightened uncertainty about how bad the situation could get, led to flight to safety in consumption and investment among consumers, investors and international trade partners etc. She also tries to interrogate the government policies and efforts to control coronavirus pandemic according to her lawmakers in many countries supported an extended social distancing policy, damning the consequences of social distancing on the economy.

Rachana Sharma in her paper "Migrants and the Reverse Migration during the COVID-19 Pandemic" highlights the social impacts of COVID-19 on the migrants and the migration process in urban India. Also, it specifically looks into the vulnerabilities faced by the migrants during the lockdown situation and migration scenario in the post-lockdown. She broadly reviews the broader discourse on the reverse migration during the current pandemic. According to her, the migrant exodus in India during the pandemic became an international concern with analysts predicting the trends and implications of reverse migration and no future migration which added a fresh air to the development and marginalisation discourse. She further argues that although migrants have always been ignored in the broader discourse of economic and social growth, but this pandemic has forced us to finally acknowledge the migrants, their existence in huge numbers in our cities and villages, their role and contributions in making up our economies on one hand and on the other hand, it has exposed some of the austere realities of inequality, marginalisation and privilege in Indian society.

Sunil Kumar in his article "Analytical study of E-Governance services during COVID-19 pandemics: A Case Study of Punjab State" tries to present analytical analysis of E-Governance services provide by state of Punjab during coronavirus pandemic. He explores the preventive measures taken to control the COVID-19 by the Punjab government through electronic services, its effectiveness and with other steps taken by government to manage this crucial situation. He suggested that there is a need of collaborative efforts towards Proactive E-Governance not only at state, country even at world level so that society can quickly recover from this crucial situation.

Renu Bala in her article "India-European Union Relations in Context of 15th Summit between the Two Entities Postponed Due to COVID-19" deals with the postponement of the fifteen annual summit between India and European Union scheduled for 13 March 2020 in Brussels due to COVID-19 pandemics. She argues that it was a very important summit between the two entities because the theme of the summit must include certain topics that would shape the future of the India-EU relations. The first India EU summit was held in Lisbon in June 2000, which marked a watershed in the evolution of this relationship. Since then, there have been many summit level interactions. But now due to Corona Virus. Both sides have agreed that due to health authorities advising against travel between regions it would be to reschedule to the 15th wise summit to a mutually convenient date.

Meenu Sharma in her article "Role of Media and Communication during COVID-19 Pandemic" analyze the role of media and other source of communication during the coronavirus pandemic. She argues that nowadays media works as a bridge between government and society. Media have been recognised as robust power to form how we experience this world. During COVID-19 pandemics media played a very significant role in making people aware about the situation, and encourage them to do positive action. She presented role of different kinds of media like digital media and print media and social media with their impact during the pandemics. She used various articles reports and working papers and secondary data to justify her findings.

Sukhvinder Kaur in her paper "Environment/Ecological Effects of Covid-19 Pandemics" highlights the impacts of lockdown period on the environment and our eco system. According to her, while the whole world is now struggling with the pandemic COVID-19, besides this, it has caused worldwide changes in the environmental conditions. It is because most of the countries has imposed lockdown as a measure to keep social distancing in order to save precious human lives. It has caused reduction in air, vehicular, water and noise pollution to some extent. Air Quality Index has been lower during this period and water quality parameters were showing improvements. Similarly it has caused change in behaviour of Animals and Birds, who are feeling freer now, indicating its impact on other Ecosystems also. She advocates that reduction in pollution in these days has saved lives of thousands of people who loses their lives due to pollution related diseases every year all over the World. By giving references of so many studies she highlighted that the present positive change in the environment is just a temporary relief because once lockdown's are over and normalcy returns. The conditions may worsen, if productions are increased to boost economy without taking environment protection measures.

Tejinder Kaur Dhaliwal &
Bali Bahadur

Historicising Pandemics

1

Hazardous Journey into Economic Uncertainty in Developing Nations: an insight into Pakistan's fight against COVID-19

Raja Adnan Razzaq

Throughout recent history the Indian subcontinent has been a victim of a variety of both pandemics and epidemics. Poor sanitation condition, lack of fresh drinking water in remote areas, questionable hygienic culture and above all malnutrition were amongst the major causes of the aforementioned diseases. Major pandemics during the colonial era included the Cholera outbreaks in 1817, 1829, 1852 and 1881, the Bombay Plague in 1896 and Influenza in 1918.[1]

At the time of partition in 1947, Cholera posed a devastating threat in both India and Pakistan. Many moving refugees in search of a promised land lost their lives due to riots, rigorous winters, heavy rains and flooding causing Cholera epidemic mostly in refugee camps. The death rate in one refugee camp in West Punjab, of approximately 150,000 refugees, was reported as 600 a day.[2] Despite being a nascent provincial government with very limited resources, the West Punjab authorities under Governor Francis Mudie did whatever they could to provide relief to the suffering refugees. The infected inmates were immediately separated from the other refugees and were provided with necessary medical care. The healthy ones were inoculated in the reception camps and were provided with warm clothing and food and were thoroughly briefed about personal hygiene. After the acute period of partition related hazards the Pakistan government did manage to bend down the devastation levels of pandemics and epidemics with the help of the international health organisations such as WHO,

UNICEF, OXFAM, Red Cross etc and by improving the hygiene standards over a period of time.

However, Pakistan's trek record for fighting epidemics and pandemics has not been up to the mark or parallel with other developing countries in the past. In fact, Pakistan and Afghanistan are the only remaining countries where poliomyelitis or generally known as Polio is still considered as endemic viral infection.[3] There are plethora of factors responsible for this medical embarrassment but the prime factor in this regards are the conspiracy theories, mostly frivolous, related to possible side effects of the vaccines including sterilisation in order to reduce the Muslim population by the western 'infidels'. This was further strengthened when the Americans traced Osama bin Laden through a vaccination drive in Abbotabad.[4] Many workers associated with the polio vaccination departments have been killed in cold blood in recent years which has forced the authorities to suspend the vaccination drives several times. Before Corona pandemics the former Indian subcontinent was terrorised with the Dengue fever which resulted in a larger number of casualties in India, Pakistan, Bangladesh and Sri Lanka. Having no vaccine for the Dengue made it difficult for the health authorities to cure or to prevent the disease from spreading but somehow the Pakistan Government with the help from the Sri Lankan experts made necessary arrangements to cure the Dengue patients and established many Dengue centers at tahsil levels to isolate the patients until they were fully recovered. If we compare governmental responses to both diseases it is quite evident that since there was no conspiracy theory associated with Dengue, it was relatively easy for the provincial and central governments to eventually overcome the epidemic fever.

The Corona pandemic/COVID-19

Mankind has suffered a lot because of global pandemics in the past until they managed to harness the disease, courtesy the manmade vaccines for Plagues, Spanish Flu, Smallpox, Swine Flu, Cholera, AIDS, Ebola etc. The novel Corona Virus is still at a stage where the world is searching for a vaccine for the unprecedented disease. The World Health Organisation (WHO) is hoping to deliver around two billion vaccine doses by the end of 2021[5] until then the only cure available is precautionary measures especially self-isolation and by maintaining social distancing.

The Corona Virus is believed to be originated from Wuhan in China somewhere in December 2019 and since it showed symptoms like common Pneumonia it was locally named as Wuhan Pneumonia.[6] Later on it was named as Novel Corona Virus or 2019-n COV then Severe Acute

Respiratory Coronavirus 2(SARS-CoV-2). The current name COVID-19 was adopted by the WHO on 12th February 2020.[7] Apart from being a deadly disease it has invited conspiracy theorists from around the world who had reasons to believe that it was a manmade disease created to depopulate the overcrowded world. Some would even associate it with religious prophecies and will have the audacity to provide documented proofs to cement their frivolous arguments.

The second tier of 'intellectuals' surfaced with some possible remedies based on herbal medicines, primitive rituals mostly religious and some experimental medicines used for common cold, pneumonia and malaria. Apart from these, the fake news around the world associated with COVID-19 created panic and fear. It has triggered Sinophobia wave in many European countries where Chinese minorities faced racist tirades and even physical assaults.[8] However, the death of the Chinese doctor and the whistle blower Li Wenliang provided some relief for the Chinese communities living abroad.[9] Even the US President Donald Trump was trolled for naming the virus as the 'Chinese Virus' during official meetings and public gatherings.

As of 9th November 2020 there were 50,954,334 confirmed cases with 1,264,969 deaths and 35,909,960 recovered patients around the world. In Pakistan, there have been 346,489 confirmed cases of COVID-19 with 6986 confirmed deaths and 318,881 recovered patients as reported to WHO.[10] Apart from taking lives, this virus has crashed many bullish economies in the world; it destroyed the hegemony of the mighty oil economy, global shutdowns creating unemployment, food shortages, abruption of educational activities and sports, travel bans which resulted in shortage of medicine and other medical related equipments. Just when the world thought that they have controlled the virus, the hydra has raised its head once again. The Director General WHO Dr. Tedros Adhanom Ghebreyesus on 26th October 2020 informed the world through a media briefing that during the last week there was highest number of COVID-19 cases reported so far especially from the northern hemisphere. He further added that there aren't any magical solutions to this outbreak and only science continues to tell us the truth about this virus as how to contain it, suppress it and stop it from returning.[11] The world is getting ready for the second wave of corona virus with the approaching winters and unfortunately without any reliable vaccine to fight one of the deadliest viruses of modern times.

Pakistan's Response to COVID-19

Pakistan is a developing economy with very limited resources to cope with such pandemics. The Pakistanis were following the developments in the outbreak of virus in China which later shifted to Europe when the first case of COVID-19 was reported from Pakistan on 26th February 2020. The 22-year old patient Mr. Yahya Jafri of Karachi city was infected during his stay in Iranian holy city of Qum as a pilgrim.[12] These returnees from Iran pricked another heated debate in the power corridors. Earlier the Pakistan government was adamant not to evacuate around 500 Pakistani students in Wuhan universities despite enormous pressure from the students' families and the opposition block.[13] They feared, and rightly so, that these stranded students in Wuhan who have been residing within the vicinity of the epicenter might be the disease carriers. On the other hand, the government was quite quick to allow Pakistani pilgrims from Iran into Pakistan through Taftan border which brought-in first known case of COVID-19 in Pakistan. In this mismanagement of returnees from a badly hit country one federal minister for Overseas Pakistanis and a very close friend of PM Imran Khan Mr. Zulfi Bukhari was heavily criticised for allowing the infected pilgrims to enter into Pakistan without following the proper SOPs. The government, however, denied any administrative negligence in this regard.

Under pressure from the opposition parties and the orthodox religious parties primarily the Sunnis, the Khan's government closed its borders with Iran and Afghanistan on 16th March 2020 and banned all flights from Iran with effect from midnight between 27th and 28th February 2020.[14] The government also set up a quarantine centre at Taftan on the Pakistan-Iran border. The government, however, had responded to the global pandemic by establishing a core committee on COVID-19 which met on 15th January 2020 and had decided to reinforce the Points of Entries (POEs) to screen the incoming passengers, this unfortunately was not very effective on borders where people were crossing on foot or by local transport. National Security Committee (NSC) met on 13th March 2020 which resulted in the creation of National Command and Operation Centre (NCOC) on 27th March 2020 under the command of Federal Minister for Planning and Development Asad Umar and Major General Asif Mehmood Goraya as DG Operations and Planning.[15] The NCOC closely worked with both civil and military leadership and took major decisions to fight the Corona pandemic in Pakistan. On the advice of NCOC the Pakistan government announced major lockdown throughout Pakistan on 2nd April 2020 banning all public gatherings, educational and sports related activities, congregational prayers, religious and social festivals and at the same time ensured implementation of decisions taken at the highest levels with the help of law enforcement agencies.[16] Initially, there was some resistance shown by the religious elements that were against the banning of congregational prayers in mosques but were timely dealt with by the government authorities. Situation improved after Saudi government's decision to ban the Umrah services for Muslim pilgrims from around the world. Later on in order to avoid spread of disease on a large scale the Saudi government decided not to allow foreign Muslims to come to Saudi Arabia to perform the Hajj in the year 2020. The Hajj was performed with only a thousand selected locals and people belonging to other nationalities and that too after following all the necessary SOPs.[17] It was a very positive and thoughtful decision by the Saudis as it not only reduced chances of spread of virus on a large scale, it also made the religious elements all over Muslim world to realise the gravity of the situation and in response they started cooperating with the authorities.

The major lockdown did bend the curve in government's favour as there was considerable decrease in the Corona positive cases. The peak of the disease was noticed in June-July but by the end of August there was a remarkable decline in corona positive cases in Pakistan. But the pandemic exposed the already depleting health resources in Pakistan. Initially, the main task was to address the panic in the public because of its novelty and non-existence of a reliable vaccine. This was somehow managed through a vigorous campaign on print and electronic media, cellular networks, radio and social media by creating awareness about the disease negating frivolous rumors. But the actual shortage of necessary medical equipment such as ventilators, isolation wards and quarantine centre made things worse for the government. Even the developed countries like England, America and EU countries were facing the same shortages so it was not possible for the Pakistan government to import ventilators from foreign countries on such a short notice. This shortage of equipment was compensated by the dedicated and selfless efforts made by the doctors, paramedical staff, nurses who worked long hours to provide relief to the patients kept in isolation centers. These heroes were vulnerable to exposure and unfortunately many young doctors died because there was not enough or adequate Personal Protection Equipments (PPEs) to be provided to the frontline doctors and in case of infection there were a very limited number of epidemiologists working in the country during the early days of the pandemic. The young doctors did complain about the non-availability of the PPEs but they did not stop working. The government responded by providing them with necessary equipment donated by foreign countries especially China on priority bases. In order to encourage the doctors the government doubled their salaries and acknowledged their services and sacrifices through media campaigns such as 'we care' to appreciate their services for the noble cause.[18] The government was doing all in her capacity to provide relief to Corona patients even in the most remote areas. Special modifications were done in government hospitals to accommodate corona patients. During the acute period the NDMA instructed major hotel chain to modify their infrastructure to act as quarantine centers. 35 tertiary hospitals were designated for COVID-19 in whole of Pakistan i.e. 10 hospitals in Baluchistan, 3 in AJK, 4 in Gilgit Baltistan, 4 in Sindh, I in Islamabad, 7 in Khyber Pakhtun Khwa and 6 in Punjab. The government made 215 isolation and 23,557 quarantine facilities throughout the country.[19] The government of Pakistan was well aware of its financial constrains with regards to providing necessary medical care essential in Covid-19, therefore they encouraged local manufacturers and scientists to prepare protective gears including masks, sanitisers and ventilators. A Pakistani company 'Poulta' came up with a locally made ventilator based on AI model which was presented before the National Disaster Management Authority (NDMA) and Pakistan Engineering Council (PEC) for approval. The cost of the said ventilator was much less than the imported ventilators. Currently, most of the public sector hospitals in Pakistan are equipped with ventilator and oxygen units. In order to provide a volunteer force to monitor the corona patients and to provide food and medical assistance during complete lockdown, a Corona Relief Tiger Force (CRTF) was announced by the Prime Minister Imran Khan.[20] The Tiger Force was to work under the local Deputy Commissioners.

The PM though authorised the complete lockdown but he remained concerned for those less fortunate daily wage labourers who were left with no jobs and had no savings to feed their families in the crucial months during the pandemic. Unlike the developed countries where the government after enforcing lockdown provided food and other essentials at the door step, a large number of people in Pakistan have to earn everyday to survive. Therefore, the PM made exception for people who were associated with small businesses and required very limited public interaction in order to arrange possibilities for them to make their livings.[21] The government also allocated 144 billion rupees to be distributed among the people whose business was shut down because of lockdown. In this connection every deserving family after registration received a lump sum amount of 12,000 rupees to be utilised in four months.[22] This benefitted those local daily wagers who were permanently residing in their respective areas. But in big cities like Karachi, Lahore, Peshawar and Rawalpindi cities a large number of these daily wagers who had come to find work were people from villages and far flung areas such as GB, Quetta, Mianwali etc. When they couldn't find work or were asked to leave because of lockdown and Corona, it become very hard for them to survive in a city that forced them to go back to their ancestral places. They often used public transport to travel and if one of them was exposed to the virus, he became a carrier and then infected many others travelling with him. Once they reach home in remote areas where many people even refuse to believe the very existence of corona virus and therefore did not maintain required social distancing, it spread in no time effecting thousands daily.

Though the government was quick to ban the inter city transport to avoid any possible spread of virus but it was hard for the government to enforce complete lockdown. According to a careful estimate around 2300 smart lockdowns had been implemented in the country.[23] When situation improved the authorities also experimented with micro-smart lockdown limited only to specific streets where corona patients were spotted after tests. This helped both the authorities and the general public at large. There was a rise in Corona cases in early August in Pakistan because of relaxation in travel restrictions, reopening of schools, colleges, marriage halls and restaurants and the crowded shopping malls were reopened only to be closed during weekends. The Eid-ul-Adha was celebrated in the first week of August, people were allowed to travel back to their homes and the animal mandis were permitted in all the major cities of Pakistan which resulted in an increased number of Covid patients all over Pakistan.

By mid September 2020, the government along with private organisations, national and international NGOs, members of civil societies, electronic and print media agencies and the military worked like a team and managed to control the spread of virus to an extent that the government decided to lift the lockdown in almost all the major cities of Pakistan. Although the educational institutions, restaurants and other businesses that attract a large number of people were allowed to operate but they were forced to observe all the necessary SOPs. Failing to exercise these required SOPs resulted in heavy fines and even closure of businesses. The teamwork of all the major institutions of the state was rewarded when the WHO declared Pakistan as one of the seven countries that the world needs to learn from while dealing with corona situation.[24]

Luckily Pakistan has managed to curb the pandemic despite its financial and technological limitations but the danger of a possible second wave is not yet over. With the reopening of educational institutions, resuming of the congregational prayers, reopening of recreational spots, restaurants etc, there is a considerable rise in the Corona positive cases in populated localities. In order to check the level of spread of virus the government is still enforcing smart and micro-smart lockdowns and is also carrying out sentinel testing in schools, colleges and other high risk areas in order to keep record of the ratio of increase or decrease in the Covid positive cases. Since there is no internationally recommended vaccine available yet, the best defence against this pandemic is to take precautionary measures including social distancing, personal hygiene and by religiously following the SOPs apart from learning to live with it until there is a reliable vaccine to be available globally.

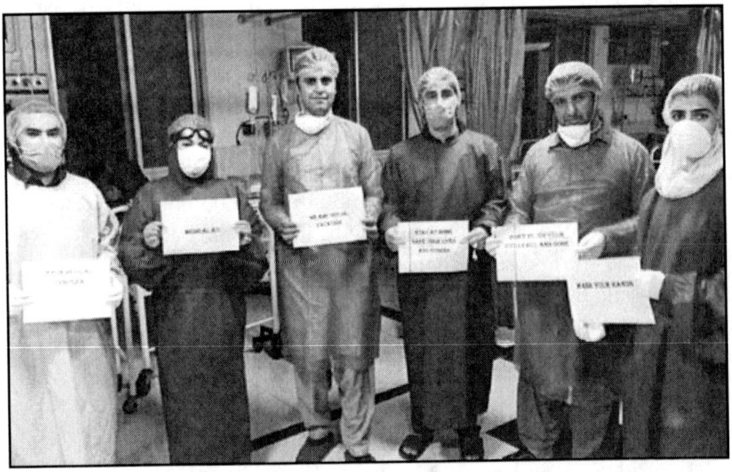

Pakistan has lost 42 doctors to corona

PM Imran Khan at the National Command and Operation Centre

References

1. Swetha G., Anantha Eashwar U.M., Gopalakrishan S.: "Epidemics and Pandemics in India throughout History: A Review Article", *Indian Journal of Public Health Research and Development*, Vol. 10, No. 8, January 2019, p. 1504.
2. Ilyas Chattha: "After the Massacres: Nursing Survivors of Partition Violence in Pakistan Punjab Camps", *Journal of Royal Asiatic Society*, Vol. 28, Issue 2, April 2018, pp. 273-93.

3. Muhammad Suleman Malik, Muhammad Afzal, et al.: "Disease Status of Afghan Refugees and Migrants in Pakistan", *Frontiers in Public Health*, 7:185, doi: 10.3389/fpubh.2019.00185. See also polioeradication.org.
4. Chuck Pfarrer: *Seal Target Geronimo: the inside story of the mission to kill Osama bin Laden* (New York, 2011). The alleged Osama bin Laden's compound in Abbotabad in KPK was under surveillance by the Americans for quite some time but in order to be sure of Laden's presence in the said compound DNA samples had to be retrieved. In order to materialise the retrieval of DNA samples a Pakistani Dr. Shakil Afridi was recruited by the CIA who used the vaccination drive for the collection of samples from the targeted area. Based on the results of DNA, a raid was conducted on 2nd May 2011 where Osama bin Laden was allegedly killed and his body was retrieved by the Navy Seals of USA. Dr. Afridi was later arrested within weeks and was charged with treason. He was sentenced to 33 years in prison but his sentence was reduced to 23 years on appeal. The involvement of a Pakistani doctor, associated with the vaccination drive, in a CIA led operation within the territorial boundaries of Pakistan had pricked anger and resentment towards the people associated with such vaccination related drives especially in the tribal areas.
5. https://www.who.int/initiatives/act-accelerator/covax
6. https://www.who.int/csr/don/05-january-2020-pneumonia-of-unkown-cause-china/en/. The Country Office of WHO in China was informed on 31st December 2019 of cases of pneumonia of unknown etiology in Wuhan city of Hubei province. Within three days 44 patients were reported to WHO from the Huanan seafood market in Wuhan.
7. Saddam Hussein: "Pakistan's Fight against Covid-19: Lessons to be learned', working paper, *Center for Research and Security Studies (CRSS)*, 2020, Islamabad, Pakistan, p.9. See also Harapan H, Itoh N., et al., "Corona virus Disease 2019 (COVID-19): A literature review", *Journal of Infection and Public Health*, 2020.
8. https://www.aljazeera.com/news/2020/02/18/coronavirus-prompts-hysterical-shameful-sinophobia-in-italy/. Yuebai Liu, 'Coronavirus prompts 'hysterical', shameful Sinophobia in Italy', 18th February 2020 for Aljazeera.com.
9. https://www.bbc.com/news/world-asia-china-51403795. Dr. Li, an ophthalmologist working in Wuhan Central Hospital sent out a warning message to his fellow doctors and staff about the deadly virus on 30th December 2019 but was soon questioned by the local police and was told not to spread rumors that can cause unrest. Later on the authorities however apologised to Dr. Li. He got infected while treating corona patients and died on 7th February 2020. His death invited sympathetic responses from around the world. He was rightly labeled as the whistle blower and was appreciated for his early warnings and his decision to continue treating the corona patients till his death.
10. www.worldometers.info/coronavirus/?fbclid=IwAR2Ak_lT4Q9jx0z8_1H2ojos GD2hqedekLDBOkPQv6CGWR0xV-KSKLrYO3Y.
11. For a complete account of his media briefing on 26th October 2020 please visit https://www.who.int/director-general/speeches/detail/who-director-general-s-opening-remarks-at-the-media-briefing-on-covid-19—26-october-2020.

12. *Daily Jang*, Karachi, 27th February 2020.
13. *The Economic Times*, Mumbai: "Pakistan refuses to air lift and evacuate its citizens from China", 5th February, 2020. The Chinese Ambassador to Pakistan H.E. Yao Jing thanked the Pakistani government for not evacuating the Pakistani students from Wuhan.
14. *Anadolu Agency* (AA) Ankara Turkey: "Pakistan suspends flights to Iran amid corona virus fear", by Aamir Latif, 27th February 2020. As for Afghanistan, the government of Pakistan decided to close Pak-Afghan border at Torkham on 16th March 2020 to avoid a possible spread. The Additional Assistant Commissioner Landi Kotal Mr. Shamsul Islam under instructions from the provincial and central governments set up 11 quarantine centers to isolate at least 300 possible effected patients from Afghanistan. For details on this please see *The Nation*, Pakistan, "Thousands struck at Pak-Afghan border" by Ahmad Nabi, 16th March 2020.
15. Press Releases dated 27th March 2020 and 3rd April 2020, Prime Minister's Office, Islamic Republic of Pakistan, www.pmo.gov.pk; Saddam Hussein, "Pakistan's Fight against Covid-19: Lessons to be learned", *ibid*, p.12.
16. *The News*: "Govt extends lockdown to April 14 to fight corona virus", 2nd April 2020.
17. *The Daily Jang*, 31st July 2020: The Pakistani diplomats in Saudi Arabia represented Pakistan during the Hajj.
18. *Express Tribune*, 12th May 2020.
19. Saddam Hussein: "Pakistan's Fight against Covid-19: Lessons to be learned", *ibid.,* p.14.
20. *The Nation*, 28th March 2020.
21. *Reuters*: "Pakistan to start easing lockdown amid sharp corona virus spread", by Asif Shahzad, 7th May 2020. https://www.reuters.com/article/us-health-coronavirus-pakistan-idUSKBN22J1MX.
22. *Dawn*, 27th March 2020. The government initiated 'Ehsaas Kafalat Program' with 144 billion rupees for deserving families and another 200 billion rupees for daily wage workers.
23. Saddam Hussein, *ibid,* p.15.
24. The WHO listed Pakistan amongst seven countries including Italy, Thailand, Mongolia, Mauritius and Uruguay, that the world should learn from to fight Corona and other future pandemics. The WHO DG Dr. Ghebreyesus while addressing the media on 7th September 2020 stated that "Pakistan developed the infrastructure built up over many years for polio to combat COVID-19. Community health workers who have been trained to go door to door vaccinating children for polio have been utilised for surveillance, contact tracking and care". For a detailed account of media briefing please visit https://www.who.int/director-general/speeches/detail/who-director-general-s-opening-remarks-at-the-media-briefing-on-covid-19 —7-september-2020; *Express Tribune*, 12 September 2020.

2

The Pandemics in India: Past and Present

Raj Kumar

The world has passed through many epidemics and pandemics since time immemorial. Only in last 100 years period, modern world has witnessed three pandemics: Spanish flu (1918), Asian influenza (1957), and Hong Kong influenza (1968). Among these, Spanish influenza considered to be the most deadly infectious disease in the history of modern world, which killed millions of people globally.[1] In 1920s, Edwin Oakes Jordan, had estimated the global mortality of 21.5 million due to Spanish influenza.[2] After the consideration of certain facts, recent studies have recalculated the mortality of Spanish influenza (worldwide), which was much more than it was recorded in 1920s. Johnson believed that global mortality due to Spanish influenza may fall in the range between 50 to 100 million worldwide.[3] According to the Taubenberger K. Berger, the global mortality of Spanish influenza was between 40-50 million.[4] The total estimated death toll due to Spanish influenza (1918-19) by the scholars is presented in the Table 1. On the basis of the studies of past pandemics, scientists feared of a severe pandemic, similar to Spanish influenza, which could occur anytime in future. In their opinion in such unwanted situation, developing countries will suffer immensely as compared to developed countries. The fear of scientists turned into reality, when present pandemic COVID-19 suddenly, emerged from Wuhan city of China and soon the entire world came into the grip of this infectious disease within 3-4 months.

The fear of the experts, basically, had two reasons; first, the severity and huge mortality in the past due to Spanish influenza in countries like India under colonial rule. Secondly, the lack of resources to tackle with the pandemic situation in developing countries as compared to the developed countries of the modern world. The paper analyses the opinion of scientists on the future of developing countries in next pandemic. India alone had lost around 18 million people out of 50 million worldwide, due to Spanish influenza, occurred 102 years back.[5] Out of 18 million 13.8 million deaths were reported only from British-controlled provinces of India.[6]

Table 1: Mortality due to Spanish Influenza pandemic in 1918-19: Worldwide

Location	*Published death toll (per 1,000)*	*Published death rate*
Africa	~2,375,000	~18.20
America	~15,40,000	——
Asia	26,000,000-36,000,000	——
Europe	~2,300,646	4.8
Oceania	85,000	——
Global Total	>48,798,038~50,000,000-100,000,000	~2.5-5.0

Source: Niall P.A.S. (2002): "Updating the Accounts of Global Mortality of the 1918-1919 'Spanish' Influenza Pandemic", *Bulletin of the History of Medicine*, Vol. 76, No. 1, pp. 110-114. Ian D. Mills (1986): "The 1918-1919 Influenza Pandemic- The Indian Experience", *Indian Economic and Social Historical Review,* pp. 1-40.

Although the experts believed that world could encounter such pandemic but, they were not certain about the time, and location of its occurrence.[7] David M. Morens and Anthony S. Fauci had the views that in case of future pandemic, the developing countries of the world will not have the access to same level of prevention and medical care as compared to developed countries. So, in such a case developing countries will share the greatest burden of any future pandemic.[8] Dr. Daniel Lavanchy, coordinator of epidemic disease control at the World Health Organisation, Geneva in 1999, reported: "Many developed countries including United Kingdom, France, Belgium and Switzerland have a plan in place. Others such as the Netherland, Germany, China and Japan, are currently making preparations. However, some developed and many developing countries have yet to take action." According to him, the particular impact of the pandemic will be on developing countries, where influenza vaccine, antiviral drugs, and health professional will be in short supply. He wanted these developing countries to be prepared like developed countries. Dr. Stephen (Commonwealth Fund), New York warned: "New data from the 1819 pandemic showed the appalling impact in the areas such as sub-Saharan Africa and India." He estimated 17 million deaths alone in India.[9] Sungwon Yoon believed, in case of any future pandemic, developed countries will be in a better position as compared to the developing countries because, developed countries possess global manufacturing capacity of vaccine and other medical equipments, which is not true in the case of developing countries. So, the mortality in developing countries was predicted much higher in a case of future pandemic.[10] Unlike other scholars, Gracia- Sastre and Whitley were quite optimistic about enormous scientific advancement and unequaled opportunity to use preventive measures against future risk of influenza pandemic as compared to 100 years ago.[11]

On the basis of the literature review discussed above we try to find out the loss of lives, due to the present pandemic COVID-19 in India (a developing country) and compare it with the major developed countries of the world including US, till date. Thus, the objective of this paper is to elaborate in detail the comparison of death toll in India during Spanish influenza (1918) and COVID-19 (till date), as compared to the developed countries, against the feared prediction of experts about the huge loss of lives in future pandemic in developing countries. In the following section, we discuss the spread and loss of human lives caused by Spanish influenza (1918-19) and COVID-19. Further the mortality rate of developed countries is compared with the mortality rate of India due to COVID-19. Subsequently, we come to the conclusion that how far the prediction of the experts about future pandemic proved true.

We see that during Spanish influenza (1918-19) all the sections of Indian society were hit very hard.[12] No other part of the world suffered as severely as India in the last quarter of 1918.[13] Mills estimated that second wave of Influenza (out of three) in September (1918), which lasted around for a brief period of four months, took the lives of 17-18 million people in India.[14] So, death toll during Spanish Influenza in India was much higher than any other part of the world.[15] Table 2 presents the mortality rate of India during pandemic Spanish influenza.

When we talk about Spanish influenza the spread of disease can be attributed to different sources in India. The World War-I was at its last leg and a ship of Indian soldiers from Mesopotamia reached Bombay on 29 May, 1918. The soldiers were the carriers of H1N1 Influenza from the trenches on the Western front (Europe). No one in India was even slightly aware about the dreadful time India was heading for. Seven sepoys including one posted at the docks at Bombay were admitted to hospital with the symptoms of Influenza. Soon, the spread of disease was witnessed in every part of India through railway filled with the soldiers who had returned to their home land after fighting for British Empire from 1914-1918.[16] Many of them were infected and ill due to the spread of influenza in Europe in early months of 1918.

According to Major Norman White (Sanitary commissioner India, 1918), "railway was the major culprit in spreading the infection in India. The postal department was another important agency in disseminating

Table 2: Mortality of the 1918-1920 Influenza Pandemic: India

Location	*Population*	*Published death toll (per 1,000)*	*Published death rate*	*Recalculated death rate*
India	305,693,000	18,500,000	—	6.1

Source: Niall P.A.S. (2002): "Updating the Accounts of Global Mortality of the 1918-1919 'Spanish' Influenza Pandemic", *Bulletin of the History of Medicine*, Vol. 76, No. 1, pp. 110-114. Ian D. Mills (1986): "The 1918-1919 Influenza Pandemic- The Indian Experience", Indian *Economic and Social Historical Review*, pp. 1-40.

infection, mainly, through the railway postal service. Lucknow, Lahore Shimla and other cities are said to have been infected in this manner". In a short span of time, whoever travelled by rail, road or water, was a carrier of infection unknowingly.[17] Spanish influenza in India in first wave remained mild and the disease was not considered threat, because of its low mortality rate.[18] In the second wave Influenza also reached coastal areas of India. The people assumed the disease will not last long but, in a few months it took the lives of millions of people in India.[19] Mortality was very severe in India in second wave. It took heavy toll in the Bombay in October, 1918. A great number of deaths was seen in November (1918) in Northern and Central Provinces. Bengal was hit very severely in the month of December. In Bengal, the situation became worse as it is stated that rivers were clogged with the dead bodies due to lack of firewood for the last rites of Hindus.[20]

Exactly, 102 years after the Spanish influenza, a lethal pandemic due to a new type of Corona virus emerged in December, 2019 and threatened the entire world. In the last week of December, 2019 China identified Corona virus (with unknown etiology), and isolated this new virus on 7 January, 2020. Thereafter, Chinese authorities informed World Health Organisation (WHO), country office in China about this new virus. Very soon the cases related to corona virus started emerging in different parts of the world, with travel history from Wuhan city of China.[21] The number of cases of Corona virus reached 581 globally on 23 January, out of which 571 cases were reported from China (majority from Wuhan, Hubei with seventeen deaths) alone. World Health Organisation in its third report assessed that the risk of this virus was to be very high in China, high at the regional level and high at the global level.[22] World Health Organisation released an advisory to international air travellers to use certain precautions, as there may be chances of human-to-human transmission of disease due to Corona Virus so, passengers should abstain from direct unprotected contact with live animals and surfaces. Apart from cleanliness of hands, they were advised to avoid close contact with people with symptoms of Corona virus.[23] Since then, World Health Organisation released several international travel and health advisories to the international community time to time. On 11 February, 2020, World Health Organisation named Corona Virus Disease of 2019 as COVID-19.[24] World Health Organisation declared the novel COVID-19 outbreak a global pandemic on March 11, 2020. The scientists around the world are trying hard to develop a vaccine to fight deadly disease but, their efforts could not bring a desired result till date. Since then virus has affected 215 countries of the world and affecting millions of people worldwide and it will continue with the catastrophe until any vaccine to cure the virus is developed. In the opinion of experts in medical field, it can take 1-2 years to prepare the vaccine.

Table 3: Deaths due to COVID-19 (till October 07, 2020) and Spanish influenza

Location	*Confirmed Cases*	*Confirmed deaths COVID-19*	*Published death toll (per 1000) Spanish influenza*
America	17,262,755	5,74,122	~15,40000
Europe	6,337,722	241,444	2,3000,646
Asia	11,331, 996	205,567	26,000,000-36,000,000
Africa	1,206,767	26414	~2,375,5000
Oceania	31,872	940	85000
World (Total)	35,537,491 (*Source*: WHO)	1,042,798 (*Source*: WHO)	>48,798,038

In order to analyze and establish the comparison of post and present pandemic, COVID-19 and Spanish Influenza (1918-19) respectively, we collected data from WHO official site and research papers on Spanish Influenza. The COVID-19 data has been collected till October 7, 2020 from its inception in December, 2019.

In this section, the detailed comparison of past pandemic Spanish Influenza and present pandemic COVID-19, are presented in terms of death toll and percentage. The Table 3 shows, death toll due to Spanish Influenza during 1918-19 and COVID-19 till October 7, 2020 since its inception in December, 2019 of five continents of the world. We observe from the table that the highest number of COVID-19 are confirmed cases are found in America, followed by Asia as of October 7, 2020, whereas the lowest cases are observed in Oceania. While, considering death toll due to COVID-19, we observe that the highest number of deaths are witnessed in America, with death toll 574,122 followed by Europe with death toll 241,444, whereas Asia comes at number third place with death toll 2,05,567. The lowest number of death toll is witnessed in Oceania. While comparing death toll of COVID-19 with Spanish Influenza, we see that in this pandemic, highest

Table 4: The Mortality Rate in Developed Countries and India Due To COVID-19

Country	*USA*	*Italy*	*UK*	*France*	*Belgium*	*Spain*	*Germany*	*Canada*	*India*
Population (in 1000s) (*)	3,26,687.50	60,421.76	66,460.34	66,977.11	11,433.26	46,796.54	82,905.78	37,057.76	**13,52,617.33**
Percentage of deaths	0.0630	0.0595	0.0637	0.4788	0.0882	0.0685	0.01163	0.0257	**0.0077**

Source: WHO. (*) *Source:* World Bank.

death toll was witnessed in Asian countries, followed by Africa, Europe, America and Oceania fell at the last place. Therefore, from this table we observe that the effect of Spanish Influenza was more in developing countries of Asia and Africa. The COVID-19 effect on developed countries of America and Europe was apparently opposite to the prediction of the scholars about future pandemic. For the final conclusion, death rate (i.e. percentage) of main developed countries is compared with India, displayed in Table 4. The reason behind selecting India for this study for the comparison with developed countries was mainly due to India's immense loss of human lives due to Spanish Influenza a century ago. It is observed from this table that the highest COVID-19 death rate is witnessed in France i.e. 0.4788, followed by Belgium, USA and UK. On the other hand death rate in India is 0.0077, which is quite low as compared to the death rate in the developed countries.

Thus, in this paper we conclude that, although scientists had predicted that in any future pandemic developing countries would be at high risk and hard hit as they were not prepared as compared to developed nations. However, our study shows that developing country like India with second largest population of the world, has quite lower mortality rate due to COVID-19 as compared to the developed countries like Italy, France, USA, UK, Spain, Belgium etc. The results of the present study are completely opposite to the predictions made by the experts. The criteria of this prediction was the rich resources and better healthcare system of developed countries and their preparations to meet such unwanted situation in future. They could easily procure the vaccine to stop the spread of pandemic. Hence, these countries will perform much better in pandemic situation. On the other hand, developing nations in the absence of better healthcare systems and lack of resources will pay heavy price in such times as they would not be able to save their population from the new disease. However, despite being second highest populated country in the world, the better performance of India is attained by following timely guidelines/advisories released by the government regarding the precautions such as washing hands, wearing mask, and maintaining social distance, etc. along with effective lockdowns and above all compliance of the people.

References

1. Source Economic, Political Weekly, and No August: 'Panic on the Pandemic', *Economic and Political Weekly*, 44.33 (2009), 5–6.
2. Johnson, Niall P. S. (2002): "Updating the Accounts of the 1918-20 "Spanish" Influenza Pandemic" *Bulletin of the History of Medicine*, Vol. 76, No. 1, p. 108, JSTOR.

3. Johnson Niall P. S. (2002): "Updating the Accounts of the 1918-20 "Spanish" Influenza Pandemic", p. 115.
4. Jeffery K Taubenberger: 'Symposium Keynote Address/: Fixed and Frozen Flu: The 1918 Influenza and Lessons for the Future Author (s): Jeffery K. Taubenberger Source/: *Avian Diseases*, Vol . 47, Special Issue . Proceedings of the Fifth International Symposium on Avian Influenz', 47.2003 (2020), 789–91.
5. Ian D. Mills (1986): "The 1918-1919 Influenza Pandemic- The Indian Experience", *Indian Economic and Social Historical Review,* 23, p. 30.
6. Siddharth Chandra and Eva Kassens-Noor: 'The Evolution of Pandemic Influenza: Evidence from India, 1918-19', *BMC Infectious Diseases*, 14.1 (2014), 1–10 <https://doi.org/10.1186/1471-2334-14-510>.
7. Martin J. Balaser (2006): Pandemics and Preparations, *The Journal of Infectious Diseases*, Vol. 134, supliment 2. Seasonal and Pandemic Influenza: at the crossroads, A Global opportunity, p. S70.
8. David M. Morens and Anthony S. Fauci: 'The 1918 Influenza Pandemic: Insights for the 21st Century', *The Journal of Infectious Diseases*, 195.7 (2007), 1018–28 <https://doi.org/10.1086/511989>.
9. Susan Mayor: 'Flu Experts Warn of Need for Pandemic Plans', *BMJ (Clinical Research Ed.)*, 321.7265 (2000), 852 <https://doi.org/10.1136/bmj.321.7265.852>.
10. Sungwon Yoon: 'Ideas, Institutions, and Interests in the Global Governance of Epidemics in Asia', *Asia-Pacific Journal of Public Health*, 22.SUPPL. 3 (2010) <https://doi.org/10.1177/1010539510373131>. 1295
11. Adolfo García Sastre and Richard J. Whitley: 'Lessons Learned from Reconstructing the 1918 Influenza Pandemic', *The Journal of Infectious Diseases*, 194.s2 (2006), S127–32 <https://doi.org/10.1086/507546>.
12. Tommy Bengtsson and Alain Gagnon: 'Revisiting Mortality Crises of the Past: Introduction', *Genus*, 67.2 (2011), 1–7 <https://doi.org/10.4402/genus-370>. p. 3.
13. Mangesh G. Korgaonker: 'The Indian Experience', *The New Economy in East Asia and the Pacific*, 2003, 103–23 <https://doi.org/10.4324/9780203643020>.
14. Ian D. Mills (1986): "The 1918-1919 Influenza Pandemic- The Indian Experience", *Indian Economic and Social Historical Review,* 23, p. 30.
15. John Parfet: 'Pandemic Preparedness', *BioProcess International*, 7.7 (2009), 136 <https://doi.org/10.1201/b16072-19>.Ingo
16. Amit Kapoor (2020): "An unwanted shipment: The Indian Experience of the 1918 Spanish flu", *The Economic Times,* 3 April https://economictimes.indiatimes.com/news/politics-and-nation/an-unwanted-shipment-the-indian-experience-of-the-1918-spanish-flu/articleshow/74963051.cms?from=mdr
17. Shenoy, K (2020): "Railways spread Spanish flu in 1918", TOI, 22 March, https://timesofindia.indiatimes.com/city/kochi/railways-spread-the-spanish-flu-in-india-in-1918/articleshow/74759235.cms

18. Ruby Bala (2011): "The Spread of Influenza Epidemic in Punjab (1918-1919)", *Proceedings of Indian History Congress,* Vol. 72, Part-I.
19.
20. David Killingray (2003): "A New 'Imperial Disease': The Influenza Pandemic 1918-19 and its Impact on the British Empire, *Caribbean Quarterly,* www.jstor.org/stable/40654422S
21. WHO, Situation Report-1, 21 Jan.
22. WHO, Situation Report-2, 22 Jan.
23. WHO, Situation Report 24 Jan cross check
24. https://www.who.int/emergencies/diseases/novel-coronavirus-2019/technical-guidance/naming-the-coronavirus-disease-(covid-2019)-and-the-virus-that-causes-it

COVID-19:
Conceptualisation and Issues

3

Genetic Comparison of Novel Coronavirus to SARS and MERS: A Review

Navpreet Kaur

Coronaviruses belong to the family of Coronaviridae which includes a cluster of single-stranded, non-segmented, positive-sense enveloped RNA viruses with largest genomes (25-31 kb) where it is sub-categorised under a subfamily of Coronavirina that are involved in human and vertebrate's diseases. These viruses are known to cause illness that varies between a common cold to more severe diseases like severe acute respiratory syndrome (SARS) and the Middle East respiratory syndrome (MERS). The corona-viruses are further classified into generas of Alphacoronavirus, Betacorona-virus, Deltacoronavirus and Gammacoronavirus. The analysis phylogenetic relationships and genomic structures confide the COVID-19 belongs to the genera Betacoronaviruses (Mousavizadeh and Ghasemi, 2020).

The fresh surfacing of a novel coronavirus epidemic with a rare viral pneumonia in Wuhan, China was reported in December 2019 which latter flushed the world in early 2020. The World Health Organisation (WHO) declared the COVID-19 eruption a global pandemic in March 2020. Despite meticulous global restraints and quarantine efforts, the frequency of COVID-19 continues to rise, with more than 3364535 laboratory-confirmed cases and over 239236 deaths worldwide as of 3rd May 2020. The genomic structure of the COVID-19 has a close genetic similarity to that of severe acute respiratory syndrome-related coronaviruses which belong to order of beta-corona-viruses and like SARS-virus it also uses the ACE-receptors to enter into the cells.

Genetic Map of COVID-19

Coronaviruses are single-stranded (positive-sense) RNA viruses associated with a nucleoprotein that is encompassed in matrix protein which forms its capsid. The surface glycoproteins from capsid projects like club-shaped projections are shown in Figure 1 and 2. A few coronaviruses also contain hemagglutinin-esterase protein (HE) 4. The GpC content is variable among different lineages of coronaviruses ranging from 32 percent to 43 percent. The genes like ORF1ab, spike (S), envelope (E), membrane (M) and nucleocapsid (N) are conserved ones, although there are a variable number

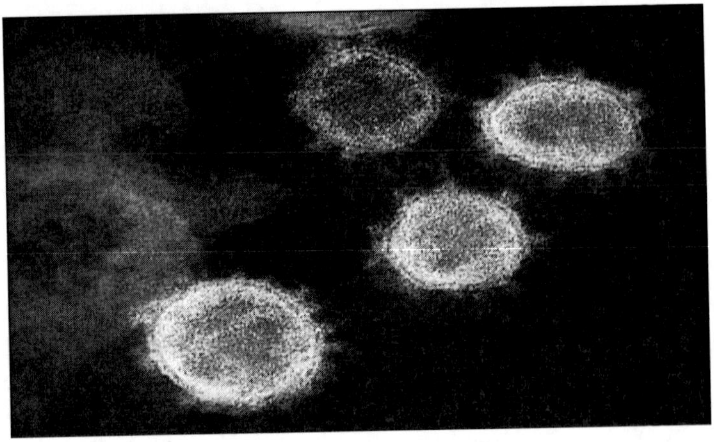

Figure 1: The Transmission electron microscope image of SARS-CoV-2.

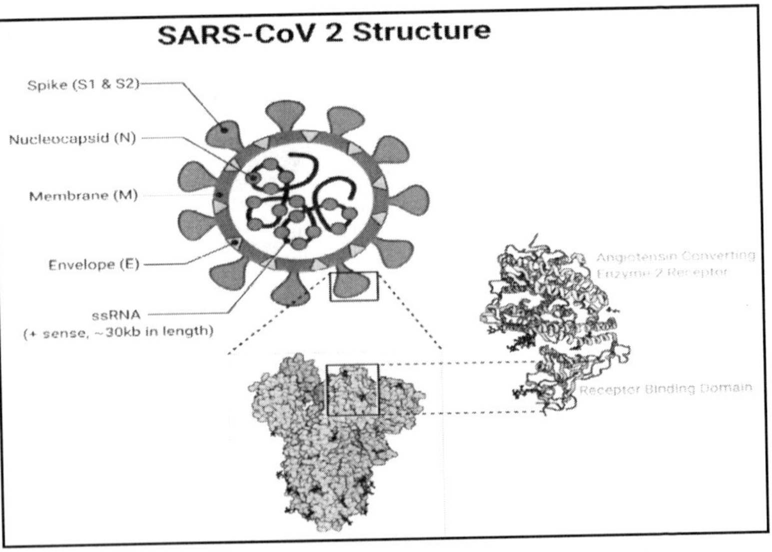

Figure 2: Structure of SARS- CoV 2 (Cascella et al, 2020).

of open reading frames in between them. A large gene encodes a replicase (ORF1ab) is followed by the four major structural proteins encoding genes occur in an order as 5'-ORF1ab, S, E, M, and N -3'(Huang et al, 2020 and Wu et al, 2020).

There are eleven ORFs (Open reading frames) with the full length of 29,903 bp in its genomes and first ORF (ORF1a/b) encodes 16 non-structural proteins (nsp1-16). A frameshift between ORF1a and ORF1b translates about two-third of the genome into two polypeptides: pp1a and pp1b which are processed by virally encoded chemotrypsin like protease (3CLpro) and Papin-like proteases into 16 nsps. The structural proteins [spike (S), membrane (M), envelope (E), and nucleocapsid (N)] of the virus are translated from the sgRNAs by an open reading frame 10 and 11 that comprise of one-third of the genome (Czub et al, 2005 and Van et al, 2012). The detailed genomic structure of SARS-COVID-19 is depicted in Figure 3.

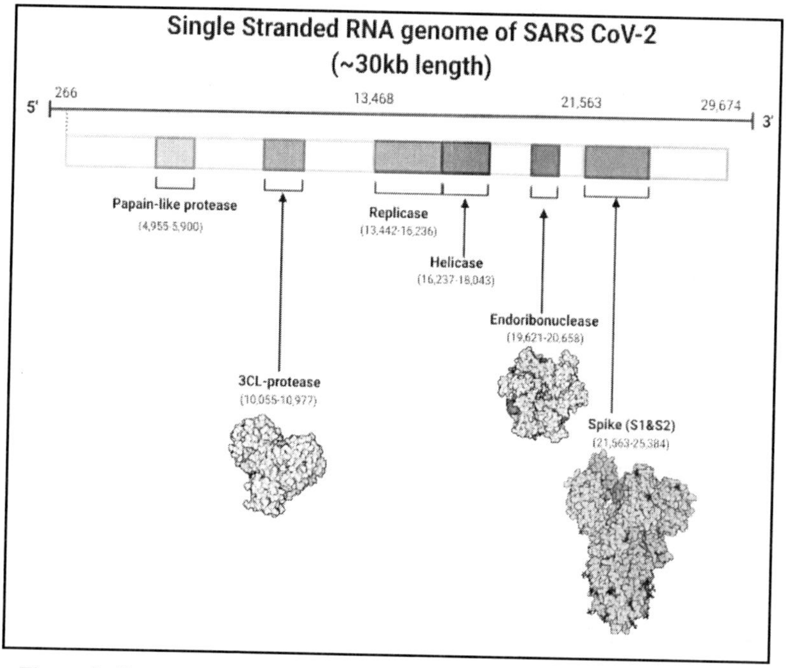

Figure 3: Single-stranded RNA genome of SARS-CoV2 (Cascella et al, 2020).

The membrane of the virus has three or four viral proteins among which membrane (M) glycoprotein is most abundant spanning the membrane bilayer thrice, leaving a long COOH terminus (cytoplasmic domain) inside and short NH2-terminal domain outside the virion (CAM et al, 1998). The spike protein (S) constitutes the peplomer which is mainly an antibody neutraliser. The spike proteins are type I membrane glycoprotein. The molecular interaction (predominantly by M) between the membrane proteins determines the formation and composition of the membrane protein. However, the non-infectious spikeless virions are produced in the presence of tunicamycin (CAM et al, 1998 and Woo et al, 2010).

The low heterogeneity among the sequences of SARS-CoV-2 establishes its evolution from a common ancestor as it has an average substitution rate for 10-4 substitutions per year per site (Su et al, 2016 and Lu et al, 2020). Subsequently, so far, the variant number with an addition or deletion is 4007 with the mutant numbers of 3951, 82, 10 and 20 respectively (https://bigd.big.ac.cn/ncov). And with a continuous spread of the COVID-19, these numbers are ever-changing. One of the mutant isolated from Japanese COVID-19 patient had a deletion of eight amino acids in viral polyprotein 1ab (pp1ab) protein encoded by ORF1ab gene and patient did not show critical symptoms (Cardenas et al, 2020).

The presence of two mutations of SARS-CoV-2 could confer lower stability of the protein structures that are identified as NSP6 (amino acid position 3691) and ORF10 adjacent regions (amino acid position 9659) respectively (Bevenuto et al, 2020).

Another two mutations with a higher mutation rate of 30.53 percent and 29.47 percent for nt28144 in ORF8 and nt8782 in ORF1a respectively categorises the SARS-CoV-2 virus as type L (28144T) and S (28144C) based on the different amino acid of Leucine and Serine in nt28144 (Wang et al, 2020). The L type with a mutation rate of 70 percent was more prevalent than the S type that has a mutation rate of 30 percent where the latter was indicated to be the ancestral version and was less aggressive and contagious (Xiaolu et al, 2020). The University of Cambridge found three central variants distinguished by amino acid alteration, named A (8782T, 28144C), B (derived from A, 8782C, 28144T), and C (derived from B, 26144T) in 160 different human SARS-CoV-2 genomes, with A being the ancestral type according to the bat out-group coronavirus (Forster et al, 2020). The A and C type predominates Americans and Europeans, whereas the B type was most commonly found in East Asia.

Recently, with reverse genetics researchers have cloned and resurrected the novel coronaviruses that is an attractive alternative to obtain infectious virus strains and a method to provide researchers with infectious virus strains without valuable clinical samples (Thao et al, 2020).

Comparison of SARS-COV-2 (COVID-19) with SARS-COV, and MERS-COV

The genome of coronavirus consists of 50UTR (untranslated regions) and 30UTR that are involved in RNA-RNA interaction in inter- and intra-molecular interactions. The first ORF (Pb1ab) at the 5' end encodes non-structural proteins in COVID-19, SARS-CoV and MERS-CoV which 7096, 7073 and 7078 amino acids long respectively. The length of spike protein is variable as its 1273 amino acids long for COVID-19 and 21493 amino-acids for SARS-CoV and is 1270 amino acids long for MERS- CoV. The COVID-19 is about 79 percent similar to SARS-CoV while it's about 50 percent similar to MERS and the difference is in the arrangement of the envelope protein (E), membrane protein (M) and nucleocapsid protein (N) whereas 96.3 percent identity with a bat coronavirus (Lu et al, 2020 and Paraskevis et al, 2020). The closest relatives of SARS-CoV-2 are several viruses originated from bats, such as Bat-CoV RaTG3, Bat SARSr CoV-ZC45, Bat SARSr CoV-ZXC21 as suggested by phylogenetic analysis suggests that the closest relatives and therefore, bats are assumed to be the original host of SARS-CoV-2. However, there are suspicions of an intermediate host, who transferred the novel coronavirus to human because the sequence of bat virus Bat-CoV RaTG3 and SARS-CoV-2 has a minor difference (Lu et al, 2020 and Zhou et al, 2020). This doubtful intermediate host was suggested to be the Pangolin by Chinese researchers based on genetic analysis (Cyranoski et al, 2020). A recent study has instituted that it can easily infect ferrets and cats, but weakly infectious to pigs, dogs, ducks and chickens (Shi et al, 2020).

The spike protein of COVID-19 (SARS-CoV-2) is primed by enzyme protease TMPRSS2 which then binds to ACE2 (the angiotensin-converting enzyme 2) receptors and thus enters into the cell. This entry process is similar to SARS. The entry of the virus into the cell is followed by uncoating of the genome which is later transcribed, translated and replicated at the cytoplasmic membranes. The 20 kb replicase gene encodes a huge protein complex that comprises of 16 viral subunits and cellular proteins by both continuous and non-continuous RNA synthesis (Sola et al, 2015). The various other enzymes are RNA dependent RNA polymerase, RNA helicase, coronavirus replicase, putative sequence-specific endoribonuclease, 30- to-50 exoribonuclease, 20-O-ribose methyltransferase, ADP ribose 10-phosphatase and, in a subset of group 2 coronaviruses, cyclic phosphodiesterase (Ziebuhr 2005 and Almaza'n et al, 2006). The translated proteins assemble at the cell membrane and genomic RNA is then incorporated. The mature particles are formed by budding from the internal cell membrane (McIntosh, 2009).

The receptor of SARS-CoV-2: Angiotensin-converting enzyme II (ACE2)

The host infection and transmission capacity are determined by the envelope spike (S) protein (Lu et al, 2020). The spike proteins of SARS-CoV-2 and SARS-CoV have a highly similar three-dimensional structure of the receptor-binding domain (RBD) thus invading through the receptor ACE2 (Chen et al, 2020). The *in-vitro* studies from HeLa cells with or without ACE2 expression suggests the virus can enter humans, Chinese horseshoe bats, civets, pigs to mice except that of the mouse as an entry receptor (Zhou et al, 2020).

ACE2 are a type I membrane protein receptors expressed in the lungs, stratified epithelial cells of upper oesophagus, myocardial cells, cholangiocytes, intestine, absorptive enterocytes from ileum and colon, kidney proximal tubule cells and testicle (Ding et al, 2004; Liang et al, 2020 and Zhao et al, 2020). Thus, all these cells highly expressing ACE2 receptors may be potential to be invaded by SARS-CoV-2. Moreover, the Surface plasmon resonance analysis revealed transmission capacity of SARS-CoV-2 is stronger as its affinity of human ACE2 protein binding to novel coronavirus S protein is 10 to 20 fold higher than that of SARS-CoV S protein (Wrapp et al, 2020). The strong interaction of SARS-CoV-2 RBD with ACE2 receptors was also verified by molecular modelling techniques (Chen et al, 2020). The viral S protein interacts with the cell surface receptor ACE2 which may activate the downstream renin-angiotensin-aldosterone system (RAAS) as ACE2 is one of the crucial components of RAAS.

Viral Pathogenesis

Human Betacoronaviruses (SARS-CoV-2, SARS-CoV, and MERS-CoV) have analogous genotype and phenotype but the genetic and phenotypic differences can sway their pathogenesis. There are several comorbidities such as cardiovascular diseases, diabetes and cerebrovascular diseases. The abnormalities like coagulation activation, myocardial injuries, cellular immune deficiency, secondary bacterial infections, and hepatic and kidney injuries have been reported (Chen et al, 2020). Lymphopenia and sustained inflammations have been recorded in majority cases of severe disease and death. Most of these observations of SARS-CoV-2 patients are similar to that of the 2003 SARS epidemic (Liu et al, 2020).

Vaccines and Antiviral Drugs

At present, COVID-19 associated pathologies have no medicine or anti-virus vaccine and clinical management includes infection prevention, control measures and supportive care. Based on S protein evaluation various vaccines and antiviral drugs have been evaluated. The vaccines can include full length S protein, Recombinant S protein or can be Recombinant RBD protein (Du et al, 2009). The various antiviral therapies designed based on S protein structure include S cleavage inhibitors, S protein inhibitors, RBDeACE2 blockers, protease inhibitors, neutralising antibodies, fusion core blockers, and small interfering RNAs (Du et al, 2009). Although the countries are focused on vaccine development against SARS-CoV-2 yet existing medicines have been re-purposed. The antivirals weaken the virus entry to cell and prevent them from multiplying have been foremost treatment till date. Antibiotics can be used in the case of a secondary bacterial infection although have no role in treating COVID-19 patients. Since the first appearance of the disease in December 2019 in China, the effectiveness of different types of drugs that were used previously to treat other diseases to include malaria and HIV drugs, antivirals, blood plasma derivatives and arthritis drugs and newly developed DNA vaccines was tested which are listed in Table 1.

Table 1: The Virus Drugs and Vaccines Tested For Their Effectiveness and Efficacy against SARS-CoV-2

Therapies				
Sl. No	***Drug***	***Generic name/ Developed by***	***Target receptor/ Target Patients***	***Reference***
1.	IFN ribaverin	Toyama Chemical		Chen et al, 2020
2.	losartan		ACE blockers (Angiotensin receptor 1 (AT1R) blockers)	Gurwitz 2020
4.	Remdesvir	[GS-5734], Gilead Sciences	Against Ebola Virus (Blocks the viral replication through pre-mature termination of RNA transcription)	Sheahan et al, 2017; Liu et al, 2020; Wang et al, 2020 and Holshue et al, 2020
5.	Favilavir	Toyama chemicals	Nose and throat patients, Approved in Japan in 2014 for flu	Elfiky et al, 2020 and Li et al, 2020;
6.	Chloroquine and hydroxychloro quine		Against Malaria, Chemoprophylaxis, rheumatoid arthritis and lupus	Dong et al, 2020 and Gao et al, 2020
7.	Lopinavir/riton avir	Kaletra by AbbVie	Protease inhibitor	Que et al, 2003 and Chu et al, 2004

(Contd...)

8.	Tocilzumab	Actemra	Rheumatoid arthritis	Dong et al, 2020 and Zhang et al, 2020
9.	Darunavir	Anti-Viral HIV-1 protease inhibitor	Inhibits the replication and inhibits the efficacy	Dong et al, 2020
10	Ivermectin		Anti-parasitic	Caly et al, 2020
11.	Blood Plasma	Recovered patients	Presence of neutralizing antibodies was used in Spanish Flu.	Cheng et al, 2005; Duan et al, 2010 Griensven et al, 2016 and Chen et al, 2020
12.	DNA vaccine	Entos Pharmaceutica ls	Fusogenic nano-medicine	Abd El-Aziz et al, 2020
13.	AT-100 Human Surfactant Protein D [rhSP-D]	Airways therapeutics	Reduces the inflammation and infection in the Lungs.	Crouch, 2000
14.	Virus-Like Particles (VLP)	Medicago (Canada)	A multi-protein structure that resembles the native virus surface proteins.	Roldao et al, 2010
15.	I-Mab	Biopharma by TJM2	Against cytokine release syndrome	Vornhagen et al, 2018
16.	TZLS-501	Tiziana Life Sciences	Monoclonal Antibodies	Rayner et al, 2020
17.	ChAdOxl nCoV-19	The University of Oxford and Italian Pharmaceutica ls Advent SRL.	Attenuated Adenovirus	Alharbi et al, 2017

The changes in COVID-19 sequence might boost its virulence and its transmittance among people. Although it is expected to become less virulent due to genetic tailback for RNA viruses recurrent human to human transmissions (Cascella et al, 2020).

Conclusion

Drug discovery against SARS-CoV-2 is an exigent process but is imperative. To counter the pandemic spread to 199 countries of the world the development of anti-virus vaccine is crucial. Due to the high similarity of the virus to its families efforts have been made to provide vaccines and medicines for COVID-19. Therefore, more structural details of surface proteins and details about the basis of replication, structure and pathogenicity of COVID-19 are need of an hour for discovering a novel way to the vaccination. This likely will hasten the development of drugs and/or vaccine against SARS-CoV-2. Furthermore, it is very essential to go on with WHO guidelines to avoid the spread of COVID-19.

References

- Abd El-Aziz, Tarek Mohamed, and James D. Stockand. 2020: "Recent progress and challenges in drug development against COVID-19 coronavirus (SARS-CoV-2)-an update on the status." *Infection, Genetics and Evolution,* p. 104327.
- Almaza´n F, DeDiego ML, Gala´n C, Escors D, A´lvarez E, Ortego J, Sola I, Zuñiga S, Alonso S, Moreno JL, Nogales A. 2006, "Construction of a severe acute respiratory syndrome coronavirus infectious cDNA clone and a replicon to study coronavirus RNA synthesis." *Journal of Virology,* 80 (21), pp. 10900-10906.
- Benvenuto D, Angeletti S, Giovanetti M, Bianchi M, Pascarella S, Cauda R, Ciccozzi M, Cassone2020: "Evolutionary analysis of SARS-CoV-2: how mutation of Non-Structural Protein 6 (NSP6) could affect viral autophagy". *The Journal of Infection.*
- Caly, L, Druce JD, Catton MG, Jans DA, Wagstaff KM. 2020: "The FDA-approved Drug Ivermectin inhibits the replication of SARS-CoV-2 in vitro". *Antiviral Research*, p. 104787.
- CAM de Haan, Kuo L, Masters PS, Vennema H, Rottier PJM. 1998: "Coronavirus particle assembly: primary structure requirements of the membrane protein". *Journal of Virology*; 72(8), pp. 6838-50.
- Cao B, Wang Y, Wen D, Liu W, Wang J, Fan G, Ruan L, Song B, Cai Y, Wei M, Li X. 2020: "A Trial of Lopinavir–Ritonavir in Adults Hospitalised with Severe Covid-19". *New England Journal of Medicine.*
- Cardenas-Conejo Y, Linan-Rico A, Garcia-Rodriguez DA, Centeno-Leija S, Serrano-Posada H. 2020: "An exclusive 42 amino acid signature in pp1ab protein provides insights into the evolutive history of the 2019 novel human-pathogenic coronavirus (SARS-CoV-2)." *Journal of Medical Virology.*
- Cascella M, Rajnik M, Cuomo A, Dulebohn C, Di Napoli R. 2020: "Features, evaluation and treatment coronavirus (COVID-19)". *In Statpearls [internet].* StatPearls Publishing.
- Chen L, Xiong J, Bao L, Shi Y. 2020: "Convalescent plasma as a potential therapy for COVID-19".*The Lancet Infectious Diseases*, 20(4), pp. 398-400.
- Chen N, Zhou M, Dong X, Qu J, Gong F, Han Y, Han Y, Qiu Y, Wang J, Liu Y, Wei Y, Yu T. 2020: "Epidemiological and clinical characteristics of 99 cases of 2019 novel coronavirus pneumonia in Wuhan, China: a descriptive study". *Lancet* 2020; 395(10223), pp. 507-513.
- Chen Y, Guo Y, Pan Y, Zhao ZJ. 2020. "Structure analysis of the receptor binding of 2019-nCoV". *Biochemical and biophysical research communications.*
- Chen Y, Liu Q, Guo D. 2020: "Emerging coronaviruses: genome structure, replication, and pathogenesis". *Journal of Medical Virology*; 92, pp. 418-423.
- Cheng Y, Wong R, Soo YO, Wong WS, Lee CK, Ng MH, Chan P, Wong KC, Leung CB, Cheng G. 2005: "Use of convalescent plasma therapy in SARS patients in Hong Kong". *European Journal of Clinical Microbiology and Infectious Diseases*, 24(1), pp. 44-46.
- Chu CM, Cheng VC, Hung IF, Wong MM, Chan KH, Chan KS, Kao RY, Poon LL, Wong CL, Guan Y, Peiris JS. 2004: "Role of lopinavir/ritonavir in the

treatment of SARS: initial virological and clinical findings". *Thorax,*59(3), pp. 252-6.

- Crouch EC. 2000. "Surfactant protein-D and pulmonary host defense". *Respiratory Research,*1(2), pp. 93-108.
- Cyranoski D. 2020. "Mystery deepens over animal source of coronavirus". *Nature*, 579 (7797), pp. 18-19.
- Czub M, Weingartl H, Czub S, He R, Cao J. 2005: "Evaluation of modified vaccinia virus Ankara based recombinant SARS vaccine in ferrets". *Vaccine*; 23(17-18), pp. 2273-79.
- Ding Y, He L, Zhang Q. 2004: "Organ distribution of severe acute respiratory syndrome (SARS) associated coronavirus (SARS-CoV) in SARS patients: implications for pathogenesis and virus transmission pathways". *The Journal of Pathology,*203(2), pp. 622-30.
- Dong L, S Hu and J Gao. 2020: "Discovering drugs to treat coronavirus disease 2019 (COVID-19)". *Drug Discoveries and Therapeutics*, 14(1), pp. 58-60.
- Du L, He Y, Zhou Y, Liu S, Zheng B-J, Jiang S. 2009: "The spike protein of SARS-CoVda target for vaccine and therapeutic development". *Nature Reviews Microbiology*, 7(3), pp. 226-36.
- Duan K, Liu B, Li C, Zhang H, Yu T, Qu J, Zhou M, Chen L, Meng S, Hu Y, Peng C. 2020: "Effectiveness of convalescent plasma therapy in severe COVID-19 patients". *Proceedings of the National Academy of Sciences*, pp. 202004168.
- Elfiky AA. 2020: "Anti-HCV, nucleotide inhibitors, repurposing against COVID-19". *Life Sciences*, 248, pp. 1174-77.
- Forster P, Forster L, Renfrew C, Forster M. 2020: "Phylogenetic network analysis of SARS-CoV-2 genomes". *Proceedings of the National Academy of Sciences of the United States of America.*
- Gao J, Tian Z and Yang X. 2020: "Breakthrough: Chloroquine phosphate has shown apparent efficacy in treatment of COVID-19 associated pneumonia in clinical studies".*Bioscience Trends,*14(1), pp. 72-73.
- Griensven VJ, Edwards T, de Lamballerie X, Semple MG, Gallian P, Baize S, Horby PW, Raoul H, Magassouba NF, Antierens A, Lomas C. "Evaluation of convalescent plasma for Ebola virus disease in Guinea". *New England Journal of Medicine*, 374(1), pp. 33-42.
- Gurwitz D. 2020: "Angiotensin receptor blockers as tentative SARSCoV- 2 therapeutics". *Drug development research,* pp. 1-4. https://doi.org/10.1002/ddr.21656.
- Holshue ML, DeBolt C, Lindquist S, Lofy KH, Wiesman J, Bruce H, Spitters C, Ericson K, Wilkerson S, Tural A, Diaz G. 2020: "First Case of 2019 Novel Coronavirus in the United States". *New England Journal of Medicine*, 382(10), pp. 929-936.
- Huang R, Xia J, Chen Y, Shan C, Wu C. 2020: "A family cluster of SARS-CoV-2 infection involving 11 patients in Nanjing, China". *The Lancet Infectious Diseases.*

- Li H, Wang YM, Xu JY, Cao B. 2020: "Potential antiviral therapeutics for 2019 Novel Coronavirus". *Chinese Journal of tuberculosis and respiratory diseases*, 43(3), pp. 170-172.
- Liang W, Feng Z, Rao S, et al. Diarrhoea may be underestimated: a missing link in 2019 novel coronavirus. *Gut* 2020.
- Liu C, Zhou Q, Li Y, Garner LV, Watkins SP, Carter LJ, Smoot J, Gregg AC, Daniels AD, Jervey S, Albaiu D. 2020: "Research and development on therapeutic agents and vaccines for COVID-19 and related human coronavirus diseases". ACS Publications.
- Lu R, Zhao X, Li J, Niu P, Yang B, Wu H, Wang W, Song H, Huang B, Zhu N, Bi Y. 2020: "Genomic characterisation and epidemiology of 2019 novel coronavirus: implications for virus origins and receptor binding". *Lancet*, 395(10224), pp. 565-74.
- McIntosh K, Peiris JSM. 2009: "Coronaviruses. Clinical virology". 3rd ed. American Society of Microbiology, pp. 1155-71.
- Mousavizadeh L, Ghasemi S. 2020: "Genotype and phenotype of COVID-19: Their roles in pathogenesis". *Journal of Microbiology, Immunology and Infection,*https://doi.org/10.1016/j.jmii.2020.03.022.
- Paraskevis D, Kostaki EG, Magiorkinis G, Panayiotakopoulos G, Sourvinos G, Tsiodras S. 2020: "Full-genome evolutionary analysis of the novel coronavirus (2019-nCoV) rejects the hypothesis of emergence as a result of a recent recombination event. *Infection, genetics and evolution: journal of molecular epidemiology and evolutionary genetics in infectious diseases,* 79, 104212.
- Que TL, Wong VC, Yuen KY. 2003: "Treatment of severe acute respiratory syndrome with lopinavir/ritonavir: a multicentre retrospective matched cohort study". *Hong Kong Medical Journal*, *9*(6), pp. 399-406.
- Rayner CR, Smith PF, Hershberger K, Wesche D. 2020: "Optimizing COVID-19 candidate therapeutics: Thinking Without Borders". *Clinical and Translational Science.*
- Roldao A, Mellado MC, Castilho LR, Carrondo MJ, Alves PM. 2010: "Virus-like particles in vaccine development". *Expert review of vaccines*, 9(10), pp. 1149-76.
- Sheahan TP, Sims AC, Graham RL, Menachery VD, Gralinski LE, Case JB, Leist SR, Pyrc K, Feng JY, Trantcheva I, Bannister R. 2017: "Broad-spectrum antiviral GS-5734 inhibits both epidemic and zoonotic coronaviruses". *Science translational medicine*, 9(396).
- Shi J, Wen Z, Zhong G, Yang H, Wang C, Huang B, Liu R, He X, Shuai L, Sun Z, Zhao. 2020: "Susceptibility of ferrets, cats, dogs, and other domesticated animals to SARS-coronavirus 2". *Science* (New York, NY).
- Sola I, Almazan F, Zuniga S, Enjuanes L. 2015: "Continuous and discontinuous RNA synthesis in coronaviruses". *Annual review of virology*, 2, pp. 265-88.
- Su S, Wong G, Shi W, Liu J, Lai AC, Zhou J, Liu W, Bi Y, Gao GF. "Epidemiology, Genetic Recombination, and Pathogenesis of Coronaviruses". *Trends in microbiology,* 24(6), pp. 490-502.

- Thao TT, Labroussaa F, Ebert N, V'kovski P, Stalder H, Portmann J, Kelly J, Steiner S, Holwerda M, Kratzel A, Gultom M. 2020: "Rapid reconstruction of SARS-CoV-2 using a synthetic genomics platform". *BioRxiv*, published online February 21.
- van Boheemen S, de Graaf M, Lauber C, Bestebroer TM, Raj VS, Zaki AM, Osterhaus AD, Haagmans BL, Gorbalenya AE, Snijder EJ, Fouchier RA. 2012: "Genomic characterisation of a newly discovered coronavirus associated with acute respiratory distress syndrome in humans". *MBio*, 3(6), pp. 00473-12
- Wang C, Liu Z, Chen Z, Huang X, Xu M, He T, Zhang Z 2020: "The establishment of reference sequence for SARS-CoV-2 and variation analysis". *Journal of Medical Virology, 92*(6), pp. 667-674.
- Wang M, Cao R, Zhang L, Yang X, Liu J, Xu M, Shi Z, Hu Z, Zhong W, Xiao G. 2019: "Remdesivir and chloroquine effectively inhibit the recently emerged novel coronavirus (2019-nCoV) in vitro". *Cell Research*, 30(3), pp. 269-271.
- Woo PCY, Huang Y, Lau SKP, Yuen K-Y. 2010: "Coronavirus genomics and bioinformatics analysis". *Viruses*, 2(8), pp. 1804-20.
- Wu F, Zhao S, Yu B, Chen YM, Wang W, Song ZG, Hu Y, Tao ZW, Tian JH, Pei YY, Yuan ML. 2020: "A new coronavirus associated with human respiratory disease in China". *Nature*; 579(7798), pp. 265-9.
- Xiaolu. T, Changcheng. W, Xiang L. 2020: "On the origin and continuing evolution of SARS-CoV-2". *National Science Review.*
- Z Jie, He H, Xi H, Zhi Z 2020: "Expert consensus on chloroquine phosphate for the treatment of novel coronavirus pneumonia". *Zhonghua Jie He He Hu Xi Za Zhi*, 43(3), pp. 185-188.
- Zhang Q, Wang Y, Qi C, Shen L, Li J. 2020: "Clinical trial analysis of 2019-nCoV therapy registered in China". *Journal of Medical Virology*, *92*(6), pp. 540-545.
- Zhao Y, Zhao Z, Wang Y, Zhou Y, Ma Y, Zuo W. 2020: "Single-cell RNA expression profiling of ACE2, the receptor of SARS-CoV-2". published online January 26.
- Zhou P, Yang XL, Wang XG, Hu B, Zhang L, Zhang W, Si HR, Zhu Y, Li B, Huang CL, Chen HD.2020: "A pneumonia outbreak associated with a new coronavirus of probable bat origin". *Nature,* 579(7798), pp. 270-3.
- Ziebuhr J. 2005: "The coronavirus replicase. Coronavirus replication and reverse genetics". *Springer*, pp. 57-94.
- Wrapp D, Wang N, Corbett KS, et al. 2020: "Cryo-EM structure of the 2019-nCoV spike in the prefusion conformation". *Science,*367(6483), pp. 1260-1263.
- Alharbi, N.K., et al. 2017. "ChAdOx1 and MVA based vaccine candidates against MERS-CoV elicit neutralizing antibodies and cellular immune responses in mice". *Vaccine*, 35(30), pp. 3780-3788.
- Vornhagen AS. 2018: "Cytokine release syndrome". *J Immunother Cancer*, 6(1), p. 56.

4

To Fight COVID-19 Using Machine Learning Approach: A Challenge

Harveen Kaur, Harpreet Kaur and Amandeep Singh

Serious Acute Respiratory Syndrome Coronavirus two (SARS-CoV-2), the causative operator of novel coronavirus (COVID-19 or 2019-nCoV), came to the surface in late 2019. It is believed that COVID-19 emerged from the Hubei Province of China called Wuhan. It spread at a very fast pace from Person to Person and soon became a Pandemic. It is rumored to be first derived from bats and soon got transmitted to humans via raccon dog being the intermediate host. The significant indications of SARS-CoV-2 incorporate fever, shortness of breath and cough [1]. No clinically proven drug or vaccine exists to cure it which leads to a lot many deaths throughout the world and is still causing the high number of deaths across the world. Despite precautious measures taken by the government, there has been no full stop to it. As the number of patients is increasing with each passing day there is a burden on healthcare systems to provide them a required medical aid. It no doubt will release the burden on healthcare systems if an approximate number of future possible cases are made known to them in advance so that precautious measures can be taken beforehand and the medical aid for the future patients can somehow be arranged and managed. It has become urgency for the non-clinical techniques to come into action such as Data Mining and Machine Learning. Data Mining Plays a major role in collecting past data and analyze that data to give predictive results for the future. Based on the past number of cases and throughout rise in cases the future can be predicted depending on government policies laid such as a strict lockdown or a lockdown with relaxation. In past decades many pandemics came into being such as EBOLA, Spanish flu and data mining though less refined in its techniques was then also used to do future analysis. Developed Mining techniques these days are effective non-clinical techniques for collecting past records of cases, the circumstantial rise or fall in the number of cases which in turn are a data set for future case predictive analysis. Many Machine Learning Predictive techniques exist with practical results and here in this paper, a study of decision tree algorithm, Naïve Bayes algorithm, k-means algorithm and Random Forest Algorithm is done to make it easy to choose one according to the available data set, depending on term i.e. long term or short term prediction and many other factors.

Literature Review

Till Date many of the different and advanced researches had been done on the analysis and prediction of COVID-19 virus. Some of the research works done on the prediction of COVID-19 using Machine Learning Algorithms are described below.

L. J. Muhammad, Md. Milon Islam, Usman Sani Sharif and Safial Islam Ayon in 2020 in paper [1] proposed Predictive Data Mining Model for Novel Coronavirus (COVID-19) Infected Patients Recovery. In this research, the prediction of an infected patient's recovery is done. This model predicted the number of days that a patient will take to recover from Covid-19 Pandemic. They have tried to figure out the maximum and the minimum number of days required for the patient's recovery. The algorithms that have been applied to the data set of South Korea patients are the Decision Tree, Support Vector Machine, Logistic Regression, Random forest, K-Nearest Neighbor, Naïve Bayes Algorithms. Out of these Decision Tree, Data Mining Algorithm stands out with an accuracy of 99.85 percent. Parikshit N. Mahalle, Nilesh P. Sable, Namita P. Mahalle and Gitanjali R.Shinde in 2020 in paper [2] proposed Multimodal data techniques for Covid-19 prediction. They discussed and analyzed different predictive analytic techniques available for analysis of changes over time. Besides analyzing techniques for prediction and forecasting a comparison of them was also done to analyze their state-of-art. Random forest Algorithm, Gradient boosting Model, K-means Algorithm, FB Prophet Algorithms have been compared. As a result of comparison, FB Prophet Algorithm comes up as the one with efficient prediction results for the next 3 months.IsraAl-Turaiki, MonaAlshahrani, TahaniAlmutairi in 2016 in paper [3] built predictive models for MERS-CoV infections using data mining techniques. Here in this paper Decision tree algorithm was studied to understand which age group is likely to get infected and to understand the recovery of MERS-Cov and it came up with the result that the healthcare workers are safe from getting infected as on timely bases they are vaccinated due to the reason that most of the time they are in contact with the infected patients. Despite this they stay safe due to these timely vaccinations. This model gave accuracy between 53.6 percent and 71.58 percent. Ali Keshavarzi in 2020 in paper [4] stated Coronavirus Infectious Disease (COVID-19) Modeling: Evidence of Geographical Signals. Here in this paper 10-fold testing was performed with latitude, longitude, age and sex as leading parameters. A comparison of Decision Tree, Naïve Bayes, Random Forest and Logistic Model Trees algorithms was done based on these parameters and the accuracy of these models was rated according to Kappa Statistics and researcher came up with the result that Random Forest Algorithm outperforms the rest with highest kappa value of 0.9083 followed by Decision Trees Algorithm with 0.8854 of kappa statistics value. Celestine Iwendi, Ali Kashif Bashir, Atharva Peshkar, R. Sujatha, Jyotirmoy Chatterjee, Swetha Pasupuleti, Rishita Mishra, Sofia Pillai, Ohyun Jo in 2020 in paper [5] proposed Boosted Random Forest Algorithm to predict the health of Covid-19 infected patient. Here in this paper the geographical, travel, health history of patient is fed as an input to this random forest algorithm. All these factors decide out the severity of the case and the chances of recovery. Random Forest Algorithm provably gives accurate results even when the datasets are not so balanced. As a result of this research it was found that there exist a precise correlation between the gender and death of patient. Random Forest Algorithm has an accuracy of 94 percent. Shashank Reddy Vadyala, Sai Nethra Betgeri, Eric A. Sherer, Amod Amritphalein 2020 in paper [6] presented the model for the Prediction of the Number of COVID-19 Confirmed Cases Based on K-Means-LSTM. In this research, the hybrid model was constructed to predict the Covid-19 cases. The hybrid algorithm of K-Means and Long-short-Term-Memory Algorithm has been made to create a K-Means LSTM Combinational Algorithm for short term prediction. This model was specifically constructed to predict the rise or fall in the Covid-19 cases in USA in the near future. This hybrid model successfully came up with high accuracy showing up RMSE of 601.20. This model surpassed SEIR model.

Sanjay Kumar Sonbhadra, Sonali Agarwal, P. Nagabhusha in 2020 in paper [7] targeted specific mining of COVID-19 scholarly articles using one-class approach. Here K-Means Algorithm was implemented not for predicting the Covid-19 cases but for mining Covid-19 scholarly articles. This research was targeted to make it easier for researchers to extract the best suited article using machine learning approach. In the world full of knowledge sources it has become difficult to easefully extract the best suited article, K-Means clustering algorithm came to rescue and was proven by the researchers that K-Means Algorithm is well suited for custom extraction of data. Akib Mohi Ud Din Khanday, Syed Tanzeel Rabani, Qamar Rayees Khan, Nusrat Rouf, Masarat Mohi Ud Din in 2020 in paper [8] proposed Naïve Bayes algorithm for detecting Covid-19 using Clinical Data. Clinical dataset of 212 patients was taken into consideration. A perfect ratio 70:30 was done of dataset, from which 70 percent of portion of data represents data for training model and remaining 30 percent of data corresponds to test the model. 10 fold strategy of cross-validation was performed to estimate the accuracy of model. Naïve Bayes model outperforms rest of Machine learning algorithms by showing up accuracy of 96.2 percent followed by random forest algorithm with an accuracy of 94.3 percent.

Various Machine Learning Algorithms to Predict COVID-19

Machine Learning Algorithms came to the surface as a non-clinical approach to curb the growth of Covid-19 by doing a beforehand prediction with good accuracy. Here below four of major machine learning prediction algorithms i.e. Decision Tree Algorithm, Naïve Bayes Algorithm, Random Forest Algorithm, K-Means Algorithm have been covered.

Decision Tree Algorithm

Decision Tree Algorithm is a supervised Learning Algorithm which works effectively for both categorical and continuous input variables. Decision Tree is basically a Learning and Classification based algorithm. In the Learning phase Decision Tree learns from the Categorised Samples and as a result a learned decision tree is formed. The resultant decision tree is further used for the purpose of classification to classify the data. For the purpose of prediction in Covid-19 Decision Tree follows up the following steps:

Step 1: A complete Dataset is obtained and is worked upon if it is not up to the mark or complete.

Step 2: Follows the Greedy Iterative Approach to make a decision tree.

Step 3: With Iterative approach Dataset is partitioned based on the best suitable attribute to form a decision tree.

Step 4: Next Iteration: Decision tree obtained is again subjected to the process of Iteration and a Suitable attribute with maximum of gain ratio is chosen as splitting attribute and a decision tree is made to split to form a Tree like structure.

Step 5: Iteratively Decision tree is made to split based on maximum gain ratio attribute chosen at that level of tree and Decision tree thus formed is well suitable for classifying and predicting.

This Model effectively predicted the rise or fall in number of Covid-19 cases for South Korea and many other countries. Ali Keshavarzi [4] have shown up that latitude and longitude are the important classifying parameters and with the use of these parameters a flowchart is created for the purpose of prediction. Symptomatic and Age are the basic parameters taken into consideration for prediction [1]. Here below Figure-1 describes the greedy iterative approach of Decision tree for Symptomatic and Age parameters. It can clearly be seen that how these two parameters helps in the prediction of the condition of COVID-19 Positive patient by forming a tree like structure.

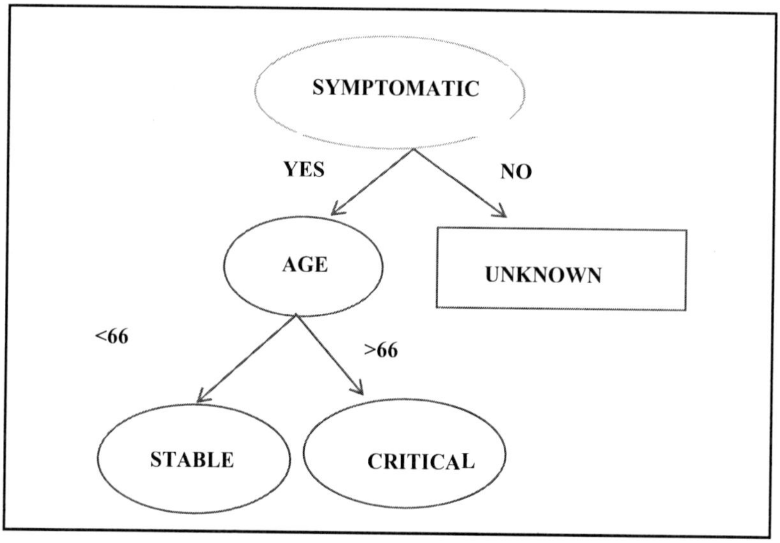

Figure 1: Greedy Iterative approach of Decision Tree for Classifying and Prediction [3].

This algorithm is known for providing the highest accuracy in predicting with 99.85 percent of efficient accuracy [1]. The Machine learning models discussed in this paper were built on 10-fold cross validation and therefore can be compared. Isra Al-Turaiki et.al [3] in their paper have compared Naïve Bayes Algorithm and Decision Tree Algorithm and came up with the results that Naïve Bayes algorithm gives high accuracy of 71.58 percent when compared to Decision Tree Algorithm for Recovery parameter. In contrast to this Decision Tree gives high accuracy of 55.69 percent on comparing with Naïve Bayes Algorithm for Stability as a parameter. Table 1 depicts the Results of the above comparison for Recall, Precision and Accuracy for Recovery Parameter whereas Table 2 depicts the Results of the comparison for Stability parameter.

Table 1: Performance Evaluation for Recovery [3]

Algorithm	*Accuracy*	*Precision*	*Recall*
Naïve Bayes	71.58%	79.4%66.5%	60.4%83.4%
Decision Tree J48	68%	86%61.3%	45.2%92.2%

Table 2: Performance Evaluation for Stability [3]

Algorithm	*Accuracy*	*Precision*	*Recall*
Naïve Bayes	53.63%	56.9%41.1%	67.5%43.1%
Decision Tree J48	55.69%	54.9%43.9%	89.5%15.3%

Decision Tree Algorithm works well for predicting the maximum and the minimum number of days for COVID-19 patients to recover. A Dataset with missing values reduces prediction accuracy.

A. Naïve Bayes Algorithm

Naïve Bayes is a classification algorithm used to calculate the probability of the occurrence of an event based on prior knowledge of its occurrence, and therefore is a well suited algorithm for predicting Covid-19 cases in near future. Here for the purpose of prediction in Covid-19 Naïve Bayes Algorithm follows up the following steps:

Step 1: Data Collection.

Step 2: Relevant Dataset for the purpose of research.

Step 3: Preprocessing: Preprocessing of the dataset is done to give a structure to the unstructured data by removing extras of punctuations, brackets and many such sort of extras in the dataset to get a refined dataset.

Step 4: Feature Engineering: In Feature Engineering features from the refined dataset are extracted and their probabilistic values are estimated. TF/IDF, Bag of Words are the few of extraction techniques used in case of feature engineering.

Step 5: Machine Learning: Traditional and the most efficient Naïve Bayes machine learning prediction algorithm calculates posterior probability for each of the class and the class with highest of posterior probability value is the outcome of prediction.

Figure 2 Describes the graphical representation of the Processing steps followed by Naïve Bayes Algorithm to depict Covid-19.

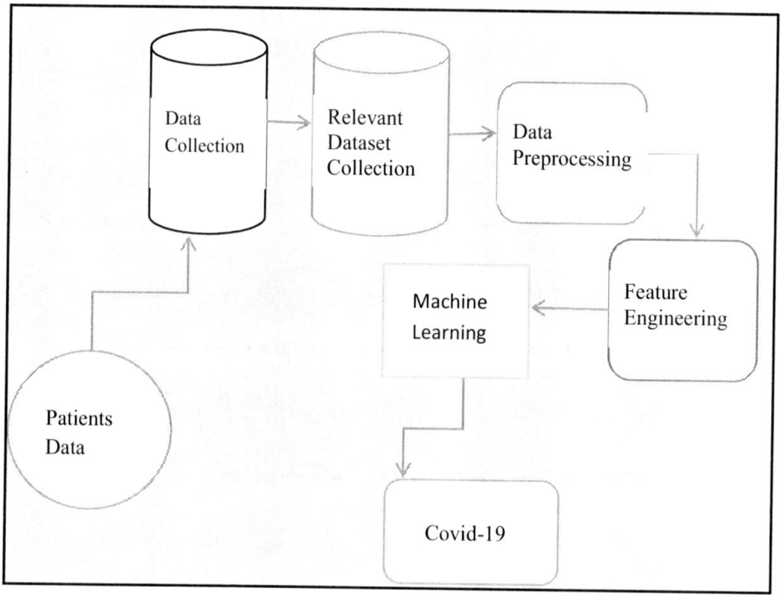

Figure 2: Processing steps to predict COVID-19 [8].

Naïve Bayes doesn't work efficiently in case of an over fitting dataset. To get accuracy in prediction whole of the data needs to be fed into as it works efficiently when the whole of the data is used for experimentation. It can be said that the efficiency of this model depends on the amount of data fed into. Akib Mohi Ud Din Khanday et.al [8] in their paper compared Naïve Bayes algorithm with Decision Tree and Random Forest Algorithm. Table 3 depicts the values that these algorithms have got on comparing with each other for Precision, Recall, F1 Score and Accuracy. Figure 3 shows up the graphical representation of these values. The Graph in Figure 3 and the numeric values in Table 3 clearly show the results Akib Mohi Ud Din Khanday et.al [8] has got on comparing Naïve Bayes with the other two efficient Machine Learning Algorithms i.e. Decision Tree Algorithm and Random Forest Algorithm for Precision, Recall, F1 Score and Accuracy for prediction in China. It can clearly be seen in Table 3 that Naïve Bayes algorithms predicted Covid-19 cases with highest accuracy of 96.2 percent.

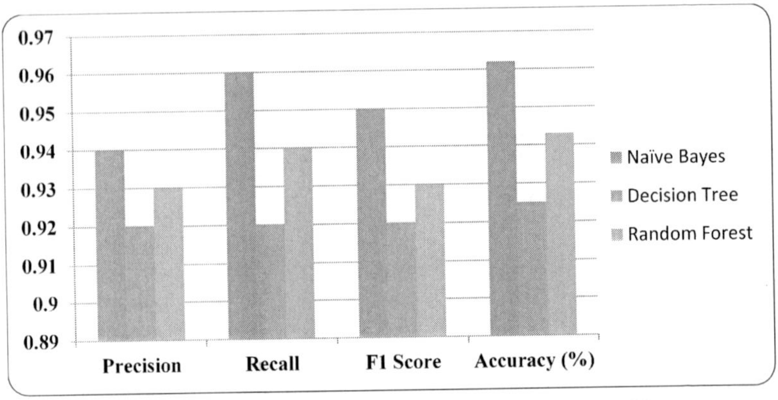

Figure 3: Evaluation of performance of Algorithms [8].

Table 3: Performance Evaluation of Algorithms based on different Parameters [8]

Algorithm	*Precision*	*Recall*	*F1 Score*	*Accuracy (%)*
Naïve Bayes	0.94	0.96	0.95	96.2%
Decision Tree	0.92	0.92	0.92	92.5%
Random Forest	0.93	0.94	0.93	94.3%

Major parameters considered were Laplace Smoothening Parameter and Gaussian Distribution Parameter [8].

B. Random Forest Algorithm

Random Forest Algorithm is more suitable for Big data where over fitting can be addressed effectively. It works more like decision tree algorithm except the fact that it works well in case of overfitting dataset whereas decision tree algorithm fails to perform when data is over fitted. This algorithm builds a forest which in actual is an ensemble of Decision trees trained with "Bagging" method. This algorithm works efficiently for both the Classification and Regression problems. Following steps are followed by Random Forest Algorithm for Predicting Covid-19 Cases:

Step 1: Data Preprocessing: Data is collected and preprocessed and the data obtained is unstructured and may have categorical values whereas random forest algorithm works on numerical data for prediction.

Step 2: Follows the Greedy Iterative Approach to make up a decision tree and these trees are then combined with the help of classifier class of random forest to form a Big Forest.

Step 3: Selecting Feature or Attribute: A Randomness is added to the Model with the increase in the levels of tree. It search for best suitable feature from the random subset of features and do splitting according to it.

Step 4: Next Iteration: Random Forest Tree obtained is further subjected to the process of Iteration and another attribute is chosen from random subset of features for further splitting.

Step 5: Towards the end of levels a tree has two categories of nodes i.e. Decision nodes and Leaf nodes. Decision Nodes may have two or more branches depicting the value of each feature and on the other hand Leaf nodes holds the result values of prediction.

Table 4 depicts the performance of major Machine Learning Algorithms based on their values for Kappa Statistics. Ali Keshavarzi [4] in his research came up with the values shown in the Table 4 for performance evaluation parameter Kappa Statistics for major machine learning algorithms when subjected to prediction environment and Random Forest Algorithm turns out to be the one with highest value of Kappa Statistics. Values that Ali Keshavarzi [4] in this research got on comparing have graphically been described in the Figure 4 below.

Table 4: Performance of Algorithms Evaluated according to Kappa Statistics [4]

Algorithm	*Kappa Statistics*
Naïve Bayes	0.8744
Decision Tree	0.8854
Random Forest	0.9083

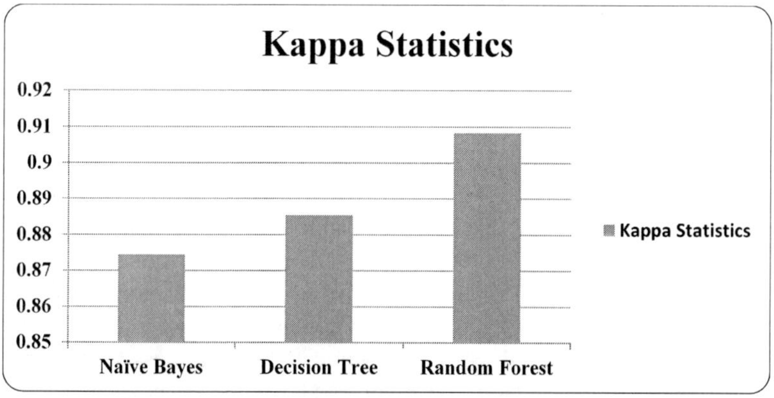

Figure 4: Performance Evaluation according to Kappa Statistics [4].

It revealed a positive correlation between death and gender of the patient. It gave the Covid-19 predictive results for China with an accuracy of 94% [5]. It predicts the severity of the patient's health; the time it will take for the patient to recover based on his geographical travel history and health factors. Parameters considered for prediction are Precision, Recall, F1 Score, Gender, Age, country, travel history of patient.

C. K-Means Algorithm:

K-Means Algorithm Works well in case of Covid-19 cases prediction as it helps in creating a cluster of datasets, therefore making it easeful for prediction purposes. Moreover K-Means Algorithm also extracts the required article easefully as it is based on clustering mechanism and therefore clusters the related data at one place thereby making it easy for the researcher to extract the specific article. For Prediction purposes this algorithm divides data into K number of predefined non-overlapping distinct groups and the new incoming patient record can be added to a particular logical group based on the severity of symptoms or other factors [7]. Here for the purpose of prediction in Covid-19 following steps are followed by K-Means Cluster Algorithm:

Step 1: Data Preprocessing: Data is collected and preprocessed, Data preprocessing is quite an important phase as the major extraction of quality features is carried out under this phase. Feature extraction plays a major role in making data fit for prediction by precisely K-Means Algorithm. Feature extraction means to compress large files thereby increasing the computational speed.

Step 2: XGBoost: Here in this step Weights are assigned to the extracted features using XGBoost algorithm.

Step 2.1: Assigning Weights: Weights value is calculated by observing the change that comes in predictive output on replacing extracted feature with some random noise.

Step 3: Clustering: Weighted features are combined with the clustering mechanism of K-Means Algorithm. Clustered features are then fed as an input to predict COVID-19 cases.

It worked efficiently for prediction in China and Louisiana State of USA for Covid-19. Root Mean Square, Activation Parameter, Batch Size, Temperature, Population density and Age are the parameters considered for prediction. Accuracy for K-Means is more when compared with SEIR model for prediction [6]. More the value for RMSE Less will be the Accuracy. Here below Graph in Figure 5 shows the Root Mean Square

Error (RMSE) values that these Covid-19 predicting K-Means and SEIR model holds for state Louisiana (USA).

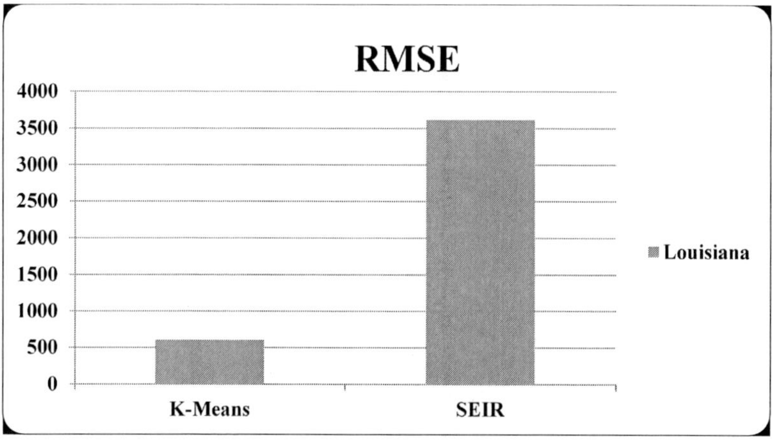

Figure 5: Root Mean Square Error value for K-Means and SEIR Model.

Conclusion

Covid-19 a serious pandemic has its effect in almost all countries all over the world. To rescue non-clinical Machine Learning prediction algorithms have been implemented to forecast the COVID-19 cases depending on the area, dataset and term of the forecast. From the above study it can verifiably be concluded that Naïve Bayes algorithm showed up highest accuracy of 96.2% when compared with the rest of three algorithms discussed. It efficiently worked upon the clinical dataset of 122 patients and Static yet real time updated dataset from GitHub data repository and is good for short term prediction. On the other hand, Random forest gives accuracy of 94.3% and works really well in case of over fitting data unlike decision tree algorithm. Despite the fact that it ensembles Decision Tree algorithm, Random forest tree algorithm works on random subset of features whereas decision tree algorithm chose the best informative attribute with maximum gain ratio for prediction. Decision tree shows up an accuracy of 92.5% in prediction when the dataset chosen is clinical and is precise, whereas its accuracy falls to 68% for recovery and 55.69% for stability when the real time updated dataset is taken from GitHub. Both the decision tree and Random forest work on latitude and longitude parameters to yield good accuracy whereas Naïve Bayes works on Patients Age, gender, travel history, health history parameters. K-Means algorithm comes to the surface when the clusters of data are to be formed based on feature selection.

It shows up a less value for RMSE and therefore gives sufficiently good accuracy. There is not any algorithm yet developed which can yield 100% of Accuracy to predict COVID-19, which in itself is a Big Challenge for researchers to work upon.

References

1. L. J. Muhammad Islam, Md Milon Usman, Sani Sharif, Ayon, Safial Islam 2020. "Predictive Data Mining Models for Novel Coronavirus (COVID-19) Infected Patients' Recovery". pp. 1-15.
2. Parikshit N. Mahalle, Nilesh P. Sable, Namita P. Mahalle, Gitanjali R. Shinde 2020. "Data Analytics: COVID-19 Prediction Using Multimodal Data". Intelligent Systems and Methods to Combat Covid-19. pp. 1-10.
3. IsraAl-Turaiki, MonaAlshahrani, TahaniAlmutairi 2016. "Building predictive models for MERS-CoV infections using data mining techniques". Journal of Infection and Public Health. Vol. 9, pp. 744-748.
4. Ali Keshavarzi 2020. "Coronavirus Infectious Disease (COVID-19) Modeling: Evidence of Geographical Signals". SSRN Electronic Journal.
5. Celestine Iwendi,Ali Kashif Bashir, Atharva Peshkar, R. Sujatha, Jyotirmoy Chatterjee, Swetha Pasupuleti, Rishita Mishra, Sofia Pillai, Ohyun Jo 2020. "COVID-19 Patient Health Prediction Using Boosted Random Forest Algorithm". *Frontiers in Public Health.* pp. 357-366.
6. Shashank Reddy Vadyala, Sai Nethra Betgeri, Eric A. Sherer, Amod Amritphale 2020. "Prediction of the Number of COVID-19 Confirmed Cases Based on K-Means-LSTM". ArXiv.
7. Sanjay Kumar Sonbhadra, Sonali Agarwal, P. Nagabhusha 2020. "Target specific mining of COVID-19 scholarly articles using one-class approach". ArXiv.
8. Akib Mohi Ud Din Khanday, Syed Tanzeel Rabani, Qamar Rayees Khan, Nusrat Rouf, Masarat Mohi Ud Din 2020. "Machine learning based approaches for detecting COVID-19 using clinical text data". *International Journal of Information Technology.* pp. 1-9.
9. Najmul Hasan 2020. "A Methodological Approach for Predicting COVID-19 Epidemic Using EEMD-ANN Hybrid Model". *Internet of Things.* Vol. XI.
10. Shinjini Ghosh 2020. "Predictive Model with Analysis of the Initial Spread of COVID-19 in India". *International Journal of Medical Informatics.* MedRxiv.
11. Talha Burak Alakus, Ibrahim Turkoglu 2020. "Comparison of deep learning approaches to predict COVID-19 infection" Chaos, Solitons & Fractals 140.
12. M. Rubaiyat Hossain Mondal, Subrato Bharati, Prajoy Podder, Priya Podder 2020. "Data analytics for novel coronavirus disease" *Informatics in Medicine Unlocked.*
13. Christopher Y. Shen 2020. "Logistic growth modelling of COVID-19 proliferation in China and its international implications". *International Journal of Infectious Diseases 96*. pp. 582–589.

14. Domenico Benvenuto, Marta Giovanetti, Lazzaro Vassallo, Silvia Angeletti, Massimo Ciccozzi 2020. "Application of the ARIMA model on the COVID-2019 epidemic dataset". *Journal Data in Brief 29*. Vol. 29.
15. Ashis Kumar Das, Shiba Mishra, Saji Saraswathy Gopalan 2020. "Predicting community mortality risk due to COVID-19 using machine learning and development of a prediction tool". pp. 1-18.
16. Fatemeh Ahouz, amin golabpour 2020. " Predicting the COVID-19 Prevalence Rate Using Data Mining".
17. Kia Jahanbin, Vahid Rahmanian 2020. "Covid-19 outbreak using Twitter and Web News Mining". pp. 1-3.
18. Jianhong Wu, Kathy Leung, Gabriel M Leung 2020. "Nowcasting and forecasting the potential domestic and international spread of the 2019-nCoV". *Elsevier.* Vol. 395. pp. 689-697.
19. Kimberlyn Roosa, Yiseul Lee, Ruiyan Luo 2020. "Real-time forecasts of the COVID-19 epidemic in China from February 5th to February 24th, 2020". *Infectious Disease Modelling.* pp. 256-263.
20. Mohammadreza Nemati, Jamal Ansary, Nazafarin Nemati 2020. "Machine-Learning Approaches in COVID-19 Survival Analysis and Discharge-Time Likelihood Prediction Using Clinical Data". Vol. 1, pp. 1-8.

Abbreviations

- COVID-19: Coronavirus Disease
- LSTM: Long Short-Term Memory
- MERS-Cov: Middle East Respiratory Syndrome Coronavirus
- RMSE: Root Mean Square Error
- SARS-CoV: Serious Acute Respiratory Syndrome Coronavirus
- SEIR: Susceptible Exposed to Infectious Recovered

World Scenario on COVID- 19

5

Urban India and COVID-19: Preparedness and Challenges

Jagsir Singh

During the period of COVID - 19 pandemic, the whole world including each and every country, state and city is focused and engaged in responding to the COVID crisis. The pandemic has posed many challenges to us at every stage. The world economy has been shaken, the pedagogy of education and its system is under dynamic shift and health system (especially public health system) is under serious questions and concerns. If we look at the patterns of the virus, the big urban centers are at high risks due to various reasons. In India, the cases of COVID-19 are increasing day by day and the main concentration of the virus is in cities. Big urban centers are suffering more but it does not mean that small cities are safe; they are also facing multiple challenges because they are already lagging behind on account of economic and other factors including employment, small scale industries and responsibility of running their families. The flow of population, finance, infrastructure and services tend to move towards big urban centers. Small cities and towns have been unequal partners in the process of urbanisation with poor planning and governance in India. Poor water supply, public sanitation, education and healthcare services make these cities hotspots of infectious diseases. Due to low testing procedures, the trend shows that small cities have less number of cases of COVID-19. On the other hand, big cities are receiving much attention with resources redirected towards testing, ventilators and hospital beds. Cities and towns which are not included in the list of big cities are finding it hard to cope up with increased demands on their physical and social infrastructure due to return of migrants. These returned migrants are usually from lower economic and social background, with no guarantee of food, livelihood, health care and sustainable long term future as to how they can survive. The present COVID-19 pandemic deconstructs the myth that we prefer cities for better life chances and health.

In the recent past, through the implementation of The Agenda 2030- Sustainable Development Goals (SDGs), we are committed to promote health, with the help of adequate, inclusive and quality public services. The global commitment and aspirations were well-intended and thought out (Hitesh Vaidya & Chetan Vaidya, 2020). However, it cannot be achieved unless we empower the very institutions at the bottom, which are preconditions for over-all development of the masses i.e. centers for education and training, public health system, etc. The pandemic crisis demonstrates the view that until investment and planning in institutions are not directly related to coming generation, we will continue witnessing similar crisis in future also.

Last one and a half century experienced a massive increase in the urban population throughout the world. Today more than half i.e. 55 percent of the world's population lives in urban areas, a proportion that is expected to increase to 68 percent by 2050 (U.N. 2018). The ongoing process has resulted in higher prevalence of urban poverty, rather than prosperity and modernisation (Smiles, 1975). As far as India is concerned, the last half of twentieth century can be considered as an era of urbanisation. According to census 2011, India's 31.16 percent people are living in cities and Punjab is included in the list of most urbanised states of India with 37.49 percent of its population residing in cities. But the infrastructure and required services are not sufficient, because the area under urbanisation is comparatively small. Without any proper planning, the overcrowded cities face grim situation on various grounds. The question of adequate services like health is a far reaching goal for many.

The present study is a modest effort to critically examine the preparedness of Indian cities to combat the pandemic like COVID-19 in general and cities in Punjab is taken as an example. It is a well known fact that urbanisation in India is oriented towards big cities. The study will explore the effects of this 'big city oriented urbanisation' on the health of people. The study will try to figure out how cities face economic hardship due to lock-down. The study is descriptive in nature. The explanations are based on secondary sources.

Urban India

Urbanisation is a transformation from agrarian rural economies to modern industrial one. It occurs due to efforts of an individual, commerce and government. Many rural migrants move towards the city for reasons of seeking economic and social mobility. After 1980s, more emphasis has been given to the urban centers. Cities have been considered engine of economic growth (Sharma and Shaban, 2006; Planning Commission, 2008; Mckinsey and Company, 2010; Abdul Shaban and Sanjukta Sattar, 2016). Now it becomes a well established fact that urbanisation is a necessary component for the overall development of nation in general and economic development in particular. The countries that urbanised most rapidly are those with most rapid urban economic growth and most of the world's largest cities are in the world's largest economies (UNCHS, 1996). This is a clear indication of the link between economic wealth and urbanisation.

India as a developing Asian country has a great amount of its inhabitants (According to Census 2011, 31.16 percent) residing in cities. Being the second most populous country in the world, growing urbanisation of India has a regional as well as worldwide impact. India is at an acceleration stage of the process of urbanisation (Jaysawal Neelmani, 2014). The urban population in India has gone up gradually from about 11 percent in 1901 to 17 percent in 1951 and then to 28 percent in 2001, now it is more than 31 percent (Census, 2011). As we have already mentioned that the pattern of urbanisation in India is characterised by continuous concentration of population and activities in large cities, the large cities exhibit distinctly lower poverty ratios. The low incident of poverty in these big cities is due to the expansion of economic opportunities and availability of semi-skilled employment.

In India, about 377 million people live in 7935 towns and cities across the country. The number of towns has significantly increased from 2219 in 1951 to 7935 in 2011. There is a high inequality in the distribution of the urban population by size class categories. About 70 per cent of the total urban population lives in 468 towns in India. According to the 2011 census, there are 53 cities in India with a population of one million or more. Lopsided urbanisation induces growth of class- 1 cities only. This trend of urbanisation leads to massive growth of slums followed by misery, poverty, unemployment, exploitation, inequality, and degradation of the quality of life. Breese termed urbanisation in India as pseudo-urbanisation wherein people move to cities not due to urban pull but due to rural push (Breese, 1969). But fascination and availability of work may also pull the people to bigger cities. Such processes compel many unskilled people from villages and small towns to large ones. The Eleventh Five Year Plan document of Government of India refers to urban centers as characterised by 'lacking adequate financial resources, growing homelessness, outdated method of urban planning', etc. (Planning Commission of India, 2008). To tackle these shortcomings, the Government takes some initiatives viz. Jawaharlal Nehru Urban Renewal Mission (JNURM) initiated in 2005-06 and smart cities project launched in 2015. There has been a significant change in the way one looks at the urban centers. Cities have been placed at the center stage of the economic thinking and as business model, driver of the spatial and national economies (Mckinsey and Company, 2010).

The other side of the same coin is that cities in India has created a socio-political condition in which 'power' is again being shifted to the hands of economically powerful (Abdul S. & S. Sanjukta). Cities in India are characterised by extreme heterogeneity in terms of their socio-economic characteristics. Big cities attained inordinately large size of population, leading to virtual collapse in the urban services and quality of life. These cities are structurally weak and formal instead of being functional entities because of inadequate economic base. Urbanisation in India happens without industrialisation and strong economic base and it is mainly a product of demographic explosion and poverty induced rural-urban migration. Large urban centers have reached at the level of saturation to generate more employment (Kundu, 1994). Since these cities are suffering from poverty, unemployment, housing-shortage, deficiency in infrastructure, they cannot include unskilled and poor migrants. Big cities grow in urban population not in urban prosperity, and culture (Nayak, 1962). These mega cities are subjected to extreme filthy slums and lack of shelter, drinking water, electricity, sanitation, etc.

Preparedness and Challenges due to COVID-19

When Government of India announced a 21 days lockdown, almost immediately, not only thousands of migrant workers come on the streets in big cities, they lost their income and even survival. Hawkers, vendors of food and other small items, labourers of construction work, small businesses and the host of other connected economies collapsed within a few hours. Migrant labourers wanted to go back to their native states because without any income, they could not pay their rents and even cannot purchase food. Due to suspension of buses, trains and all other forms of public transport, they began walking towards their respective homes. Without proper food, water and rest, they kept walking for many days. The condition of older people and children was grim because they could not walk for long. That was one side of the whole mismanagement. The sufferings of migrants are not measurable and are often invisible. In addition, they lack necessary documents to access relief measures concerning food, shelter, health, hygiene and livelihood. Moreover, with no money in hand, they have become vulnerable victims of the virus. Their future is determined by the availability of jobs, housing, food and a whole range of social and physical infrastructures. But the preparedness was not at par. The nature of our response to the crisis of negligence and lack of planning in smaller cities and towns determine the future of urban India.

Improper investment in public healthcare system purposes a challenge to COVID – 19 containment plans of India. The death toll due to the Corona Virus in India was of 356 as of April 14, 2020. India's underfunded and patches public system, with huge variations between different states, poses special challenges to the government strategies. This is the reason that there had been several reports of patients trying to flee isolation wards in government hospitals and hiding their travelling history. Even many suspected and infected persons tried to dodge the necessary home quarantine. It seems that it is difficult for Indian Government to make the people of the country understand the importance of isolation and quarantine as a mandatory response to the pandemic. The expenditure of government on health is the least in the world. 52% of households in urban areas and 44% in rural areas, private hospitals are the main source of healthcare. People have lost the faith in the government and the trust can be restored only by increasing the health expenditure.

Jalandhar, a class-I city of Punjab, has been recently added to the list of smart city under Smart City Project by Government of India. It can be considered as the city of emigrants because of sizeable number of migrants and NRIs. Due to COVID-19, thousands of these migrants and NRIs have returned to the city in the last few months, some may have been carrying the virus but without proper arrangements for quarantine and treatment, patients were transported to other cities. As a modern city of Punjab, Jalandhar must have prepared for its natives who have changed urban landscape of the city with the attribution of money from abroad.

Under lockdown, Jalandhar's sports and clothing industry, which is responsible to feed thousands of workers and their families, face the hardest time. Lockdown has put enormous stress on small businesses, their workers, and even on entire informal economy. The city's biggest second-hand clothes and other cosmetics market, which is predominantly run by women migrants from Gujarat, UP, Bihar and Punjab, face an existential threat from lockdown. During this hardest time, the most vulnerable residents are poor who have lost their jobs and they are mostly from lower caste living in slums of different parts of the city. Social/physical distancing is a cruel irony in slums. They all have lost their livelihood due to unplanned lockdown.

Conclusion

We are living in the era of technology and for the sake of technological outcome, we must give priority to planning. But urban world, as an area, having more than half of the world's population, remained relatively unplanned. Under the recent pandemic, many Indian cities have transformed their Integrated Command and Control Centers into 'COVID-19 War Rooms' where digital monitoring of quarantine measures, contact tracing, drone surveillance and mobile phone tracking have been put in place to control the virus. Some of the cities have grown smarter by using infrastructure created to collate and provided adequate datasets to respond to the cities. But without the lack of infrastructure and planning, many big cities could not be equally benefited.

The picture of urbanisation is not so much glorious as it apparently seems. Modern cities are growing in a haphazard and unplanned manner due to many reasons. We need housing, basic services, economic and social infrastructure, but this pandemic demonstrates that each city has to plan and design its future based on the needs and requirements of the citizens. In future, the cities will not be judged on their productivity, investments, infrastructure, economic strengths, beautiful public spaces, heritage, and culture, but also on how responsive the cities are towards their citizens (Hitesh Vaidya & Chetan Vaidya, 2020). Public health has to be central to city management. Benefits of water supply, sewerage and sanitation have to consider improved health impact of these services. Regional and national research and training institutions must focus on urban public health.

India's urban future lies not in the big metropolitan cities only, but in the small and medium type cities and towns. If we have proper infrastructure and services in small cities and towns, people can have social support at the time of crisis like COVID-19. The current scenario underscores the need to make cities adapt and respond to crises and threats through effective planning.

References

Abdul Shaban and Sanjukta Sattar (2016). Critical Reflection on Contemporary Urbanisation in India. *Shelter*, 17 (1), 31-39.

Breese, G. (1969). *Urbanisation in Newly Developing Countries*. New Delhi: Prentice Hall.

Census of India (2011). General Population Tables, New Delhi: Government of India.

Davis, K. & Golden, H.H. (1954). Urbanisation and the Development of Pre-Industrial Areas. *Economic Development and Cultural Change,* 3(1), 6-26. https://doi.org/10.1086/449673

Davies, K. (1965). The Urbanisation of the Human Population. *Scientific American* 213 (3) 41-53. (Reprint in) LeGates, R. (Ed.), Stout, F. (Ed.). (2011). The City Reader. London: Routledge. https://doi.org/10.4324/9780203869260

D'Souza Victor S. (1979). Socio-Cultural Marginality: A Theory of Urban Slums and Poverty in India. *Sociological Bulletin.* 28(1-2), 9-24.

Hitesh Vaidya and Chetan Vaidya. World Urban Campaign, 2020. https://www.worldurbancampaign.org/national-institute-urban-affairs-covid-19-and-cities-we-want (Retrieved September 20, 2020).

Jaysawal, Neelmani (2014). Urbanisation in India: An Impact Assessment. *International Journal of Applied Sociology*. 4(2): 60-65.

Kundu, A. (1980). *Measurement of Urban Processes: A Study in Regionalisation*. Bombay: Popular Prakashan.

Kundu, A. (1983). Theories of City Size Distribution and Indian Urban Structure: A Reappraisal. *Economic and Political Weekly, 18*(31), 1361-1368. Retrieved July 11, 2020, from www.jstor.org/stable/4372362

Mckinsey & Company (2010). India's Urban Awakening: Building Inclusive Cities, Sustaining Economic Growth. New Delhi: Mckinsey Global Institute.

Michael Spence, Patricia Clarke Annez & Robert M. Buckley (eds.) (2010). *Urbanisation and Growth.* Jaipur: Rawat Publication.

Nayak, P.R. (1962). The Challenge of Urban Growth to Indian Local Governance, in Tumer R. (eds.) India's Urban Future. USA: University of California Press.

Planning Commission (2008). Eleventh Five Year Plan, Government of India. New Delhi.

Premi, Mahendra K. (1991). *India's Population: Heading towards a Billion –An Analysis of 1991 Census*. New Delhi: B.R. Publishing Corporation.

Roy Baikunth and Vidya Yadav (2020). Homelessness Amid COVID-19: Miseries Untold and Promises Shattered: Concerted efforts from all concerned stakeholders is crucial at this juncture. https://thewire.in/author/baikunth-roy-and-vidya-yadav25/SEP/2020(Retrieved September 28, 2020)

Sharma, R.N. and Shaban A. (2006). Metropolitanisation of Indian Economy: Lessons in Urban Development. *The ICFAI Journal of Governance and Public Policy*, 1(2), 17-35.

United Nations (2019). World Urbanisation Prospects: The 2018 Revision. Population Division of the Department of Economic and Social Affairs of the United Nations. New York.

UNCHS (1996). An Urbanizing World: Global Report on Human Settlement. Oxford University Press. Oxford.

Wirth Louis (1938). Urbanism as a Way of Life. *The American Journal of Sociology*. 44(1), 1-24.

6

COVID-19: The Deglobalisation Virus

Sandeep Kaur Brar

At present, the whole world is observing a very tough time while fighting an invisible enemy; the novel COVID-19 coronavirus. It seems that the thick black clouds of Covid-19 have enveloped the whole globe, spreading its aura of terror. The whole world is praying and waiting for the time when these dark clouds will vanish so that the bright yellow sun rays touch our lives again. Every country is trying its best to slow the spread of this novel coronavirus by testing and tracing, imposing lockdowns and curfews, quarantining citizens, limiting travels and banning large gatherings. But this virus initially observed in the Wuhan province of China is now spreading like a wave around the whole world. Even the World Health Organisation has warned that the coronavirus pandemic is "accelerating" with more and more cases coming out daily.

What is COVID-19

Covid-19 is a respiratory illness that can easily spread from person to person. It is a new strain that was discovered in 2019 and has not been previously identified in humans. Researchers believe that corona viruses are zoonotic, which means they are transmitted from animals to humans. The novel coronavirus, also known as COVID-19, is a new strain of coronavirus. The disease caused by this novel coronavirus was first identified in Wuhan, China and has been termed as Coronavirus Disease 2019 (COVID-19). In this *CO* stands for Corona, *VI* stands for virus and *D* for disease. Further, researchers relate this virus to the family of viruses like SARS (Severe Acute Respiratory Syndrome) and some kind of common colds. At present, there is not a specific vaccine or treatment for Covid-19. This virus spreads primarily through droplets of saliva or discharge from the nose when the person infected from Covid-19 coughs or sneezes. That is why the best way to prevent the transmission of this virus is by practicing respiratory etiquettes (e.g. by coughing or sneezing into a flexed elbow), maintaining physical distance, washing our hands or using an alcohol based sanitizers frequently and not touching our face. Starting from Wuhan, the epicentre of SARS-COV-2, this virus has reached nearly 213 countries till date. According to the report of World Health Organisation (WHO), 202,733 deaths and at least 2,959,929 known infections have been linked to this Covid-19 (WHO, April 28, 2020). To acknowledge the global spread of this virus, the World Health Organisation decided to declare it a pandemic.

How is COVID-19 a Pandemic

Mankind has observed various pandemics throughout the history. A pandemic is an epidemic on a global level. Currently, the world is struggling with the fifth pandemic in 21st century - the COVID-19 pandemic. On March 11, the World Health Organisation (WHO) upgraded the status of Covid-19 outbreak from epidemic to pandemic. By doing this upgradation, WHO indicates that the outbreak of this virus is now a worldwide phenomenon. On March 11, 2020, Dr. Tedros Adhanom Ghebreyesus, Director General of WHO stated at a media briefing in Geneva:

> *Pandemic is not a word to use lightly or carelessly. It is a word that, if misused, can cause unreasonable fear, or unjustified acceptance that the fight is over, leading to unnecessary suffering and death. Describing the situation as a pandemic does not change WHO's assessment of the threat posed by this virus. It doesn't change what WHO is doing, and it doesn't change what countries should do.*

He assured that WHO has been assessing the novel coronavirus outbreak around the clock and is "deeply concerned both by the alarming levels of spread and severity, and by the alarming levels of inaction." Acknowledging it a first pandemic caused by coronavirus, Tredos further stated that the world need not to fixate on the word "pandemic", but to focus instead on five other words or phrases, beginning with "p" i.e. Prevention, Preparedness, Public health, Political leadership and People (WHO, March 11, 2020). It seems that WHO wants every country to take quick necessary action to curb this outbreak. Highlighting the same, even the editorial of *The Lancet Journal* puts forward: "Declaration of a pandemic, combined with clear and coordinated management guidelines, might help every country limit the impact of the disease and bring it more swiftly under control" (*The Lancet,* 2020). As the world becomes more connected due to globalisation, cooperation and collaboration at global level is needed to reduce the impact of this pandemic. The outbreak of this Covid-19 pandemic clearly demonstrates that the spread of such pandemic will become more common with our increasing connectivity around the world.

How is Globalisation and COVID-19 Interrelated

Due to globalisation, the world has become a smaller place (a global village, to use a MacLuhan's phrase). It has a deeper impact on our lives as it deals with the interconnectedness of the world through new systems of communication. A. Giddens takes globalisation as "the intensification of worldwide social relations which link distant localities in such a way that local happenings are shared by events occurring many miles away and vice versa" (64). It is a set of processes that involve various interactions and movements within the political, social and economic domains. Globalisation can be employed to depict a condition, system or process of economic, ethnic and political interconnection that makes the existing boundaries and borderlines insignificant. It speeds up the world with the development of trade, capital and a new system of transportation and communication. Not only this, distant events have a deeper impact on our lives. This results in the blurring of boundaries between domestic issues and global affairs.This fact cannot be denied that globalisation, which is characterised by unparallel levels of human interaction and mobility, has facilitated the fast spread of highly contagious diseases.

Thinkers view that the spread of the novel coronavirus (Covid-19) is accelerating due to human hyper-interconnection. Undoubtedly, the spread of COVID-19 has coincided with globalisation, urbanisation and climate change. Due to globalisation, such pandemics can move from a remote town to a major city and then to the whole world at a much faster rate. It is noted that due to globalisation people are travelling more than before for both work and pleasure. According to the reports of the World Economic Forum, there were 4.2 billion air transport passenger journeys in 2018 as compared to 310 million in 1970. This increased mobility helped propel COVID-19 fast transfer from China to more than 176 countries in just three months. It demonstrates that viruses like COVID-19 freeload by hopping abroad jet travellers to convert a local outbreak into a pandemic.

Is COVID-19 Accelerating Deglobalisation

Due to the current outbreak, the era of globalisation, open borders and global supply chains are under pressure. The present situation reveals that COVID-19 pandemic has led to the waning of globalisation. To combat this pandemic, the governments of all the countries are involved in keeping people apart by sealing their international, national and regional borders.

Travels are halted and people all around the world are in effective lockdown. This pandemic has literally brought much of the world to a standstill. It seems that this virus has initiated the process of deglobalisation. Undoubtedly, COVID-19 has sounded the death knell for globalisation by paving the way for either deglobalisation or new forms of globalisation like glocalisation, virtualisation and digital globalisation.

Some economic experts think that the wave of globalisation had already started to stagnate since the 2008-09 Global Financial Crises. The term 'slowbalisation' was being used for it. According to the Annual Economic and Social Survey of United Commission of Asia and the Pacific (UNESCAP), COVID-19 crisis is going to be a bigger shock to the world economy than the Global Financial Crisis of 2008-09. Bruno Le Maire, the French Minister of the Economy and Finance, views the COVID-19 pandemic as a "game-changer" for globalisation. As all the governments adopt protectionist policies, this pandemic will surely lead to the collapse of global value chains. Even global supply chains are disrupted due to factory closures and production suspensions. This will compel the national governments to relocate production facilities in the home only to avoid reliance on foreign suppliers. Thus, this pandemic could catalyze the processes of localisation and regionalisation. Harold James, Professor of History and International Affairs, aptly points out:

> *Pandemics are not just passing tragedies of sickness and death. The omnipresence of such mass-scale threats, and the uncertainty and fear that accompany them, lead to new behaviours and beliefs. People become both more suspicious and more credulous. Above all, they become less willing to engage with anything that seems foreign or strange.*

The above statement appears true in case of COVID-19 pandemic. Richard Portes, Professor of Economics at London Business School, puts forward the same idea that things will surely change in the wake of COVID-19 pandemic as people and firms have realised the risks they had been taking. Portes further points out: "Look at trade, once supply chains were disrupted [by coronavirus], people started looking for alternative suppliers at home, even if they were more expensive… If people find domestic suppliers, they will stick with them… because of those perceived risks" (Quoted by Bloom). Thus, the present outbreak reveals an "irresponsible and unreasonable" reliance on Chinese suppliers and exposes the vulnerability of complex international supply chains.

In the similar vein, Andres Ortega quotes Bruno Le Maire, the French Finance Minister, who opines that they should reduce their dependence on great powers such as China. In America also, many companies have realised the risk their over-interdependence and attempted to control it by focussing on local alternatives. A recent report of Bank of America highlights that nearly "80 percent of the multinationals investigated plan to repatriate part of their production, known as re-shoring, a trend that COVID-19 could turn into a tidal wave" (quoted by Ortega). However, some thinkers believe that the main problem is a lack of diversification and not globalisation or China. Most of the countries lack regional and inter country trade. This pandemic can be considered as an alarm bell to diversity networks. This step of diversification might contribute in the reshaping of the global economy. Blandina Kilama, an economist aptly points out: "Maybe this crisis is going to force us to trade more amongst ourselves" (Quoted by Trumbull). European nations have also realised their over independence on India and China in the field of medical supplies. Propelling the reshoring wave, this outbreak has emphasised on production at local, regional and national level.

Thus, the spread of COVID-19 has forced us to rethink about globalisation. In an interview, Ian Goldin rightly puts up: "Dangers like pandemics are the spillovers of globalisation. Integration of China with the world economy, 1.4 billion tourists, and business travellers around the world every year are not only spreading good things, but also spreading bad things." This pandemic has shown us the good, the bad and the ugly face of globalisation. However, deglobalisation is not an answer to such global problems. Instead of blaming globalisation, an attempt should be made to recognize the weakest links of globalisation. Highlighting the same, Goldin puts forward:

> *The answer is not deglobalisation. The answer is not to build high walls. There is no wall high enough even for mighty countries like India, China and the United States to keep out the great threats in the future. These are the threats such as climate change, pandemics and financial crises. These high walls keep out ideas, technologies, vaccines and finance.*

It implies that globalisation cannot be reversed or it can be said that it is not beneficial to reverse globalisation. An attempt should be made to manage the risks of globalisation. Some scholars believe that Covid-19 will not end globalisation but change it hugely for the better. Raphael S. Cohen argues that the present pandemic will change the mechanics of globalisation and it will not spell death knell for globalisation. Asserting this view, Cohen points out:

> *Above all, the primary reason why globalisation will persist—perhaps in a modified form—is that the underlying drivers of the trend remain intact. Countries still need goods and services from one another, just as they have for thousands of years. Some states will still need natural resources; others will need access to cheap labour; still others access certain talents, skills and capital not resident within their own borders. They will need to trade, just as they have done for much of recorded history. Moreover, personal interconnections between different parts of the world formed over the past several decades of globalisation cannot be easily broken.*

As globalisation has done more good than bad, all nations need to manage the risks to harvest the benefits of globalisation. Hence, the global world which is so unregulated can be blamed for its spread, and collective action based on evidence can be the best way to stop such disasters. Therefore, nations must work together for a safer future through globalisation. The present pandemic has taught us that nations must work together for a better future in this global world and global issues like climatic changes, pollution, global warming and such pandemics can be tackled through collective actions. This pandemic is a wake-up call for collaboration. Tedros Adhanom, Director General of WHO says this repeatedly: "There is a common enemy, and we need to fight in unison" (WHO, 2020). Working together and co-ordinated will be the only key to solve such pandemics.

What Will Be the Future of Globalisation

Winston Churchill has rightly said: "Never let a good crisis go to waste." Crises teach us many lessons and can spur the creation of new technologies. For instance, the 2003 SARS epidemic spurred innovation in the digital technology of China. The current pandemic has taught us many lessons. It is time to learn from this pandemic so that the outbreak of another pandemic is prevented. This pandemic will surely trigger a wave of change that will shape our world for years to come. The world that will emerge after defeating this invisible enemy (COVID-19) will be completely different from the one we lived in before the pandemic began. Undoubtedly, there will be human, financial, economic and social crises. All countries will witness a change that will be going to reshape their international relation and relations among states.

Similarly, when this pandemic is finally gone, globalisation will resume in a new form totally different from the one we have known up to now. This is evident that the wheel of globalisation cannot be turned back as it has benefited both developed and developing countries. The world only needs to redefine the definition of globalisation in order to make it more human-centric instead of market and profit oriented. All the nations should make an attempt to recognise the weakest links of globalisation. In words of Yorck Otto, President of a business association representing small and medium sized companies:

> *The global supply chain will continue to get better and better every day. This globalisation will be refined, and hopefully it will be also covered under new humanitarian laws and regulations so that the world can be a little bit better through globalisation. (Quoted by Trumbull)*

This clearly shows building walls are not the solution to such pandemics. An effort should be made to make globalisation work more for people than even before. In other words, globalisation must be tamed and turned to glocalisation at least to lessen the impact of such pandemics. Glocalisation is a neologism derived from globalisation and localisation. It is an approach which is characterised by both local and global considerations, both being intertwined at the core. Thus, COVID-19 pandemic is not an end to globalisation, but it is going to add a smart dimension to globalisation.

As a consequence of this pandemic, a revolutionary change has also occurred in the dominant modes of communication. This pandemic has encouraged companies, multi-national co-operations, universities and schools to ask its employees to work from home. It means such preventive measures are taking us to the next phase of globalisation i.e. digital globalisation. Even in education sector, the rapid virtualisation process is taking place. In the present time of emergency, schools and universities are shifting to online teaching or other e-learning forms. Similar processes take place in the area of e-administration. Even people are connecting with others through video calling during this time. This indicates that the transition to web-based communication methods is taking place at a speedy rate. So, this fact cannot be denied that recession, virtualisation of communication, and unprecedented collective effort to find a vaccine has strengthened cooperation among the nations on a global scale.

Conclusion

It is still unclear that what will be the end result of this pandemic. It is hard to say whether there will be deglobalisation or glocalisation, or there will be a continuation of globalisation. It could equally well be possible that the end result will be the combination of these alternatives. It is really difficult to draw any predictions at this point of time. As far as the coronavirus is concerned, the only certainty is that nothing is certain in the presence of this invisible enemy. There are many "known unknowns and unknown unknowns" (Van Til). Nevertheless, this crisis has taught us a valuable lesson to spot, control and regulates the risk that seems to be an integral part of globalisation. Undoubtedly, this pandemic is a true stress test for globalisation. Presently, this pandemic has a potential to accelerate deglobalisation, but it cannot stop the long-term movement toward a more interconnected world. This crisis will surely lead to the emergence of a novel kind of globalisation which will be more diversified and human centric. Thus, it can be hoped that globalisation will surely survive the present pandemic like other epidemics and pandemics in the past—the Spanish Flu in 1918, SARS in 2003, H1N1 in 2009 and Ebola in 2014.

References

- Bloom, Jonty. 2020. "Will Coronavirus Reverse Globalisation?" *BBC NEWS*. Available at: https://www.bbc.com/news/business-52104978. Assessed on 2 April 2020.
- Cohen, Raphael S. 2020. "The Coronavirus Will Not Stop Globalisation, April 12, 2020". *Lawfare*. Available at: https://www.lawfareblog.com/coronavirus-will-not-stop-globalisation. Assessed on 20 April, 2020.
- Ghebreyesus, Dr.Tredos Adhanom. 2020. "WHO Director-General's opening remarks at the media briefing on COVID-19 - 11 March 2020."*World Health Organisation.*Available at: https://www.who.int/dg/speeches/detail/who-director-general-s-opening-remarks-at-the-media-briefing-on-covid-19—11-march-2020. Assessed on 13 April 2020.
- Giddens, A. 1990. *The Consequences of Modernity.* Cambridge: Polity Press. Print.
- Goldin, Ian. An interview with Vibja Varshney. 2020. *Down To Earth.* "Pandemics are the Spillovers of Globalisation, 03 April 2020." Available at:https://www.downtoearth.org.in/interviews/governance/covid-19-pandemics-are-the-spillovers-of-globalisation—70042. Assessed on 20 April, 2020.
- James, Harold. 2020. "A Pandemic of Deglobalisation, February 28, 2020." *Project Syndicate.*Available at: https://www.project-syndicate.org/commentary/covid-19-deglobalisation-pandemic-by-harold-james-2020-02 . Assessed on 17 April 2020.
- Ortega, Andres. 2020. "The deglobalisation Virus, March 18, 2020." *The Globalist: Rethinking Globalisation.* Available at: https://www.theglobalist.com/coronavirus-covid19-pandemic-globalisation-deglobalisation-globalism/—. Assessed on 23 April 2020.
- The Lancelot infectious Diseases. 2020. "Covid-19, A Pandemic or Not?" Editorial, Volume 20, Issue 4, p. 383, April 01, 2020. Available at: https://www.thelancet.com/journals/laninf/article/PIIS1473-3099(20)30180-8/fulltext. Assessed on 13 April 2020.
- Trumbull, Mark. 2020. "Why COVID-19 is likely to change globalisation, not reverse it, March 9, 2020." *The Christian Science Monitor.* Available at: https:/

/www.csmonitor.com/Business/2020/0309/Why-COVID-19-is-likely-to-change-globalisation-not-reverse-it. Assessed on 23 April 2020.

- Van Til, Frederik. 2020. "Three Scenarios for Globalisation in a Post-Covid-19 World, 01 April, 2020." *The Clingendael Spectator*. Available at: https://spectator.clingendael.org/en/publication/three-scenarios-globalisation-post-covid-19-world. Assessed on 15 April 2020.

7

COVID-19 Pandemics a Global Disaster

Rupinder Kaur

In the earth from the past of a decade, there was plenty of the situation occur at that time we think that this is the last time for the earth, but after that humans are surviving from the attacks. The starting of the pandemic firstly visible in 1918 to 1920 the given name is Spanish flu also known as (H1N1). At that period, the death's count in between 1.7 to 10 crore or the bigger than that, these recodes are collected from Wikipedia it may vary. In this first time happened that the more deaths of the human due to the virus not to war. In all the world 70 percent of the population is infected with a virus. After 37 years this flu came back with the name Asian flu in the year 1957-58 in this time death tally is 20 lakh people came in the catch of the virus and die due to this time the name of the virus is (H2N2). The symptoms of the virus slightly change and but deadly too. In the year 2002 virus name SARS had arrived and this time footprint of this pandemic was smaller as compared to before, the worldwide death was around 774. But the virus changes itself and the person who was infected from the virus having problems related to respiratory. In 2009-10, swine flu came and also known as (H1N1/09). There were 1 lakh 51 thousand 7 hundred deaths all around the world but there was no vaccination that has been made for this virus. After some time virus is demolished himself.

The outbreak of coronavirus disease 2019 (COVID-19) has created a global health crisis that has had a deep impact on the way we perceive our world and our everyday lives. Not only the rate of contagion and patterns of transmission threatens our sense of agency, but the safety measures put in place to contain the spread of the virus also require social distancing by refraining from doing what is inherently human, which is to find solace in the company of others. Within this context of physical threat, social and physical distancing, as well as public alarm, what has been (and can be) the role of the different mass media channels in our lives on individual, social and societal levels?

Mass media have long been recognised as powerful forces shaping how we experience the world and ourselves. This recognition is accompanied by a growing volume of research, that closely follows the footsteps of technological transformations (e.g. radio, movies, television, the internet, mobiles) and the zeitgeist (e.g. cold war, 9/11, climate change) in an attempt to map mass media major impacts on how we perceive ourselves, both as individuals and citizens. Are media (broadcast and digital) still able to convey a sense of unity reaching large audiences, or are messages lost in the noisy crowd of mass self-communication? Do social media provide solace or grounds for misinformation, (de)humanisation, and discrimination? Can we harness the flexibility and ubiquity of media technologies to increase the public's adherence to the safety measures suggested by global health organisations to combat the spread of COVID-19? How can different media industries and channels for mass communication promote adaptive responses to foster positive health attitudes and adherence to preventive measures.

After 10 years this virus came back and collapsed all the world economy and all the factories are almost closed. This time the name of the virus is coronavirus also known as the (COVID-19 / SARS-2). It is an infectious disease caused by severe acute respiratory syndrome coronavirus (SARS-CoV-2). The COVID-19 was first identified in December 2019 in Wuhan, the capital of China's Hubei province, and has since spread globally, after that in the ongoing 2019–20 coronavirus pandemic. As of 27 April 2020, more than 30.4 lakh cases have been reported across 185 countries and territories, resulting in more than 211,000 deaths. More than 894,000 people have recovered. General symptoms include fever, cough, fatigue, shortness of breath, and loss of smell. The time from exposure of symptoms is typically around five days but may range from two to fourteen days. Suggested measures to prevent infection regular hand washing, maintain physical distance from others, and from those how have symptoms, coughs, cold and don't touch face. In addition, the use of a face mask or n-95 mask to prevent from COVID-19. The majority of cases result in mild symptoms, viral pneumonia, multi-organ failure, or cytokine storm. More concerning symptoms include difficulty breathing, persistent chest pain, confusion, difficulty walking, and bluish skin. In recommendations wear mask use. At present, there is no vaccine or specific antiviral to cure COVID-19. Governments around the globe involve the treatment of symptoms, supportive care, isolation, and experimental measures. The World Health

Organisation declared the 2019–20 coronavirus outbreak a Public Health Emergency of International Concern on 30 January 2020 and a pandemic on 11 March 2020. It takes a large impact over the economy some of the country's never upcoming from this strike. Almost all countries closing national borders during the past month, the movement of people and tourism flows have come to a screeching halt. Millions of workers in these countries are facing the bleak prospect of losing their jobs. Governments are considering and rolling out large stimulus packages to avert a sharp downturn of their economies which could potentially plunge the global economy into a deep recession. Global stock markets fell the lowest since 2008 on 24 February 2020 due to a significant rise in the number of COVID-19 cases outside mainland China. With falls of several percent in the world's major index global market crashed March 2020. As the virus spreads, conferences, and events across the world like technology, fashion, and sports are being cancelled or postponed. As the financial impact on the travel and trade industry is yet to be estimated, it is likely to be in the billions and increasing. In India, the some of the native countries most of the population is below the poverty line and most of the people doing labour to fulfil the needs of the family. Some of the people doing work in the fields and one man is working and other family members depends on the person. Some of the serves shows that lack of nutrition kids face some of the problems in the hole life span. That's the biggest challenge in front of the Indian government and some of the other countries because India is a farming country most of the people depend on farming.

Respiratory virus infections cause a broad and overlapping spectrum of symptoms collectively referred to as acute respiratory virus illnesses or more commonly the 'common cold'. Although mostly mild, these ARIs can sometimes cause severe disease and death. These viruses spread between humans through direct or indirect contact, respiratory droplets and fine-particle aerosols droplets and droplet nuclei with aerodynamic diameter 5μm Although hand hygiene and use of face masks, primarily targeting contact and respiratory droplet transmission, have been suggested as important mitigation strategies against influenza virus transmission, little is known about the relative importance of these modes in the transmission of other common respiratory viruses. Uncertainties similarly apply to the modes of transmission of COVID-19.

Some health authorities recommend that masks be worn by ill individuals to prevent onward transmission (source control). Surgical face masks were originally introduced to protect patients from wound infection and contamination from surgeons (the wearer) during surgical procedures, and were later adopted to protect healthcare workers against acquiring infection from their patients. However, most of the existing evidence on the filtering efficacy of face masks and respirators comes from in vitro experiments with non biological particles, which may not be generalisable to infectious respiratory virus droplets. There is little information on the efficacy of face masks in filtering respiratory viruses and reducing viral release from an individual with respiratory infections, and most research has focused on influenza.

Here we aimed to explore the importance of respiratory droplet and aerosol routes of transmission with a particular focus on corona viruses, influenza viruses and rhinoviruses, by quantifying the amount of respiratory virus in exhaled breath of participants with medically attended ARIs and determining the potential efficacy of surgical face masks to prevent respiratory virus transmission.

The primary outcome of the study was virus generation rate in tidal breathing of participants infected by different respiratory viruses and the efficacy of face masks in preventing virus dissemination in exhaled breath, separately considering the respiratory droplets and aerosols. The secondary outcomes were correlation between viral shedding in nose swabs, throat swabs, respiratory droplets and aerosols and factors affecting viral shedding in respiratory droplets and aerosols.

Impact on Global Economy

The coronavirus (COVID-19) outbreak has already brought considerable human suffering and major economic disruption. In China, containment efforts have involved quarantines and widespread restrictions on labour mobility and travel, resulting in unplanned delays in restarting factories after the Lunar New Year holiday and sharp cutbacks in many service sector activities. These measures imply a sizeable output contraction whilst the effects of the outbreak persist. Subsequent outbreaks in other countries, including Korea and Italy, have also prompted containment measures such as quarantines and border closures, albeit on a smaller scale. The unpleasant consequences of these developments for other countries are significant, including the direct disruption to global supply chains, weaker final demand for imported goods and services, and the wider regional declines in international tourism and business travel. Risk aversion has increased in financial markets, with the US 10-year interest rate falling to a record low and equity prices declining sharply, commodity prices have dropped, and business and consumer confidence have turned down. Relative to similar episodes in the past, such as the SARS outbreak in 2003, the global economy has become substantially more interconnected, and China plays a far greater role in global output, trade, tourism and commodity markets. This magnifies the economic spill over's to other countries from an adverse shock in China. Even if the peak of the outbreak proves short-lived, with a gradual recovery in output and demand over the next few months, it will still exert a substantial drag on global growth in 2020. Before the COVID-19 outbreak, activity data remained soft but survey indicators had begun to stabilise or improve in both manufacturing and services. Financial conditions had also strengthened following moves to increase monetary policy accommodation and reduce trade policy tensions. Preliminary estimates suggest that global GDP growth slowed further in the fourth quarter of 2019, to just over 2½ percent (at an annualised rate on a PPP basis), with strikes, social unrest and natural disasters affecting activity in several countries. Growth remained close to trend in the United States, but demand fell sharply in Japan following the consumption tax increase in October and stayed weak in economies strongly exposed to the slowdown in global trade, including Germany. Growth continued to be subdued in many emerging market economies, with GDP growth slowly easing in China and large non-performing loans and over-leveraged corporate balance sheets weighing on investment in India. Industrial production continued to stagnate in late 2019, and the growth of consumer spending lost momentum despite continued steady employment gains. The pace of the decline in global car sales moderated through 2019, but demand has subsequently tumbled again, with provisional data suggesting a monthly decline of 10 percent in sales in January 2020, with a 20 percent decline in China. Global trade also remains very weak. Merchandise trade volumes contracted in the fourth quarter of 2019, and declined in 2019 as a whole, the first calendar year fall since 2009. Container port traffic and air freight traffic were also weak ahead of the coronavirus outbreak, and further sharp falls seem likely in the near term. Survey measures of manufacturing new export orders had begun to turn up but fell back in the flash PMI surveys for February, particularly in Japan and Australia. Investment data are also soft, held back in part by continued high uncertainty and weak expected future growth. Aggregate investment growth in the G20 economies (excluding China) slowed from an annual rate of 5 percent early in 2018 to only 1 percent last year. The higher tariffs imposed on US-China bilateral trade over the past two years are an important factor behind the weakness of global demand, trade and investment. The US-China "Phase One" trade agreement in January is a welcome development that should help to alleviate some of these effects. Nonetheless, the commitment by China to purchase an additional cumulative USD 200 billion of goods and services from the

United States over 2020-21 (relative to a 2017 baseline of around USD 180 billion) will be challenging to achieve without distorting third-party trade, and bilateral tariffs remain substantially higher than two years ago. Overall, the Phase One agreement reduces the drag on global GDP growth in 2020 and 2021 from the measures implemented over the past two years by around 0.1 percentage point per annum.

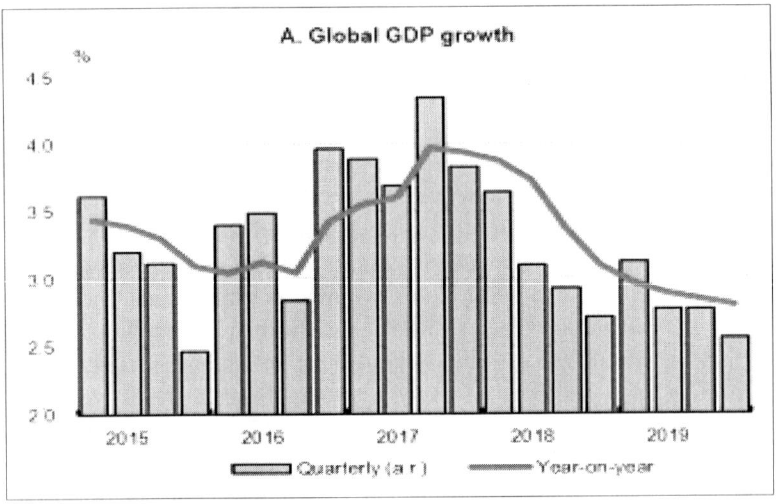

Corruption on This Time

Governments, businesses, civil-society organisations and citizens are facing an unprecedented challenge and are asked to be resilient and find effective measures to address the health and non-health-related implications of COVID-19. As this unparalleled crisis puts healthcare systems, people's safety and the economy under strain, it is imperative that transparency and accountability remain at the heart of the global response. This generation will be judged on how this situation is handled, and we need to make sure good governance is at the core of a new social and economic order.

At this time when the whole world is continues its battle against COVID-19, China has sent Personal Protective Equipment (PPE) kits in poor quality as they have the main supplier of these kits, which were found to be unusable as they failed the safety tests. On the other hand, the ones which failed the quality checks, were given to the Indian government as contributions by private companies. Of the 1.7 Lakh kits that arrived in India on April 5, about 50,000 failed the quality test, a person aware of the matter told ET.

Amidst rising complaints about the low-grade Chinese exports of a range of medical gear to fight the COVID-19, China on Wednesday asked all the countries to trade in these items through reputed Chinese firm clear by the government and vowed to punish those involved in counterfeit behaviour. As its factories resume operation after over two-month of the harsh battle against the coronavirus, China is busy tapping into the vast business opportunities of sell overseas of key remedial goods, especially ventilators and personal protection equipment (PPE), from corner to corner the world, including India, where both personal and government bodies are placing orders for the import of these stuff. Also Read - Hetero ties up with Gilead for Remdesvir Advertisement Several countries including Italy and Spain have complained about the low quality of medical materials including PPE, test kits and ventilators, cast a dark over Chinese exports. The Chinese government has forced strict limits on its firm to certify quality exports. Answer to questions about value concern lift up by a numeral of countries related to medical gear imports from China, Foreign Ministry spokesman Zhao Lijian told a media briefing here that the Chinese government is facilitate the arranged exports. On that time China check the shops and check the products and file the case against it. In this they found 1 crore poor quality products like masks and other things which are used in the corona disaster.

This decision of ICMR not to use testing kits from China has annoyed angry reaction from China, which termed Indian conclusion as unreasonable and careless. China gave itself self-certification that Chinese the system have validate the equipment produced by the two Chinese firms namely, Guangzhou Wondfo Biotech and Zhuhai Livzon Diagnostics. Similar to a classic retailer who would like to save his coat after supply bad quality products, China has nearly charge Indian medical practitioners of not having enough expertise to use the equipment. China said "The tests needed to be carried out in a professional manner to produce accurate results. There are strict needs for the storage space, shipping and use of COVID-19 antibody speedy test kits. Any process which is not passed out by professional in accordance with the product condition will lead to the test accurateness variations". Noticeably, with such a declaration, China has attempt to disgrace the Indian medical professionals by doubtful their capability and information level. This is a off-putting declaration made with the purpose of evasion from the accountability of a dealer, which needs to be powerfully destined.

Previously, when country like Spain discarded the testing kits from China due to superiority issues, China responded by offer to substitute or else return them. When India discarded test kits, China has termed it an careless judgment. Do this signify that China has different yardstick for different country and views India's decision with contempt. It is usual practice for major producers to sub-contract the production to small sub-contractors, if there is a large order beyond the capacity of the producers to supply at the stipulated schedule. Many people now surprise, that faced with the enormous order circumstances, many miniature Chinese producers could also have formed the test kits as sub-contractors to the major suppliers from China and the value of these test kits might not have been subjected to strict quality ensure and manage. This aspect needs to be instigated. In any case, the main producers and the government of China are accountable for the quality of the test kits, particularly when exported.

Instead of simply explanation as to why the test kits have unsuccessful to give consistent results in India, Chinese producers should have verified and prove the trustworthiness of the test kits, China has simply called India's decision as negligent. On the other hand, one may not be mistaken if he would conclude that only China has been negligent.

A number of European countries have complain about the value of the tools being supplied by China to facilitate contract with the coronavirus outbreak. Over the weekend, The Netherlands recall thousands of mask import from China because of excellence issues, even as Spain complained about faulty import test kit supplied by a Chinese producer, media information said. China's overseas organisation said several countries had raised worries about the value of goods import from China, and acknowledged that there might be some problems. "A great amount of Chinese manufacturers are working continuous to help other countries save lives. Our seriousness and aid is real. If trouble take place in this procedure, the Chinese side will talk to related department," China's distant organisation spokeswoman Hua Chunying tell a information discussion on Monday. Meanwhile, New York Governor Andrew Cuomo said on Tuesday that states across the US are "fighting" amongst themselves to source essential medical supplies as coronavirus cases in the country surge daily and "ironically" most entity are look to buy from China.

Impact on Education

In a matter of weeks, coronavirus has changed how students are educated around the world. Those changes give us a hint at how education could change for the better and the worse in the long term. The coronavirus spreading rapidly across globally have taken swift and decisive actions to mitigate the development of a full-blown pandemic. In the past few weeks, there have been multiple announcements at schools and universities. As of March 13, the estimated that over 42 crore students are affected due to school closures announced or implemented in 39 countries. These risk control decisions have lead students into home studying situations, especially in some of the most heavily impacted shows all around the countries. These changes have certainly caused a degree of problem, but they have also prompted new examples of educational modernisation. Even though it is too early to critic how reactions to corona virus will affect education systems around the world, there are signs suggesting that it could have a lasting impact on the path of learning innovation and digitisation.

The lockdown has generated uncertainty over the exam cycle. May be universities may face impact in terms of a slowdown in student internships and placements, lower fee collection that can create hurdles in managing the working capital. Another major concern is that it can affect the paying capacity of several people in the private sector, which is catering to a sizeable section of the students in the country.

- Student counselling operations are also affected.
- Several institutions may pause faculty hiring plans for existing vacancies which in turn affect quality and excellence.
- Structure of schooling and learning includes teaching and assessment methodologies and due to closure, it will be affected.
- Technology may play an important role in the lockdown period like a study from home and work from home. In India, some private schools could adopt online teaching methods. Low-income private and government schools may not be able to adopt online teaching methods. And as a result, there will be completely shut down due to no access to e-learning solutions. In addition to the opportunities for learning, students will also miss their meals and may result in economic and social stress.
- Higher education sectors are also disrupted which again pave an impact on the country's economic future. Various students from India took admissions in abroad like the US, UK, Australia, China, etc. And these countries are badly affected due to COVID-19. Maybe there is a possibility that students will not take admissions there in the future and if the situation persists, in the long run then there will be a decline in the demand for international higher education also.
- Another major concern is employment. Students who have completed their graduation may have fear in their minds of

withdrawal of job offers from the corporate sector due to the current situation. The Centre for Monitoring Indian Economy estimates unemployment shortage from 8.4 percent in mid-March to 23 percent in early April. In the urban unemployment rate is 30.9 percent. We can't ignore that technology plays a crucial role in the educational system and the demand for the current situation is this only.

Conclusion

As every action there is an equal and opposite reaction, we pollute the nature very badly and it hits back with this impact. If at this time we ignore it after that it will be worse than this. Globally the circumstances of economy, business, education; virus breaks the backbonc of it. As in past, economy revives from their worst impact but the lives of the people cannot be. As this unparalleled crisis puts healthcare systems, people's safety and the economy under strain, it is imperative that transparency and accountability remain at the heart of the global response. This is to fight against Corona virus together not be corrupted. COVID-19 is a Global disaster so whole world are in this grip. At this time we can say that "Prevention is better than cure".

References

1. https://en.wikipedia.org/wiki/Listofepidemics
2. https://medicaldialogues.in/latest-industry-news/quality-issues-china-asks-countries-to- import-covid-19-medical-kits-through-authorised-chinese-firms-only-64890
3. https://www.oecd.org/berlin/publikationen/Interim-Economic-Assessment- 2-March-2020
4. https://www.wionews.com/opinions-blogs/covid-19-outbreak-why-china-is-wrong-to-blame-india-for-rejecting-the-faulty-test-kits-296781
5. WHO Collaborating Centre for Infectious Disease Epidemiology and Control, School of Public Health, Li Ka Shing Faculty of Medicine, The University of Hong Kong, Hong Kong, China.

8

The World After 2020

Seema Kapoor

On opening the windows of the past, we witness three main pandemics; 1918 Spanish Flu, 1957 Asian flu and 1968 Hong Kong Flu. Spanish Flu was the severest as it killed around 50 million people worldwide. Spanish Flu has marked the history with its pangs and is remembered even today. But that time population was about a quarter, the size of what it is today and infectious diseases were still the main killer of people. It was a world that did'nt know virus diagnostic test and no really good treatment very well.

After a century, the world is again facing a contagious disease called COVID-19. It is spreading rapidly across nations and countries responded with lockdown but the situation is worsening.The virus that causes COVID-19 is mainly transmitted through droplets generated when an infected person coughs, sneezes, or exhales. These droplets are too heavy to hang in the air, and quickly fall on floors or surfaces.You can be infected by breathing in the virus if you are within close proximity of someone who has COVID-19, or by touching a contaminated surface.

This crisis is alarming, in part, because it has several new and unfamiliar features. A global medical emergency caused by a virus we still do not know and yet as time has passed, it has also become clear that much of what is most distressing about this crisis is not new at all. Striking variations in COVID-19 infections and outcomes appear to reflect existing economic inequalities. Remarkable mismatches between the social values of what "key workers" do and the low wages they receive follow from the familiar failure of the market to value adequately what really matters. As countries are firefighting the Covid-19 pandemic, one thing is becoming clear, the post-coronavirus world will be different in many ways economically, socially and health wise. ... It will play a major role in all aspects of life in education, e-governance, commerce, health and artificial intelligence.

Less global, more isolated. Even before COVID-19, the decades-long trend toward ever-more globalisation of trade, investment, supply chains and people flows was beginning to grind to a halt. We began to look closer to home in terms of the products we produce and consume, the people with whom we interact, and where we get our energy and our money.The reaction of developed economies to the coronavirus will only strengthen this consensus, as all things international will be viewed as incurring unnecessary and dangerous risks. What was a growing "anti-globalisation" consensus is poised to crystalise into a "de-globalisation" reality.We are being told this de-globalisation will make us all more resilient. But it will also make us less prosperous — with less choice and higher prices. It may also make us less secure, as international cooperation will decrease and the potential for international conflict will increase.

Less density, more distance. Urbanisation is likely to be the other major casualty of the coronavirus. Unlike globalisation, the trend of ever greater-urbanisation was unaffected by the global financial crisis. Even America — the land of all things suburban joined the global march into cities. People were attracted to cities not only for economic opportunity but also for the urban lifestyle. After coronavirus, people will be more fearful of crowded trains and buses, cafes and restaurants, theatres and stadiums, supermarkets and offices. Crowded spaces are the lifeblood of cities. But now crowds are seen as major health risks. People who have the ability to exit the city will increasingly be tempted to do so. People who cannot leave will feel at increased risk, hunker down, and reduce their movements and contacts.

De-urbanisation would harm economic growth because cities generate enormous scale economies and have proved to be remarkably effective incubators of creativity and innovation. This could be particularly true in developing economies where the movement of people from rural areas to rapidly expanding cities has been perhaps the key driver of poverty reduction. But the shrinking of cities will have other adverse effects too, from reducing cultural vibrancy and cosmopolitanism to exacerbating climate change. In addition to being more productive, cities also tend to be more environmentally sustainable. A world that is less global and less urban would be far less appealing to me, personally. But it is also a world that would hurt economic prosperity, reduce shared understanding among disparate people, and increase the prospect of conflict among them. Our immediate reactions to COVID-19 will lead us to want both to de-globalise and to de-urbanise. But we must take fully into account the profound longer-term costs of doing so. Globalisation

A Fragile Economy

Lockdown is placing pressure on the global economy. We face a serious recession. This pressure has led some world leaders to call for an easing of lockdown measures. The economics of collapse are fairly straightforward. Businesses exist to make a profit. If they can't produce, they can't sell things. This means they won't make profits, which means they are less able to employ you. Businesses can and do (over short time periods) hold on to workers that they don't need immediately: they want to be able to meet demand when the economy picks back up again. But, if things start to look really bad, then they won't. So, more people lose their jobs or fear losing their jobs. So they buy less. And the whole cycle starts again, and we spiral into an economic depression.

Education Disruption

COVID-19 has caused education disruptions and prolonged school closures all around the world, which affected 90 percent of the world's student population and led most countries to think about alternative ways of providing education to ensure that learning never stops. Keeping education continuity in mind, most countries rushed to online distance education using online platforms, e- learning, and ICTs, which set off an unplanned and rapid shift in the education sector, opened the door to many opportunities, highlighted existing and new disparities and gave rise to several challenges.

In regards to this rush to online and distance education, the World Economic Forum cited Wang Tao, Vice President of Tencent Cloud and Tencent Education, to highlight that " the way forward is to further harness available technologies and the internet in education and that online education will become an integral component of school education". World Economic Forum.

This has pushed education stakeholders to think out of the box to provide unconventional and alternative education modalities based on the use of the internet, radio and TV, which resulted in some constructive and positive changes as well as concerns on ensuring quality of distance education provided. Key recommendations include:

- Education systems should explore new methods to train and prepare teachers and educators, so they may attain the required skills and competencies to keep up with the changes in the field of education.

- Education systems should review and upgrade the range of skills provided to students in a way that would better equip and prepare them for the future.
- Educational systems should undertake new measures for benchmarking the quality of education and tackling the current digital divide.
- It is essential and inevitable to develop a worldwide framework for coordination and cooperation and initiate effective and operative partnerships between public and private institutions with the aim of providing equitable and quality education to all students around the world.

Education is undergoing unprecedented difficulties and challenges during the pandemic. However, the current crisis can be turned into an opportunity by building a more resilient education system. To achieve this transformation, we should exert effort to capitalise on IT, provide vocational training for teachers and enhance their capacities, review assessment methods, engage in a comprehensive digital transformation, build effective partnerships and review old educational philosophies, as well as the goals and outputs of the educational system, to be in line with recent developments as well as with labour market requirements.

Elderly Care

Older persons are particularly susceptible to the risk of infection from COVID-19, especially those with chronic health conditions such as hypertension, cardiovascular disease and diabetes. Older persons are not just struggling with greater health risks but are also likely to be less capable of supporting themselves in isolation. Although social distancing is necessary to reduce the spread of the disease, if not implemented correctly, such measures can also lead to increased social isolation of older persons at a time when they may be at most need of support.The discourse around COVID-19, in which it is perceived as a disease of older people, exacerbates negative stereotypes about older persons who may be viewed as weak, unimportant and a burden on society. Such age-based discrimination may manifest in the provision of services because the treatment of older persons may be perceived to have less value than the treatment of younger generations. International human rights law guarantees everyone the right to the highest attainable standard of health and obligates governments to take steps to provide medical care to those who need it. Shortages of ventilators, for example, necessitate the adoption of triage policies and protocols based on medical, evidence-based and ethical factors, rather than arbitrary decisions based on age.

Health

Hospital care will undergo a major change. There will be clear instructions for medical practitioners about hospital admissions during emergencies. Many countries have already introduced health insurance to cover medical care. According to Sayed Shafuddin, "Services like the NHS in the UK, which is under tremendous pressure, may also undergo a review to balance critical care with outpatient treatment. Some NHS trusts had already outsourced MIR scans and physiotherapy care. This may be taken to the next level to include other investigations before hospitals intervene. The mental health sector, which has always been under-resourced in many countries, will assume a priority to cope with the trauma and stress of the current pandemic. More funding may be allocated for research into new vaccines to control the outbreak of future pandemics mimicking SARS and Covid-19."

New international health protocols will be negotiated for co-operation in early warning and information sharing between countries. These will focus on agreed reporting systems, supervised controls and cooperation in drawing up common contingency plans for accidental leaks of pathogens, radiation and viruses. A more transparent regime will also be in place to monitor research on viruses and their research sponsors.

Questions will be raised why countries with advanced health systems did not act early to respond to the warnings about the spread of a global pandemic. These concerns were raised as early as 2018 on the centenary of the Spanish Flu. The billionaire philanthropist Bill Gates recently said in a TV interview on the Daily Show with Trevor Noah that although he predicted in 2017 that a global pandemic was around the corner, he had no idea that it would be so soon. Neither the US National Institute of Allergy & Infectious Diseases which is headed by Dr Anthony Fauci, nor the Gates Foundation invested sufficiently in developing effective vaccines for the known strains of coronavirus. There is now a race among the worlds leading pharmaceutical companies to find an anti-Covid-19 vaccine which is safe for everyone. Opponents of Big Pharma say that the pandemic is being used as a smoke screen to advance their agenda of making trillions of dollars by pushing the vaccines globally and making them a part of every individuals annual drug management programme. There may also be associated risks with the development of a new vaccine, and if the virus returns next winter.

Information Technology

This sector will see the highest growth. Heavy reliance on the internet during Covid-19 forced major IT giants to adjust their public websites to allow clients access to increased cyber communication. Companies such as Zoom and Skype, which provide web-based conference servicing saw their shares rise in the stock market. Home entertainment giants Netflix and Disney gained new subscribers in millions. Google and Apple joined hands to compile statistics on coronavirus. In the post-corona phase these giants are likely to invest more in IT services.

Countries may also use IT to monitor the movement of citizens through tracking software in mobile phones or chips embedded in driving licences and photo ID cards. Police may be given limited access to citizens financial, employment and criminal records at the click of a button on their mobile instruments. Any outcry for privacy will be outweighed by considerations of security and health. Human rights defenders will be worried about the power this could give to authoritarian governments for silencing opposition and blackmailing them into submission. In established democracies, there would be legislation to define the limits and mandates of authorised government agencies, which will have the power to monitor citizens movements under law, and a mechanism will be available to citizens to challenge misuse through courts. With the passage of time, the location of every individual will be traceable through satellite, just as machine-readable passports contain all the relevant information about their holders on government portals.

Tourism Industry

After staying in their homes for months, holidaymakers will want to have a break provided the places they are going to visit are free from infection hazards. Tourism will comeback but will take time. The reopening of tourism will also help the return of regular and budget airlines and associated travel-related services to enable thousands of dormant workers back to work, and bring these businesses into liquidity.

Countries which have invested heavily in the tourism sector such as the Gambia, Barbados, Trinidad and Tobago, Spain, Portugal, India, Egypt, Tunisia and Turkey will work closely with the hotel and resort operators to ensure that they provide an insulated and infection-free environment to tourists. In such places tourist resorts will be self-inclusive and locals will not be allowed in. Service staff will be admitted only after they have been tested periodically to ensure they are free from any infection or illness.

There will be new visa rules for visitors in most countries. States where the virus has peaked and life has returned to normal will impose visa restrictions on nationals of those countries where the pandemic has not reached its peak. Countries may even require a new coronavirus health insurance or vaccination certificate, if a vaccine is developed and marketed worldwide, before a visit visa is issued to overseas visitors. In such a scenario, health considerations and precautions might place at a disadvantage old-age pensioners who have both time and resources to undertake frequent holiday trips compared to working families.

The Workplace

Office workers were already used to open workspaces and hot-desking. This pandemic has taken the notch a step further. It has shown how admin costs can be saved by managers by making staff work from home. There will be less waste of time for workers commuting to offices and spending money on lunches and coffee breaks. Businesses where large inventories and stocks are not required to be stored will rent small office spaces and encourage staff to work from home. Firms will hire workers for 3 days instead of the traditional 5 day a week to share the employment pie with a large number of people looking for employment. Travel agents may disappear from high-streets, as most would start working on e-ticketing from home.

Business travel will reduce considerably resulting in greater reliance on virtual meetings and reduction in business class seats in airlines. A positive outcome of this will be less carbon footprint for international companies using air-miles to do business.The lesson from the coronavirus disease is poignant. It is a new struggle for the survival of the fittest in humanity's post-modern evolution. It implies that if you haven't got the strength as an individual or as a nation to beat the economic, financial and social pressures that confront you, the lease on your survival in a highly competitive world is due to run out soon. Is the world prepared for this grim scenario? Humanity demands that in the march of civilisation we take our weak and vulnerable along with us, even if we have to carry them on our shoulders. But this needs international consensus not to remain just a wish, but to become a reality.

References

- Shafuddin Sayed, Pages 247-257 | Published online: 17 Jun 2020 The world after Covid-.19
- World Economic Forum. April 2020. The COVID-19 pandemic has changed education forever. This is how. https://www.weforum.org/agenda/2020/04/

coronavirus-education-global-covid19-online-digitallearning/19 https://doi.org/10.1080/00358533.2020.1760498

- Allen, J., Burns, N., Garrett, L., Haass, R. N., Ikenberry, G. J., Mahbubani, K., Menon, S., Niblett, R., Nye, J.S. Jr., O'Neil, S. K., Schake, K., & Walt, S. M . (2020, March 20). The Coronavirus pandemic will change the world forever. *Foreign Policy* https://foreignpolicy.com/2020/03/20/world-order-after-coroanvirus-pandemic/ [Google Scholar]
- Georgieva, K. (2020, March 20). The great lockdown: Worst economic downturn since the Great Depression – Statement by Kristalina, Managing Director of IMF. Press release. https://www.imf.org/en/News/Articles/2020/03/23/pr2098-imf-managing-director-statement-following-a-g20-ministerial-call-on-the-coronavirus-emergency [Google Scholar]
- Harari, Y. N. (2020, March 20). The world after Coronavirus. Financial Times, 445. https://www.ft.com/content/19d90308-6858-11ea-a3c9-1fe6fedcca75 [Google Scholar]
- Kissinger, H. (2020, April 3). The Coronavirus pandemic will forever alter the world order. *Wall Street Journal*. https://www.wsj.com/articles/the-coronavirus-pandemic-will-forever-alter-the-world-order-11585953005 [Google Scholar]
- Roy, A. (2020, April 3). The pandemic is a portal. *Financial Times* https://www.ft.com/content/10d8f5e8-74eb-11ea-95fe-fcd274e920ca [Google Scholar]

9

Effect of COVID-19 on India

Navjot Kaur

Coronavirus ravages the economic foundations of world trade. According to the WTO, the world trade is expected to fall by between 13 percent and 32 percent in 2020, thereby indicating the world economy is expected to face recession. Trade cannot flourish without commensurate policies to revive the economy. A combination of fiscal, monetary and trade policy measures is, thus, required to revive the economy and trade in these uncertain times. I am sure the world will come out of the crisis and give birth to a new phase of an improved and inclusive world. India's trade has been severely impacted. People have a sudden loss of their income, causing a major drop in demand. To rescue the economy, India has announced impressive fiscal and monetary stimulus packages. This pandemic has strong foreign and trade policy effects. This Research Report not only captures vital economic impact on India but also throw light at other aspects that effects India.

The Indian economy has been hit hard by the ongoing Coronavirus pandemic-driven global crisis. The entire world is passing through great uncertainty. There are, primarily, two major challenges that the Indian economy is facing at this juncture. First is to save the country from the spread of Coronavirus (COVID-19), which is a health emergency. Saving lives is the most important, the principal concern of the government. Second is to save the economy from the unfolding economic uncertainty due to the dual effects of the Coronavirus pandemic and the global and national lockdown. Many economies may face negative per capita income growth in 2020 due to the Coronavirus pandemic. India's trade has been severely impacted. People have been facing a sudden loss in their incomes, causing a major drop in demand. To rescue the economy, India has announced a range of fiscal and monetary stimulus packages. The present health-cum-

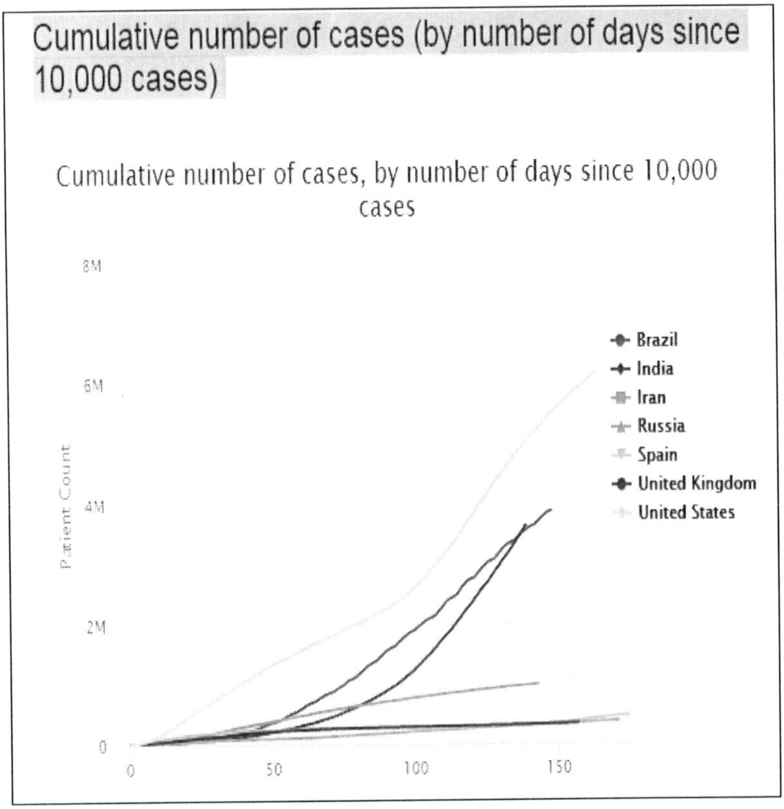

Source: Worldometers.com

CHART I: Total no. of Covid-19 Cases of Top 7 Countries.

economic crisis throws up several important challenges. If the spread of the virus and the consequent loss of life is minimised, either through newly invented vaccines or medicines, economies will rebound sharply. Countries are, therefore, heavily engaged in inventing the vaccines, and also injecting appropriate fiscal and monetary stimulus measures. These two will then become major factors supporting the recovery in the coming months.

At the moment, businesses are very vulnerable to the unfolding economic crisis. People have been facing a sudden loss in their incomes, causing a major drop in demand. To rescue the economy, India has announced a range of fiscal and monetary stimulus packages. The major aim of this stimulus is similar to the traditional Keynesian prescription of 'pump priming', whereby income transfers to people having higher marginal propensity to spend can boost up the sagging demand.

Finance Minister Nirmala Sitharaman said that the Government will spend as much as Rs 20 lakh crore to tackle the impact of the coronavirus on the economy. He said that the Government will focus on land, labour, liquidity and laws. The Finance Minister focused on providing relief to micro, small and medium enterprises (MSMEs), non-banking finance companies (NBFCs), power distribution companies (DISCOMs) and the real estate sector.

Need For This Study

This study examines the impact of Covid-19 on India, taking various perspectives, for instance, Change in Macro economy of the India, Change in Technology (Technology Innovation) and how these will help India to find solutions to limit the impact of Covid-19.

As a result, this study help the reader (person or organisation) how to align future strategy with the given economic conditions and hence he/she is at a better position to manage the negative future consequences.

Aim of the Study

(1) To know about the current and future Political environment, as a result of Covid-19.

(2) To know about the current and future Economic environment, as a result of Covid-19.

(3) To know about the current and future Social environment, as a result of Covid-19.

(4) To know about the current and future Technological environment, as a result of Covid-19.

(5) To know about the current and future Legal environment, as a result of Covid-19.

(6) To know about the current and future Environmental environment, as a result of Covid-19.

Overall, PESTLE analysis is used to do the impact of Covid-19 on India.

Research Methodology

Resources of Data Collection: Primary research is done (but limited to only 5 persons) to know about the changes they felt about current Covid-19 Pandemic.Most of the research is Secondary and sources are largely Government driven data sources. Pestel Analysis is used:

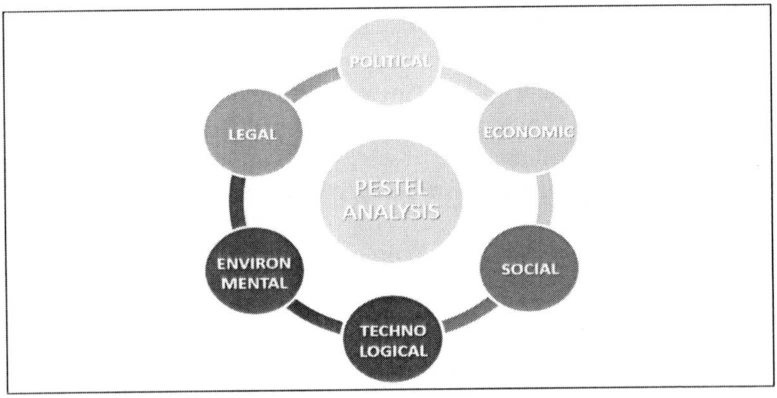

Figure 1: Pestle Analysis.

So we cover these aspects to know about what are the Covid-19 impact on India.

Political Impact of COVID-19

India has announced a 21-day national lockdown, beginning March 25, to prevent the spread of the Covid-19 pandemic in the country. Barring essential services such as food supplies, healthcare, banking, and law enforcement, everything is shut down during this period. This also means that a very large share of India's 400 million-plus workforce will not be able to access the labour market and make earnings. This unforeseen calamity has the potential to fundamentally change India's political economy landscape.

Political Aspects means the current government influence on the country's current environment.

This includes certain aspects like:

- Trade restrictions & fund stimulus by government to revive economy.
- Labour laws during Covid-19 pandemic.

Fund Stimulus by Government

Governments all over the world have announced plans to protect their economy as many nations announced stay at home orders in a bid to stop the spread of the coronavirus.

- **Stimulus Package**

  RoW: Japan has announced a stimulus package which is more than 21 percent of its GDP. The United States (US) (13.3 percent), Australia (10.8 percent) and Germany (10.7 percent) follow.

India: Narendra Modi's mega plan, combined with previously announced plan, is roughly 10 percent of the GDP. This is the fifth-largest among the G-20 economies.

Direct Cash Payments

The lockdowns in various countries were disruptive to many, but it was catastrophic to workers. Many governments across the world paid cash to workers so they could survive. Many nations like Canada, US, Hong Kong, Japan and Thailand have followed this policy. Canada is already providing CAN$2000 for four months (from April) to those who have lost their jobs, are sick or have to stay at home. In the US, eligible persons apply for a one time payment of $1,200. Hong Kong is providing a cash handout of HK$10,000 for each permanent resident aged 18.

In case of India, no new scheme was announced on Wednesday. The poor received modest benefits from the first stimulus package — 500 each to women Jan Dhan account holders, 1,000 for senior citizens, poor widows and the disabled. It also hiked the payment for MNREGA and front loaded PM-KISAN payments. However, on Wednesday, it was announced that Rs 1,000 crore from the money donated to PM CARES fund will be used to take care of migrant labourers. This money will be used by the State and UTs to provide accommodation, food, medical treatment and transportation to the migrants.

Financial assistance to corporations

Due to the shutdown, many corporations were unable to function, and some have become too big to fail. The US created a $500 billion dollar fund to bailout failing corporates. This includes helping aviation, healthcare and sectors of national importance. The French government is all set to provide a bailout of 7 billion euros to Air France-KLM. In April, The French finance minister Bruno Le Maire said that the government had earmarked 20 billion euros for bailouts.

On the other hand, the Finance Minister announced a scheme to provide liquidity to power distribution companies. She announced a Rs 90,000-crore loan "against State (government) guarantee" to power distribution utilities (discoms) to mitigate the liquidity crisis in the power sector. To provide relief to the real estate sector, the FM announced easing in regulations for those projects that were stalled. The Housing and Urban Affairs Ministry will advice States/UTs and their regulatory authorities to extend the registration and completion data *suo moto* by six months for all registered projects expiring on or after March 25, 2020, without individual applications, she said.

Labour Laws

There are four major central legislations that form the core of labour laws in India.

- **Factories Act, 1948:** The main objectives of this act is to ensure safety measures on factory premises, and promote the health and welfare of workers.
- **The Shops and Commercial Establishments Act, 1961:** It aims to regulate hours of work, payment, overtime, a weekly day off with pay, other holidays with pay, annual leave, employment of children and young persons, and employment of women.
- **The Minimum Wages Act, 1948:** It sets the minimum wages that must be paid to skilled and unskilled labours.
- **Industrial Disputes Act, 1947:** It relates to terms of service such as layoff, retrenchment, and closure of industrial enterprises and strikes and lockouts.

Many state governments were focused on repealing labour laws. States like UP, MP and Gujarat have suspended labour laws for the next three years. The suspension of labour laws will automatically result in the loss of many of the rights that employees have won after long struggles. The three states have similarly repealed labour laws with a few variations. The governments of UP and Gujarat have announced that most of the labour laws will be cancelled for the next 1000 days while maintaining a few basic rules. One of the major amendments to the labour law is to increase working hours from 8 hours to 12 hours and overtime working hours to 72 hours per week. The governments have provided for companies to recruit or dismiss up to 100 workers as per their requirement without promising any security. This gives employers the right to "hire and fire" according to their interests. The BJP-ruled chief ministers of the three states, justifying such anti-worker amendments and the repealing of the laws, have said that they are **"part of the process of attracting foreign companies withdrawing from China to their states".** However, the people who observe the dynamics of the international labour market and industrial sector are well aware that such a move is not likely to happen in the near future.

Solutions

For sustainable industrial growth in India, there is a need for holistic labour laws reforms, which would enable firms to expand, while keeping the interest of labours intact, thereby resulting in the formalisation of the Indian economy.

Short-Term Steps

- With respect to Covid-19 pandemic, the central and state governments in India should follow what most governments have done across the world.
- The government should partner with the industry and allocate a percentage of the GDP towards sharing the wage burden and ensuring the health of the labourers.

Long-Term Steps

The government has proposed four labour codes:

- Labour Codes on Wages
- Labour Code on Industrial relations
- Labour Code on Occupational safety, health and working conditions
- Labour Code on Social Security and Welfare

Economic Impact of COVID-19

Economic Aspects means the change in country's economic conditions:

This includes certain aspects like-

- Industrial Activity
- Inflation Rate
- GDP and sectoral impact

This global pandemic turnedeconomic crisis affects India's economic and national security. The effects of the crisis on trade and foreign policy are not only complicated but also widespread.

The financial crisis has begun with the US-China trade war, and then the rise of Coronavirus pandemic accompanied by the global and national lockdown has occurred. As a result, we see a fall in global trade, capital flows and remittances; disruption in supply chains; contraction in outputs; rise in unemployment; and then rise in poverty. Barring few, countries across the world have already entered into recession. Several business units may have to shut down and face bankruptcies, and with the fall in business orders, both international and domestic, the value of the currency may deteriorate further. In other words, economic recession can lead to long term damage to the Indian economy MSMEs.

The first signs of the imminent tectonic shifts that COVID-19 would cause became visible when there is sharp reductions in GDP growth in advanced economies (AEs) ranging from (-) 3.4 percent to (-) 14.2 percent and in emerging markets (EMs) between 2.9 percent and (-) 6.8 percent (year-on-year or y-o-y basis) in Q1:2020 have been exacerbated in the ensuing months by a collapse in manufacturing as reflected in purchasing managers' indices (PMIs), which have plunged into contractionary territory.

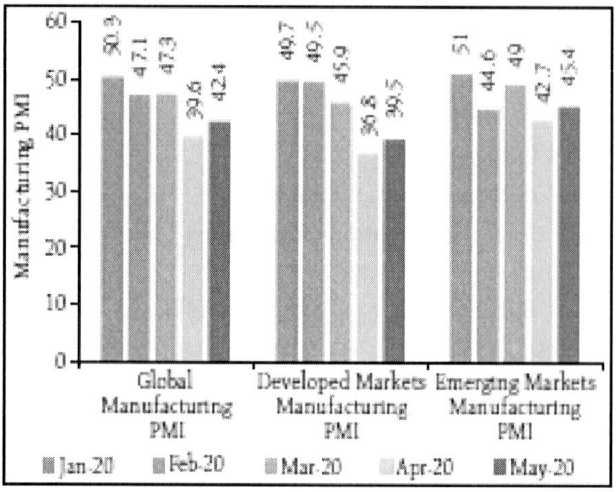

Source: RBI Financial Stability Report.

Chart II: World's Manufacturing PMI.

Industrial activities

In view of the preventive measures and announcement of nation-wide lockdown by the government to contain spread of COVID-19 pandemic, a large number of the industrial sector establishments were not operating from the end of March, 2020 onwards. This has had an impact on the items being produced by the establishments during the period of lockdown. With the lifting of restrictions in the subsequent periods, industrial activity is resuming. The Figure 1 tells us that activities related to Mining, Manufacturing, and Electricity are halted and in future these sectors might still have sluggish growth.

Table 1: Index for Industrial Production

(Base : 2011-12=100)

Month	Mining (14.372472)		Manufacturing (77.63321)		Electricity (7.994318)		General (100)	
	2019-20	2020-21	2019-20	2020-21	2019-20	2020-21	2019-20	2020-21
Apr#	107.8	78.7	126.2	41.5	162.9	125.5	126.5	53.6
May#	110.1	87.5	135.8	83.6	176.9	150.6	135.4	89.5
Jun#*	106.5	85.4	129.0	106.9	173.6	156.2	129.3	107.8
Jul	100.2		133.7		170.5		131.8	
Aug	92.0		128.4		165.7		126.2	
Sep	86.4		126.0		158.7		122.9	
Oct	99.5		126.3		145.8		124.0	
Nov	112.7		130.6		139.9		128.8	
Dec	120.9		135.4		150.3		134.5	
Jan	124.3		137.9		155.6		137.4	
Feb	123.3		134.2		153.7		134.2	
Mar	131.0		111.6		146.9		117.2	
Average								
Apr-Jun	108.1	83.9	130.3	77.3	171.1	144.1	130.4	83.6
Growth over the corresponding period of previous year								
Jun#*	1.5	-19.8	0.3	-17.1	8.6	-10.0	1.3	-16.6
Apr-Jun	3.0	-22.4	2.4	-40.7	7.3	-15.8	3.0	-35.9

Source: Ministry of Statistics amd Programme Implementation.

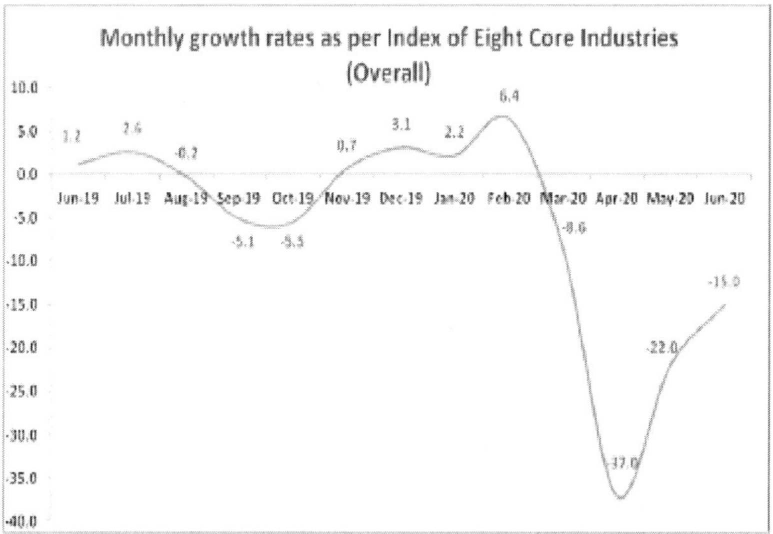

Source: Office of Economic Advisor.

Chart III: Growth Rate of 8 Core sectors (Manufacturing Industry).

The growth rate of Index of Eight Core Industries for June 2020 declined by 15.0 percent (provisional) compared to decline of 22.0 percent (revised) in previous month of May 2020. Its cumulative growth during April to June, 2020- 21 was -24.6 percent.

High frequency indicators of services sector activity for May-June indicate signs of a modest resumption of economic activity, especially in rural areas, although at levels lower than a year ago. Notably, the decline in passenger vehicle sales moderated to (-) 49.6 percent in June from (-) 85.3 percent in May, indicative of tentative urban demand, and faster recovery of sales in rural areas. On the other hand, domestic air passenger traffic and cargo traffic continued to post sharp contraction. Construction activity remained tepid cement production fell and finished steel consumption moderated sharply in June. Imports of capital goods a key indicator of investment activity – declined further in June.

Exports and Imports

India's merchandise exports contracted for the fourth successive month in June 2020, although the pace of fall moderated on improving shipments of agriculture and pharmaceutical products. Imports fell sharply in June in a broad-based manner, reflecting weak domestic demand and low international crude oil prices. The merchandise trade balance recorded a surplus in June (US$ 0.8 billion), after a gap of over 18 years. On the financing side, net foreign direct investment moderated to US$ 4.4 billion in April-May 2020 from US$ 7.2 billion a year ago. In 2020-21 (till July 31), net foreign portfolio investment (FPI) in equities at US$ 5.3 billion was higher than US$ 1.2 billion a year ago. In the debt segment, however, there were outflows of US$ 4.4 billion during the same period as against inflows of US$ 2.0 billion a year ago.

Consumer Price Index (CPI) or Inflation

Table 2: Inflation Rates

Indices	*Jul. 2020 Prove*			*Jun. 2020 (Final)*		
	Rural	*Urban*	*Combd.*	*Rural*	*Urban*	*Combd.*
CPI (General	7.04	6.84	6.93	6.34	6.12	6.23
CFPI	9.89	9.05	9.62	8.84	8.58	8.72

Source: Ministry of Statistics and Programme Implementation.

Headline CPI inflation, which was at 5.8 per cent in March 2020, was placed at 6.23 percent in the final estimates for June 2020. Inflation pressures were evident across all sub-groups. Households one year ahead inflation expectations were lower than their three months ahead expectations in the July 2020 round of the Reserve Banks survey, indicating their anticipation of lower inflation over the longer horizon. Producers sentiments on input prices remained muted as their salary outgoes fell.

Gross Domestic Production and Growth

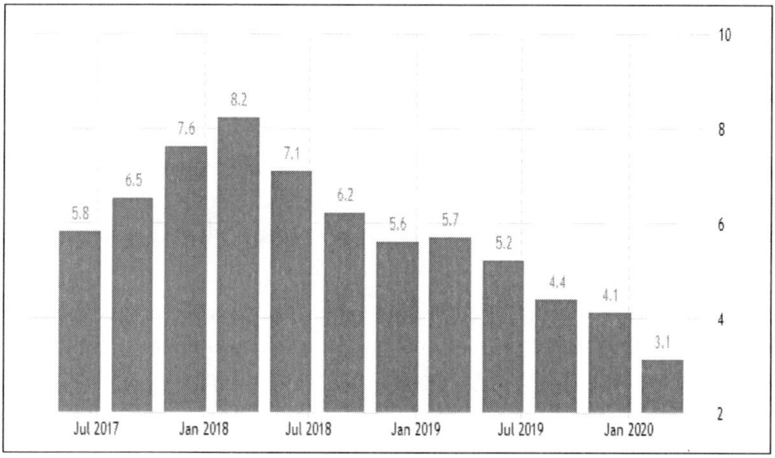

Source: Tradingeconomics.com

Chart IV: GDP Growth Rate.

Real GDP or Gross Domestic Product (GDP) at Constant (2011-12) Prices in the year 2019- 20 is now estimated to attain a level of Rs 145.66 lakh crore, as against the First Revised Estimate of GDP for the year 2018-19 of Rs 139.81 lakh crore, released on 31st January 2020. The growth in GDP during 2019-20 is estimated at 4.2 percent as compared to 6.1 percent in 2018-19.

Professional forecasters veered towards a consensus that India's economy will face its worst recession in 40 years, contracting by at least 5 percent this fiscal, which will partially reflect the unfolding impact of the pandemic on the economy. S&P Global Ratings said the Indian economy will contract 5 percent in FY21, assuming that the ongoing outbreak in India will peak in the September quarter while Swiss Bank UBS said India's economy could shrink 5.8 percent during the current financial year amid weaker-than-expected domestic economic activity and the ongoing global recession. Earlier, S&Ps Indian arm Crisil, Fitch Ratings and Goldman Sachs projected India's economy to contract 5 percent in FY21.

Social Impact

Social stress caused by lockdown has many faces and reasons resulting from travelling restrictions and disruption of cultural celebrations, limited healthcare facilities and interruption in regular immunisations in hospitals leading to anxiety and fear among the population, social distancing with friends and family, closure of places of entertainment and leisure, unplanned closure of schools and colleges affecting both students and parents regarding the academic year and the loss of quality education. Inadequate infrastructure, leading to ill-equipped healthcare employees who are fighting endlessly to treat patients and protect themselves from infection at the same time are all quite visible. This major loss and unpreparedness is an aftermath of the negligence of healthcare sector since years. Incapacitated hospitals and distressed primary healthcare are significant reasons behind so much distress among the people for a disease which could be prevented with a little care and precaution.

Focus has mostly been on testing, treatment and prevention of COVID-19 but people and communities are going through various social problems as well in adjusting to the current lifestyles and fear of the disease across nations. Conditions have all the more affected the other half of the population globally and particularly in India where abrupt lockdown has brought millions below the poverty line struggling for basic needs like food and shelter which then leads to unequal share in domestic responsibilities, to violence against the vulnerable members of the household.

The issue of migrant workers was one of the most cruel and highlighted issue in this pandemic where millions were rendered unemployed and stranded without money, food and shelter, crisscrossing the country's highways to return to their villages and several meeting with accidents and deaths on their way COVID-19 pandemic brought whole world to an uncertain but equal state. The living condition of all became similar in some sense; including living with minimal resources, travelling less, more time at home with family, keeping distance with your neighbours, etc. made most of us socially equal. It is expected that in short term this all will hold similar impact on many, but situation may change to large extent with each passing day in long term. As economy cannot stand still for long time, it should walk if not allowed to run. Imagine a situation when farmers are not able to harvest their crops in April, due to non-availability of labour from UP and Bihar.

Technological Impact

Technology impact of Covid-19 on India is mostly positive and it includes following aspects:

- Technological Innovation
- Research & development
- Automation

In the wake of COVID-19 pandemic, consumers in India have reported major increase in the use of digital and low-touch activities across categories like delivery services, at-home entertainment, education, food, staples, shopping, communications, health and fitness. The COVID-19 crisis has highlighted the weaknesses and the strengths of India's large businesses. Now executives have an opportunity to make changes that will see their companies through the downturn and position them for long-term success. On digital technology and analytics, adoption of these technologies can generate enormous value and cited a McKinsey Global Institute estimate in 2019, according to which such technologies could create some USD 1 trillion of value in India alone.

COVID-19 has accelerated India's digital reset

- Coronavirus propelled the use of contactless digital technology across India.
- The digital-first reset has set the foundations for improving governance.
- Indian states have increased the use of robots and drones.

The country was already on a digital-first trajectory with one of the highest volumes of digital transactions in the world when the pandemic struck, and further propelled the use of contactless digital technology.

Data from the apex Reserve Bank of India (RBI) show that India is now clocking around 100 million digital transactions a day with a volume of 5 trillion rupees ($67 billion), about a five times jump from 2016. RBI expects this to further grow five-fold to 1.5 billion transactions a day worth 15 trillion rupees ($200 billion). Much of this is powered by the United Payment Interface (UPI), a real-time payment system developed by the National Payments Corporation of India and monitored by RBI.

This digital-first reset of a country of 1.3 billion people is not only technological advancement but, more importantly, it is the foundation of a new mechanism for the deliverance of goods of governance. Embedded in this programmatic use of technology by the state are two promises which have historically been difficult to fulfil in India – speed and the plugging of leakages. The use of digital technology led to savings of nearly $23 billion, 98 percent of this by eliminating erroneous beneficiaries.

Change in Workspace Post COVID-19

Contactless access control

The first step toward resuming office life in the post-Covid-19 world will involve identifying and making adjustments to the areas where employees could come in close contact with others – for example, the entrance and check-in areas. Moreover, contact-free access control can also track visitors entering the office premises and automatically generate digital passes for visitors without requiring any human intervention.

Automated thermal cameras for temperature screening

As mandated by most state governments, companies must conduct temperature screening of every employee at the office entrance. When done manually, this process is time-consuming, causes long queues outside the entrance, and violates the social distancing rules. With advanced technologies such as thermal imaging and artificial intelligence, body-temperature screening of employees can be carried out in a completely automated and non-intrusive manner.

Using AI to help combat COVID-19

Artificial Intelligence (AI) has reshaped many major industries such as banking, e-commerce, and more. It has the potential to transform healthcare too. It can help mine patient data and analyse it, ensure early detection, find patterns, facilitate correct diagnosis, design the right treatment, conduct research, help create drugs and molecules faster, help make quicker decisions — all life-saving applications when it comes to healthcare, especially in today's times of Coronavirus.

The COVID-19 pandemic has exposed a clear digital divide: those companies which had already invested in digital operating models/ enablement have fared much better than those which had not. In fact, for many businesses, the continuity of operations critically depends on their digital capabilities.

Boards and markets are taking note, and consequently digital transformation is likely to be one of the most strategic topics on the boardroom agenda. The question now is how soon organisations can shift to the new digital business and operating models.

Legal Impact of COVID-19 Pandemic

Legal Aspects means the laws protecting the Interest of Public and organisations.

This includes certain aspects like-

- Consumer Protection Laws
- Health and Safety Laws
- Employment Laws

The nationwide lockdown has been central to the government's strategy to combat the COVID-19 pandemic. With businesses closed, supply chains disrupted, timelines extended and contracts terminated, this exercise has caused the organised sector unprecedented economic losses. In the unorganised sector, there has been a complete breakdown with little or no legal recourse for those who are affected. While the lockdown has helped contain community spread of the disease, a legal and legislative audit of this exercise has evaded scrutiny so far. As we are now in the seventh week of the lockdown, it is imperative and timely that we assess its underlying legislative soundness.

Laws Governing Lockdown

The lockdown has been carried out by State governments and district authorities on the directions of the Union Ministry of Home Affairs under the Disaster Management Act of 2005, which was intended "to provide for the effective management of disasters and for matters connected therewith or incidental thereto". Under the Act, the National Disaster Management Authority (NDMA) was set up under the leadership of the Prime Minister, and the National Executive Committee (NEA) was chaired by the Home Secretary. On March 24, 2020, the NDMA and NEA issued orders directing the Union Ministries, State governments and authorities to take effective measures to prevent the spread of COVID-19, and laid out guidelines illustrating which establishments would be closed and which services suspended during the lockdown period.

Taking a cue from the guidelines, the State governments and authorities exercised powers under the Epidemic Diseases Act of 1897 to issue further directions. For instance, the Health and Family Welfare Department of Tamil Nadu issued a government order on March 23, 2020, to impose social distancing and isolation measures which directed "suspected cases and foreign returnees" to remain "under strict home quarantine" and people "to stay at home and come out only for accessing basic and essential services and strictly follow social distancing norms". Subsequently, on March 25, the earlier order was extended for a period of 21 days, in accordance with the directions of the NEA. District authorities such as the Commissioner of Police, Greater Chennai, have consequently issued orders to impose Section 144 of the Criminal Procedure Code in public places.

Cumulatively, these orders constitute the legislative umbrella governing the lockdown that has been in place since March 24. The invoking of the Disaster Management Act has allowed the Union Government to communicate seamlessly with the States. However, serious questions remain whether the Act was originally intended to or is sufficiently capable of addressing the threat of a pandemic. Also, the use of the archaic Epidemic Diseases Act reveals the lack of requisite diligence and responsiveness of government authorities in providing novel and innovative policy solutions to address a 21st century problem. Another serious failing is that any violation of the orders passed would be prosecutable under Section 188 of Indian Penal Code, a very ineffective and broad provision dealing with disobedience of an order issued by a public servant.

Environmental Impact

This aspect consider the change in environment post Covid-19

- Air Quality
- Survival of Wild Life

The lockdowns enforced due to the COVID-19 pandemic led to large improvement in air quality in India, say scientists who suggest that such interventions may be used as a possible emergency measure to combat severe air pollution episodes like those witnessed in Delhi-NCR region during the winter months.

Ahead of the World Environment Day on June 5, experts have outlined several environmental factors that saw improvements in India as a result of the lockdowns, namely, air quality, noise pollution, water quality, and biodiversity among others due to reduced industrial and human activities. Since then the lockdown has been extended many times with gradual lifting of restrictions.

According to two studies, published in the journal Geophysical Research Letters in May, the levels of two major air pollutants, including nitrogen dioxide, drastically reduced since lockdowns were enforced worldwide in response to the COVID-19 pandemic.

In India, satellite data has shown a significant drop in particulate matter or aerosol levels after the COVID-19 lockdown over most parts of the country. Field measurements show that there is a substantial reduction in the concentration of suspended particulate matter (PM), a major component of air pollution, in the atmosphere due to reduced human activities as a consequence of the lockdown," he said.

The scientist explained that multi-spectral measurements of aerosol absorption, in addition to data available from Central Pollution Control Board (CPCB), indicate that the drastic decrease in pollution levels is mainly due to a reduction in fossil fuel burning emissions.

This pandemic restricted worldwide to take required actions in various developed and developing nations such as strict lockdown in Wuhan, China; 21-day complete lockdown in India; extensive travel restriction, Italy; Pubs, bars, theater have been closed in London, worldwide effect on transportation, decline in growth of aviation industry and railways, strategy like work from home has been adopted. All of these steps showed positive impact on environment globally. Developmental activities caused threat to present environmental condition but recently due to COVID-19 outbreak industrial and transportation activities has been banned which made the surrounding environment more cleaner than previous condition. This is one of the positive side of this pandemic as New York reduce approx. 50 percent pollution, coal use is decline by 40 percent in China, air quality index has been improved in Europe as satellite image showed fading of NO_2 emission, similar case monitored in Spain and UK.

In India, due to restriction of industrial activity and zero effluent discharge results in better river water quality. In India, cities like Delhi as per system of air quality and weather forecasting and research (SAFAR) showed average air quality index followed by Bengaluru, Kolkata, and Lucknow. Real time water monitoring data of CPCB, the average water quality of Ganga and Yamuna has been improved and become suitable for bathing, propagation of wildlife and fisheries. Impact on carbon neutrality reveals that impose of lockdown to restrict the spread of COVID-19 showed fall in GHG and CO_2 emission across the continents. Scientist and researchers estimates 5 percent fall in carbon output in 2020. However, this fall in emission could be short term and have minor impact on the concentration of CO_2 in atmosphere. The world needs to adopt renewable energy sources to maintain balance in the ecosystem and to improve energy efficiency. Once the world get out of this pandemic then huge pressure will be employed on environment. Thus, it is better to implement strict regulations and rules for environment protection and industries to avoid detrimental effect of anthropogenic activity.

Many researchers have hypothesised that the drop in air pollution levels may currently be saving a significant amount of lives, not only by reducing individuals susceptibility to Covid-19, but also by preventing some of the worlds seven million annual deaths due to air pollution exposure. Still, the dangerously high levels of NO_2 in many urban areas before Covid-19 has likely resulted in far more virus deaths compared to the lives saved by this current drop in emissions. The pandemic and the subsequent decreases in air pollution levels due to the quarantine have illuminated a severe issue regarding ongoing high levels of air pollution.

Future Prospects

The terrifying reality is that despite human activity essentially coming to a complete standstill, current estimates suggest that carbon dioxide (CO_2) levels will only decrease by roughly 5.5 percent in 2020 compared to 2019. To put this in perspective, to meet the goal of limiting the global increase in temperature to 1.5ºC, which many experts agree would stave off the worst effects of climate change, global CO_2 emissions would need to decrease by 7.6 percent each year. Similarly, air pollution and NO_2 levels are expected to rise to their normal unhealthy levels when quarantines are lifted.

Its ironic that this devastating respiratory virus has illuminated another respiratory crisis. May India make the recent decreases in air pollution that have provided a glimmer of hope during these difficult times permanent, rather than a temporary glimpse at what is possible.

References

- Ministry of Statistics and Programme Implementation. "Consumer price index numbers on base 2012=100 for rural, urban and combined for the month of July 2020". Available at: http://www.mospi.gov.in/press-release
- The World Bank. "Indicator of GDP Growth". Available at: https://data.worldbank.org/indicator/NY.GDP.MKTP.KD.ZG?end= 2019&locations=IN&start=1961&view=chart
- Business Today 2020. "India's weak manufacturing PMI for July one of the worst globally". Available at: https://www.businesstoday.in/current/economy-politics/india-weak-manufacturing-pmi-for-july-one-of-the-worst-globally/story/412002.html
- Markit Economics 2020. "IHS Markit India Manufacturing PMI". Available at https://www.markiteconomics.com/Public/Home/PressRelease/8d0d0f3599b74c2a9027b7d28643afff
- Reserve Bank of India. Available at: https://www.rbi.org.in.
- World Economic Forum 2020. "COVID-19 has accelerated India's digital reset. Available at: https://data.worldbank.org/indicator/NY.GDP.MKTP.KD.ZG?end=2019&locations=IN&start=1961&view=chart

- Economics Times 2020. "Technology services and its changing role during the Covid-19 era. Available at: https://cio.economictimes.indiatimes.com/news/enterprise-services-and-applications/technology-services-and-its-changing-role-during-the-covid-19era/75490056
- Money Control 2020. "Technology and digital reach will change the face of healthcare post Covid-19". Available at: https://www.moneycontrol.com/news/coronavirus/technology-and-digital-reach-will-change-the-face-of-healthcare-post-covid-19-5320271.html
- Economic Times 2020. "Impact of Covid-19 on the Indian Economy". Available at: https://bfsi.economictimes. indiatimes.com/blog/impact-of-covid-19-on-the-indian-economy/4241
- Financial Express 2020. "COVID-19 crisis: Continued spread of Coronavirus pandemic poses risk to Indian economy, says IMF official". Available at: https://www.financialexpress.com/economy/covid-19-crisis-continued-spread-of-coronavirus-pandemic-poses-risk-to-indian-economy-says-imf-official/2009181/ . Assessed on 21 August, 2020

COVID-19 Pandemic and Human Rights and Women's Issues

10

COVID-19 in India: An Analysis of Human Rights Perspective

Jaspal Kaur

COVID-19 pandemic characterised as a spread of new disease in the world by the World Health Organisation (WHO). It has been recorded as one of the perilous events after the World War-II in the 21st century, which claimed more than eight lakh lives. An outbreak of a new fatal disease came into being in December 2019 when a cluster of pneumonia cases caused by coronavirus emerged in Wuhan (China). It is leading to a public health crisis swiftly with 4,995,996 confirmed cases and 327,821 deaths.[1] WHO has declared it as a Global Public Health Emergency of International Concern under Article 6.1 and Article 12.1 of International Health Regulations (IHR) 2005[2] on 30 January, 2020? To achieve health protection, states are endorsed to take additional measures under Article 43 of IHR at international level. States have included legislative and regulatory measures in response to COVID-19. The GOI has also followed the additional measures to combat the COVID-19 pandemic. Indian Prime Minister Mr. Narendra Modi had announced a nationwide lockdown on 24th March, 2020 under the Section 6 (2)(i) and 10 (2)(i) of The National Disaster Management Act, 2005 in tandem with the Epidemic Disease Act of 1897.

Under lockdown all the offices of GOI, state/union territories, their autonomous bodies, and corporations were ordered to remain closed. Besides, the commercial, private and industrial establishments were also directed to be closed down. However, the Ministry of Home Affairs subsequently exempted the essential goods and services from national lockdown. The essential services like defence, treasury, public utilities (including petroleum, CNG, LPG), disaster management, power generation, post offices, national information centers, water, sanitation, police, telecommunications, banks, print and electronic media, pharmaceuticals etc. have been excluded from the purview of the lockdown. Union and state governments instructed the police to act with restraint while enforcing the lockdown monitoring the movement of people, "but not to that of essential goods".

In order to combat COVID-19, GOI had taken several preventative measures with good intention to combat COVID-19 expansion. However, the large chunk of the population had left unprepared for daily needs due to the abrupt decision of lockdown. The migratory labourers had entrapped at their workplaces and left with no option/s moving back to homes. The citizens were harshly treated by the police. Moreover, the health system was exposed, substantiated by the deaths of doctors, and their protest/strikes. The hospitals were not in a position to provide the basic healthcare facilities given the lack of medicines, equipment etc. Moreover, the people suffering from the COVID-19 have been stigmatised. The Human Rights Watch has been increasingly concerned about the stigmatisation of individuals and a rise in vigilante violence. In this background, the main focus of this paper is to examine and analyse COVID-19 and how it has become rationale for human rights violation in India?

Pandemic: Historical Moorings

Throughout the recorded history, communicable diseases had ravaged the humankind's hunter-gatherer days. However, during the shifting from hunter-gatherer to agrarian life about 10,000 years ago had created communities that made them more vulnerable to epidemics and pandemics. The same period was more characterised by diseases like Influenza, leprosy, malaria, tuberculosis, smallpox etc. In the course of history, it has been said that there were several epidemics which had taken place including the latest five declarations of international public health emergencies. The list of the same included -Antonine Plague (165 A.D.); Cyprian Plague (250 A.D.); Justinian Plague (541 A.D.); Leprosy (11th Century); The Black Death (1350); The Great Plague of London (1665); First Cholera Pandemic (1817); The Third Plague Pandemic (1855); Russian Flu (1889); Spanish Flu (1918); Asian Flu (1957); HIV/AIDS (1981); SARS (2003); Swine Flu (2009); Polio (2014); Western Africa Ebola (2014); Zika Virus (2015) and another Ebola (the Democratic Republic of the Congo-2019). COVID-19 is the new entry in the list of pandemics, declared officially by the WHO.

COVID -19: Origin and Expansion

COVID-19 is an infectious disease caused by a newly discovered coronavirus. 'CO' stands for corona, 'VI' for virus and 'D' for disease. Earlier, this disease was referred to as '2019 novel coronavirus' or '2019-nCoV'. The COVID-19 is a new virus linked to the same family of viruses SARS-CoV-2 as Severe Acute Respiratory Syndrome (SARS) and some types of common cold. The most likely ecological reservoirs for SARS-CoV-2 are bats, but it is believed that the virus jumped the species barrier to humans from another intermediate animal host. This intermediate animal host could be a domestic food animal, a wild animal, or be a domesticated wild animal which has not yet been identified.[3] In general, coronaviruses are very stable in a frozen state which has shown survival for up to two years at -20°C and thermolabile, which means that they are susceptible to normal cooking temperatures (70°C).[4]

Coronaviruses are a large family of zoonotic viruses that cause illness ranging from the common cold to severe respiratory diseases. Zoonotic means these viruses are able to be transmitted from animals to humans. There are several coronaviruses known to be circulating in different animal populations that have not yet infected humans. COVID-19 is the most recent one to cause human infection. Most coronavirus infected people have been experiencing mild to moderate respiratory illness, pneumonia, severe acute respiratory syndrome, kidney failure, death etc. The older people and people with underlying medical problems like cardiovascular disease, diabetes, chronic respiratory disease, and cancer are more vulnerable to develop serious illness. The corona virus spreads primarily through the droplets of saliva or discharge from the nose when an infected person coughs or sneezes. The time for exposure to onset of symptoms is usually between two and 14 days, with an average of five days.

The first case of novel corona was identified at Wuhan, Hubei province, China on 31st December, 2019. The Chinese authorities had informed to WHOs China office about a cluster of 44 patients of pneumonia cases with unknown causes. Out of 44 patients, 11 were severely ill, while the remaining 33 patients were in stable condition.[5] Most of them were connected to the Huanan seafood wholesale market.[6] The causal agent has not yet been identified or confirmed. On January 7, China had identified a new novel Coronavirus which is considered to be the cause of the outbreak. February 11, WHO assigns the novel coronavirus its official name as COVID-19. After China, Thailand confirmed COVID-19 cases followed by Japan, South Korea to almost all the countries of seven continents except Antarctica in the world.

The COVID-19 has affected the entire world, originating from Wuhan. Meanwhile, the epicenter of pandemic has been shifted to Europe from

China having the highest death tolls in Italy, Spain and France based on the data collected by Johns Hopkins University.[7] Table 1 shows 24,854,140 corona infected cases with the total 838,924 deaths have been reported by the WHO (2020, August 30). The USA is the worst affected country. A substantial number of affected cases have been reported in USA i.e. one-fourth of the total cases, followed by Brazil and India among top ten countries which have been infected by the corona menace. (Table 1)

Table 1: Reported Cases and Deaths by Country

Sl. No.	*Country*	*Total Cases*	*Total Deaths*
	World	24,854,140	838,924
1.	USA	5,855,521	180,689
2.	Brazil	3,804,803	119,504
3.	India	3,542,733	63,498
4.	Russian Fed	990,326	17,093
5.	Peru	629,961	28,471
6.	South Africa	622,551	13,981
7.	Colombia	590,520	18,767
8.	Mexico	585,738	63,146
9.	Spain	439,286	29,011
10.	Chile	408,009	11,181

Source: https://covid19.who.int/table[8]

Present Scenario of COVID-19 in India

The novel coronavirus infection has also been infiltrated into India through China. Hitherto 5.8 million cases have been reported in India by 30 August 2020. Due to massive population density, poor socio-economic conditions and inadequate healthcare resources, India has been turned into its epicenter. WHO has recently reported that the future of the pandemic depends on how India would handle it.[9]

India confirmed its first arrival in Kerala on January 30, 2020 by the Ministry of Health and Family Welfare. The patient happened to be an Indian student from the Chinese university. It has also been analyzed that most of the Corona cases available have a travel history to infected countries or come in contact with a person who travelled recently abroad. Table 2 highlighted the sizable number of infected cases and death of coronavirus happened to be in five states. It has been found that 51 percent of the total reported cases and 69.16 percent of total deaths due to coronavirus were reported in the five states. Maharashtra is placed in the top slot; followed by Andhra Pradesh, Karnataka, UP and Tamil Nadu.

Table 2: COVID-19 State-wise Status

Sl. No.	*States*	*Total Cases (percentage in Parenthesis)*	*Total Deaths (percentage in Parenthesis)*
1.	Maharashtra	193889 (24.79)	24399 (37.84)
2.	Andhra Pradesh	99129 (12.67)	3884 (6.02)
3.	Karnataka	88110 (11.26)	5589 (8.66)
4.	Uttar Pradesh	54666 (6.99)	3423 (5.30)
5.	Tamil Nadu	52721 (6.74)	7234 (11.22)
6 .	India	781975 (100)	64469 (100)

Source: Ministry of Health and Family Welfare (Government of India).

Redressal Mechanism by the Government of India

COVID-19 is a pan India biological health emergency given no specific therapeutics or vaccines for the treatment of the disease are available. The GOI has taken proactive measures in line with global approaches and guidelines from the MOHFW and Ministry of Home Affairs. As given the reported massive infected cases and deaths, the GOI had taken several preventive measures. In the very beginning, PM Narendera Modi had declared the public curfew followed by several other measures like isolation, social distancing, lockdown, ban on domestic and foreign travelling etc. However, the major chunk of the population left unprepared for such preventive measures. Therefore, in order to meet their daily needs, the citizens had to come and consequently met with the police highhandedness and resulted in partly human rights violation. The preventive measures taken by the GOI were as follows:

Isolation

Isolation refers to the separation of infected persons to protect the non-infected persons, and usually occurs in hospital/home settings. Quarantine is one of the oldest and most effective tools of controlling communicable disease outbreaks. This public health practice was used widely in fourteenth century Italy, when ships arriving at the Venice port from plague-infected ports had to anchor and wait for 40 days (in Italian: quaranta for 40) before disembarking their surviving passengers.[10]

COVID-19 spread made it mandatory for the government to implement home quarantine but quarantine is not easy to implement due to inadequate infrastructure to quarantine people safely. In India, large scale home isolation is nearly impossible as homes are not big enough to isolate members who are exhibiting symptoms or tested positive. The largest chunk of Indians has either one or two rooms' houses.[11] Overcrowding made it impossible to have an assess of home quarantine.

Secondly, a large number of migratory workers dependent on daily earning, left no money in hand, became unemployed and victims of corona virus while returning back to homes. So it is very difficult for them to isolate themselves, they were already running on hand to mouth basis. They did not follow quarantine rules. As a result they were punished under Sections 269, 270 and 271 of Indian Penal Code with imprisonment of six months and fine. So, social isolation/quarantine is a violation of Right to equality, Right to life and to move freely throughout in India.

Social Distancing

Social distancing is a non-pharmaceutical infection prevention and control intervention implemented to avoid/decrease contact between those who are infected with a disease causing pathogen and those who are not, so as to stop or slow down the rate and extent of disease transmission in a community.[12] Social distancing is designed to reduce interactions between people in a broader community, in which individuals may be infectious but have not yet been identified hence not yet isolated. In the absence of sufficient measures are deemed to be insufficient, 'community-wide containment' may need to be implemented. Community-wide containment is an intervention applied to an entire community, city or region, designed to reduce personal interactions, except for minimal interaction to ensure vital supplies.

The social distancing is a misnomer, which implies physical separation to prevent the viral spread but it is nearly impossible for the poor.[13] In India, COVID-19 is an infection coming from the rich and infecting the poor, and yet, the poor have to bear a large part of the burden and risk. However, social distance remains a distant reality for the hundreds of thousands of domestic workers, safai karamcharis, delivery people and others engaged in the unorganised sector. Physical interaction is vital to their survival and work from home is an unaffordable luxury.

Lockdown

Lockdown is a new arsenal response to classical public health measures of prevention and control which was first imposed in Wuhan province at the peak of pandemic on 23rd January, 2020 and later extended to 15 cities across China. The rationale for lockdowns is to slow down the spread of the disease, flatten the curve to match the capacity of the healthcare system, and allow time for its strengthening.[14] Singh, R. & Adhikari, R. (2020) in their study recommended a protocol of three consecutive lockdowns of 21 days, 28 days and 18 days spaced by 5 days of suspension[15] to bring the number of infections below 10 where explicit contact tracing followed by quarantine may be successful in preventing resurgence. Prime Minister of India has announced a countrywide lockdown for three weeks starting at midnight on 24 March to slow the spread of Covid-19. This is the largest lockdown announced since the beginning of the outbreak as per health experts. The Prime Minister of India ordered nationwide lockdown in four phases:

(1) **Phase-I (24 March-14 April):** All persons were required to obey the curfew. All transport services, educational institutes, industrial establishments and hospitality services were suspended except essential services like police, medical services, media, home delivery professionals and firefighters. Any person violating this containment will be liable to be proceeded against as per the provisions of Section 51-60 of the Disaster Management Act, 2005 besides legal action under Section 188 of the IPC.

(2) **Phase-II (15 April-3 May):** Prime Minister of India extended lockdown up to 3rd May with conditional relaxation allowing agricultural business, public works programme, cargo transportation vehicles and banks with govt, centres would reopen while maintaining social distance. Lockdown areas were classified into three zones:

   (a) Red zone indicating the presence of infection hotspot

   (b) Orange zone indicating some infection

   (c) Green zone with no infection

(3) **Phase-III (4 May-17 May):** Ministry of Home Affairs (MHA) and GOI extended lockdown for 2 weeks with some relaxation. Normal movement is allowed in green zone with buses limited to 50 percent capacity, orange zone would allow only private and hired vehicles but no public transportation while no relaxation in red zone.

(4) **Phase-IV (18 May-31 May):** Lockdown was further extended by MHA and National Disaster Management Authority (NDMA). In this phase Red zone was divided into Containment and Buffer zone.

COVID-19 and Human Rights

After the outbreak of COVD-19, the WHO called all the governments at global level to take urgent and aggressive actions to stop the spread of the virus. So the government should prioritise human rights perspective while responding to COVID-19. It should not violate people's right to human dignity, freedom of movement, freedom of trade, occupation and profession, and access to healthcare, food and water. According to Article 25.1 of the Universal Declaration of Human Rights (UDHR), affirms everyone has the right to a standard of living adequate for the health of himself and of his family. Article 12.1 of the International Covenant on Economic, Social and Cultural Rights, States parties recognize that the right of everyone to the enjoyment of the highest attainable standard of physical and mental health. The right to health is closely related to other human rights, as contained in the International Bill of Rights, including the rights to food, housing, work, education, human dignity, life, non-discrimination, equality, the prohibition against torture, privacy, access to information, and the freedoms of association, assembly and movement. These and other rights and freedoms address integral components of the right to health.

The right to health provides that health facilities, goods, and services should be:

- available in sufficient quantity,
- accessible to everyone without discrimination, and affordable for all, even marginalised groups;
- acceptable, meaning respectful of medical ethics and culturally appropriate;
- Scientifically and medically appropriate and of good quality.

The Siracusa Principles[16] adopted by the UN Economic and Social Council in 1984, and UN Human Rights Committee general comments on states of emergency and freedom of movement provide authoritative guidance on government responses that restrict human rights for reasons of public health or national emergency. Any measures taken to protect the population that limit people's rights and freedoms must be lawful, necessary, and proportionate. States of emergency needed to be limited in duration and any curtailment of rights needs to take into consideration the disproportionate impact on specific populations or marginalised groups.

It has been reported by a non-government organisation named Hola Bon Renaissance (HBR) Foundation in Africa is challenging Government's response to COVID-19. HBR has approached the Constitutional Court seeking a declaration that the lockdown currently underway in South Africa is unnecessary and unconstitutional as it has violated peoples' rights to human dignity, freedom of movement, freedom of trade, occupation and profession, and access to healthcare, food and water.

Migration

In India, the four hour short notice for the shutdown effectively trapped the 470 million migrant workers in no man's land. In India, 80 percent of the workforce is employed in the informal sector and one-third working as casual labour.[17] The closure of all but essential services made it impossible for daily wagers to live in the rented shanties of big cities but the labourers who live on margins panicked and sparked an exodus to their native place. They undertook several hundred kms journey on foot as the transportation service both by buses and trains were suspended during 21 days lockdown. The journey turned into fatal for some which was reported to be at least 22 migrants but the actual figure may be much higher.[18] One of the workers died on as he attempted a walk of 270 km journey back home. About 22 migrants have died, though the actual count may be much higher. One 39-year-old, who set off on foot from Delhi to his hometown in Madhya Pradesh, collapsed and died after walking around 200 kilometers. He had worked at a restaurant in Delhi that closed due to the spread of COVID-19. Another migrant, who had subsisted on just one meal in two days, told a reporter wryly: "If coronavirus doesn't kill us, hunger will!" but this is the violation of fundamental rights of Indian constitution as free migration is enshrined in clauses (d) and (e) of Article 19 (1) and guarantee all citizens to move freely throughout the territory of India. But the question arises why the arrangement for their migration has not been made, secondly, why night shelters, community kitchen, toilet facility and free food-the basic requirement for mankind has not been provided.

Police Assault

Instead of helping distressed and poor citizens who were laid off, facing poverty, hunger, deprivation of basic necessities etc. during their way back to homes on foot hundreds of kms, that have become a serious cause of concerns and cases of human rights violation. While the people were moving on the roads, the Indian police personnel and security forces were assaulting and using excessive force to clear the streets and roads. The people were beaten with batons while others have been publicly maltreated by forcing them to do squats, push-ups, crawl or roll around on the streets. Many people had succumbed to death given the lack of basic necessities like water, food, medicines, rather were sanitised with the chemicals. Many deaths had also taken place given the lack of food accessibility.

Lack of Healthcare Services

Indian Council of Medical Research (ICMR) -the apex body of medical research declared that there was no community transmission of Pandemic Coronavirus but the situation changed overnight with millions of migrant workers heading home due to loss of jobs, shelter (small industries and landlords apparently asked them to vacate) and fear of starvation. It was very difficult for the administration to maintain the social distance for quarantining a large population effectively, providing food and medical support. At the time of the Pandemic outbreak India realised a poor healthcare system.

A health system or healthcare system includes the organisation, financing and provision of healthcare services to a population. India has a three tier system of Public health system i.e. Primary (first point of contact for patient), Secondary (provided by specialist on referral from primary care provider) and tertiary (highly specialised medical care) care. It also includes private practitioners and private hospitals to provide care to 80 percent outpatients and 60 percent inpatients. Thus, all services at government facilities, like preventive and primary care, diagnostic services, and outpatient and inpatient hospital care, are delivered free of charge. In practice, severe shortages of staff and supplies limit access to care. As per World Health Organisation norm of doctor-to-population ratio is 1: 1,000 and nurse-to-patient ratio is 3:1,000 but India has 1:1,674 doctor-to-patients ratio and nurse-to-patient ratio 1.7:1,000 which results in acute shortages and uneven distribution of doctors and nurses in India.[19] The staff who danger their lives and work day long and nights have raised concerns over the shortage of supplies such as personal protective equipment and purchasing it privately at inflated price.

On 30th March the announcement of making Mahatma Gandhi of Medical Sciences, Sewagram in rural Maharashtra as the nodal centre for the treatment of COVID-19 brought a wave of shock as the hospital was unprepared. It had only two ICU beds and was running out of personal protective equipment with only a small stock they had bought at an inflated price.[20] At Jhansi Medical College in Uttar Pradesh the doctors are provided with PPE and nurses had paid salary for the last seven months who went on strike for one day at the time of the outbreak of coronavirus. On 28 March, Rudra Arpan Chatterjee, a fellow in clinical immunology and rheumatology at the Sanjay Gandhi Postgraduate Institute of Medical Sciences in Lucknow, shared a letter from the vice chancellor of KGMU on Twitter. The letter asked the staff to give up a day's salary to fund the supply of PPE. Punjab, healthcare workers were using diluted sanitisers and cloth masks, even as the state's health minister insisted that it was well-prepared for the pandemic. The fears were not unfounded: a doctor at KGMU recently tested positive for the novel coronavirus, and is now under treatment.[21] A similar situation persists in Bihar, where 83 junior doctors have developed symptoms of COVID-19, but are forced to continue treating patients.

In addition to virus infection stigma, medical professionals in India are also facing another insidious threat i.e. ostracisation by the public, who fear that they could serve as vectors for the novel coronavirus. Many doctors have been asked to vacate their rented homes by their landlords as they believe that doctors staying at their houses may make them more susceptible to Covid-19.[22] Some doctors have faced threats and harassment as they attempted to travel to work under the nationwide lockdown. An anonymous female doctor in Telangana was abused, assaulted, and hauled to a police station while attempting to answer a last-minute call from the hospital for a shift. It has been reported that it is not a matter of concern in India only but severely affected countries by Coronavirus such as Italy, Spain and the United States, strained healthcare systems have also reached at their breaking points. Shortages of masks and other forms of PPE have become widespread, putting medical professionals at severe risk. At Mount Sinai Hospital, in New York City, the epicenter of the outbreak in the United States, some nurses resorted to using black plastic trash-bags as PPE. On 24 March, Kious Kelly, a 48-year-old nurse manager at Mount Sinai, died after contracting COVID-19. A scarcity of medical workers has also plagued countries that are struggling with the COVID-19 pandemic. The government of the United Kingdom asked 65,000 retired nurses and doctors to return to work, along with final-year medical students as Ruth May, chief nursing officer for England, said in a statement to the media. So it is a matter of human concern the Right to life is a fundamental and human right of all. It includes service providers also who spare their life to save others. Their safety is a matter of concern. The authorities should also ensure their safety so that they can make their efforts to save others.

Conclusion

COVID-19 had engulfed more than 50,000 lives so it is a challenge to public health and development. COVID-19 outbreak had exposed shortcoming in the public health system and social welfare which makes it hard to protect its population from transmission of diseases. Government should ensure that everyone can access essential healthcare including migrants, asylum seekers and refugees. The Corona virus knows no borders and reminds us of global connectedness and shared responsibility. Thus, all the government should give more emphasis on the health system by prioritising Right to health to all and human rights.

Referemces

1. Sharma, A., Tiwari, S., Deb, M. K., & MARTY, J. L. (2020). Severe Acute Respiratory Syndrome Coronavirus-2 (SARS-CoV-2): A global pandemic and treatments strategies. *International Journal of Antimicrobial Agents*, 106054.
2. World Health Organisation (2020). " COVID-19 as a Public Health Emergency of International Concern (PHEIC) under the IHR", Available at https://extranet.who.int/sph/covid-19-public-health-emergency-international-concern-pheic-under-ihr, assessed on 27 August, 2020.
3. World Health Organisation. (2020). Coronavirus disease 2019 (COVID-19): situation report, 82, available at https://www.who.int/docs/default-source/coronaviruse/situation-reports/20200221-sitrep-32-covid-19.pdf?sfvrsn=4802d089_2 assessed on 28August 2020.
4. World Health Organisation (2020). "Pneumonia of Unknown cause-China" available at https://www.who.int/csr/don/05-january-2020-pneumonia-of-unkown-cause-china/en/, assessed on 28 August 2020.
5. Secon, H., Woodward, A., & Mosher, D. (2020). A comprehensive timeline of the new coronavirus pandemic, from China's first COVID-19 case to the present. *Business Insider*.
6. COVID, C. (19). Dashboard by the Center for Systems Science and Engineering (CSSE) at Johns Hopkins University (JHU). 2020. Available at https://coronavirus.jhu.edu/map.html. Assessed on 28 August 2020.
7. World Health Organisation (2020). WHO Coronavirus Disease (COVID-19) Dashboard, available at https://covid19.who.int/table , assessed on 30 August 2020.
8. Pal, R., & Yadav, U. (2020). COVID-19 pandemic in India: present scenario and a steep climb ahead. *Journal of Primary Care & Community Health*, *11*, 2150132720939402.
9. Cetron, M., & Simone, P. (2004). Battling 21st-century scourges with a 14th-century toolbox. *Emerging infectious diseases*, *10*(11), 2053.
10. Thakur, Arul (2020). Why Home Quarantine is Difficult in India, available on - https://timesofindia.indiatimes.com/india/why-home-quarantine-is-difficult-in-india/articleshow/74704620.cms- assessed on 30 August 2020.
11. Ministry of Health and Family Welfare- Government of India (2020). "Advisory on Social Distancing Measure in view of spread of COVID-19 disease" available at https://www.mohfw.gov.in/pdf/SocialDistancingAdvisoryby MOHFW.pdf #:~:text=Socialpercent20distancingpercent20ispercent20apercent 20non, duepercent20topercent20thepercent20disease, assessed on 31[St] August 2020
12. Dr. Sudharshini Subramaniam Dr. Vijay Gopichandran Dr. Vinod H Krishnamoorthy (2020). Social distancing for the poor? Near impossible, write three doctors available on https://www.thenewsminute.com/article/social-

distancing-poor-near-impossible-write-three-doctors-120399 on 17 March 2020, assessed on 20 August 2020

13. Lau, H, Khosrawipour V, Kocbach P, Mikolajczyk A, Schubert J, Bania J et al. The positive impact of lockdown in Wuhan on containing the COVID-19 outbreak in China. *Journal of Travel Medicine* 2020
14. Singh, R., & Adhikari, R. (2020). Age-structured impact of social distancing on the COVID-19 epidemic in India. *arXiv preprint arXiv:2003.12055*.
15. Human Rights Dimensions of COVID-19 Response- https://www.hrw.org/news/2020/03/19/human-rights-dimensions-covid-19-response#_Toc35446577
16. COVID-19 and India's Nowhere People -The lockdown, and loss of jobs, lays bare the plight of India's millions of internal migrants- https://thediplomat.com/2020/04/covid-19-and-indias-nowhere- people/
17. India: COVID-19 Lockdown Puts Poor at Risk-Ensure All Have Access to Food, Health Care https://www.hrw.org/news/2020/03/27/india-covid-19-lockdown-puts-poor-risk
18. Parliament of India, Rajya Sabha. The Functioning of Medical Council of India (Ministry of Health and Family Welfare), Report No. 92, March 8, 2016; accessed Oct. 13, 2016
19. India's under-supported force of healthcare professionals is crumbling under the pressure of COVID-19 available at https://caravanmagazine.in/health/india-under-supported-health-care-workers-crumbling-pressure-covid-19

11

Human Rights amid the COVID-19 Outbreak

Navneet Saini

Human rights is a notion that has been persistently developing all through the history of humans. They are entrenched to the stability and progress of various countries all over the globe. Human rights are the rights inherent to all human being irrespective of race, religion, ethnicity, sex, language and culture. Human rights include the right to life and freedom, liberty from slavery and torture, independence of speech and expression, the right to work and many more. Hence, these are the basic rights that provides a sense of freedom to each and every person on this earth. These rights are generally based on shared values like dignity, equality, fairness and independence.

In this era of globalisation, these principles achieve more significance not only in defending human beings from the ill-effects of change but also in making sure that all human beings are permissible a share of the benefits. Immense emphasis has been placed on international conventions and their execution in order to guarantee observance to a universal standard of adequacy.

Human rights must lies at the heart of all anticipation, vigilance, restraint and management endeavours from the beginning only to maintain communal health as well as harmony within the society. This paper look at the concerns and challenges of human rights that come into view over and over again as states act in response to COVID-19 outbreak. This paper also put emphasis on the human rights concerns which are at stake when the country enforced preventive measures to look after the collective health, such as quarantines, travel bans and other such restrictions, access to information along with the responsibility of states to make sure the access to preventive care, goods and services for the public.

COVID-19 Outbreak

The most recent danger to global health is the ongoing outbreak of the respiratory disease that was recently given the name Coronavirus Disease 2019 (Covid-19). This disease was recognised in December 2019 (WHO, January 5, 2020). The World Health Organisation has announced Covid-19 a pandemic, thereby pushing the intimidation beyond the global health emergency (WHO, March 11, 2020). It is a hinge moment for the whole world. Covid-19 is a highly infectious disease that transfers from human to human. Generally, it spreads all the way through the droplets of saliva or discharge from the nose when an infected individual coughs or sneezes. As this virus progresses through the body, the patient needs the standard oxygen treatment. Albeit, countries all over the world are battling against this virus that started from Wuhan city in China. All the countries who have been continuously hit by this deadly virus are now practicing special procedures in an endeavour to make compulsory social distancing to slow down the spread of Covid-19. Many countries have stopped the mass gatherings, close down the colleges and universities and shut down the public spaces like big malls, pubs and clubs. The countries which are going through a bad phase due to the Covid-19 attack have also announced complete lockdown situation, thereby enforcing the people to stay indoors for their safety and society at large. India, China, France, Italy, New Zealand, Poland and United Kingdom have implemented the world's largest and most restrictive mass quarantines (Kaplan Juliana, Frias Lauren and McFall-Johnsen Morgan, April 17, 2020).

The whole world is witnessing a worst situation in the midst of disease and death. This virus is new and there is no vaccination available to control its adverse impact. In this situation, experts, scientists and authorities have come up with the idea of self-isolation. Self-isolation is basically a kind of social distancing. Both self-isolation and quarantine are the two methods that are intended to prevent people who are suffering from this virus or are known to have had contact with people who are infected from passing on this lethal virus to the rest of the population. Hence, social distancing is taken as a wider measure that can stop the integration of people, thereby preventing the infections to multiply among the population with each passing day. Social-distancing is therefore acting as a weapon to save this whole world from the attack of this invisible virus.

Moreover, certain groups of people such as aged people and people with pre-existing medical conditions appear to be at bigger threat of stern illness and demise if they come in contact with any infected person (Centers for Disease Control and Prevention, 2020). In this way, people having diabetes and high blood pressure are more likely to have Covid-19. In addition, deprived sections of society are also more vulnerable owing to the fact that their poor socio-economic strata debarred their access to adequate water and safe sanitation. In this situation of additional barriers in their way to keep health and protection, these people almost lies at the risk zone to protect themselves against this fatal virus. In designing significant responses to Covid-19, it is imperative that states should act carefully as this virus can put an adverse impact upon specific groups of people. The requirements of such definite groups should be taken into account and their episodes should be analyzed conscientiously in order to make essential changes in plans and strategies on a regular basis to save them from the attack of Covid-19.

The whole human race has been continuously facing the outrageous effects of coronavirus since January, 2020. However, Covid-19 is not the first pandemic that has affected our world. Disease and illnesses have plagued humanity since the earliest days. Around twenty major pandemics have occurred over time (World Economic Forum, March 15, 2020). The 1918 Spanish flu remains the deadliest in modern history, killing at least 50 million people and infecting more than 500 million. It was the mother of all pandemics (Taubenberger, Jeffrey K. and Morens, David M., 2006). Like nowadays, no vaccine was available then, thereby leaving the public health authorities to declare closures, quarantines, good quality hygiene, disinfectant and social distancing in order to battle with the spread of the disease. Schools, restaurants, and businesses were closed at that time due to this flu. Public gatherings were also banned. People were told to isolate and quarantine themselves to save their lives. Though, the world is totally different than it was hundred years ago. Nowadays global communication and sharing of information has made things much more easier than in 1918. Moreover, the efficacy of the measures adopted during Spanish Flu gives us hope that the current measures will also limit the impact of the Covid-19 pandemic.

Objectives of the Study

1. To look at the concerns and challenges of human rights that emerged during COVID-19 outbreak.
2. To throw light on the human rights concerns which are at stake when the nation enforced preventive measures to look after the communal health, such as quarantines, travel bans and other such restrictions, access to information as well as the liability of states

to make sure the right to use preventive care, goods and services for the public.

3. To put forward some recommendations in order to alter this unhappy situation across the nation.

Methodology

This study is based on the secondary data collected through review of literature. To achieve the above objectives, the available literature on related issues have been explored with the help of journals, articles, news reports etc.

The reports of people facing additional barriers while exercising their human rights due to quarantines, travel bans and other such restriction, access to information etc. have been reviewed to have deeper insight into the issue of human rights obligations amidst Covid-19 outbreak.

Preventing People's Contact during COVID-19

Quarantines

Quarantine is the state of parting the people who may have been exposed to or are showing warning signs of any contagious ailment. This method is generally used as a reaction to manage the reach of communicable diseases, including in countries' responses to COVID-19. Quarantines are used for people or groups who do not have any symptoms of any infectious disease but are exposed to the disease or attack of the virus. Quarantine method usually keeps the infection away from others.The practice of quarantine started during the 14th century in an attempt to defend the coastal cities from the wave of plague. In Venice, ships arriving from infected ports were obligatory to be seated at anchor for forty days of time before landing. This practice, known as quarantine, was derived from the Italian words *quaranta giorni* which stands for forty days (Centres for Disease Control and Prevention, 2012).

Reports point out that quarantines of different degrees have been continuously used in India in response to Covid-19. This practice of quarantines have been constantly influencing the cities as well as regions. Around 50 people including doctors were quarantined in Bikaner when a woman who was tested positive for Covid-19 died suddenly. Approximately, twenty family members of the deceased, fifteen neighbours' and several hospital staff members were quarantined after the death of the patient (India Today, April 6, 2020). Quarantines have been continuously putting an impact upon the individuals' freedom of movement. There have been reports of people facing additional hurdles in putting their human rights into practice due to the quarantine procedures. People have been facing difficulties in accessing basic necessities such as food, hygiene supplies and healthcare.

According to BBC's report of Vikas Pandey, large number of people are living under the scared state and people easily accept as true any kind of rumor they watch on the platform of social media. He further revealed a report in which a person who was quarantined due to the infection has been continuously facing the stigma even after the end of his quarantine period. Even vegetable and milk vendors have rejected to visit and deliver any essential goods to his house. Similarly, there are numerous cases in which people have been facing similar type of discrimination. People have stopped talking to the people kept under quarantines. Every person fears of getting the infection of coronavirus from such quarantined people. Reports have revealed that people have somewhere stopped being human in this course of Covid-19 (BBC NEWS, April 8, 2020).

Quarantines have been putting an impact upon people living in poverty. These people have insufficient resources to purchase food articles, health items and other supplies as well. They cannot go to work in such conditions and they may also have limited savings to last through a period of unpaid leave. According to the reports, the lockdown has unduly harmed the marginalised communities because of loss of livelihood and shortage of foodstuff, shelter, wellbeing and other indispensable needs. The responsibility of government have increased in this situation in order to protect the wellbeing and safety of the populace. The truth is that quarantines have left thousands of migrant workers trapped in difficult situations where there are not even rail and bus services for them to cater their diverse needs. The closing of state borders have caused several troubles in the delivery of important goods, thereby leading to price rises and a fright of scarcity in the whole state. About thousands of homeless people have been suffering badly in the desire of getting safety and shelter. Unfortunately, the actions of police personnel's in order to punish those violating the orders have reportedly resulted in mistreatment and exploitation against people in need in this way (Human Rights Watch, March 27, 2020).

The National Commission for Women (NCW) has received large number of complaints of domestic violence especially when the whole nation is struggling under the biggest lockdown to break the chain of coronavirus. The commission has recorded more than twofold increase in gender-based violence in the country during this lockdown period. The total complaints from women increased from 116 in the first week of March (that is, March 2-8), to 257 in the final week (that is, March 23-April 1). It is quite evident that the cases of domestic violence have actually doubled than what it was before the period of lockdown. The NCW chief Rekha Sharma stated that the cases of domestic violence are quite higher in Bihar, Haryana, Punjab and Uttar Pradesh. Moreover, the foremost reason for the increase of domestic violence is that the men stays at home during this lockdown period and they are taking out their aggravation and dissatisfaction upon women and they also decline to contribute in household work. On the other hand, women are unable to share their pain with anyone while staying within the four walls of home (Outlook India, 2020, April 7, 2020).

Travel Bans and Restrictions

The World Health Organisation (WHO) recommend against the application of travel or trade restrictions to countries experiencing COVID-19 outbreaks, except in limited circumstances, because of the risks of this approach. According to their most recent guidance, "restrictions may interrupt needed aid and technical support, may disrupt businesses, and may have negative social and economic effects on the affected countries"; furthermore, "restricting the movement of people and goods during public health emergencies is ineffective in most situations and may divert resources from other interventions" (WHO, February 29, 2020). Amid rising cases of Covid-19, many infected countries announced the travel restrictions and bans to control the spread of Covid-19. These measures can also impact the right to the freedom of movement, which comprises the liberty to leave any country and the right to not be arbitrarily deprived of the right to enter one's own country as well. India has also closed its border with neighbouring Myanmmar to respond to the coronavirus outbreak since countries across South Asia reported an increase in Covid-19 cases (Jamkhandikar, Shilpa, March 11, 2020).

According to the Indian Bureau of Immigration, all incoming passengers through air, land and sea has been barred by India except for essential goods and services. The government has taken the step of suspension of all the international flights arriving and departing from India in order to control the situation of the country amid Covid-19 outbreak (The New York Times, April 15, 2020). The imposed bans on travel to and from areas with high numbers of COVID-19 cases have been regularly impacting people trying to reach their homes and families. Migrant labourers have been protesting against the restrictions of lockdown across India. When thousands of migrant workers came out on the streets in the southern state of Kerala with the intention to reach their home and families, the authorities had a tough time in dispersing them for their own safety. Similarly, Delhi and Uttar Pradesh governments had finally made the arrangements to bring the migrants home by arranging few buses. In this way, the overwhelming majority was turned away at some places of the country (The New York Times, March 29, 2020).

Access to Information

The most imperative factor in controlling the reach of coronavirus is to empower the citizens with the accurate information and taking precautions as per the advisories being issued by Ministry of Health and Family Welfare. Providing accurate information to the people in relation to the major health problems is the responsibility of the authorities. In addition, the methods of preventing and controlling any ailment is considered as the liability of these main concerns to the core commitments of the right to maintain health. Information accessibility is therefore measured as a key dimension of the accessibility of health care. It also takes into account the right to ask for, obtain and communicate information pertaining to health issues. Hence, all the communities are permitted to obtain appropriate, timely and significant information about the nature and stage of the health risk during the time of any distress. Such relevant information should be accessible in the languages to meet up the diverse needs of those affected by the infection the most.

The catchy songs of hand washing have been frequently awaking the people about the correct ways of hand washing during this Covid-19 pandemic to control the increase of coronavirus cases. However, false and fake online information have been regularly putting large number of people in distress. At this crucial moment, when our doctors, health workers and police personnel have been doing their duty 24x7 for the well-being of people, then some individuals' fake posts are changing the whole game of communal safety and welfare. Hence, the reality is that misleading information is more dangerous than the virus itself. The facts are in line with the declaration of World Health Organisation. WHO has declared the amount of fake news and misinformation about the Covid-19 epidemic as an 'infodemic'. WHO director general, Dr. Tedros Adhanom Ghebreyesus in a press conference said, misinformation has been "making the work of our heroic workers even harder" (Global Data Thematic Research, February 26, 2020).

In order to control the spread of the coronavirus, all relevant information should be conveyed to the affected communities time to time to make them aware about the nature of the health crisis. Nevertheless, failures to create a sense of trust among the public can intensify the sense of vulnerability, resentment and annoyance, thereby weakening the public health comeback and putting the wellbeing of others at threat, and may represent the violation of human rights as well.

Preventive Care, Goods and Services

During the Covid-19 outbreak, this is the responsibility of the states to ensure that preventive care, goods and services must be available and accessible to all persons. The World Health Organisation has also cautioned that rigorous and rising interruption to the worldwide supply of personal protective equipment (PPE) - caused by growing demand, terror buying, hoarding and mishandling is putting lives at threat due to the coronavirus infection. As we know that health workers depend upon personal protective equipment to guard themselves and their patients from being infected and infecting others. However, shortages are making even the doctors, nurses and other healthcare workers severely ill while handling the patients of Covid-19 due to the limited access of supplies for their usage such as aprons, medical masks, face shields, gowns, gloves and respirators. The World Health Organisation has also informed the governments as well as the industries to boost up their manufacturing by 40 percent to meet up the growing demand at the world level (WHO, March 3, 2020).

Recommendations

1. Government should take appropriate measures so that healthcare facilities are available to all the people in the country without any kind of discrimination. Hence, healthcare should be accessible, reasonably priced, culturally apt and of good quality.
2. Government should also make sure that health workers have access to suitable personal protective equipment while dealing with patients suffering from this deadly virus.
3. Government should make definite awareness campaigns for the public and take appropriate steps to address how victims of domestic violence can contact services available for help in times of distress amid coronavirus outbreak. These victims should also be ensured that services are accessible to all victims of domestic violence especially to those victims who are residing in those parts which are under restrictions of movement or are under the quarantine time period due to the COVID-19 infection.
4. Government should also make sure to the public that their response measures to COVID-19 do not differentiate against any particular religious or ethnic groups. The state responses should be

all-inclusive and value the human rights of marginalised groups as well particularly those who are suffering due to some disabilities or are aged people.

5. Government should also make more efforts to struggle with the growing problem of stigma and discrimination that generally exists within the society. In order to achieve better results, government should provide appropriate training to the health workers on COVID-19 by making use of mass media along with higher education networks to spread out public awareness on the subject of human rights, and thereby making people realise that this pandemic identifies no boundaries and distinguishes no difference of caste, race, ethnicity and religion.
6. During the imposition of quarantines or lockdowns in the country, government should make sure the access to provisions, water, health facilities and care-giving support especially to the poor people.
7. Majority of aged people and people with disabilities rely upon the incessant community services and their support. Therefore, government should ensure that the public agencies, community organisations and other essential service providers who are working in this direction should continue their services in order to meet the requirements of aged people along with people in disabilities.
8. The strategies of government should be made in such a way as to minimize the interruption in services and build up reliant sources of comparable services for the welfare of the public. The disruption in the community-based services may affect the society in negative sense especially the persons with disabilities or elderly people, which can show the way to harmful health outcomes as well.

Conclusion

The quick spread of COVID-19 has brought the whole world to its knees. The virus has been a great leveler, affecting people irrespective of their prosperity and communal status. It has raised fears in the minds of all the infected countries that it may impact them badly if they did not take any required steps timely to adequately respond to it. Many countries have announced complete lockdown situation, thereby enforcing the people to stay indoors for their wellbeing. Indian government has taken the nation-wide lockdown decision timely to fight with Covid-19. In this time of crisis, national cooperation and solidarity are the keys to achieve success in this battle of Covid-19. All the citizens should follow the rules and regulations which are made for their own welfare and protection by the government. The response must itself be rights-respecting and should take account of long-term as well as immediate needs, keeping in mind the particular needs of specific, marginalised groups.

References

- BBC NEWS. 2020. "Coronavirus: India Home Quarantine Families Face Discrimination, 8 April 2020". Available at: https://www.bbc.com/news/world-asia-india-52201706
- Centers for Disease Control and Prevention. 2012. "Quarantine and Isolation". Available at:https://www.cdc.gov/quarantine/historyquarantine.html
- Centers for Disease Control and Prevention. 2020. "Coronavirus Disease 2019". Available at:https://www.cdc.gov/coronavirus/2019-ncov/need-extra-precautions/people-at-higher-risk.html
- Global Data. 2020. "Covid-19 Outbreak: How Misinformation Could Fuel Global Panic, 26 February, 2020". Available at: https://www.pharmaceutical-technology.com/features/covid-19-outbreak-how-misinformation-could-spark-global-panic/
- Human Rights Watch. 2020. India: COVID-19 Lockdown Puts Poor at Risk, 27 March 2020". Available at:https://www.hrw.org/news/2020/03/27/india-covid-19-lockdown-puts-poor-risk
- India Today. 2020. "50 People, including Doctors, Quarantined in Bikaner as Woman Tests Positive for Covid-19 after Death, 6 April 2020".Available at:https://www.indiatoday.in/india/story/50-people-including-doctors-quarantined-in-bikaner-as-woman-tests-positive-for-covid-19-after-death-1663681-2020-04-06
- Jamkhandikar, Shilpa. 2020. "India Cancels Almost All Visas, Closes Myanmar Border, as Regional Coronavirus Cases Rises, 11 March 2020". Available at:https://www.reuters.com/article/us-health-coronavirus-southasia-idUSKBN20Y16B
- Kaplan Juliana, Frias Lauren and McFall-Johnsen Morgan. 2020. "A Third of the Global Population is on Coronavirus Lockdown- Here's Our Constantly Updated List of Countries and Restrictions, 17 April 2020".Available at: https://www.businessinsider.com/countries-on-lockdown-coronavirus-italy-2020-3
- Outlook India. 2020. "Domestic Violence Cases Across India Swell Since Coronavirus Lockdown,07 April 2020". Available at:https://www.outlookindia.com/website/story/india-news-rise-in-domestic-violence-across-all-strata-of-society-in-the-coronavirus-lockdown-period/350249
- Taubenberger, Jeffrey K. and Morens, David M. 2006. 1918 Influenza: The Mother of all Pandemics. CDC, Centers for Disease Control and Prevention.
- The New York Times. 2020. "India's Coronavirus Lockdown Leaves Vast Numbers Stranded and Hungry, 29 March 2020". Available at: www.nytimes.com/2020/03/29/world/asia/coronavirus-india-migrants.html
- The New York Times. 2020. "Coronavirus Travel Restrictions, Across the Globe, 15 April 2020". Available at: www.nytimes.com/article/coronavirus-travel-restrictions.html

- World Economic Forum. 2020. "A Visual History of Pandemics, 15 March 2020". Available at: https://www.visualcapitalist.com/history-of-pandemics-deadliest/
- WHO. 2020. " Pneumonia of Unknown Cause, 5 January 2020". Available at: https://www.who.int/csr/don/05-january-2020-pneumonia-of-unknown-cause-china/en/
- WHO. 2020. "Updated WHO Recommendations for International Traffic in Relation to COVID-19 Outbreak, 29 February 2020". Available at: https://www.who.int/ith/2019-nCov advice for international traffic-rev/en/
- WHO. 2020. " Shortage of Personal Protective Equipment Endangering Health Workers Worldwide, 3 March 2020". Available at: www.who.int/news-room/detail/03-03-2020-shortage-of-personal-protective-equipment-endangering-health-workers-worldwide
- WHO. 2020. "WHO characterizes COVID-19 as a Pandemic, 11 March 2020". Available at: www.who.int/emergencies/diseases/novel-coronavirus-2019/events-as-theyhappen

Health Issues and Challenges during COVID-19 Pandemics

12

COVID-19: Public Health Emergency in India during Pandemic

Arti Sharma

In the beginning of year 2020, the world witnessed deadly cases of 'pneumonia of unknown origin'. The outbreak of disease started in the Wuhan city, Hubei Province of China during the early weeks of December 2019 (Lu H et.al, 2020). It is suggested that the disease has a zoonotic origin as large number of the people who developed symptoms were exposed to wet animal market in Wuhan city. The area later on exclusively recognised as the epicentre of the disease and linked to the spread of the virus across the world. However, till date, no reliable evidence of coronavirus origin reservoirs has been proved (M. Bassetti et.al, 2020). On January 30, 2020, India reported its first case in a student who returned home for a vacation from Wuhan University in China in Karela (P S Gopikrishnan Unnithan, India Today). On the same day after reporting of cases by several countries in Europe, Asia and the America, WHO declared the disease as a public health emergency (WHO[1]). With the outbreak of disease, the global political commitments shifted towards the emerging health emergency. Scientists and renowned labs across the world focused its research on identification, recognition, origin of transmission and sequencing of the unknown virus. The International Committee on Taxonomy of Viruses (ICTV) study group and WHO announced official name to novel corona virus as SARS-CoV-2 (Severe Acute Respiratory Syndrome Coronavirus-2) and the disease as COVID-19, short for "coronavirus disease 2019" (WHO[2]). After analysing the situation on March 11, 2020 with transmission of the virus in more than 114 countries, affecting 118,319 individuals and 4292 deaths, the WHO revised the status of the COVID-19 from public health emergency to global pandemic with very high risk (WHO[3]).

COVID-19 showed some unique clinical features that are different from common flu. The virus targets the lower as well as the upper respiratory tract. The symptoms usually appear in infected individual after an incubation period of 5 days. However, the period from onset of the symptoms to death ranges from 6 to 41 days with an average of 14 days. The period is dependent on the age of the patient and its immune response. The most common symptoms of COVID -19 includes fever, cough and fatigue, while other symptoms comprise sputum production, headache, haemoptysis, diarrhoea, dyspnoea, and lymphopenia (Huang, C. et al, 2020).

The preparedness for the ongoing coronavirus disease 2019 including its transmission in India demands setting up of effectively equipped and dedicated healthcare facilities to manage sick patients along protecting healthcare workers and the environment. There is an urgent need of the facilities to be kept ready during the epidemic period for training of health professionals and for managing cases. The health system have to surge capacity for such critical care units and preferably government or private hospital should have at least one such facility available at local level in each district of the country. To meet the stringent requirements of health sector to mitigate the pandemic situation there is urgent need of increase in GDP share for health sector. In financial year 2019-20, the government spent of India on healthcare is 1.6 percent of GDP. The National Health Policy of India, 2017 articulates to increase investment to 2.5 percent of GDP by 2025 in the sector (National Health Policy, 2017). The allocation is still far below than that of model developing and developed countries. Current health services and resources are not adequate to meet the emergency situation during the pandemic. If India wants to defeat the virus it is important understand virus transmission behaviour and analyse and strengthen the public health services.

On the basis of recent experiences of pandemics, mental and psychosocial issues are also considered as a part of the public health parameter during the outbreak. The WHO is releasing timely advisory guidelines to be implemented by countries on mental health and well-being of all age groups especially of elderly people and children, migrants and healthcare workers in community. In Indian concern the factors are important to consider because of population diversity.

Objectives

1. The first objective of the study is to find the various reasons for transmission of COVID-19 at various entry points that are responsible for fast transmission of the virus in India.

2. To study the preparedness of India to mitigate the pandemic situation.
3. The study will unfold the health issues of COVID-19 as well as mental and psychosocial health aspects associated with the pandemic.

Materials and Methods

1. The review article is based on secondary data only. It includes a systematic literature search on Google Scholar, PubMed, World Health Organisation databases, Ministry of Health and Family Welfare databases and studies of Indian Council of Medical Research.
2. The Article includes the literature study till April 29, 2020 only.

Transmission in India

The casualty ratio of the SARS-CoV-2 is less than the two recent epidemics due to SARS-CoV-1 and Middle East respiratory syndrome (MERS)-CoV, but the virus has greater transmissibility and rapidity of the spread (Lai CC et.al, 2020). Considering the risk of importation of COVID-19 through air travel from infected countries, the WHO provided advisory guidelines to countries for screening of passengers at entry and exit points. The guidelines provided for screening of the signs and symptoms of respiratory infection with focus on thermal screening to detect potential suspects, home quarantine guidelines and laboratory tests for the confirmation of infection (WHO[4]). Government of India (GOI) took many initiatives to prevent transmission of the virus. Restrictions have been put on international passenger traffic, advisory guidelines issued to states and UTs for traffic across borders. However, a research paper published in IJMR, India indicated that airport screening may not be able to sufficiently detect COVID-19-infected travellers. The statistical analysis indicated that the 46 percent of infected travellers would not be detected by thermal screening at airport, depending on incubation period. Moreover there is no accurate, rapid test for COVID-19 that could be deployed in this setting (Manda Sandip et.al, 2020). The study set true in this scenario as the subclinical cases became root cause of transmission of cases in the country. In the same direction GOI announced lockdown in all the states and union territories to curb spread of the virus by social distancing on March 23, 2020 to April 14, which was again extended to May 3, 2020. The cases of disobeying of social distancing are continuously appearing in the country because of unplanned lockdown. Even the lockdown measures are difficult to follow in crowded metro-cities like where cases are surging at high rate.

In the absence of a licenced vaccine or effective therapeutics for COVID-19, it is difficult to prevent or delay the local outbreaks in India. The health ministry is advising good personal hygiene with respiratory etiquettes; avoid close contact with people, regular monitoring of health and to contact a doctor immediately if cough, fever or problem in breathing arises. The information dissemination and help regarding COVID-19 infection, the helpline has been launched (Resources, MoHFW).

Despite of the theses best possible efforts, the transmission of COVID-19 is surging in India, yet rate of transmission is lower than the global rate. As per the situation reports of Ministry of Health and Family Welfare from March 22, 2020 (the day of Janata Curfew and subsequent lockdown) to April 29 the number of confirmed cases has raised from 360 (319 Indian Nationals and 41 Foreign Nationals reported from 23 States/UTs across India.) to 31,332 in 32 states and UTs (Press Information Bureau[1]).

As on April 29, 2020, India has only clusters of cases among individuals with travel history, their family members and other individuals who came in close contact with the COVID-19 positive cases. In India, risk of community transmission is very high because of its dense population, "pessimistic" behaviour of people who have a travel history to infected countries or contact with the infected don't undergo home quarantine. Religious assemblies, social gatherings, venders and various help groups serving the community's obvious necessities being unaware of their clinical conditions are pushing India toward community transmission. If a COVID-19 outbreak happens in a community, it may last for a long time and the mortality rate will be much higher in India as compared to epicentre countries like Italy, Spain, Germany, UK and USA.

Health Concerns in India

WHO and National Centre for Disease Control (NCDC), India emphasizes that the SARS-CoV-2 virus infects people of all ages. However, two groups of people are at a higher risk of getting severe COVID-19 disease. These are older people with above age group of 60 years and those with underlying medical conditions such as chronic heart disease, respiratory diseases, neurological conditions, and weakened immune system, people with organ transplant and people with cancer undergoing active chemotherapy or radiotherapy (NCDC guidelines).

Another unavoidable health feature related to the pandemic situation is psychosocial health and mental well-being of vulnerable groups including elderly people, children and migrants. Generalised fear, anxiety and stress related to COVID-19 pandemic can deteriorate the health of such individuals.

Health Concerns Related to COVID-19

Since the outbreak emerged in India around three months ago, the number of cases has undergone a steady rise. India reported first death of COVID -19 patient of 76 years old man in Karnataka with medical history of hypertension, diabetes and asthma and appendicitis on March 12, 2020. As on April 29, 2020, demise of 1008 individuals has been observed. During the pandemic, positive news for the nation is high recovery rate of 24.5 percent with 7695 total recovered individuals (Press Information Bureau[1]).

Dr Harsh Vardhan, Union Health Minister, MoHFW in a press release on April 6, 2020 revealed data of COVID-19 on the basis of the gender distribution and different age groups. According to the report out of 4067 confirmed cases 76 percent are male and 24 percent are female. It indicates the COVID-19 positive cases are 3 times more in male compared to female. About half of the confirmed cases belong to age group below 40 years (47 percent of confirmed cases) but the death rate in the age group is least (7 percent of total death). 34 percent of confirmed cases are of age group between 40 to 60 years with almost similar death rate of 30 percent. Only 19 percent positive individuals are above age of 60 but the mortality rate in the age group is quite high with 63 percent. Gender distribution analysis report of 109 deaths due to COVID-19 indicates that death in male is 2.7 times more than female (73 percent male and 27 percent female) (Press information bureau[2]). The data analysis again is in line with suggested WHO and NCDC view. None of the reports issued by MoHFW, after April 6, 2020 till date has revealed such information again in public sector.

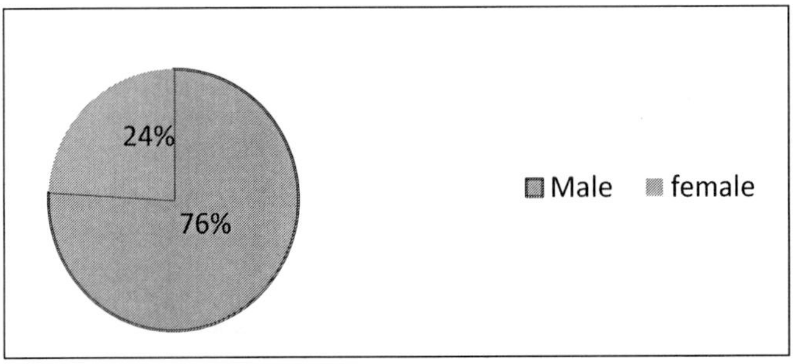

Source: Data analysis of total confirmed COVID -19 cases as on April 6, 2020 by MoHFW.

Figure 1: Gender Distribution of Confirmed Cases of COVID-19.

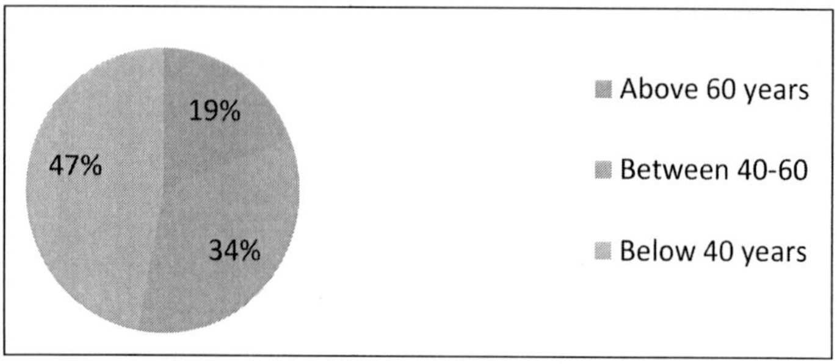

Source: Ibid.

Figure 2: Age Group Distribution of Confirmed Cases of Covid-19.

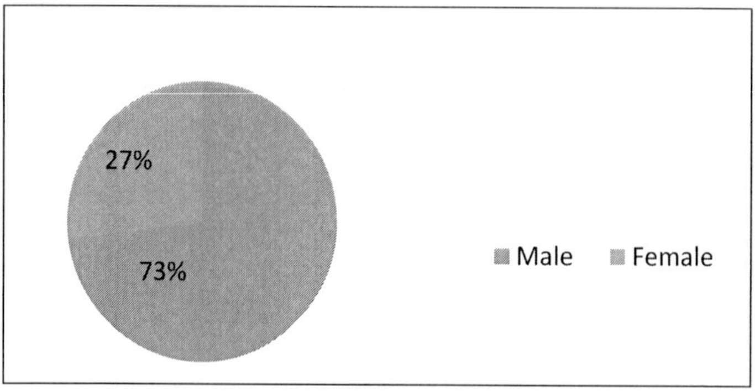

Source: Ibid.

Figure 3: Gender distribution of deaths due to Covid-19.

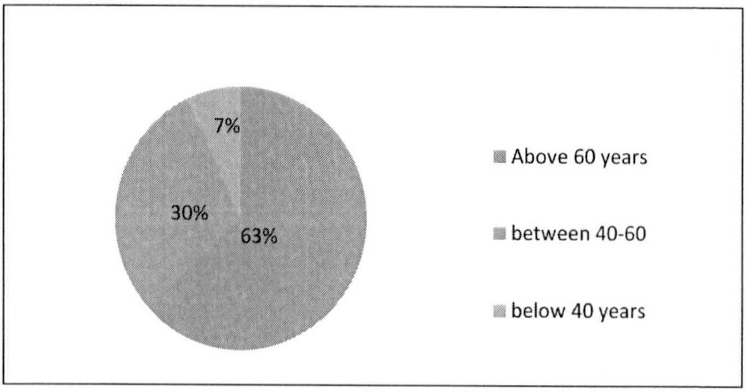

Source: Ibid.

Figure 4: Age Group Distribution of Deaths Cases Due to COVID-19.

During these 3 months of outbreak, India has strengthened its health care system by increasing testing labs from 1 to 230 government aided and 87 private labs with more than 16,000 collection centres. GOI is also planning to scale up the government labs to 300 and increase daily testing capacity of 55,000 to 1 lakh per day by end of May, 2020. To deal with health crises, the nation has organised 1.9 lakh isolation beds, more than 24,000 ICU beds and more than 12,000 ventilators (Press information bureau[3]). WHO appreciated the efforts of GOI at global platform for its control and preparedness against the challenge thrown by the corona virus. However, the country is facing criticism over its low testing and faulty imported test kits. India is doing testing of individuals at random and in identified hot spots. But reality is that without extensive testing it is impossible to know the real situation of affected people. This situation is highlighted in a publication on Sentinel surveillance among severe acute respiratory illness (SARI) in India. According to the research paper (Gupta Nivedita et.al, 2020), in 41 sentinel sites where 104 confirmed cases reported from 52 districts in 20 States/Union Territories from February 15, 2020 to April 2, 2020, the 39.2 percent (40 patients) COVID-19 cases did not report any history of contact with a known case or international travel. Current stock of imported and indigenous test kits is also matter of worry as it is not adequate to meet the testing requirement of 1.37 billion populations of India.

In the wake of the COVID-19 outbreak, Ministry of AYUSH, India is also recommending the self-care guidelines for preventive health measures and boosting immunity with special reference to respiratory health. These measures are supported by Ayurvedic literature and scientific publications. While there is no medicine for the disease as of now, it is good to take preventive measures which boost our immunity in these times. The ministry is promoting daily practices to boost immunity by providing general measures including Daily practice of Yogasana, Pranayama and meditation, Ayurvedic Immunity Promoting Measures, Simple Ayurvedic Procedures for dry cough and sore throat.

Mental and Psychosocial Health

On the basis of recent experiences of pandemics, psychological issue is also considered as a part of the public health response during the outbreak. The COVID-19 pandemic is triggering widespread concern as fear and stress toward the uncertain situation. The mental health issue facing each and every person in country is how to manage and react to the stressful situation that everyone is facing in their lives and communities. Common causes of psychological stress during pandemics include, fear of falling ill and dying, fear of losing work and livelihoods, fear of being placed in quarantine. WHO takes the impact of the crisis on people's mental health very seriously and is monitoring the situation together with national authorities, while providing information and guidance to governments and the public. The disturbing effects of COVID-19, including social distancing, anxiety and fears currently dominating our daily lives.

The MoHFW is releasing timely advisory guidelines on the psychological crisis related to mental health and well-being of all age groups especially of elderly people and children and migrants in community. The outbreak of the disease and its consequences cause anxiety and stress in old age and children. So it is advised to take care of the mental health of the vulnerable group by engagement in different task and good communication with friends and family while maintaining social distancing.

Impact on children mental health

Children are likely to experience worry, anxiety, irritability, anger and fear of the unprecedented situation. Schools have been closed as part of necessary measures, so children have no longer provided by the opportunity to be with their friends and get that social support that is essential for good mental well-being. Being at home may place some children at high risk of exposure to the disturbing pandemic situation and unpleasant family environment. Children being more perceptive to change may develop symptoms of disturbed mental health.

National Institute of Mental Health and Neuro Sciences under MoHFW provided simple strategies that can address the needed attention to resolve their fears by being honest with children, explaining what is happening in a way that they can understand, make routine of learning at home, engage in indoor activity, keep them in contact with their friends and manage their anxiety (awareness material, MoHFW[1])

Mental health of the elderly people

Elder people are more vulnerable to COVID-19 outbreak as they conceive situation extremely frightening and very fear-inducing. The mental health impacts for these populations can include anxiety and feeling stressed or angry. Its impacts can be particularly difficult for older people who may be experiencing cognitive decline or dementia. And some older people may already be socially isolated and experiencing loneliness which can worsen mental health.

On a positive note, the government broadcasting simple tips to manage mental stress of elderly people that people can initiate themselves. These include many of the strategies like spending time with family, getting involved in daily activities, spending time in recreation activities and exercise, connecting to the loved ones and avoiding listening to news. (Awareness material, MoHFW[2]).

Mental Health of Healthcare Workers

Frontline healthcare workers such as doctors and nurses are experiencing additional mental health problems. The stress is because of using strict biosecurity measures such as use personal protective equipment, need for constant awareness and attentiveness, strict procedures to follow and higher demands in the work settings. The fear of transfer of infection to their loved ones put frontline workers in additional stress. To support the healthcare workers fighting COVID-19 GOI has announced insurance policies. Although videos and documentaries for motivation, salutation and respect are broadcasting in public domain but till there is lack of training programmes for stress management of such workers.

Psychosocial Health

COVID-19 is creating psychosocial disturbance as the disease involves the unfamiliar threats that is difficult to detect and measure in community. The psychosocial disturbance during the outbreak a community health indicator. In India the disturbance is faced majorly by migrants, frontline health workers and police personnel. The national response to reduce the pandemic-related adversities is considered as an essential component in national policy to mitigate the pandemic situation.

The one of the most vulnerable targets during the situation in India are migrants, mobile populations, and seasonal workers. They face a unique set of challenges. The psychosocial needs of migrants and displaced persons are taken into consideration in governments' responses. Among this group people leave their native places in search of better opportunities and earnings, psychosocial issues are prevalent. The fear of neglect and ignorance by the local community and concerns for their families at innate places create various social, psychological and emotional traumas during the situations (Resources, MoHFW).

Additionally, the generalised fear and fear-induced over-reactive behaviour is also common among the people. The suspected and ill people, who refuse to seek care, follow precautionary measures and non-cooperation with health workers is impeding infection control. During the current situation, there have been instances of critical service providers including members of healthcare and police security services being targeted and attacked by public. In this context, the Union Cabinet on April 22, 2020 has approved amendment in the Epidemic Diseases Act, 1897 to protect healthcare service personnel and property including their living/working premises against violence during epidemics (Promulgation of an Ordinance to amend the Epidemic Diseases Act, 1897).

It is important to control the COVID-19 related psychological and psychosocial health disorders by proper and comprehensive management and attention to vulnerable groups of community. Adhering to all the rules and guidelines mentioned by WHO and GOI is only possible way to overcome the existing situation of COVID-19 associated stress.

Conclusion

COVID-19 is a potentially fatal disease and cause of global public health concern. India, with 17.7 percent of total global population, is at grave risk of community transmission due to inadequate health supplies and negligent behaviour of few individuals. As the disease continues to spread in several countries, the pandemic has just begun in India. The trajectory of the pandemic is entirely unclear. The gaps in public healthcare system and preparedness pose a challenge to India's COVID-19 containment plans. Extraordinary measures needed for healthcare preparedness to reduce morbidity and mortality. Besides the disastrous effect of human mortality, there are equally distressing conditions of psychosocial crises in vulnerable groups of society. Microorganisms because of their ingenuity affected humankind in past and present. It is undeniable that they will continue to cause pandemics in future also. So it is important to strengthen biomedical research and healthcare system in India to meet health emergencies. The COVID-19 pandemic has created opportunities to build an improved response mechanism in health sector for future health crises.

References

1. Awareness material, MoHFW[1], 2020. "Taking care of mental health of children during COVID-19" posted on April 1, 2020. Available from: https://www.mohfw.gov.in/pdf/mentalhealthchildrean.pdf
2. Awareness material, MoHFW[2], 2020. "Taking care of mental health of elderly during COVID-19" posted on April 1, 2020. Available from: https://www.mohfw.gov.in/pdf/mentalhealthelderly.pdf
3. Guidelines for elderly and high risk groups to safeguard from COVID-19 Outbreak (1753503/2020/O/O IDSP-NCDC), available from: https://ncdc.gov.in/WriteReadData/l892s/95494121881585916857.pdf.

4. Gupta, Nivedita et.al. "Severe acute respiratory illness surveillance for coronavirus disease 2019, India". *Indian J Med Res,* April 27, 2020, Epub ahead of print available from: http://www.ijmr.org.in.
5. Huang, *C., et al,* 2020. "Clinical features of patients infected with 2019 novel coronavirus in Wuhan, China". *The Lancet,* Volume 395, issue 10223, pp. 497–506, February 15, 2020. Available from https://doi.org/10.1016/S0140-6736(20)30183-5.
6. Lai, CC et.al, 2020, " Severe acute respiratory syndrome coronavirus 2 (SARS-CoV-2) and coronavirus disease-2019 (COVID-19): The epidemic and the challenges), *Int J Antimicrobial Agents* 2020; 55 : 105924.
7. Lu H. et. al. 2020. "Outbreak of Pneumonia of Unknown Etiology in Wuhan China: the Mystery and the Miracle". *Journal of Medical Virology* 92: 401-02.
8. M. Bassetti et.al. "The Novel Chinese Coronavirus (2019nCoV) Infections: challenges for ghting the storm". *Eur. J. Clin. Invest.* (2020) e13209, available from: https://doi.org/10.1111/eci.13209.
9. Mandal Sandip et. al. 2020, "Prudent public health intervention strategies to control the coronavirus disease 2019 transmission in India: A mathematical model-based approach". *Indian J Med Res,* April 10, 2020, Epub ahead of print Available from: http://www.ijmr.org.in.
10. Ministry of Health and Family Welfare, Government of India. National Health Policy 2017. Available from: https:// www.nhp.gov.in/nhpfiles/national_health_policy_2017. pdf, accessed on March 28, 2020.
11. Ministry of Health and family welfare, Resources: citizens. "Ministry of AYUSH Ayurveda's immunity boosting measures for self-care during COVID-19 crisis" posted on April 7, 2020 available from: https://www.mohfw.gov.in/pdf/ImmunityBoostingAYUSHAdvisory.pdf
12. P S Gopikrishnan Unnithan, India Today, "Kerala reports first confirmed coronavirus case in India". January 30, 2020.
13. Press information bureau, Govt. of India, press release, posted on: "Promulgation of an Ordinance to amend the Epidemic Diseases Act, 1897 in the light of the pandemic situation of COVID-19": Posted On: 22 APR 2020 by PIB Delhi, Available from:https://pib.gov.in/newsite/PrintRelease.aspx? relid=202493.
14. Press information bureau[1], Govt. of India, press release, posted on: April, 29, 2020, available from: https://pib.gov.in/PressReleseDetail.aspx?PRID=1608549.
15. Press information bureau[2], Govt. of India, press release "Ministry of Health and Family Welfare: Updates on COVID-19" Posted On: 06 APR 2020, available from: https://pib.gov.in/PressReleasePage.aspx?PRID=1611676#
16. Press information bureau[3], Govt. of India, press release, "India has acquired enough strength and resources to take on the worst challenge thrown by the corona virus: Dr. Harsh Vardhan" posted on: 23 APR 2020, available from: https://pib.gov.in/PressReleasePage.aspx?PRID=1617656.
17. Resources, Ministry of Health and Family Walefare, Available from: https://www.mohfw.gov.in/
18. World Health Organisation[1] 2020. "Novel Coronavirus (2019-nCoV) Situation Report-11". Available at:https://www.who.int/docs/default-source/coronaviruse/situation-reports/20200131-sitrep-11-ncov.pdf?sfvrsn=de7c0f7_4.

19. World Health Organisation[2] 2020. "Novel Coronavirus (2019-nCoV) Situation Report-22" Available from https://www.who.int/docs/default-source/coronaviruse/situation-reports/20200211-sitrep-22-ncov.pdf?sfvrsn=fb6d49b1_2.

20. World Health Organisation[3] 2020. "Novel Coronavirus (2019-nCoV) Situation Report-51". Available from:

https://www.who.int/docs/default-source/coronaviruse/situation-reports/20200311-sitrep-51-covid 19.pdf?sfvrsn=1ba62e57_10.

21. World Health Organisation[4] 2020."Updated WHO advice for international traffic in relation to the outbreak of the COVID-19". Available from:

https:// www.who.int/ith/COVID-19_advice_for_international_traffic /en/, accessed on February 11, 2020.

13

Harsh Impacts of COVID-19 on Sex Worker's Health and Socio-Economic Conditions

Akwinder Kaur Aulakh

Everyone has been aware the term COVID-19 who lived in the 2020. The COVID-19 pandemic has created a lot of stress and panic across the world. The COVID-19 is an infectious disease caused by severe acute respiratory syndrome corona virus. This disease was first identified in 2019 and has spread globally; resulting in the 2019-20 corona virus pandemic. The pandemic affected more than 210 countries and territories in early 2020. The epicenter of COVID-19 virus occurred in Wuhan, China. The pandemic affected the 11 million people worldwide. In India, first confirmed case of coronavirus infection reported in Kerala on 30 January 2020. Observing the sharpen increase in COVID cases; PM Narendra Modi announced the 'Janta Curfew' on 22nd of March to break the continue chain of novel corona virus and there was complete nationwide lockdown from March 24. The lockdown during the pandemic proved drastic and the situation is expected more challenging in low-income countries with weak health and economical system. This is compounded by the fact that many healthcare system in India were poorly prepared for COVID-19, with critical care wards and protective gear that were insufficient to deal with a flux of serious cases. At present, approximately 31 lakh corona infected cases and 57,000 deaths in India (The Indian Express, 25 Aug. 2020).

During the pandemic, people regularly struggle for life and survival. Impact of it can be seen in each aspect of life i.e. social, economic, medical, religious and educational. After long period of lockdown of 5 months, India is now going in the phase of unlocking with the challenges of survival from the consequences of pandemic. The country is reporting multi-dimensional health, social and economic effects of COVID-19 and the ensuing policy responses to contain the diseases on global scale. The pandemic has triggered increasing unemployment and major economic loses. Some aspects of the society badly affected during pandemic. Sex work industry is one of facing the brutal consequences of pandemic.

Sex Work Industry in India

Sex workers, usually referred as prostitutes, have occupied an anomalous position in societies traced in the each civilisation on the earth.Throughout the history, people have exchanged the commodity of sex for money to survive against poverty, to empower themselves against miserable life circumstances and to challenge societal norms. Sex work is exchange of sexual services, involving sexual acts, between consenting adults for remuneration, with term agreed between seller and buyer. People of the different gender, ethnic and socio-economic backgrounds carry out sex work for often complex and overlapping reasons. Poverty and deprivation of opportunities fuelled by discrimination, gender inequality, social exclusion, racism, colonialism, social and economical inequality and oppression lead people into sex work. The changeable attitudes towards this profession from time to time and society to society make it more complex. The double standard of people's thinking makes it an illicit activity and society always looked at sex work as immoral and destructive. The tag of "fallen women" attached with the sex workers proved a curse for them and shows the plight of women in the trade.

As per UNAIDS survey of 2016, there are approximately 657,800 sex workers in India and around 5 lakh customers visit red light areas. In India, sex work falls under the bracket of the informal sector and sex workers are mostly daily wagers.Sex workers are most vulnerable among the margins. The moral codes conducted by the society regulated them to margins; they are exploited and their rights are violated every day. Sex work is often not recognised as work and is so highly stigmatised in many contexts. Imogen Tyler in "Stigma: The machinery of inequality" argues that it is critical to be aware that stigmatisation occurs when there are significant power imbalance- stigma is literally a form of power. The marginalisation of sex workers through government policy enables stigma to be reproduced and reinforced, which increases their vulnerability. Sex workers have faced considerable barriers to accessing the financial safety nets available to the workers in other occupations.

Sex Work and COVID-19: Pandemic of Margins

Diseases and disasters may not much differentiate while infecting the human bodies, but the uneven social structure do render non-uniformity of pandemic impacts upon people. Pandemic highlights the inequalities unseen and hidden prior the crisis. This has been seen due to the crisis of HIV (Human Immunodeficiency Virus) in 1999, Severe Acute Respiratory Syndrome (SARS) in 2003, outbreak of Ebola in 2014, the spread of Zika in 2016 and many others. Marginalised communities are always worst hit during the crisis. Pandemic in India represents a grim reality of poor and marginalised section suffering from the denial of rights amidst the crisis. Groups already criminalised and marginalised effecting in the pandemic. They are unable to support their families and facing the challenges related to health services, rents and food. The abruptly announced lockdown in India had disastrous consequences for millions of such marginalised populations. Lack of access to food and other essential daily supplies, loss of livelihoods, increase in gender-based violence etc. are some of the fallouts of pandemic.

For one of the world's most marginalised, vulnerable and stigmatised group of people like sex workers such human rights violations and abuses are daily reality or risk in many countries worldwide. Sex work suffers due to the COVID-19 pandemic and sex workers experiencing many hardships. Both sides of the coin proved drastic. Choose to work in pandemic endanger their lives and decision to stop the work is difficult for survival. Sex workers are facing extreme poverty and hunger due to the lockdown amidst the pandemic. Government has not come to their aid. Sex workers have to choose between earning an income and risking their own and their loved ones' health has been extremely stressful. Amidst the pandemic, sex workers and their clients are self-isolate. As a result, they are increasingly vulnerable and unable to provide for themselves and their families. Sex workers who are homeless, use drugs, or are migrants with insecure legal or residency status face greater challenging in accessing health services or financial relief, which increase their vulnerability to poor health outcomes and longer term negative economic impacts.

A recent report by the International Committee on the rights of sex workers in Europe (ICRSWE) highlights the discriminatory and exclusive nature of government's pandemic recovery schemes across continents (Wheeler, 2020). Sex workers faced serious human rights abuse and violation such as violence, extortion, harassment and denials of rights to health, housing and other essential services. A recent study conducted in Delhi with 5000 registered sex workers shows that over 60 percent (3000 sex workers) have returned to their home states due to the loss of livelihood amid the pandemic after enduring weeks of struggle for basic facilities like food, shelter and medicines. For sex workers, forced by criminalisation, stigma and discrimination to live in the shadows, the crisis is more hidden and makes their condition more dramatic.

Impact of COVID-19 on Sex Workers

In India, the prohibitionist approach of criminalising sex work has been adopted. It has led to a vicious cycle of social insecurity, economic exploitation and public exclusion. Sex workers could surge the number of cases of COVID-19, there has been a decrease in the number of clients. This has had a devasting impact on sex workers who solely rely on this work to make a living. The socio-economic and health disadvantages sex workers experienced due to the existent stigma and discrimination that they face. As the crisis deepens day by day there is no income, no support or no work for sex workers. The pandemic has completely snatched their livelihood. Their survival is at the risk due to the stoppage of work in the lockdown. Some fallout of pandemic that sex workers facing during the pandemic are:

Economic Insecurity

Sex workers' incomes have been impacted drastically (Wyton, 2020). Sex workers represent an important group that exemplifies the vulnerability of workers in the informal labour sector. The COVID-19 pandemic has placed many sex workers in a particularly difficult situation. Like other precarious workers, sex workers generally cannot access labour protection such as paid sick leave and unemployment insurance. They are experiencing loss of income due to appointment cancellations, decries demand for services, workplace closures and sickness. Since sex industry does not offer a salary, sick days or benefits, there is little to no safety net for sex workers when they are unable to work. Stigma and criminalisation means that sex workers might not seek, or be eligible for, government-led social protection or economic initiatives to support small businesses. "Poverty will kill us before the coronavirus," said an Indian sex worker (Dutt, 2020).

International Committee on the Rights of Sex Workers in Europe report notes that sex workers are in the "economic margins" and often have less savings and government support to fall back on. Sex workers do not qualify for employment insurance. During the current pandemic and are forced to work in risky situations in order to survive and feed their families. Sex workers are daily earners. Pandemic directly affected their earning and they are without food or regularly struggling for providing food for themselves and their families. The Pandemic resulted in sudden homelessness and struggle to pay for the rent of hotels rooms. There is the added burden of paying rents for a one-room apartment which is nearly Rs. 4000. Many sex workers who can't afford have given up such rooms and visit the client's residence that can be unsafe. For the shelter, they have to spend their nights at clients' homes and forced to offer free sexual services. They are unable to pay their children school fees which effect the education of their children.

Challenges to Access Health Services and Supplies

The pandemic crisis severely affected the health of sex workers. Loss of money and unaffordable transportation had direct impact on the health-care access for the sex workers. The pandemic time is critical to continue to monitor sex workers' access to health and social services which has negative impact on their health. Many people living with HIV (PLHIV), who are more susceptible to COVID-19, couldn't access Anti-Retroviral Therapy (ART) due to the complete lockdown. They are struggling to continue treatment during the lockdown period. Due to the lack of identification documents to access food supplies, medicines and other daily essentials, sex workers living with HIV are unable to access the essential medicine. There is also an interruption to condom and lubricants supplies. Some are purchasing condoms from NGO centers are temporarily closed in some urban areas during pandemic. Many sex workers working on the street consider themselves alien to the city and do not know that they had the right to access sexual and reproductive health services in government health institutions.

Food insecurity is also a barrier to taking the drugs daily and can decrease their efficacy. The patients have been advised to take medicine with highly nutritious food that includes protein supplements. She has less money to buy food. The antiviral drug she takes for HIV can bring on pain, weakness and nausea. But due to the lockdown it has become difficult for them to source medicine. This could lead to increases in HIV incidence during this crisis. Sex workers also face heightened risks from STDs/STIs. The waning demand for sexual services as a result of the pandemic and economic recession has led the remaining clients to take advantage of their increased bargaining power to demand riskier acts, including unprotected sex, for less pay. In turn, decreased accessibility of sexual and reproductive health services during the pandemic deepens STD/STI related risks.

Vulnerability to Violence

Sex workers vulnerability to violence had increased significantly since COVID-19, particularly physical and sexual and threats by police. Globally, sex workers are witnessing rising reports of intimate partner violence that accompany the confinement of people to their living quarters (Bradbury-Jones & Isham, 2020). As stay at home measures are put in place, there are report from several countries of increased incidence of intimate partner or domestic violence. Women in abusive relationships and their children face an increased likelihood of exposure to violence as people stay at home. As women's care burden has increased, livelihoods are affected, access to basic necessities is reduced, social and protective networks are disrupted and services for survivors are diminished, there is increased stress in the household. This leads to the potential for an increased risk of violence. As a result of the COVID-19 pandemic, sex workers all over the world are experiencing hardship, a total loss of income and increased discrimination, violence and harassment.

There is a punitive crackdown against sex workers by police. Increased policing exposed the sex workers identity and also beating them. There are frequent raids at their homes and enforced to COVID-19 testing. There hidden identity has been revealed. Police threatened and arrest them. Police arrests, fines, violence, disruption in aid by law enforcement and compulsory deportation has been reported by sex workers across diverse settings, fuelling concerns that the pandemic is intensifying stigma, discrimination and repressive policing. Sex workers who live in brothels have been arrested and taken into quarantine centers (Maundu, 2020). They are facing quite challenging to sleep on the street and even physical or sexual violence and robbery from the street youths.

Psycho-Social Impacts of Pandemic

A number of key stressors related to the pandemic negatively affecting the psycho-social well beings. Sex workers are anxious about contacting the coronavirus, especially because they often lacked family and peer support networks. Decline in income and food insecurity further add their stress and anxiety. Many workers are experiencing stress and anxiety for going to work, resulting in some workers staying home or quitting their jobs (Bhattarai, 2020). They feel depressed because of the increased stigma they were facing from the community. Dramatically reduction in the income, worried about meeting the demands financially supporting themselves and their families, working from clients residence revealed their identities openly, giving free services to the clients to get a home to sleep and reduction in the prices of sexual services regularly are prominent reasons for the depression.

Exploitation of Human Rights

Human rights law mandates that human rights are inalienable, universal, interdependent and indivisible. India is signatory to numerous international agreements on rights of women that prohibits discrimination by gender but failed to satisfactorily protect the human rights of women, particularly sex workers. The professional services of the sex workers considered essential for the society to control rape and sexual harassments but publically they kept away from the rights of workers by playing the dirty politics of 'shame'. Sex workers faced serious human rights abuse and violation such as violence, extortion, harassment and denials of rights to health, housing and other essential services.

Exclusion from Government Protection Mechanism

In the wake of COVID-19 pandemic, sex workers are subject to government indifference and apathy of the judicial system in the country. Governments reproduce and reinforce stigma when they pursue policies that defines sex workers as either victims or deviants and do not allow them to be part of decisions that are fundamentally about them. They are rarely benefited with the government schemes and plans. Migrants sex workers are completely excluded from the government schemes and going back to their hometowns during the pandemic. They are unaware that they had the right to seek public support because they are migrants to the city in which they now living.

Since the start of the pandemic, authorities have been providing aid in the form of essential food commodities to economically underprivileged citizens including sex workers. Government has launched special schemes for farmers and others groups below the poverty line. In an effort to protect the marginalised, the government announced various schemes valued at $22.5 billion. However, the government only provides for those who are able to produce ration cards and other essential documents that is not possible in the case of sex workers. Many sex workers have lack an identity card to prove that they meet the eligibility criteria. More than 50 percent of sex workers across India do not have ration cards or any such documentation. Sex workers are reporting a lack of access to national social protection schemes and exclusion from emergency social protection measures being put in place for other workers, particularly where sex work is criminalised.

Survival: A Challenge for Sex Workers in Pandemic

With decreasing demand for in–person services due to the pandemic, sex workers are continuously finding the alternative sources for livelihood.

Some of them are trying to adapt the pandemic and have taken sex work digitally through WhatsApp and online payment gateways. But it is only for the higher class category sex workers who have been able to earn with the use of phone and internet sex. They have continued providing online audio and video services on phone. But many of them are not tech-savvy and do not know how to find clients online. They have lack of mobile phones or digital connectivity. For lower class sex workers, forced by criminalisation, stigma and discrimination to live in the shadows, the crisis is more hidden and makes their condition more dramatic. They have started roadside hotels like selling dosa, fishes, vegetables and flowers for survival.

Conclusion and Implication for Policy and Programming

There is a need to take immediate, critical action grounded in human rights principles to protect the health and rights of sex workers. Emergency financial support for the sex workers facing destitution, particularly migrants who are unable to access residency based financial support. Able them to access the national social protection schemes for sex workers. Government should take initiatives for providing the homeless sex workers to appropriate emergency housing and need to engage in policy development that can better protect sex workers, combating marginalisation and stigmatisation and improving overall protect sex workers, occupational health and safety of those working in the industry. They should carry out meaningful consultations with sex workers to establish a framework that respect their human rights and improves their safety and working conditions. The state should allocate targeted relief funds to ensure that sex workers who lose income because of COVID-19 regulations, are able to access social services. Here some priority actions highlight to address these risks:-

Proper Preventive Information and Distribution of Hygiene Kits and Masks- Some sex workers have good awareness about masks and hand washing measures, some in particular are unaware about it and frequently unable to comply with the guidance due to the poverty. NGOs' providing sex workers with these essential and also be scaled up across cities.

Ensure sexual and reproductive health services- Sex workers linked with some NGO programmes are continuing receive good access to condoms, HIV and STI test even during the COVID-19; but many are excluded from these services who have not contacted with NGOs. Sex workers are facing increasingly vulnerable situations in which the risk of sexually transmitted infections will be heightened during the pandemic which scaled up the need of health services during the pandemic.

Tackle physical and sexual abuse perpetrated by police and male peers- Sex workers reported a high risk of verbal, sexual and physical abuse from police and male peers that has been unleashed by the COVID-19 crisis. Awareness – raising and positive policing practices should be urgently provided to police to tackle the problem. Sex workers provided with information and support regarding their rights. There is need of proper policy implementation for stop physical abuse and robbery by street gangs.

Invest in psychosocial support services, including through social workers and youth volunteers- Sex workers in this business stem from traumatic family backgrounds characterised by the death of parents, domestic violence, extreme poverty or family separation. These psycho-emotional stressors are often compounded by stigma surrounding their current situation and are for many being exacerbated further under covid-19. They have provided with sufficient social protection packages and also need moral support to combat the stress and anxiety.

References

- Elene Lam. 2020. "Migrant sex workers left behind during COVID-19 pandemic". *Canadian Journal of Public Health.* Vol. CXI, No. 4 July. pp. 482-484.
- Geetanjali Misra, Ajay Mahal, & Rima Shah. 2000. "Protecting the rights of Sex Workers: The Indian Experience". *Health and Human Rights.* Vol. V, No. 1 pp. 88-115.
- Haveripeth Prakash. 2013. "Prostitution and its impact on Society- A Criminological perspective". *International Research Journal of Social Sciences.* Vol. II, No. 3 March. pp. 31-39.
- Joshua Kimani, Joyce Adhiambo, Rosemary Kasiba. 2020. "The effect of COVID-19 on the health and socio-economic security of sex workers in Nairobi, Kenya: Emerging intersections with HIV". *Journal of Global Public Health.* Vol. XV, No. 2 May. pp. 1-10.
- Jacqueline Lewis. 2020. "Sex workers are criminalised and left without government support during the coronavirus pandemic". Available at: https://theconversation.com/sex-workers-are-criminalised-and-left-without-government-support-during-the-coronavirus-pandemic-141746 . Assessed on 20 July 2020.
- Jacob Koshy. 2020. "Commercial sex work could spike COVID-19 cases in India". Available at: https://www.thehindu.com/news/national/coronavirus-commercial-sex-work-could-spike-covid-19-cases-in-india-says-study/article31608856.ece . Assessed on 17 May 2020.
- Lynzi Armstrong. 2020. "COVID-19 illuminates discriminatory sex work policies". Available at: https://www.opendemocracy.net/en/beyond-trafficking-and-slavery/covid-19-illuminates-discriminatory-sex-work-policies/. Assessed on 9 June 2020.

- Lucy Platt, Jocelyn Elmes & Rachel Stuart. 2020. "Sex workers must not be forgotten in the COVID-19 response". Available at: https://www.ncbi.nlm.nih.gov/pmc/articles/PMC7228722/. Assessed on 15 May 2020.
- Namita Bhandare. 2020. "Covid-19's impact on sex workers and their families". Available at:https://www.hindustantimes.com/columns/covid-19-s-impact-on-sex-workers-and-their-families/story-mp8WTXShUuzIgUiFHchVJI.html . Assessed on 7August 2020.
- Ndirangu Ngunjiri. 2020. "COVID-19 Impact on Female Commercial Sex Workers in Developing Countries". Available at: https://www.researchgate.net/publication/340644463_COVID-19_Impact_on_Female_Commercial_Sex_Workers_in_Developing_Countries . Assessed on April 2020.
- Nicole Karlis. 2020. "Sex workers are stressed, anxious and depressed amid COVID-19 pandemic". Available at: https://www.salon.com/2020/03/22/sex-workers-are-stressed-anxious-and-depressed-amid-covid-19-pandemic/ . Assessed on 22 March 2020.
- Neeta Kantamneni. 2020. "The impact of COVID-19 pandemic on marginalised populations in the United States: A research agenda". *Journal of Vocational Behavior.* 8 May 2020.
- Oxford Human Rights Hub. 2020. "Indian Government Fails to protect Sex Workers during COVID-19 Crisis". Available at : https://ohrh.law.ox.ac.uk/indian-government-fails-to-protect-sex-workers-during-covid-19-crisis/ . Assessed on 12 June 2020.
- Peter Newman & Adrian Gupta. 2020. "How to Have Sex in an Epidemic Redux: Reinforcing HIV Prevention in the COVID-19 Pandemic". *Journal of AIDS and Behavior.* Vol. XXIV, 4 June, pp. 2260-2264.
- Priyadarshee Mukhopadhyay. 2020. "Criminalisation and COVID-19: Acute Social Insecurity and the critical condition of Sex Workers in India". Available at: https://www.jurist.org/commentary/2020/07/priyadarshee-mukhopadhyay-covid-sex-workers/ Assessed on 8 July 2020.
- Priyanka Tripathi & Chhandita Das. 2020. "Social Distancing and Sex Workers in India". *Economic & Political Weekly*. Vol. 55, No. 31 August. https://www.epw.in/journal/2020/31/commentary/social-distancing-and-sex-workers-india.html
- Prashasti Awasthi. 2020. "Sex workers braving lockdown only to stare at an uncertain future". Available at: https://www.thehindubusinessline.com/news/variety/sex-workers-braving-lockdown-only-to-stare-at-an-uncertain-future/article31277892.ece . Assessed on 7 April 2020.
- Shirin Choudhary. 2020. "COVID-19: Loss of work, Lack of support push thousands of sex workers to a corner". Available at: https://www.newsclick.in/COVID-19-Loss-Work-Lack-Support-Thousands-Sex-Workers-Corner . Assessed on 28 April 2020.
- Tara Boghosian. 2020. "COVID-19 and the Untenable Criminalisation of Sex Work". Available at: https://www.onlabor.org/covid-19-and-the-untenable-criminalisation-of-sex-work/ . Assessed on 29 April 2020.
- Tanika Godbole. 2020. "Sex Workers in India find new ways to earn amid coronavirus pandemic". Available at: https://www.dw.com/en/sex-workers-in-

india-find-new-ways-to-earn-amid-coronavirus-pandemic/a-54526927 . Assessed on 11 August 2020.

- UNAIDS. 2020. "Sex workers must not to be left behind in the responses to COVID-19". Available at: https://www.unaids.org/en/resources/presscentre/pressreleaseandstatementarchive/2020/april/20200408_sex-workers-covid-19 . Assessed on 8 April 2020.

14

Impact of COVID-19 on Mental Health of Students in Kashmir: A Sociological Reminder during Covid-19 Pandemic Lockdown

Nelofar Ara & Sukanya Das

Trepidation, worry and constant agonising are normal responses to be perceived or real threats and at times when we are faced with uncertainty. So it is normal and understandable that people are experiencing fear in the context of the COVID-19 pandemic. But with the global development of the corona virus disease (COVID-19) outbreak, many psychological issues which accompany this pandemic have rapidly compounded its public health burden (Torales et al, 2020). Emerging research assessing the mental health implications of COVID-19 has identified a heightened pervasiveness of moderate-to-harsh self-reported or fake news's create the depressive nature among the general public (Wang et al, 2020) sparkling the pervasive effects of indistinctness and health-related fears. Added to the fear of contracting the virus in a pandemic such as COVID-19 are the significant changes to our daily lives as our movements are restricted in support of efforts to contain and slow down the spread of the virus. But when we are going to talk about students the susceptible levels of psychological agony and downstream negative academic consequences are prevalent under normal circumstances (American College Health Association: 2019). As a result of physical estrangement measures implemented in response to COVID-19, tertiary educational institutions have shifted to an emergency online learning format, which would be expected to further intensify academic stressors for students. It is reasonable to undertaking that students may experience reduced motivation toward studies, enlarged pressures to learn separately, rejection of daily routines and potentially higher rates of drop-out as unswerving consequences of these measures (Wickens: 2011). Thus, by increasing academic stressors in a population with heightened aggravate levels and a potentially reduced ability to rely on typical coping strategies the COVID-19 pandemic has placed an unequalled mental health saddle on students. The pandemic has revealed an attention on inequality every where the world around: School closures and social isolation have affected all students every where, but particularly those living in poverty like as in Kashmir which is the territory of a developing country (India) and most of the people here are depend on agricultural economy and tourism. And especially during these days (the days of COVID-19 Pandemic) due to physical isolation people didn't move anywhere because of the deaths occurred or the threat of spreading this pandemic disease (COVID-19) which also damages the economy in the Kashmir Valley to a large extent. Adding to the damage of the students in to their learning or education due to the shortage in resources because of poverty, a mental health crisis is emerging as many students have lost access to services that were offered by schools. And not only this but the teachers are also facing pressing issues, how can they help students to recover and stay on track throughout the year even as their own lives are likely to continue to be disrupted by the pandemic. No doubt that the students from the hottest countries of the world during the summer, their formal schooling stops, and learning loss happens at roughly the same rate for all students. But what about the students who are from the cold places like as Kashmir is where in winter season the temperature goes down to minus and formal schooling stops and learning loss happens at roughly the same rate for the students and also the schools remains off in summer and not only this but because of political disturbance the curfews, strikes, shutdowns in the valley the students face a different types of psychiatric traumas. Also the instructions has been uneven during the pandemic, as some students who have the broadband facilities are able to participate in online learning while others have faced obstacles such as lack of internet access that have hindered their progress in education because every year the students in Kashmir face internet problems but especially or we can say it strictly from 4th August 2019 because of the reason of abolition of Article 370-35A[1] the whole network was completely shut down and after a long time only the 2-G[2] network become available with which most of the students are unable to take online classes. And it is common among the Students in Kashmir that they forget some of what they learned in school because of these problems and also because of the closing of schools for a long time. But now there's a big difference between summer as well as winter learning loss and pandemic-related learning loss also makes the condition worse because of internet problems. Horace Mann once referred to schools as the 'great equalizers,' yet the pandemic threatens to expose the fundamental inequities of inaccessible learning. According to a 2015 Pew Research Center analysis, 17 percent of teenagers have difficulty of carrying out the homework assignments because they do not have consistent access to internet connection.

Students Mental Health and Educational Challenges

The unending COVID-19 pandemic has resulted in many social isolation trials intended to keep individuals physically distanced from others for the probable future. Even though these initiatives are essential to avoid the spread of the novel corona virus, but they may be causing pervasive mental health effects, including melancholy and solitude among all ages of individuals alike, according to experts. Students faced many challenges when COVID-19 forced most schools to shift online. Mental health issues have increased, that impact on well-being may be exaggerated by another effect of school closures. School closures may be especially unruly for children from lower-income families, who are disproportionately likely to receive mental health services entirely from schools. The Covid-19 pandemic may worsen accessible mental health problems and lead to more cases among children and adolescents because of the unique amalgamation of the public health crisis, economic decline or social isolation. Persistent stress changes the elemental and physical structure of the brain, impairing cognitive skills like interest, concentration, reminiscence and creativeness. While distress informed practices were widely used before the pandemic, they're likely to be even more integral for the students experience economic hardships and mourn the loss of family and friends. According to Jena Lee, MD, (medical director of pediatric consultation at University of California, Los Angeles) 'Daily configuration is important to everyone, but predominantly to children in their psychological and emotional development,' 'the reliability of schedules, predictable rules, penalty and set opportunity teach children how to perform, develop self-discipline and impulse control'. Clinically, we often see an exacerbation of behavioural problems in our pediatric patients when their schedule is disturbed. The level of this challenge depends on the family's aptitude to provide support and configuration at home, which further depends on the family's unique possessions and stressors, Lee noted. It has been considered that children are the great imitators of their parents and elders. They learn by watching the adults and since they will often be at home together now, they will observe what the adults in the home say or how they implement structure, ensure steadiness and deal with their own emotions but also if their parents are not good with each other or torture each other physically as well as verbally in front of their school going children then it can create a big mental trauma for their children and here it can also be expected that it will become a root for the cycle of abuse as nowadays one of the news is more common in most of the newspapers that domestic violence is growing very fast during the days of COVID-19 pandemic. So teaching every parent the importance of daily structure and reliability in their responses to their children's behaviours or living peacefully in front of their children is a precedence which is not easily possible especially during these days of COVID-19 Pandemic. According to Sarah K. Lipson, PhD, (assistant professor in the department of health law, policy and management at Boston University School of Public Health) research over the past decade has shown a steady increase in the pervasiveness of depression among students across the United States. 'For students who are besieged with nervousness, which has surpassed melancholy as the most common mental health concern on college campuses, the ambiguity regarding the corona virus is something we really need to be worried about, since it has the potential to amplify already high rates of anxiety,' Lipson said. There are many more things that create different type of mental or psychological traumas for students as well as for teachers as a whole like as every day change in the rules, regulations or restrictions by UGC.

UGC[3] Guidelines Related to Covid-19 Virulent Disease

Some Common Guiding Principle

(1) All universities may follow a six-day week model to reimburse the failure for the lingering session of 2019-20 and the next session 2020-21.

(2) The universities should prepare e-content or e-lab experiments and upload the same on their websites.

(3) The link provided by Ministry of Human Resource Development for practical laboratories to make possible the students of science/ engineering/ technology streams may also be suitable for such purposes.

(4) Every institute should develop efficient classroom and video conferencing facility and all teaching staff should be trained with the use of the technology.

(5) In order to conquer such challenges in future, the faculty should be effectively qualified for the use of ICT and online teaching tools, so that they complete about 25 percent of the

syllabus through online teaching and 75 percent syllabus through face to face teaching.

(6) The universities may formulate a proforma to record the Travel history of the students and staff for the period when they were away from the university due to lockdown, so that necessary safety measures may be taken in precise cases, if it is mandatory.

(7) In view of the present circumstances and future suspicions:

- The universities may adopt and implement these Guidelines in a clear manner by making alterations, trappings, modifications, amendments to deal with particular situation(s) in the best interest of students, educational institution and the entire education system,
- In case of educational institutions located at places where the Government (State or Centre) have obligatory margins on gathering of public, the institutions may plan accordingly.

All the guidelines that were suggested by UGC are not only increasing the pressure on students but the teachers are also facing different traumas. Especially the female teachers and girl students from rural areas like as from Kashmir, are facing double or triple times more psychiatric problems than any other because of the shortage of the facilities available and more dependence on men. As during these days of COVID-19 Pandemic the movement of people is completely restricted and at this time the women in this rural patriarchic society (Kashmir) can only move when there man can arrange any left for them or went with them. It can also become a big mental trauma for the women if there is the shortage or not availability of men at the time of urgent need and can also increase a large number of drop-out rate among girl students in Kashmir valley or in any other territory of India or the world around who are facing the same problem.

The recent condition of Covid-19 is creating psychiatric problems not only for the students reading in first, second or third level but for the students at all levels whether of secondary level, higher secondary level or of college level or of university level. At all levels each and every student is facing different psychiatric or mantal health problems. For college or university students, who are more serious about their career or bright future, experience a lot miscarriage and distress contributed by the uncertainty and abrupt disruption of the semester in addition to the anxiety caused by school closure. As more universities transitioning to inaccessible learning after the spring break, some students suffer from poor mental health due to the commotion of academic schedule (Agnew et al, 2019). Many students have to stop their research projects and internships when universities evacuated them from campus. Moreover, disruptions of their research projects and internships endanger their programme of study or delay their graduation which in turn fuels concern among college students. Many college or private college students have lost their on-campus jobs due to the emigration and the awaiting problems of room fees can worsen their economic hardship and mental health outcomes. They also have concerns and fears of infection and transmission of COVID-19 to their family members if they want to move from home to university or return to home. Although the overall impact on education and mental health of the university environment is still unknown, it is expected to be very considerable (Araujo et al, 2020). Considering the usual high incidence of emotional disorders in university students, it can be expected that the current situation may cause a notable impact on this population (Auerbach et al, 2016). Students with different streams or subjects like as: Students of music and dance, medical science, wrestling, astronomy and astrobiology, engineering and technology, art or calligraphy, earth science, Students having physical problems, Students of supports etc are also facing different types of mental traumas because they cannot concentrate properly or missing the concentrations on their subjects especially the students having eyesight problems cannot continue their study through laptops and smart phones as because of the side effects of these electronic instruments. Given the anticipated impact of the situation on our community, it is decisive to examine the experience of members of the university community during the COVID-19 crisis and detention in order to develop measures and execute psychological interventions appropriately accustomed to this situation. That may help alleviate the probable adverse effects on education and mental health among the university members.

There are some studies which explain that due to this world wide man-made deadly disease (COVID-19) the students are facing different types of psychiatric problems:Paula Odriozola González et al (2020) in *'Psychological effects of the COVID-19 outbreak and lockdown among students and workers of a Spanish university'*, addresses that the students from Arts & Humanities and Social Sciences & Law showed higher scores related to anxiety, depression, stress and impact of event with respect to students from Engineering & Architecture. University staff presented lower scores in all measures compared to students, who seem to have suffered an important psychological impact during the first weeks of the COVID-19 lockdown. Yusen Zhai, Xue Du (2020) in '*Addressing collegiate mental health amid COVID-19 pandemic*', states that college students encounter unique challenges leading to poor mental health in the wake of the COVID-19 outbreak. Before the pandemic started, one in five college students experienced one or more diagnosable mental disorders worldwide. The fact that the COVID-19 pandemic affects cloistered mental health underscores the burning need to understand these challenges and concerns in order to inform the development of courses of action and public health messaging that can better support college students in this crisis. Titan M. Alon, Matthias Doepke, Jane Olmstead-Rumsey, and Michèle Tertilt (2020) in '*The Impact of COVID-19 on Gender Equality*', states that the economic decline caused by the current COVID-19 outbreak has considerable implications for gender equality, both during the recession and the successive recovery. Compared to expected recessions, which affect men's employment more relentlessly than women's employment, the employment drop related to social distancing measures has a large impact on sectors with high female employment shares. In addition, closures of schools have massively increased childcare needs, which have a predominantly large impact on working mothers. The effects of the crisis on working mothers are likely to be unyielding, due to high returns to experience in the labour market. Beyond the instantaneous crisis, there are contrasting forces which may eventually encourage gender equality in the labour market. Pradeep Sahu (2020) in '*Closure of Universities Due to Corona virus Disease 2019 (COVID-19) in Impact on Education and Mental Health of Students and Academic Staff*', states in light of mounting concern about the current COVID-19 pandemic, a growing number of universities across the world have either postponed or canceled all campus events such as workshops, conferences, sports and other activities. Universities are taking exhaustive measures to avoid and protect all students and staff members from the highly infectious disease. Faculty members are already in the process of transitioning to online teaching platforms.

Conclusion

In order to diminish the inexorable realities of the COVID-19 pandemic around the world it is important to take the actions that can support a helpless student population to rally round to reduce the generally global mental health lumber connected with this period of astonishing disturbance and vagueness. Educational institutions should continue to help the students. First, in addition to isolated education, student advising should continue and conversion to telecommunication (e.g., phone call, online meeting) in order to provide academic support for students. Faculty and staff should consider offering virtual office hours to students, and they need to work together to maintain the connection and help students process and address academic concerns caused by the commotion of the semester. Second, for students whose internships or research projects were affected by the pandemic, internship site supervisors and research advisors should actively engage in helping students seek substitute plans, enabling them to work from home to exploit internship and research experiences. Third, universities should work on pioneering methods to support students to move research projects and capstones forward so that students can fulfill graduation requirements; meanwhile, university career centers should control to asset services, enduring to ease career growth for college students. One more thing that is very important is government should think very keenly about the fee strictures of the students whether in private schools, colleges or universities or in government institutions because during these days of COVID-19 people are also facing a big turndown in economic sector and idea or the rule of free and compulsory education does not works. As according to the Article 26 of the Universal Declaration of Human Rights (UDHR): 'Everyone has the right to education. Education shall be free, at least in the elementary and fundamental stages. Elementary education shall be compulsory. Education shall be intended for the full growth of human personality and to the intensification of respect for human rights and fundamental freedoms'. (Universal Declaration of Human Rights, Article 26). Education of today is going to be very costly that can improve more drop-outs among students because nowadays if we want to educate our future generation then we have to have arrange all the facilities like laptops, smart phones, broadband connections if needed or at the time of week network connections we have to have arrange the broadband connections for our children no matter how much costly it will be or whether do we have the monetary recourses or not. There should be proper online psychotherapy for both teachers as well for parents. Parents can play a big role in controlling their school going children from different types of mental traumas which they are facing through this unexpected change in education system. Parents can become the good counsellors for their children at home as according to researchers child is a great imitator of their parent and at this time parents cannot salt away their children from the traumas faced but can also stop the cycle of abuse like as domestic violence, drug addiction or loneliness as because of social isolation procedures in place in much of the world, it has be converted into a common aspect of daily life. Research has revealed that solitude or social isolation increases threat for hopelessness and apprehension and heightens approach of nervous tension are the factors that adds to degeneration of physical health and poor health behaviours, including substance abuse, poor nourishment as well as poor sleep quality, according to Louise C. Hawkley, PhD, of the National Opinion Research Centre at the University of Chicago. Also parents who distinguish that their school going children are in state of anguish mentally or emotionally or facing any other type of agony will want to have at their dumping contact information for counsellors, social workers and others to whom they can refer their child or the patient.

References

1. Agnew, M., Poole H., Khan A (2019). '*Fall break fallout: exploring student perceptions of the impact of an autumn break on stress*'. *Student Success*/ ssj.v10i3.1412.
2. Antony, M.M. et al (2020). '*Psychometric properties of the 42-item and 21-item versions of the Depression Anxiety Stress Scales (DASS) in clinical groups and a community sample.*' Psychol. Assess. 1998; 10:176–181.
3. Araújo F.J.O et al (2020). '*Impact of Sars-Cov-2 and its reverberation in global higher education and mental health*'. Psychiatry Res. 2020; 288.
4. Auerbach, R.P et al (2016). '*Mental disorders among college students in the World Health Organisation World Mental Health Surveys*'. Psychol. Med. 2016; 46:2955–2970.
5. Paula Odriozola-González et al (2020). *'Psychological effects of the COVID-19 outbreak and lockdown among students and workers of a Spanish university*', Aug; 290 (2020): 113108. Pub; online 2020 May 19.
6. Sahu, Pradeep (2020). *Closure of Universities Due to Coronavirus Disease 2019 (COVID-19): Impact on Education and Mental Health of Students and Academic Staff*, by Monitoring Editor: Alexander Muacevic and John R Adler, v 12(4): e7541, 2020 Apr 4; Published online.
7. Titan, M. Alon, et al (2020). '*The Impact of COVID-19 on Gender Equality*, NBER Working Paper No. 26947, April 2020: JEL No. D10, E24, J16, J22.
8. Wang, C.et al (2020): '*Risk management of COVID-19 by universities in China*'.J. Risk Financ Manag. 2020 doi: 10.3390/jrfm13020036.
9. Zhai, Yusen, Du Xue (2020): '*Addressing collegiate mental health amid COVID-19 pandemic*', Jun; 288: 113003. Psychiatry Research Pub; online 2020 Apr 17.
10. https://HYPERLINK "http://www.hindustantimes.com/more-lifestyiles/" www.hindustantimes.com/more-lifestyiles/HYPERLINK "https://www.google.com/url?sa=i&url=https://www.hindustantimes.com/more-lifestyle/curfews-strikes-shutdowns-kashmir-schooling-now-more-challenging-as-coronavirus-cases-surge-in-the-valley/story-kauVvSc8fUFasJILaHSJaI.html&psig= AOvVaw3f9PsmafIUD_c8JCjUEINp&ust=1597489445939000& source=images &cd=vfe&ved=2ahUKEwiLmPelxprrAhWKSysKHT9PAPIQr4kDegUIARCeAQ" Curfews-strikes-shutdowns-Kashmir
11. https://www.edutopia.org/article/inside-look-truma-informed-practices
12. https://www.healio.com/psychiatry/pandimic/news/online/
13. https://jamanetwork.com/journals/jamapediatrics/
14. https://www.medscape.com/indx/
15. https://www.washingtonpost.com/health/children
16. https://www.washingtonpost.com/health/children

17. https://www.ugc.ac.in/pdfnews/5369929/Letter-regarding-UGC-Guidelines-on-Examinations-and-Academic-Calendar.pdf
18. https://www.healio.com/authors/jgramigna/news/online/

Notes

1. Article 370 of the Indian constitution gave special status to Jammu and Kashmir, a region located in the northern part of Indian subcontinent which was administered by India as a state from 1954 to 31 October 2019 and a part of the larger region of Kashmir which has been the subject of dispute between India and Pakistan.
2. 2G or 3G is the short form for second generation cellular network. 2G cellular networks were commercially launched on the GSM standard in Finland by Radiolinji(now part of Elis Oyj)in 1991.
3. UGC- University Grants Commission came into existence on 28th December,1953 and became a statutory organisation of the government of India by an Act of parliament in 1956, for the corporation, determination and maintenance and research in university education.

Effects of COVID-19 on Education

15

Staggering Impact of COVID-19 on Global Education

Rajveer Kaur

In December 2019, Wuhan city, capital of the Chinese province Hubei witnessed the outbreak of new respiratory tract disease (Sahu, P., 2020). On January 23, 2020 to reduce the transmission of virus, the Chinese government had taken several measures and one such measure was complete lockdown (Xiang, YT et al., 2020). Slowly, the virus affected other countries too and that might be because of visitors or international trades. In February 2020, the International Committee on Taxonomy of Viruses (ICTV) termed this virus as SARS-COV-2(Severe acute respiratory syndrome coronavirus). In January 2020, WHO (World Health Organisation) named the disease as COVID-19 (Coronavirus disease in 2019) (WHO, 2020). The virus is said to be natural and it has an animal origin. The common symptoms of such virus include fever, cough, unable to breathe properly and loss of smell. There are various modes by which virus can be transmitted. It can be transmitted from an infected person when he coughs or sneezes. The virus gets transmitted through those expelled droplets and these droplets gets enter through nose, eyes, mouth to a person who is in close contact with the infected one. It can also be transmitted from various surfaces when a person gets in touch with it. According to National Institutes of Health's website, the virus remains for about two or three days on plastic and stainless steel, 24 hours on cardboard, in aerosols for about three hours (Amy Carmosino, 2020). In February 2020, Italy was the largest city that was prone to the identified culprit (Spina, S et al., 2020). In April 2020 total no. of 213 countries were infected in which 2,883,603 patients were prone to the syndrome and total no. of deaths were 1,98,842 (WHO, 2020). In March 2020, no. of cases in China was reduced but Europe became the center. The government of every nation has taken various measures to fight against the invisible enemy. Shopping malls, educational institutions, large gathering places were closed (Bedford, J, et al., 2020). To protect the people from such evil disease self-isolation, quarantine, social-distancing started playing the major role (UNESCO, 2020). To get rid of COVID-19, a team of doctors in every nation has focused on preparing the vaccine for it but till date no such antiviral drug came into being (Chahrour, M, et al., 2020).

As most of the world population consists of teenagers, so universities, colleges and educational institutions were shut down. The decision regarding the closure of educational institutions was taken as a result of drop in flu patients who were infected during the swine flu outbreak in 2009 in the UK. The closure of institutions has resulted in intermittent learning, conceded nourishment, childcare hitches and subsequent economic cost to families who cannot work (UNESCO, 2020). In February 2020, only China and few other affected countries decided to close the educational institution but later on in month of March, almost every country has closed its schools, colleges and universities. As a result of which 80 percent of the world's student population was deprived of their education. All the exams, conferences, seminars, workshops, etc. were cancelled or postponed (Chahrour, M, et al. 2020). In many places, face to face teaching mode has been replaced by online mode. The online mode has both merits as well as demerits. On the one hand, online teaching maintains a link between student and institution while on the other side, there occur many problems that can be faced by students as well as a teacher. The education sector has been affected very drastically as it will impact the number of admissions in national and international institutions, assessment criteria and psychological health of a students and teachers (Gewin, V., 2020).

MAJOR PROBLEMS FACED

Online Mode of Teaching

Shifting from face-to-face mode to a new mode might be exciting for faculty as well as students, but it has created various glitches.

Switching to an online mode not just requires a laptop, mobile or internet connection but it requires how to handle technology i.e. how to use different tools like Google Classroom, Skype, WhatsApp, You Tube, etc. For faculty who are already familiar with it can do the task in a sophisticated way but those who are not techno-savy may not easily understand or cope with the latest applications required. The same is true for students, a student may have all the things required for a particular lecture but what if he or she doesn't know how to operate it (Kyungmee Lee, 2020). A class of about 50 or 60 students can easily join a group on skype or any other application for the online class. But a class of 200 or above cannot do so. A teacher cannot deliver his lecture to the whole class at the same time as was the case for manual classes. Posting a video to 200 students cannot be a great job as there will be no face-to-face interaction and the students may lose interest in that.

Some courses cannot be taught online. For example, Art, music and many other courses. Art and craft teacher cannot figure out the mistakes of his students properly. So such types of courses are a challenge to universities, colleges and schools. Moreover, there are special courses for a student with a disability. So, what about their courses? How an instructor will teach if a child cannot hear or see (Disability Rights Texas, 2020).

Online mode is a time-consuming task. Since it requires time for logging into certain applications and then requesting others to join. There might be sometimes the problem of connection or network.

Online modes hinder the communicational skills of a pupil. Such students in future will have theoretical knowledge but he will fail to pass that bunch of knowledge to others.

There is less interaction between teachers and students during an online class. A teacher or mentor will not have a proper watch on the child what he or she might be doing during the whole class. Whether a child may be mentally absent, he might be working on other applications such as using WhatsApp, playing games, or doing something else. It is difficult to conduct class tests online. There is a risk that students might perform in a test by cheating. So, a teacher cannot have a proper look at all of them or on all of their activities (Kyungmee Lee, 2020).

Since in every course, there are plenty of subjects. So, switching daily from one subject class to another on mobile or laptop throughout the entire day will affect their mental health. No physical activity is involved in such a process. So, in this way, they will feel a kind of burden.

There are many economically weak areas. So, for them attending classes is quite difficult as they cannot afford smartphones or laptops. While in some areas there is a problem with an internet connection so, many children get deprived of that (Emma Dil, et al, 2020).

Theoretical, as well as practical knowledge plays an equivalent role in the education of a child. Some subjects cannot be just taught theoretically. For example, consider the case of the subject of botany, in which to get knowledge about a flower, it will be better if its practical knowledge is to be imparted. Same is the case for a medical student and a budding engineer. Moreover, in every curriculum, there is a weightage of a practical subject also. So, how the total no. of practicals are going to be complete.

As parents plays the inevitable role in the upliftment of a child. Considering the case of a pupil who is in primary class and whose parents might be uneducated, such child can't give his performance better in an online class. On the other hand educated parents can help better during the online class of a child.

Online modes are most suitable for higher level student, a small pupil cannot easily access the apps. COVID-19 has left gap in childcare as working parents leave children alone in house and hence a child gets deprived of social and emotional balance.

Books are the most loyal friend of a student. Online modes cannot replace them. Reading a material from a book is quite stress-free than from an online source.

As the early childhood education which is usually for the students of age group 3-4 years and it includes kindergartens, preschools, nursery schools etc. Closure of such schools because of COVID-19 stops the development of child's cognitive skills. In Japan, a decision was taken to close all schools but it exempted the daycare facilities. Under such circumstances, five people who were working in preschool in Kobe tested positive for coronavirus. As a result, out of hundred students, one student was also tested positive for the virus.

The interruption in Primary education results in 67 percent loss of literacy ability among students (UNESCO, 2020).

Student's Feedback Regarding Transformation from Face-To-Face Classes to Online Classes

To study the effect of COVID-19 on education, a Google form was created and sent to students studying in different colleges and Universities. The feedback has been taken from students studying in different countries (India, Canada, New Zealand and Spain). Total no. of 54 responses has been included in the data. 17 responses were received from Canada, 1 from Spain, 2 from New Zealand and 34 from India. (Fig. 1)

1. No. of students attending online classes: Out of total no. of students, 96.3 percent of them are attending online classes while 3.7 percent students do not attend them. So, in a nutshell COVID-19 has linked students with technology. (Fig. 2)

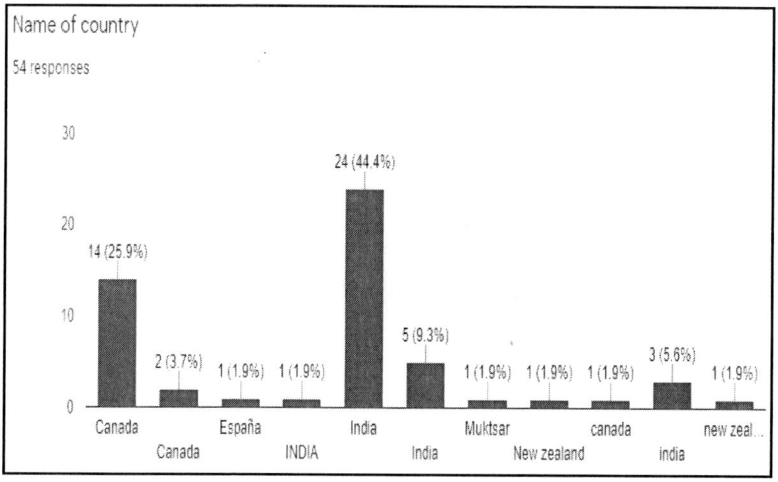

Fig. 1

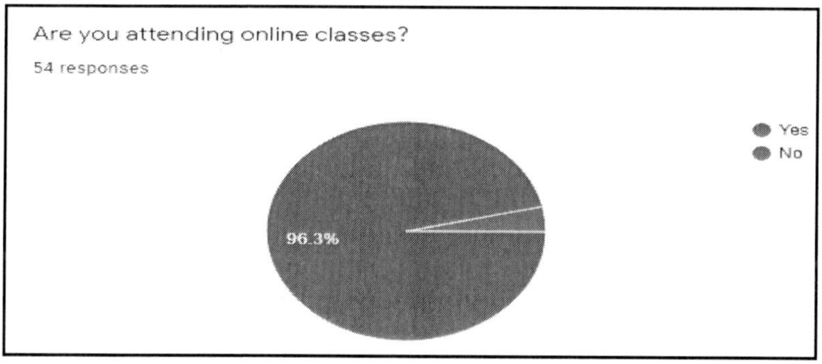

Fig. 2

2. Time-consuming: According to 64.8 percent of total responses, online classes do consume a lot of time while 35.2 percent think that it is not. (Fig. 3)

3. Interaction with Teacher: According to 74.1 percent of total student's responses, the interaction with teachers in case of manual classes is better than online classes. Only 25.9 percent thinks that it is better than classroom teaching. (Fig. 4)

4. Access to Online Classes: 66.7 percent of total student's responses think that not everyone can easily access the online classes in context of affording mobiles, laptops and internet connectivity while 33.3 percent thinks that they can afford. (Fig. 5)

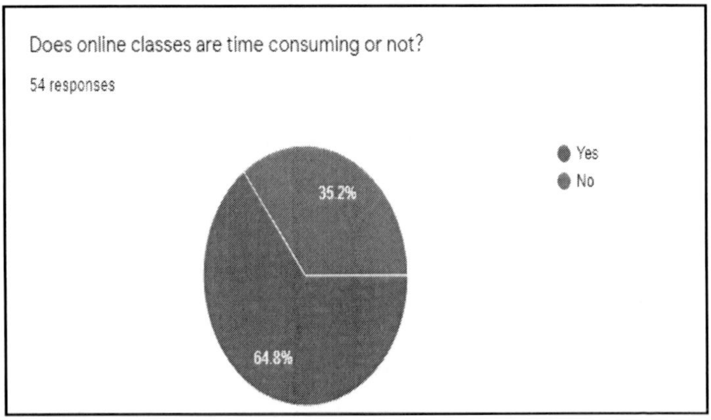

Fig. 3

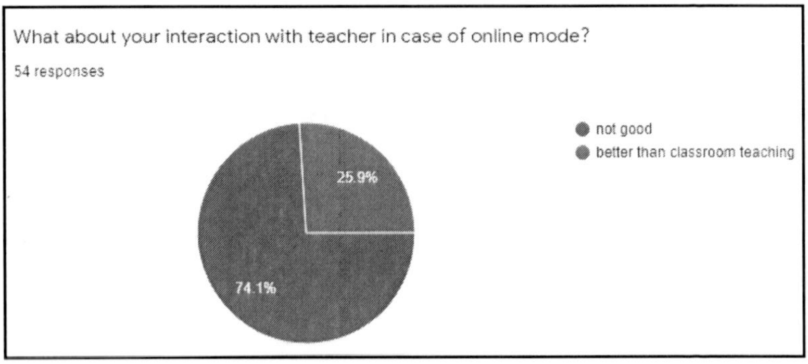

Fig. 4

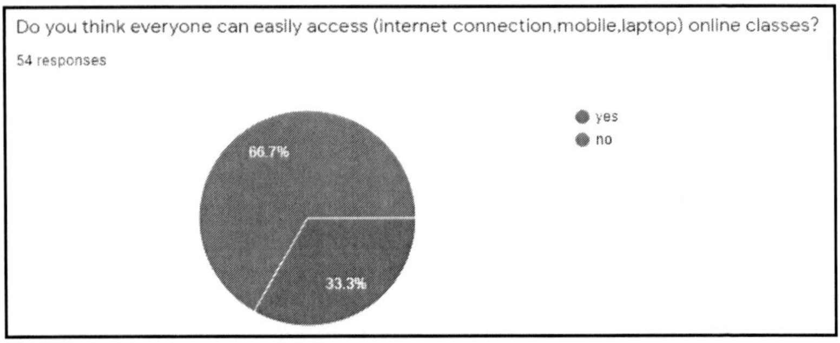

Fig. 5

5. Practical Knowledge: 70.4 percent of total students think that online classes don't impart practical knowledge which is crucial for many subjects while 29.6percent thinks that there is no requirement for such practical knowledge. (Fig. 6)

6. Technology: 64.8 percent of the total students think that it is difficult to cope with technology for many while 35.2 percent thinks that it is an easy task.

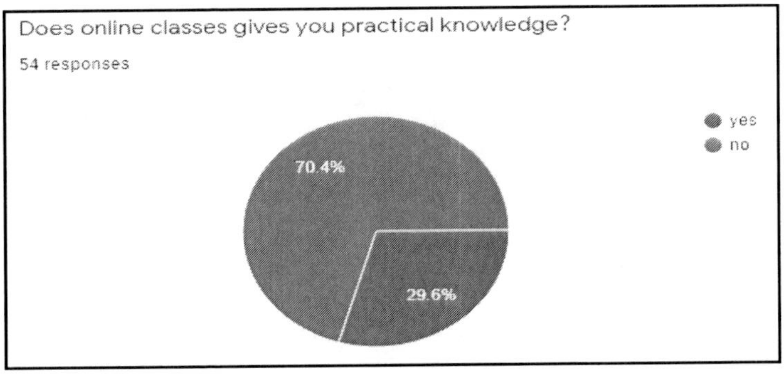

Fig. 6

7. Weaker Sections of Society: Out of total no. of student's responses, 90.7 percent think that weaker sections of the society cannot afford laptops, smartphones which are essential for online classes. Only few disagree with the statement. (Fig. 7)

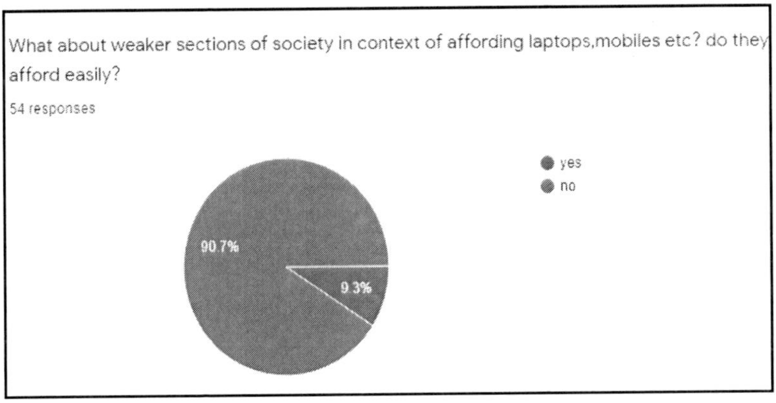

Fig. 7

8. Presence of students during online classes: 59.3 percent of students think that many students of their class bunk online classes. Whenever a teacher gets online for his particular class, many students don't attend them while 40.7 percent thinks that the problem is not same for every class. (Fig. 8)

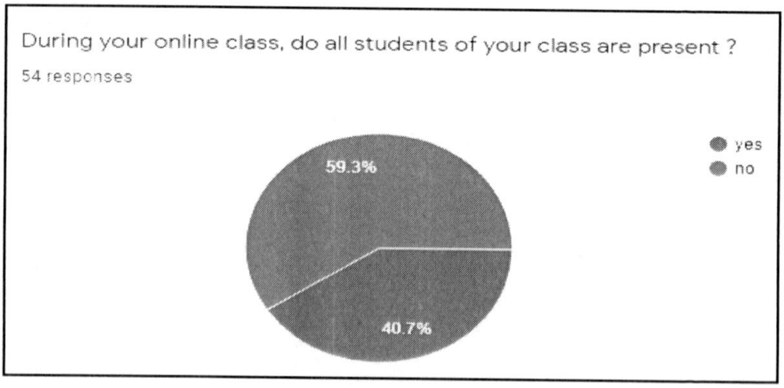

Fig. 8

In a nutshell, there are various challenges that a student is facing during an online class as discussed earlier.

Evaluation and Assessment

COVID-19, has not only affected the teaching mode but the cancellation of many exams had put a huge impact on the assessment. The assessment was given to show the progress report of a child to his/her family. But due to complete lockdown barrier has been imposed on it (Emma Dil, et al., 2020). As earlier, the assessment was given based on mid-semester examination, class tests and assignments, etc which was quite an easy task. Checking class tests, mid-semester examinations manually was easy. Assessment based on online tests, assignments is a challenging task (Disabilty Rights Texas, 2020). Evaluating student's test online of 100's is a perplexing task before a teacher. Moreover it is not a fair mode as a child can even indulge in the cheating process (George R. Watson, 2010). Even a teacher has to reset all the evaluation criteria for marking the assessment of a child online, which might be a cumbersome process (Raaheim, A, et al., 2019).

Admission Process

Taking admission to a particular course is based on the quality of education, infrastructure etc. So, before taking admission a student and his parents check manually about a school or college, and to get feedback from students already studying in that particular institution was easy. But due to the outburst of COVID-19, confusion prevails in the mind of students and parents. Hence it is going to affect the number of admissions in a particular institution (Scott Jaschik, 2020).

In the case of international students, they were free to select any country for their careers. But due to the alarm of COVID-19, fear creates in the mind of the student whether to leave his home country or not. In such circumstances, home is the optimum place to live (Ellie Bothwell, 2020). The virus has created fright in the minds of many that will such type of virus may come in the future? What about the students who will go abroad for studies? What about their safety, livelihood? So, govt. of any nation still has not assured the safety of the international student in a proper manner. International students who are already away from their homes are self-isolating themselves to keep safe (Ruby Cheng, 2020). And in such a situation, they cannot properly focus on their studies. COVID-19 affects the career as well as the cerebral health of a child. Student of this year is going to graduate late and even they are going to face the global recession due to COVID-19.

Response of different Countries regarding closure of Schools, Colleges and Universities (UNESCO. 2020).

Sl. No.	*Country/ Territory*	*Response*
1.	India	As on March 16th, country was in lockdown as a result of which all schools, colleges and universities were closed. All the examinations (CBSE, ICSE, PSEB board) were postponed. As per UGC (University Grants Commission) guidelines, universities too have postponed the exams.
2.	Singapore	Home based learning was started with the exception of students whose parents can't find proper accommodation.
3.	Russia	On 14th March, The Russian ministry of Education recommended schools to accept the remote learning process. But the Moscow region familiarized lithe process of attendance in which regular classes would be conducted with the exception that parents who wish to make their child stay at home can do so by attending online classes. But due to increasing cases of COVID-19, all Russian schools too went under lockdown.
4.	Mexico	The Secretariat of Education extended the time period of Easter break. As originally it was planned to be from 6th to 17th April. But that has been shifted from 20th March to 20th April.
5.	Lesotho	Closure of schools till April 17th was decided but on the other hand it has planned to provide school meals to students.
6.	Jordan	Since March 14th 2020, country was in lockdown and the minister of Education proclaimed induction of TV channels to broadcast different levels of education.
7.	Japan	As on 5th March, 18,923 schools were closed.
8.	Italy	Italy closed its all school and Universities
9.	Indonesia	Minister of Education and Culture of Indonesia, Nadiem Makarim has launched an educational TV show and advised students to study through it till end of year.

(Contd...)

10.	Fiji	All schools and Colleges will be closed till June 2020.
11.	China	The origin country of COVID-19 was the first country to close its all educational institutions for near about 200 million students. According to UNESCO, on 13th March few schools were reopened but majority of the schools were not in favor of reopening.
12.	Chile	According to Chilean President, the country will close its institutions only if there will be confirmed cases of virus among students
13.	Australia	According to Australian Health Protection Principal Committee, few private schools were closed but the rest of schools, colleges and universities remained open. But on 23 March, many universities were closed and classes were conducted online.
14.	United States	On April 10th, a decision was taken to close all schools which have affected about 55.1 million students. By May 2nd, in about 47 states, four territories, and the District of Columbia, schools were ordered to close the buildings for the present academic year. Even the CARES Act was passed by President Donald Trumph. According to this Act, economic relief was given to student loan borrowers.
15.	Urugay	On 14th March, it was decided that schools will only be closed if there would be positive cases for virus among students. But later on, a complete shutdown of schools was done for two weeks. Schools provided meal to students but there were no classes.
16.	Sweden	Earlier schools were opened but on March 17th, government decided to close all schools and universities and advised them for online learning.
17.	Egypt	For students of 1st primary to 3rdpreparatory, schools were closed. 1st and 2nd secondary grades students will give their exam from homes. For 3rd Secondary students, examinations will be held in schools.
18.	Finland	For parents who are working in important sectors of country, their children can attend schools as usual. Schools are also open for early education children whose parents cannot take care of their child. Contact teaching was decided for all other levels of education.
19.	Namibia	On 14 March 2020, all schools were closed. But the universities itself suspended its teaching. Reopening will only be done after the execution of stage 3 plan which is going to launch on 2nd June.

As the above data represents the present scenario of different countries in context of education. Few countries have decided to close the educational institutions for the rest of year which is going to distress the edification of a pupil.

Solutions

There exist many possible solutions that can challenge the problems faced by students and teachers due to COVID-19.

- The first step that any educational institution can put forward is the training of their teachers. Online Seminars should be scheduled in which different topics can be discussed. For example, Motivating students regarding how to cope up with COVID-19, the use of technology like how to use Google Classroom, video lessons, MOOC (Massive Open Online Course) etc.

- Orientation sessions can be arranged for the parents. Proper planning regarding the online scheduling should be done. This planning should be based on level of education, parental support, need of student and on particular zone affected (UNESCO, 2020).
- Most importantly, feedback should be taken from students regarding their syllabus, class-tests, about technology, etc.
- There should be more peer-to-peer activities as well as group discussions.
- Every event like seminars, conferences, and workshops should be postponed or cancelled and complete focus should be given on students after the lockdown.
- Different committees should be formed in all institutions like the health committee, feedback committee, activity committee, etc. so that every student remains in contact with them if they face any problem.
- The weaker sections of the society should be taken care of by every institution and if possible arrangement's in the framework of a meal, access to online classes should be made for them (Jaime Saavedra, 2020).
- The data which a particular institution shares with its students should be secured and protected. As accessing online classes is a difficult task, so care should be taken regarding the coherent time that can be given to each subject according to the level of a student. For example, Primary and secondary school students should not be given a lecture of not more than 20 and 40 minutes respectively.
- Parents should not be overloaded with the submission report of their child (UNESCO, 2020).
- After the lockdown, immediate examinations should not be conducted. Students can come to college in small groups and if needed practical knowledge should be given to them.
- Since this COVID-19 has imposed an impact on the mental health of a child, some flexibility should be given in the perspective of assessment or relaxed examination (Timmis, S, et al., 2020). Considering the cases of music, art courses, their grading should be given based on previous performance, or classes should be there after the lockdown.

- Safety comes first, so daily updates regarding virus should be sent to every child and proper psychological support should be given to them.
- In the case of international students, the government of every nation should ensure that proper financial, as well as mental support should be given to every adolescent (Sahu, P., 2020).
- Even government, bank officials, different committees should join their hands to ensure the mental state of the child.
- Regarding the Admission process, every institution should ensure that the admission committee should be active and daily updates should be sent through Facebook, You Tube channels, television, and radio about their school, university, and college. They can even take feedback from their pass out students and can use that for publicity purposes.

Conclusion

To exterminate the phase of COVID-19, academic staff and students should trace the path of their respective institutions. Every institution should provide the updated information required by its teachers, students, and parents. The safety and well-being of an individual should come before education. International students should be given the utmost importance by institution and government.

References

1. Al-Rabiaahab A, et al. (2020). "Middle East Respiratory Syndrome-Corona Virus (MERS-CoV) associated stress among medical students at a university teaching hospital in Saudi Arabia". *J Infect Public Health*. [Epub ahead of print]:10.1016/j.jiph.2020.01.005.
2. Amy Carmosino (2020). "Background & History of the Coronavirus (COVID-19)". Available at: https://psychcentral.com/coronavirus/background-history-of-the-coronavirus-covid-19/ . Assessed on 15 April 2020.
3. Bedford, J, et al. (2020). "COVID-19: towards controlling of a pandemic." [Epub ahead of print]:10.1016/S0140-6736(20)30673-5
4. Chahrour, M, et al. (March 21, 2020). "A Bibliometric Analysis of COVID-19 Research Activity: A Call for Increased Output". *Cureus* 12(3): e7357. doi:10.7759/cureus.7357.
5. Disability Rights Texas (2020). "COVID-19 and Students with Disabilities in College". Available at: https://www.disabilityrightstx.org/en/handout/covid19-college-rights/. Assessed on 28 April 2020.
6. Ellie Bothwell (2020). "The Flexible admissions could mitigate COVID-19 impact". Available at: https://www.timeshighereducation.com/news/flexible-admissions-could-mitigate-covid-19-impact. Assessed on 28 April 2020.

7. Emma Dil, et al. (2020). "As coronavirus spreads, the decision to move classes online is the first step. What comes next?". Available at: https://www.chronicle.com/article/As-Coronavirus-Spreads-the/248200. Assessed on 28 April 2020.

8. George R. Watson (2010). "Cheating in the digital age: do students cheat more in online courses?". Available at: https://www.westga.edu/~distance/ojdla/spring131/watson131.html. Assessed on 28 April 2020.

9. Gewin, V (2020). "Five tips for moving teaching online as COVID-19 takes hold". Available at: https://www.nature.com/articles/d41586-020-00896-7. Accessed on 28 April 2020.

10. Jaime Saavedra (2020). "Educational challenges and opportunities of the Coronavirus (COVID-19) pandemic". Available at: https://blogs.worldbank.org/education/educational-challenges-and-opportunities-covid-19-pandemic. Assessed on 23 April 2020.

11. Kyungmee, Lee (2020). "Coronavirus: universities are shifting classes online - but it's not as easy as it sounds". Available at: http://theconversation.com/coronavirus-universities-are-shifting-classes-online-but-its-not-as-easy-as-it-sounds-133030. Assessed on 28 April 2020.

12. Raaheim A, et al. (2019). "Digital assessment - how does it challenge local practices and national law? A Norwegian case study." *Eur J High Educ*. 2019, 9:219-231. 10.1080/21568235.2018.1541420.

13. Ruby Cheng (2020). "The COVID-19 crisis and international students". Available at: https://www.insidehighered.com/views/2020/03/19/higher-ed-institutions-arent-supporting-international-students-enough... Assessed on 28 April 2020.

14. Sahu, P (April 04, 2020). "Closure of Universities Due to Coronavirus Disease 2019 (COVID-19): Impact on Education and Mental Health of Students and Academic Staff". *Cureus* 12(4): e7541. doi:10.7759/cureus.7541.

15. Scott Jaschik (2020). "How the Coronavirus Is Affecting Admissions". Available at: https://www.insidehighered.com/admissions/article/2020/03/09/how-coronavirus-changing-admissions. Assessed on 28 April 2020.

16. Spina S, et al. (2020). "The response of Milan's emergency medical system to the COVID-19 outbreak in Italy". *Lancet*. 2020, 395:49-50. 10.1016/s0140-6736(20)30493-1.

17. Timmis, S, et al. (2020). "Rethinking assessment in a digital age: opportunities, challenges, and risks." *Br Educ Res J*. 2016, 42:454-476. 10.1002/berj.3215.

18. UNESCO (2020). "UNESCO. COVID-19 Educational disruption and response". Available at: https://en.unesco.org/themes/education-emergencies/coronavirus-school-closures. Accessed on 28 April 2020.

19. WHO (2020). "Coronavirus disease (COVID-19) Pandemic". Available at: https://www.who.int/emergencies/diseases/novel-coronavirus-2019. Accessed on 28 April 2020.

20. WHO (2020). "Naming the coronavirus disease (COVID-19) and the virus that causes it". Available at: https://www.who.int/emergencies/diseases/novel-coronavirus-2019/technical-guidance/naming-the-coronavirus-disease-(COVID-2019)-and-the-virus-that-causes-it. Accessed on 28 April 2020.

21. Xiang, YT, et al. (2020). "Timely mental health care for the 2019 novel coronavirus outbreak is urgently needed." *Lancet Psychiatry*. 2020, 7:28-29. 10.1016/S2215-0366(20)30046-8

16

A Study on Supply Shortage of Critical Primary Needs During COVID-19 Pandemic in India

Rupinderpal Kaur

World have been many times effected in history due to epidemics. This time also we all are witnessing an epidemic due to a virus known as "Corona virus" have been spread that not only effected one country but whole world. Infections are liable for somewhere in the range of 15 and 30 percent of normal colds. A corona virus was first secluded in 1937 from an irresistible bronchitis infection in winged animals. Corona viruses are sorts of infections that commonly influence the respiratory tract of warm blooded animals, including people. They are related with the regular cold, pneumonia, and extreme intense respiratory disorder (SARS) and can likewise influence the gut. Human corona viruses most normally spread from a tainted individual to others through the air by hacking and wheezing close to home contact, for example, contacting or shaking hands. Touching an item or surface with the infection on it, at that point contacting your mouth, nose, or eyes before washing your hands rarely. Cases kept on expanding exponentially and demonstrating examines announced a pestilence multiplying time of 1.8 [2]. The most serious hazard in COVID-19 is transmission to social insurance labourers. In the SARS episode of 2002, 21 percent of those influenced were social insurance labourers [4]. Till date, about 32 lakhs people around the world are infected from disease with more than 2 lakhs of deaths. It is imperative to secure human services labourers to guarantee coherence of care and to stop transmission of disease to different patients. [5]

In December, while Wuhan province was witnessing the beginning of the actual Covid-19 pandemic, India was facing massive and violent uprisings. Hundreds of thousands of Indians protested all over the country against the discriminatory anti-Muslim citizenship law [1]. This, while the specialists were invalidating the presence of network transmission of the infection regardless of the main cases showing up path back in January in India to at last declare a 21-day lockdown on the 12 PM of 24 March, with just a 4 hour notice. In India, the internal migrant workers, day labourers and the poor-deprived of resources-have decided to return to their native villages. This terrible and dangerous mass migration of poor escaping from urban areas is the most noticeable concern about health, monetary and social emergency has tripled the situation to analyze and handle. Every situation is getting tough under lockdown period, either we talk about healthcare system, the food and supply chain, earning the livelihood or the daily required things.

Accessing Healthcare System under the Lockdown

Without any doubt, this time was also a test for every country's healthcare system. How much efficient is the healthcare system in terms of medical staff, equipments, PPE kits, medicines etc. This pandemic has ruthlessly uncovered the vulnerabilities of the absolute best healthcare system. For the Indian medical system, one of the most troubled and least financed among other countries, this could be a crucial point in time; as government offices are as of now overstretched in an exceptionally broke, underfunded and uneven division of health facilities. This epidemic have welcomed us to look at the manner in which the present emergency dangers to improve durable healthcare system disparities and how broken system foundations may fall under the stress of Covid-19 cases in India. Testing is pivotal to check the degree of Covid-19 transmission in any nation. India right now has probably the least proportion of testing on the planet, which may have covered crown infection cases. According to Ferry *et al.* [4], "As of March 23rd, the total number of individuals tested for Covid-19 across the country was 17,493. The same week, South Korea was carrying out more than 5,500 tests per million people, Italy 2,500 per million, the United Kingdom close to 1,500 and France around 900". Till now we do not have sufficient equipments to test at large scale. One limitation to it could be the large number of population in comparison to other countries. If Indian government conduct even one lakh test of corona virus every day still we need approximately 37 years to test about corona virus detection. Unfortunately, may be the Indian ministry was taking into account that there will be no community transmission except the cases due to any abroad return cases.

Toward the start of its national lockdown, India just needed more testing units and regardless of whether the government has offered licences to privately owned businesses to sell them in India, the requirement on testing lies in the quantity of research centres to increase.

Kapoor et al. CDDEP (The Centre for Disease Dynamics, Economics & Policy) [9] had a detailed study on number of hospitals, beds, ventilators that are available in India in this epidemic. Table 1.1 is presenting summary of the study carried out by Gitanjali and team.

Table 1.1: Statistics of medical facilities in India

Facility	*In public sector*	*In private sector*	*Total (public+ private)*
Number of hospitals	25,778	43,487	69,265
Number of beds	7,13,986	1,185,242	18,99,228
Number of ICU beds	35,699	59,262	94,961
Number of ventilators	17,850	29,631	47,481

According to data presented by CDDEP [5], most of the beds and ventilators in India, are concentrated in seven States - Uttar Pradesh (14.8 percent), Karnataka (13.8 percent), Maharashtra (12.2 percent), Tamil Nadu (8.1 percent), West Bengal (5.9 percent), Telangana (5.2 percent) and Kerala (5.2 percent).

This data have presented data about the availability of facility before the pandemic spread out. In current situation, a country like India where chances of community spread is higher due to large and dense population. Naturally the demand of testing kits, Masks, PPE kits etc. have been increased as the medical staffs are at much higher risk than anyone else. As news from Indian Express [8] on 7th April, 2020, Around 100 specialists from Sir Ganga Ram Hospital were sent to isolate after two patients became positive for the COVID-19. Another private emergency clinic Maharaja Agrasen has sent around 80 of its staffs to isolation. The Delhi State Cancer Institute likewise needed to close its OPD for a day to sanitise the clinic and ask staffs self-isolate. Dr Satendra Singh from University College of Medical Sciences, Delhi University and the founder of Doctors with Disabilities, said," while the healthcare personnel are aware of how to protect themselves; it is lack of reciprocity from the government in their right to avail PPEs is hampering this frontline workforce. The numbers will only increase as we have failed to balance demand and supply. This has to be addressed at a war-footing to flatten the curve".

India is trying to cop-up with demand of medical equipments. India is focusing on acquiring medical supplies, including testing kits and ventilators, as priority items from China. India has received its first lot of rapid anti-body test kits from China [7]. This is commercially acquired and part of government-to-government deal. India has been trying to get testing kits from Germany, South Korea, France and Israel besides China, said sources. As many as 300,000 rapid antibody testing kits from Guangzhou Wondfo Biotech Co. and 2,50,000 from Zhuhai Livzon Diagnotics Inc, besides 100,000 RNA extraction kits from MGI Tech Co. from Shenzhen have been cleared by Chinese government. Although there is still need for more PPE kits as doctors are going on strike in demand of same as happened in one of the hospital of Amritsar in Punjab. There doctors refused to go on duty in isolation ward for Covid-19 until they get special PPE kit. Nursing staff also have blamed that senior doctor are sending them on front without any protection measures. Medical staffs are true on their part but still are saving lives with dare. India has to struggle more if the condition worsens.

Making a Living under the Lockdown

Upon the lockdown declaration, middle class Indians were seen racing to shops and markets to purchase daily required arrangements. This was especially activated by the absence of authentic arrangement to promise individuals that they would even now be able to get the grocery under the lockdown. While generally speaking, India had barely any options other than some form of a lockdown but an poorly planned and executed lockdown has made a serious issue. According to research carried by Rajagopalan *et al.*[8], most Indians work in the non-governmental sector and India has 275 million persons who live below the poverty line of $1.25 a day (approximately 3,000 rupees per month). The lockdown declaration implied that no financial action was permitted during the lockdown, causing day by day wage workers throughout the India to freeze over their capacity to earn the three-week loss of wages. Specifically, workers in urban zones are now attempting to get back to their families home towns, as trains and transports have been stopped and outskirts shut for the lockdown. Few simply did not have advance funds to save food and the phrase "I won't die of corona. Before that, I will surely die of hunger" crudely. This group is reasonably well identified and targeted across various government schemes. Two days after the declaration of the lockdown, the Union money serve, Nirmala Sitaraman, reported a boost to give extra alleviation to this gathering through plans, for example, the National Rural Employment Guarantee Scheme, that can help them to survive. The most significant part of the relief package was the arrangement of 10 kilograms of food grain and 1 kilogram of pulses for every individual every month under the public distribution system (PDS).

On March 26, the government declared to distribute a $22.6 billion relief bundles with all necessarily required food items like flour, pulses, species etc. [6]. PDS played a key job, giving 5 kg of either rice or wheat and 1 kg of pulses every month free, offered in two portions. (This is notwithstanding the prior privilege of 5 kg of eash wheat/rice per individual every month.) The relief package should meet most families' grain requirement, however the beats allotment is likely insufficient, given every month utilisation is 4-5 kg. A few states, in the meantime, have reported their own help bundles.

Given the pivotal significance of development, we can in this manner imagine that the lockdown will have completely crushing outcomes and economic conditions in country. The importance of migrant workers, an indispensable connection in India's economy, has gotten extremely evident. They have basically been overlooked by the lockdown measures. Prime minister Narendra Modi's annoucement of "Stay at home" provoked a huge hunch in labourers to get back to home, despite the fact that transport framework had just been drastically reduced.

Indian 5 percent poor families dedicate around 61 percent of their all out spending to food, while in urban territories, this deal was just 28 percent and this amount is just 5 percentages of earnings of the richest. With small savings, is probably going to affect access to food, especially among the poor [1]. With little investment funds, those family units who have a place with the most unfortunate sections of society are the most influenced by the circumstance, among which daily wagers, urban migrants, and who are left with no asset or even safe house. A second expected effect will affect all segments of society: the chain of food supply may not sustain itself.

Apart from government efforts, most of NGOs are also providing relief during this tough time. Table 1.2 is presenting few names of NGOs who are working very hard to feed hungry people.

Table 1.2: List of NGOs Working For Relief in India During COVID-19

NGO Name	*Brief Description*	*State*
MCKS Food for the Hungry Foundation	MCKS Food for the Hungry Foundation a non-profit organisation based in New Delhi. Our team's mission is simple - no one should have to sleep hungry. Over the last 15 years, we have delivered more than 1,00,00,000 meals to those in need	Head Quarters in Delhi

(*Contd...*)

Youth Feed India Program under SAFA Organisation	The Hyderabad-based not-for-profit organisation works for the urban poor by introducing sustainable livelihoods through an area-based community model. With covid-19 are helping us distribute in Hyderabad, Bengaluru, Chennai, Gurgaon, Delhi, Mumbai and North Karnataka.	Pan India
Zomato Feeding India	The not-for-profit started the 'Feed the Daily Wager' project after the announcement of the 21-day lockdown to provide food support to families of daily wage earners across cities,	Pan India
Give India	Give India is a non profit organisation in India. They are raising funds for two COVID19 programmes at the moments: 1. Donation for food parcels for daily wage earners 2. Hygiene kits for those in high risk areas	Pan India
Kashtakari Panchayat	Pune-based Kashtakari Panchayat has organised a fundraiser to support nearly 7,000 workers in Pune and the neighbouring Pimpri-Chinchwad. The funds will be used to provide safety kits, consisting of gloves, masks, soaps and sanitizers, and a month's supply of essentials, like grains, pulses, oil, sugar and tea.	
SEEDS	SEEDS is taking some burden off frontline health workers by supplementing public health systems, supplying hygiene kits and supporting the establishment of temporary quarantine facilities.	Pan India
Goonj	Goonj is also working towards long-term rehabilitation of daily wage earners, who are likely to be unemployed for an unforeseen period of time due to the pandemic. Under the programme Rahat, the volunteers aim to prepare kits with essentials such as dry rations and personal care products.	
Uttishtha Foundation	They are trying to procure test kits for COVID19 and utilize them in hard to reach/ rural areas and providing meals to the migrated workers.	Uttar Pradesh
Khushiyaan Foundation	Since the COVID-19 outbreak, Khushiyaan has been providing meals to security guards, labourers and daily wage earners around Mumbai, Thane, Airoli and Bhiwandi through Roti Ghar.	Mumbai
United Way	United Way Mumbai is a part of the 130+ year old United Way movement engaged in nearly 1800 communities, spanning 41 countries across the world.	Mumbai
Akshaya Patra Foundation	Since the COVID-19 crisis, The Akshaya Patra Foundation, in close coordination with State Governments and District Administration, has stepped in to provide relief by providing food to thousands of people across the country.	Karnataka
Uday Foundation	The current Coronavirus (Covid-19) outbreak continues to spread, Uday Foundation is providing all necessary help and services by accepting donation material such as soap for hand wash, sanitizers and one month's food supply to distrubute.	Delhi

(*Contd…*)

YUVA (Youth for Voluntary and Voluntary Action)	This NGO has been giving food to the slum dwellers and needy individuals amid coronavirus outbreak. They conducted a survey recently and identified households which are in desperate need of help -- like families of ice-cream walas, garland makers, waste collectors etc	Mumbai
Clothes Box Foundation	The organisation has launched an initiative to distribute food grains and sanitar kits to those who are worst hit by Covid-19 lockdown.	
Care India	CARE a global humanitarian organization is working with partners across over ninety countries helping the most marginalised women and girls in the fight on COVID 19. CARE India has a 1400+ team working with Government of Bihar in supporting the government in contact tracing, monitoring, infection control, laboratory and hospital strengthening for fight COVID	Bihar
Yein Udaan	It is carrying out Covid-19 relief work and have successfully provided grocery kits with essential food items to 500 Trans-women and 900 daily wage earners along with their families in the first week of lockdown.	Chennai
Jan Jagran Kendra (JJK)	For Covid-19 relief work the NGO is donating hygeine kits and emergency food supply to the economically weaker section of the society in the Hazaribagh district	Jharkhand
Bhavishya Bharat	As part of their Covid-19 relief work the organisation is distributing ration bags amongst the differently-abled.	Sikkim, West Bengal and Telangana
Humanity First	So, far, their team has helped with donating grocery items, masks, sanitizers, gloves and drinking water etc.	Punjab, Gujarat, UP and Kashmir.
National Hawker Federation (NHF)	The key initiatives in the wake of COVID-19 impact include: **Relief Camps:** As part of this initiative, 500 packets of dry ration are being distributed each day. **HawkerBazaar Express**: During this lockdown, they are now reviving Hawker Bazaar Express to help allow the street vendors to reach out to a wider market.	Udaipur, Bhubaneswar, Ranchi, Itanagar
Global Shapers Navi Mumbai Hub: Fighting COVID-19	Global Shapers is an initiative of the World Economic Forum that has dedicated its efforts to COVID-19 relief in the form of food and medical supply distribution.	Maharashtra
17000 ft Foundation	Awareness about the Covid-19 crisis and prepares students and community members with the correct knowledge and ensure the villages have all the necessary health and hygiene essentials needed to combat the disease. As part of the workshop each school will receive a Health and Hygiene Kit along with Awareness posters and material.	Leh and Kargil Districts, UT of Ladakh

(Contd...)

Paras India	At the unprecedented moment of crisis, under the project Samarpan COVID-19, PARAS is distributing food packets, fruits, sanitizers, basic medicines, producing and distributing face masks among the most vulnerable communities.	Delhi, Uttar Pradesh, Madhya Pradesh
Khalsa Aid	Khalsa aid is a NGO that provide help in each and every crisis that happen anywhere in world. As it have branches all over the world. In COVID-19 , they are providing food and shelter to the needy people a large scale	Punjab based

Source: www.investindia.gov.in

As can be seen, there are many problems and issues currently facing us with our food supply and with the food system in the light of the Covid-19 pandemic. Access to food is currently very dynamic and fluid. Changes are being introduced daily by supermarkets as the Covid-19 pandemic develops, and it remains uncertain if the Government will take the step of implementing food rationing. At this time, collective responsibilities, not just for our families, but for our neighbours and our communities need to come to the fore step.

Conclusion

In such a situation, one would hope to put national unity most importantly and to strict/ethnic/standing/class-based polarisation to the behind the stage. They face attacks and are ostracised by fear of infection, moreover other people fear of getting infection from them. What's more, it is yet to see whether and how the administration will accept the open door of this emergency to additionally gap or re-join its public. The major concern is for poor people and the minorities, who as we have seen, will be the first to experience the ill effects of this emergency. For them, the outcomes of the lockdown will be emotional.

Most of the states have been at the forefront in implementing ambitious emergency solutions for the most needy, including Kerala, Delhi, Odisha or West Bengal, despite the fact that their activity is somewhat retained with grants from the Central Government. In the more extended run, putting resources into the agricultural area would help recover the economy, by ensuring food security and lessening the urban-rural difference.

Above all, government also have to strengthen the healthcare system with two facts (1) that the quality of care can be estimated and improved and (2) that quality of care not be overlooked in pursuit for cost control. Strengthening these two facts implies ensuring that quality of healthcare system remains on the medicinal services main agenda. Agenda should be with clear identification of the risks and opportunities that are posed by the any crucial situation like here in Covid-19 phase. It additionally implies depicting how healthcare plans, medicinal services associations, and hospitals to be responsible to patients and society and, on the other hand, how people can take suitable responsibility for their own health.

References

1. Corona virus Outbreak. Available at: https://www.worldometers.info/coronavirus/. Accessed on 23 Feb 2020.
2. Ferry, M., Venkatasubramanian, G., Guérin, I., & Al Dahdah, M. et al. 2020. "The Covid-19 Crisis in India". *Dossier-Faces of Pandemic.*
3. K. Geetanjali, S. Aditi, J. Jyoti, N. Arindam, L. Ramanan. 2020, "COVID-19 in India : State-wise estimates of current hospital beds, intensive care unit (ICU) beds and ventilators", *A report—The Centre for Disease Dynamics, Economics & Policy,* New Delhi.
4. Li, Q., Guan, X., Wu, P., Wang, X., Zhou, L., Tong, Y., & Xing, X., 2020. "Early transmission dynamics in Wuhan, China, of novel coronavirus–infected pneumonia", *New England Journal of Medicine*. DOI: 10.1056/NEJMoa2001316, Vol. 1 January. Pp- 1199-1207
5. Price, C. "The UK Food System in the time of Covid-19". In chronicles-Covid-19.
6. Rajagopalan, S., & Tabarrok, A. 2020. "Pandemic Policy in Developing Countries: Recommendations for India". *Special edition, Policy Brief, Mercatus Centre, G M University.*
7. Singh, G. 2020. "Covid-19: Reserves to the rescue. *A report-Tata Centre for Development,* Uchicago.
8. Singhal, T., 2020. "A review of coronavirus disease-2019 (COVID-19)". *The Indian Journal of Pediatrics*, Vol. 87 March. pp. 1-6.
9. Somrita Ghosh. 2020. "COVID-19: Lack of PPE kits, doctors suffer". Available at- https://www.newindianexpress.com/cities/delhi/2020/apr/07/lack-of-ppe-kits-doctors-suffer-2126776.html

17

Impact of COVID-19 on Education System

Harpreet Kaur

The novel corona virus disease 2019 (COVID-19) has emerged in December, 2019 in Wuhan city of China when symptoms of respiratory illnesses followed by pneumonia were observed in most of the people belonging to seafood wholesale market (Zhu et al. 2020; Zhou et al. 2020). Subsequently, a large number of cases rapidly appeared indicating person-to-person transmission. Consequently, World health Organisation declared CoV epidemic in Wuhan in Hubei province 'a public health emergency of international concern' (PHEIC) and on March 11, 2020, World Health Organisation (WHO) announced COVID-19 as a pandemic (WHO[1], 2020). Unfortunately, the spread of this pandemic affected almost all the countries (WHO[2], 2020) developed as well as developing ones, mainly China, Europe, Iran, South Korea, and the United States which revealed the inadequate preparedness of all the wealthy nations to avoid these types of local outbreaks to become global health emergencies. Due to various development activities in this modern world such as new technological interventions, deforestations for the construction of dams and roads, mass migration of people to developed countries, high density population, globalisation of food and increase in the international travel have brought about ecological changes which facilitated the rapid spread of COVID-19 infection across intercontinental geographical limits (Tandon, 2020). Till March 29, 2020 the virus had spread to more than 177 countries and infected more than 722,435 patients, resulting in more than 33,997 deaths (Sahu, 2020). Additionally, there are still no vaccines or medicine available to protect the body from this disease.

Taking into consideration the rapid spread of COVID-19 pandemic, countries around the world have implemented measures to slow the transmission of coronavirus, from national quarantines to closure of educational institutions. To expand this, all the schools, colleges and universities took intensive measures to prevent the students and faculty members from this dreadful pandemic by postponing or cancelling the workshops, conferences, sports and other gatherings in their campus because social distancing is considered as the most useful method to interrupt the transmission of this virus. As per instructions given by WHO, national governments recommend the public for repeated hand hygiene, respiratory etiquettes, self-isolation or quarantine, social distancing and to work from home including teachers working in the educational institutions. As of March 25, 150 countries closed schools and educational institutions nationwide to breakdown the chain of transmission of COVID-19 infection which was the best possible solution to avoid infectious diseases ((Kawano & Kakehashi, 2015; Luca et al., 2018; Wheeler et al., 2010). As a result, over 91percent of the world's student population got affected with study loss and localised closures adopted by some countries impacted millions of additional learners. Colleges and universities initiated rapid transition of traditional face-to-face teaching to online teaching (Gewin, 2020, Lau et al., 2020) which adversely affected the global education system because countries were not prepared for this adverse situation especially some developing nations, facing lack of e-resources and not uptodate information and communications technology. With the passage of time, government and educational institutions tried to mitigate this problem and found various innovative teaching methods and resources. For instance, in India, ministry of education are encouraging the teachers and students to stay home and to facilitate distance learning from various resources such as Swayam, MOOC, NPTEL, e-PG pathshala, Swayamprabha, etc. However, remote teaching is a big challenge for government officials as in some areas, there is lack of technology and internet accessibility and due to global economy crisis, governments are unable to provide ICT tools to every student.

Review of Literature

The literature regarding novel corona virus disease 2019 (COVID-19) and its impact on global education system is compiled from various research articles, research papers as well as online sources as e-journals and various websites related to medical research and technology especially website of world health organisation and Indian Medical Research.

Objective of the Study

- To awaken the society towards causes and preventive measures of this infectious disease.

- To sensitise the government authorities about challenges faced by teachers as well as learners.
- To motivate the academicians to find some innovative solutions to mitigate the problems faced by students during remote learning.
- To overcome the impact of COVID-19 on the education system.
- To build resilience in our educational systems.
- To prepare the teachers and students for post-corona virus future of education.

Discussion

The severe and unprecedented impact of COVID-19 pandemic has hit the world at extreme level that governing bodies have the only solution to follow the recommendations of WHO during pandemic like public education and awareness, social distancing, home quarantine and travel restrictions (WHO, 2005). Therefore, several countries announced the lockdown in which there is temporary shutdown of industries, shopping malls, cinema halls, restaurant and large gatherings of people outside the home. In India, Prime Minister Narendra Modi ordered 21 days nationwide lockdown and further extended it till 3 May, consequently, ICSE, CBSE and other recognised boards postponed or cancelled examinations. Similarly, many top ranked colleges like MIT, Harvard, and Princeton have been closed and some standardized tests like GMAT, GRE, SATs, ACT delayed for uncertain time. It is pertinent to mention here that in this situation, education system is running on an untested and unprecedented level as many schools, colleges and universities moved online and the teachers have to become more tech savvy in a short period especially teachers related to language studies where effective communication play primary role. Undoubtedly, online teaching is not a new method of delivery for any faculty of college and university, nevertheless, some are still not techno-savvy to cope up with this mode.

At student level, the students living in remote areas have limited internet access and students belonging to underrepresented groups who do not possess smart phones, tablets and laptops, it has become a gigantic challenge to connect with their mentors. In addition, it is not a easy task to make arrangements properly to deliver courses according to the ability of different students, particularly the most vulnerable ones. Is it possible to do practical work at home without laboratories and equipments?

On the other side, it has become uncertain for teachers as well to teach students at home, their assessment and to provide them justifiable and unbiased grades. In concern to schools students, parents are feeling disrupted and stressful for their future and to teach the children at home during lockdown period. In this pandemic, lockdown and its extension has become a nationwide norm. On top of it, university graduates of year 2020 have experienced major teaching and assessment interruptions in the last semester of their studies, as a result, their careers might be severely affected due to major global recession created by a virus, COVID-19. If teachers conduct online tests, there are chances of cheating and it is difficult to examine the student individually (Watson & Sottile, 2010) and some students who do not have internet facility cannot participate in the evaluation process. Furthermore, the students studying abroad who could not travel to their home and due to closure of universities, they are studying from hostels and feel at high risk to get infected. Thus, future of many students is at risk and panic and fear to manage COVID-19 pandemic is continuously destroying the mental health of students.

To tackle the above mentioned issues, national governments tried to help students, teachers, parents and administrators by providing them various educational applications, e-resources and collaboration platforms for live-video communication such as Dingtalk, Hangouts meet, teams, Skype and Zoom. Additionally, for global education, various tools for teachers have been created for digital learning content as Thinglink, Nearpod, Buncee, Edpuzzle, etc. and various repositories for distance learning solutions. However, information and communication technology (ICT) can only be helpful if teachers are digitally literate. Secondly, there can be issue regarding the cost, supply, maintenance of the requisite infrastructure and other policies regarding effective ICT use including stable and affordable internet connectivity and security in terms of filters and site blockers. Taking into account the high cost of ICT tools, some schools have opted an approach called 'Bring your own device' in which students are allowed to bring their own smart phones, tablets, laptops, etc. However, all the families cannot afford the cost of these ICT tools, thus, these learning resources can widen the equity gaps among children. Even at the university level, institutions are unable to provide ICT services to all the students to provide equal education to all sections of society. This period (March, 2020) for education system will be unforgettable forever when the whole world is going through global learning crisis due to complete shutdown of schools, colleges and universities which will lead to the losses in learning, a tremendous increase in the number of dropouts and missed meals of about 320 million children, mostly belonging vulnerable households. The teaching and learning can be shifted to online mode but not the mid-day meals which will increase the ratio of children under malnutrition. Thus, food security is also one of the major issues related to education system.

To reckon with the challenges of education system, the government should take online feedback from students and should chalk out clear and concrete action plans to meet the demands of aspiring minds and to achieve the equity in education. Secondly, if situation of some students is not conducive to study then administrators should consider that what assurance can be offered to students for continuation of their study. All the educational institutions are trying to opt different approaches at their own level to make balance between their institution's reputation and welfare of individual students and to ensure the impartial gradation of students to enter into job market in their near future. There are so many ongoing concerns about COVID-19 pandemic although it is too early to see the direct impact of this pandemic because nobody knows that how long the present situation will continue. The outbreak of the corona virus will also affect the number of international students across the world that will directly hit the economy of prosperous nations in particular. Thus, the most difficult task for educational institutions will be managing the admissions for 2020-2021 academic year. American Council on Education estimated that the student enrolment for the coming academic year will turn down by 15 percent, including 25 percent drop in the number of international students. As a consequence, the higher education institutions will face considerable financial instability that could be troublesome for their coming future. Therefore, this is the time to pre-plan education strategies about post-Covid future of education; otherwise it would be very difficult to back-up the global education system.

Suggestions

- The government should find better possible solutions to uplift the education system in this critical situation.
- The government should provide free access of e-resources to all the students.
- The government should plan awareness programmes for digitisation and the use of online resources for teachers as well as students.
- The teachers should find some innovative ideas to connect and communicate with students in this pandemic.
- The government should make a pre-plan to deal with post-corona virus education strategies.

Conclusion

The outbreak of corona virus hit the world by plethora of means such as loss of economy, environment, health and many more sectors. However, global education system faced the digital divide at great level which put the future of millions of students at risk. COVID-19 has become a catalyst to innovate new resources for educational institutions, nevertheless, unpreparedness and rapid transition of in-person teaching to online teaching dramatically affected the education system of all the underdeveloped as well as prosperous nations. The outbreak of corona virus bring into light several innovations in the education system, however, level and quality of digital access is not accessible in some remote areas. Therefore, it is the need of the hour to design the plan of action to deal with the problem of global recession of education.

References

- Watson, G. & Sottile, J. 2010. "Cheating in the digital age: do students cheat more in online courses?". Available at: https://www.westga.edu/~distance/ojdla/spring131/ watson131. html. Accessed on March 9, 2020.
- Gewin, V. 2020. "Five tips for moving teaching online as COVID-19 takes hold". *Nature*. Nm, [Epub ahead of print]:10.1038/d41586-020-00896-7.
- https://www.aljazeera.com
- https://www.doe.in.gov
- https://www.downtoearth.org.in
- https://www.indiatoday.in
- https://www.thehindu.com
- https://en.unesco.org
- Kawano, S & Kakehashi, M. 2015. "Substantial impact of school closure on the transmission dynamics during the pandemic flu H1N1-2009 in Oita, Japan". *PLoS One*. 10: e0144839.10.1371/journal.pone.0144839.
- Luca, G.D., Kerckhove, K.V., Coletti, P., Poletto, C., Bossuyt, N., Hens, N. & Colizza, V. 2018. "The impact of regular school closure on seasonal influenza epidemics: a data-driven spatial transmission model for Belgium". *BMC Infect Dis*. 18: 29. Doi: 10.1186/s12879-017-2934-3
- Prakash, N. & Tandon. 2020. COVID-19: "Impact on health of people & wealth of nations". *Indian J Med Res*. Epub ahead of print DOI: 10.4103/ ijmr.IJMR_664_20. pp. 1-3.
- Sahu, P. 2020. "Closure of Universities Due to Coronavirus Disease 2019 (COVID-19): Impact on Education and Mental Health of Students and Academic Staff". *Cureus* 12(4): e7541. doi:10.7759/cureus.7541
- Lau, J., Yang, B. & Dasgupta, R. 2020. Will the coronavirus make online education go viral?https://www.timeshighereducation.com/features/will-coronavirus-make-online-education-go-viral. Accessed: March 24, 2020:

- Wheeler, C.C., Erhart, L.M. & Jehn, M.L. 2010. "Effect of school closure on the incidence of influenza among school-age children in Arizona". *Public Health Rep*. 125: 851-859. doi10.1177/003335491012500612
- World Health Organisation. 2005. *WHO checklist for influenza pandemic preparedness planning*. Geneva: WHO.
- [2]World Health Organisation. Coronavirus disease 2019 (COVID-19) Situation Report - 64. WHO; 2020. Available from: https://www.who.int/docs/default-source/ coronaviruse/situation-reports/20200324-sitrep-64-covid-19. pdf?sfvrsn= 703b2c4 0_2, accessed on March 25, 2020.
- [1]World Health Organisation. COVID-19 can be characterised as pandemic. WHO; 2020. Available from: https://www.who. int/dg/speeches/detail/who-director-general-s-opening-remarks-atthe-media-briefing-on-covid-19—11-march-2020, accessed on March 20, 2020.
- www.timeshighereducation.com
- Zhou, P., Yang, X.L., Wang, X.G., Hu, B., Zhang, L., Zhang, W., et al. 2020. "A pneumonia outbreak associated with a new coronavirus of probable bat origin". *Nature*. 579: 270-273.
- Zhu, N., Zhang, D., Wang, W., Li, X., Yang, B., Song, J. et al. 2020. "A novel coronavirus from patients with pneumonia in China, 2019". *N Engl J Med*. 382: 727-33.

18

Education in COVID-19: Challenges and Opportunities

Rekha

Coronaviruses are a large family of viruses which may cause illness in animals or humans. In December 2019, a new infectious respiratory disease emerged in Wuhan, Hubei province of China. It is named by the World Health Organisation (WHO) as COVID-19. 'CO' stands for corona, 'VI' stands for virus and 'D' stands for disease and 19 represents the year of its occurrence. COVID-19 is an infectious disease caused by the most recently discovered coronavirus. It has been categorised as a pandemic by the WHO. The most common symptoms of COVID-19 are fever, dry cough and tiredness. The onset of the Coronavirus pandemic globally has forced people into their homes to avoid any interaction with people and maintain social distancing (WHO, 2020).

Education in COVID-19

We are passing through a very tough phase in our life. Due to COVID-19, School, College and University education are being adverse. In this situation, many newly emerged burning issues stare at us and many alternatives will be forced to develop to substitute the old style of the education system. Due to COVID-19 pandemic, the online teaching-learning process has become more prevalent in India. This has led to the concept of 'Work from Home' and 'Study from Home' while the education sector is one of the sectors that have been affected by the virus. The COVID-19 has resulted in schools, colleges, universities shut all across the world. As a result, education has changed dramatically, with the distinctive rise of e-learning, whereby teaching is undertaken remotely and on digital platforms. During COVID-19, there are many platforms created to enable online education in India. These are supposed by the Ministry of Human Resource Development (MHRD), the National Council of Educational Research and Training (NCERT) and the Department of Technical Education. On the other hand, Google has introduced several initiatives for online education. Here's a look at what efforts Google has made for the same. Many educational institutions have shifted to online delivery of education using various online tools. Some are free and for others, one has to pay.

Review of Literature

Sood and Singh (2014) analysed both advantages and disadvantages of e-learning. According to them today the advancements in an internet support everything from textual form to streaming audios and videos. But there is a big gap between an instructor and a learner. Lone (2017) analysed with the digital India programme's vision to transform India into a digital empowered society and knowledge economy, the education sector in India is poised to witness major growth in the years to come. On the other hand, he also found various challenges for online learning i.e. lack of infrastructure and hardware facilities, lack of skilled manpower in rural areas and lack of ICT in government primary schools. Bhongade and Sarode (2018) found that through e-learning lot of opportunities can be captured but poor quality procurement practices are a barrier to growth and adoption. They also discussed that e-learning is growing at a very low rate in India as compared to the International market where it is been used at all levels. Jindal and Chahal (2018) found that online education can change the whole future scenario in education if it can be implemented in collaboration with industry, universities and government. On the other hand, innovations are required to design ways to increase the social skills of online learners. Ganai (2019) talked about various online initiatives to promote higher education are provided by the Ministry of Human Resource Development (MHRD) and the Department of Technical Education i.e. E-PATHSHALA, SWAYAM, MOOCs, NPTEL, NDL, E-GYANKOSH etc. He also discussed that through SWAYAM students of higher education from the backward rural areas can access teaching electronically. Nair (2020) found that the current crisis of online learning i.e. lack of access to quality education, lack of inclusive education and low focus on life skills. She also found that all subjects cannot be taught online especially practical.

Objectives of the Study

- To know the various opportunities of online education in COVID-19.

- To know the various challenges of online education in COVID-19.

Research Methodology

The universe of the present study is Jalandhar district of Punjab State. The present study is descriptive in nature. For the study purpose, both qualitative and quantitative methods are used for data collection. To achieve the objectives of the study, learners are selected from undergraduate classes from Trinity College Jalandhar. The reason behind selecting the undergraduate classes they are mature rather than senior secondary learners and they can able to tell the opportunities and challenges comprehensively.

Table 1: Sample Size Selected for Study

State	*District*	*College*	*Number of Learners*			*Total*
			(B.A.I)	*(B.A.II)*	*(B.A.III)*	
Punjab	Jalandhar	Trinity	25	25	25	75

Table 1 shows that sample comprises of 75 learners (25 students from each undergraduate class). Respondents are selected by simple random sampling. Primary data are collected through a questionnaire. Questionnaires are sent to learners through online platform. It is based on the objectives of the study.

The process of data collection is initiated from April-August 2020. In this period, observations are noted on the observational diary by getting information from the learners through online communication. After collecting the data, Questionnaires are edited to ensure the completeness of the responses to each question. For analyzing the data, only percentages are calculated. So, it is a great experience to talk with learners about various online tools and their opportunities as well as challenges.

Significance of the Study

As far as significance is concerned with the present study has both theoretical and practical significance. About practical significance, the findings of the present study prove fruitful for learners, teachers and software makers to make desirable softwares and apps for improvement of the higher education at a global level. On the other hand, the study focuses on quality education based on various online substitutes. The study will also help to access the role, awareness and participation of both teachers and learners on online platforms. It will be helpful to describe the challenges as well as opportunities faced by the learners. Thus, the present comprehensive study will help us to understand the challenges and opportunities of the learners regarding various online platforms.

It is observed that online platforms not only use in the time of COVID-19 even before this there was already high growth and adoption in education technology but there has been a significant surge in usages since COVID-19. During this period millions of the learners have got good opportunities through various online platforms. Here some are mentioned.

ZOOM

ZOOM is a cloud-based video conferencing service we can use to virtual meet with others either by video or audio-only or both. It is used for small, medium and large-sized teams meetings. It was launched in April 2011. After analyzing the data, it is found that 61 percent of the learners are favoured in the Zoom app. The reason behind that zoom app is easily connected with id or password rather than other apps. They can join any time in prescribed scheduled meeting or lecture. On the other hand, they observe that this app is working at the global level in various purposes like seminars, webinars, conferences, symposium and quiz etc. but for free users, the lacking of this app is based on only 40 minutes after this temporarily removed the 40 minutes limit for virtual classes, career counselling, meetings and mentoring. Since last month's Home Minister advisory that zoom is not safe, most institutes are reportedly shifting to other platforms.

GOOGLE MEET

Google Meet is also a video-communication service developed by Google. It is one of two apps that constitute the replacement for Google Hangouts, the other being Google Chat. It has very important features such as the unlimited number of meetings, video and audio preview, screen sharing with participants and messaging with participants. It was launched in 2017. After analyzing the data, it is found that 27 percent of the learners are favoured in Google Meet. According to the clarity of sound is must in this app and they can easily understand everything. On the other hand, they also respond that they can join with a single click on a prescribed link. There is no need to any id or password. This app has no limit and they can join with a long time.

GOOGLE CLASSROOM

Google Classroom is a free web service that schools and colleges can use to create and distribute lessons and grade assignments. Teachers can create an online classroom, invite students to the class then create and distribute assignments. Within the classroom teachers can track the students' progress. It was launched in August 2014. After analyzing the data, it is found that 12 percent of the learners favoured in Google Classroom. According to them by this app, they can see about their classrooms as well as their assignments and grades also.

There are some other online platforms which are provided to learners for online education but they are not aware of this. So, an effort is made to aware the learners about these online platforms such as:

MOOC

MOOC (Massive Online Courses) are free online courses available for everyone. It is a web-based distance learning programme that is designed for the participation of a large number of geographically dispersed students. It provides an affordable and flexible way to learn new skills and deliver quality educational experiences at scale. Millions of people around the world use MOOC to learn for a variety of reasons, including life-long learning, career development, e-learning and training. It was launched in September 2012.

E-PATHSHALA

The digital India campaign has prompted extensive use of ICTs in the teaching-learning process. The E-Pathshala, a joint initiative of Ministry of Human Resource Development (MHRD), Govt of India and National Council of Educational Research and Training (NCERT) has been developed e-resources including textbooks, audio, video and periodicals. The e-pathshala app is designed to achieve the student development goal (SDG). It was launched in November 2015.

SWAYAM

SWAYAM (meaning 'self') is an initiative launched by the Ministry of Education, Government of India under Digital India. It designed to achieve the three cardinal principles of Education Policy viz., access, equity and quality. The objectives of this effort are to take the best teaching-learning resources. The platform offers free access to everyone and hosts courses from 9 till post-graduation. It was launched in July 2017.

SWAYAM PRABHA

The SWAYAM PRABHA is another group of 32 DTH channels devoted to telecasting of high-quality educational programme on 24*7 basis using the

GSAT-15 Satellite. The contents are provided by UGC, CEC, IITs, NCERT, NPTEL and NIOS.

DIKSHA

The Government's DIKSHA platform offers teachers, students and parents learning material relevant to the prescribed school syllabus. Teachers have access to aids like lesson plans, worksheets and activities to create a classroom experience. Students among other things can access NCERT books for all classes. It was launched in September 2017.

At this moment we see that various opportunities on online platforms are provided by various ministries and by google in COVID-19 pandemic. Although online education is giving several opportunities to learners there are challenges also existing. Let's see the challenges observed by the learners.

Connectivity

Students in both rural and urban areas are struggling with the "homework gap" due to bad internet connection during online classes. On the other hand, most of the learners are experiencing technical difficulties because of the high usages rate of online learning systems. After analyzing the data it is found that 33 percent of the respondents say that they are not able to connect for their lectures due to low internet service.

Gadgets Shortage

After analyzing data, it is found that 28 percent of the respondents have not a personal gadget to use for online learning. Many of them are supposed to share the laptops and computers with their parents, sisters/brothers to say on track.

Physical Health Risks

After analyzing the data it is also found that 10 percent of the learners respond that they are surviving so many physical health risks such as eyestrain, headace, neck pain, back pain, muscles and joint injuries due to online education.

Computer Literacy

It is also found that 22 percent of the respondents agree with this opinion that for online learning the computer literacy is should be just because of without additional training, it's hard for teachers, students and parents to start using a learning management system (LMS) or any other digital tool.

Lack of Socialisation/Isolation

In online education most of the learners feel isolated, scared by the pandemic and friend's and instructor's disconnection. During the online lectures, it's hard to keep students engaged without a teacher's physical presence and face-to-face contact. Due to online education psychological factor is still highly affecting student's motivation and learning progress. 7 percent of the respondents respond that by online learning they feel isolated.

Conclusion

There are basically two phases of e-learning. In one phase e-learning is used for educational purpose and at other levels, it is been used for training. No doubt during COVID-19 there is so many platforms exit for online education. Through e-learning lot of opportunities can be captured and speedy development will possible. But if we see the whole picture from ground level we see that there are so many challenges also. So, the above data shows the opportunities as well as challenges faced by learners.

References

- Bhongade et. al. 2018. "Prospect of E-Learning in Indian Higher Education: Trends and Issues". *International Journal of Current Engineering and Scientific Research.* Vol. 5, No. 5 pp. 181-186.
- Ganai, Sintu 2019. "Online Programme in Higher Education in India: Challenges and Opportunities". *A Multidisciplinary Online Journal of Netaji Subhas Open University, India.* Vol. 2, No. 2 July, pp. 1-5.
- Jindal, Aman et. al. 2018. "Challenges and Opportunities for Online Education in India". *Pramana Research Journal.* Vol. 8, No. 4, pp. 104.
- Lone, Zahoor Ahmad 2017. "Impact of Online Education in India" *International Journal of Engineering Science and Computing.* Vol. 7, No. 7 July pp. 13951.
- Nair, Sulekha. 2020. "Online Education has a mountain of problems in India but it can become accessible, inclusive if states are more proactive". *First Post. July 8.*
- Sood, Manu and Singh Virender 2014. "E-Learning: Usage among Indian Students". *International Journal of Scientific & Engineering Research.* Vol. 5, No. 4, April pp. 1359.

Websites

- http://www.wbnsou.ac.in Assessed on 16 August 2020
- http://www.who.int. Assessed on 20 August 2020

- http://www.firstpost.com.Indianews Assessed on 25 August
- http://www.ijesc.org Assessed on 26 August
- http://www.ijser.org Assessed on 26 August
- http://www.pramanaresearch.org Assessed on 26 August
- http://www.ibsangsagcc.org Assessed on 26 August

Acknowledgements

I would like to show my gratitude to the Dr. (Mrs.) Jasmeet Sandhu, Retired Professor of Sociology from Guru Nanak Dev University Amritsar for sharing his pearls of wisdom with me during the research, and I thank my Director (Father Peter), Principal (Dr. Ajay Prashar) and colleagues from Trinity College, Jalandhar. Last but not least I would like to thank our family especially my husband Mr Rajinder Kumar for his insights and critics.

19

Changing Role of ICT Practices in Teaching and Learning During COVID-19 Pandemics

Roohi Sharma

In early era, we have seen that there has been a remarkable connect between human beings and technology. We humans have been continuously putting a lot of efforts in new innovations, technology advancements and its adoption. Digitalisation is rapidly increasing, it's everywhere and will keep on increasing. Also we all have seen how ICT has helped us during this pandemic whether it is availability of information or helping affected patients and helping students as well teaching during lockdown.

The Covid-19 pandemic outbreak forced many schools and colleges to remain closed temporarily. As social distancing is preeminent at this stage, this will have negative effects on learning opportunities. Educational units are struggling to find options to deal with this challenging situation. These circumstances make us realise that scenario planning is an urgent need for academic institutions. (Rieley, 2020). It is said that online mode of learning is easily accessible and can even reach to rural and remote areas also in this time of crisis. Combining face-to-face lectures with technology give rise to blended learning and flipped classroom. Students can learn anytime and anywhere. At this time, online learning serves as a panacea in the time of crisis.

The term ICT stands for Information and Communication Technology. Networking of computers gave birth to Information Technology. It includes computers, the internet, broadcasting technological, telephony etc. UNESCO consider information technology as "Scientific technological and engineering disciplines and management techniques used in information handling and processing, their application, computers and their interaction with men and machines, and associated social, economic and cultural matters."

Pelgrum and Law (2003) stated that near the end of the 1980s, the term 'computers' was replaced by 'IT' (information technology) signifying a shift of focus from computing technology to the capacity to store and retrieve information. This was followed by the introduction of the term 'ICT' (information and communication technology) around 1992, when e-mail started to become available to the general public. (Pelgrum and Law, 2003).

Changing Role of ICT in 21st Century's Teaching- Learning

- ICT helps teachers in both pre-service and in-service teachers training.
- ICT helps teachers to interact with students.
- It helps them in preparation their teaching, provide feedback.
- ICT also helps teachers to access with institutions and Universities, NCERT, NAAC, NCTE and UGC etc.
- It also helps in effective use of ICT software and hardware for teaching – learning process.
- It helps in improve Teaching skill, helps in innovative Teaching.
- It helps in effectiveness of classroom.
- It also helps in improving professional Development and Educational management as well as enhances Active Learning of Teacher Trainees.
- It is now replacing the ancient technology. As we know now-aday's students are always have competitive mind. So teacher must have the knowledge of the subject. This can be done through ICT.
- ICT helps teachers in preparation for teaching. In order to introduce ICT in pre-service teacher education different methods and strategies are applied. Different tools are used such as Word processing, Database, Spreadsheet etc.
- Various technology based plans are used to help the teachers for their practice teaching.
- ICT prepares teacher for the use of their skills in the real classroom situation and also make students for their future occupation and social life.

According to Yusaf (2005), "The field of education has been affected by ICTs, which has undoubtedly affected teaching, learning, and research." Voogt's Model of Pedagogy in the Traditional versus Information Society is worth mentioning here. Voogt (2003) and Tinio (2002) highlighted the grounded advantages of ICTs use in teaching-learning process while comparing it with Traditional Pedagogical approaches. By using ICT integrating methods and strategies to different aspects of learning one can promote more meaningful and congenial learning environment in terms of active, collaborative, creative, integrative as well as evaluative learning.

Overview of Pedagogy in the Traditional Versus Information Society

Table 1

Aspect	*Traditional pedagogy*	*Emerging pedagogy for the information society*
Active Learning	Activities prescribed by teacher Whole class instruction Little variation activities Pace determined by programme	Activities determined by the learner
Collaborative	Individual Homogenous groups Every one for him/herself	Working in teams Heterogeneous groups Supporting each-other
Creative	Reproductive learning Apply known solutions to problems	Productive learning Find new solutions to problems
Integrative	No link between theory and practice Separate subjects Disciplined based Individual teachers	Integrating theory and practice Integration between subjects Thematic Team of teachers
Evaluative	Traditional pedagogy	Emerging pedagogy for the information society

(As adapted by Voogt (2003) from (Voogt & Odenthal, 1997; Wijnenet. Al., (1999)

Tinio (2002) describes each of the pedagogic aspects in terms of implications for role of ICT uses in Teaching-learning Process as follow:

Active Learning

ICT-enhanced learning mobilises tools for examination, calculation and analysis of information in order to provide a platform for student inquiry, analysis and construction of new information. The learners therefore, learn as they do and, whenever appropriate work on real-life problems in-depth. Moreover, ICT makes the learning less abstract and more relevant to their life situations. In contrast to memorisation-based learning, this is the feature of traditional pedagogy; ICT-enhanced learning promotes increased learner engagement. ICT-enhanced learning can also be 'just-in-time' learning that the learners choose what to learn when they need. The role of a teacher is facilitator for learners.

Collaborative Learning

ICT-supported learning encourages interaction and cooperation among students, teachers, and expert regardless of where they are. Apart from modelling real world interactions, ICT-supported learning provides opportunity to work with students from different cultures, thereby helping to enhance learners teaming and communication skills as well as their global awareness. It models learning done throughout the learner's lifetime by expanding the learning pace to include not just peers but also mentors and experts from different fields. The role of a teacher is co-worker with learners as well as other fellow-teachers to create a congenial learning atmosphere for the learners.

Creative Learning

ICT-supported learning promotes the manipulation of existing information and the creation of real world products rather than the duplication of received information. The role of a teacher is creator/producer of new teaching-learning material to motivate the learners for new learning content.

Integrative Learning

ICT-enhanced learning promotes a thematic integrative approach to teaching and learning. This approach eliminates the artificial separation between the different disciplines and between theory and practice, which characterises the traditional approach. The role of a teacher is integrating the theory and practice for better output and enhancement of practical skills of the learners.

Evaluated Learning

ICT-enhanced learning is student-directed and diagnostic. Unlike static, text or print-based education, ICT-enhanced learning recognises the presence of different learning pathways to explore and discover rather than merely listen and remember. The role of a teacher is exploring and discovering the new and latest pedagogical and evaluated strategies. A thorough analysis of this models reflects one thing in obvious way that the changing role of ICTs practice teaching-learning process in integrated classroom has been undergoing a drastic shift and posed so many challenges and demands also upon in today situation of Covid-19 pandemic.

Online Learning during COVID-19 Pandemics

Most of the terms (online learning, open learning, web-based learning, blended learning etc.) have in common the ability to use a computer connected to a network, that offers the possibility to learn from anywhere, anytime, in any rhythm, with any means" (Cojocariu et al., 2014). Online learning make the teaching-learning process more student-centered, more innovative and even more flexible. Online learning is defined as "learning experiences in synchronous or asynchronous environment using different devices (e.g. mobile phones, laptops etc.) with internet access. In these environments, students can be anywhere (independent) to learn and interact with instructors and other students" (Singh & Thurman, 2019).

At present, this deadly virus spread such online platforms are needed where (a) video conferencing with at 40-50 students is possible, (b) discussions with students can be done to keep classes organic, (c) internet connections are good, (d) lectures are accessible in mobile phones and not just laptops, (e) possibility of watching already recorded lectures, and (f) instant feedback from students can be achieved and assignments can be taken (Basilisk et al., 2020).

Online learning appears to be a viable solution to fill in the void for classroom education for a period of three or four months while minimising the chances of any infection to students until classes resume. This will enable inclusive education by facilitating learning across diverse geographies in India. Moreover, it will provide an opportunity for educator to come up with customised learning solutions for every students. This online learning is more interesting, personalised and enjoyable. So, online teaching is no more an option, it is a Necessity in this global pandemic Covid-19. Betwixt all this online teaching and online learning can be termed as the panacea for the crisis. Online learning is emerging as a victor ludorum amidst this chaos. Therefore, the quality enhancement of online teaching-learning is crucial at this stage. Online education in Chinese Universities has increased exponentially after the Covid-19 outbreak. There was an overnight shift of normal classrooms into e-classrooms, that is, educators have shifted their entire pedagogical approach to tackle new market conditions and adapt to the changing situations. During this tough time, the concern is not about whether online teaching-learning methods can provide quality education, it is rather how academic institutions will be able to adopt online learning in such a massive manner (Carey, 2020).

There is a requirement of a quick shift to online learning mode; therefore, the products by Google can be really useful under such problematic situation; they are (a) Gmail, (b) Google Forms, (c) Calendars, (d) G-drive, (e) Google Hangouts, (f) Google Jam board and Drawings, (g) Google Classroom, and (h) Open Board Software (not a Google product, helps in recording meetings in the form of files). These tools can successfully be used as an alternative for face-to-face classes (Basilaia et al., 2020).

As we know changing role of ICT practices in teaching-learning P is the form of online teaching-learning process. Changing role means we shift face-to-face lectures to online classes. Online learning has many advantages in itself like digital learning, more learning engagement experience rather than the traditional learning and students get to learn the confines of their comfort zone. However, (ICT) online learning is not without it's limitations and challenges, since face-to-face interaction is usually perceived as the best form of communication as compared to the rather impersonalised nature of remote learning.

Problems Associated With Online Teaching and Learning

There are number of technologies available for online education but sometimes they create a lot of difficulties. Globally, online education has met with some success. In the case of India, we still have a long way to go before digital learning is seen as mainstream education, because students living in urban area have the facilities to opt for digital education, however, rural area students do not have the required infrastructure nor are financially strong to avail the resources required for digital education.

Not every student has a computer or fast streaming internet at home. This leads to issues with attendance and participation in online sessions. A survey of IIT Kanpur revealed that 9.3 percent of its 2,789 students were not able to download material sent by the Institute or study material. Only 34.1 percent of them had Internet connection good enough for streaming real-time lectures.

In a survey, Apporva Jha, a student of sociology at Delhi's Ambedkar University, highlights the issue of connectivity and Internet as a key challenge for most students. "Many students survive on 1 GB or 2 GB daily data plans on their phones not everyone has Wi-Fi at home and they have to manage their entire course work on that. Students feel lack of community technical problems and difficulties in understanding instructional goals are the major barriers for online learning (Song et al., 2004). In a study, students were found to be not sufficiently prepared for balancing their work, family and social lives with their study in an online learning environment. Students were also found to be poorly prepared for several e-learning competencies and academic-type competencies. Also, there is a low level preparedness among the students concerning the usage of Learning Management Systems (Parkes et al., 2014). There is a glaring disadvantages as examination have to be postponed. Examination cannot be conducted online. It is not only just the question of imparting continuous and uninterrupted learning during the outbreak of Covid-19 pandemic but also the most important challenge for the instructor is to focus on the overall elements of a well-developed course.

Possible Solutions for Problems

A lot of issues are attached to online teaching-learning but we cannot ignore its importance also specifically at the time of crisis. Technical problems can be solved through pre-recording video lectures, testing the content. One solution to this challenge is for the instructor to implement a learning environment that encourage collaboration. Providing learners with the opportunity to collaborate, share and create will increase the learner's use of various technologies, enhance their e-learning experience and support self-directed and ongoing learning (Clark and Mayer, 2011; Li & Irby, 2008). Student should be provided access to support devices that can help them solve technical problems via call, email or live chat. Students should pay attention to their instructor during the process of solving the issues. Personal attention should be provided to students so that they can easily adapt to this learning environment. Social media and various group forums can be used to communicate with students. Educators must spend a lot of time in making effective strategies for giving online instructions, which facilitate feedback from students, make learners ask questions and broaden the learner horizon for the course content (Keeton, 2004). Make sure there should be breaks set in the time table so that learners get relax in breaks set and also save their data. Institutions must focus on pedagogical issues and emphasise collaborative learning, case learning, and project-based learning through online instructions (Kim, Bonk, 2006).

The challenges to educational institutions in teaching-learning is not only finding new technology and using it but it also reimagining its education, thereby helping students and academic staff also who are seeking guidance for digital literacy then only they can use the technology effectively.

Objectives of the Study

1. To explore the changing role of ICT practices in teaching-learning in the time of crisis.
2. To explore the growth of online teaching-learning.
3. To conduct a strengths weakness opportunities and challenges analysis of online learning with changing role of ICT practices in teaching-learning and correlating it with Corona virus pandemic.

To give some suggestions for the success of online mode of teaching-learning using technology during a crisis like situation which is occurring presently.

SWOC Analysis of Online Teaching-Learning with Changing Role of ICT: Correlating it with COVID-19 Pandemic

A great deal of research and development has been conducted to bring Information and Communication Technology (ICT) to its present state of learning application. Although ICT has been an integral part of the National Curriculum for over a decade, some commentators argue that there is still no consistency in its use (Selwyn & Bullon, 2000).

In the last few years, e-learning has started gaining popularity in all over the world. Many course are provide affordable courses to students via Massive Open Online Courses (MOOC). Still, there are a lot of institutions in India were reluctant toward online teaching and learning process through ICT. If we correlate it with present situation, the challenges posed by the COVID-19 pandemic introduced everyone to a new world of online and remote teaching-learning process with the changing role of ICT practices in teaching-learning process. The SWOC Analysis of online teaching-learning as shown in figure 1. Also, to conduct smooth teaching learning programmes a list of online etiquettes was shared with students and proper instructions for attending classes were given to them (Saxena, 2020).

Strengths

There are many strengths of online teaching-learning, which is why it is becoming so popular. The most obvious are that it allows people to take classes regardless of where they live or what their schedules may be (often called "anytime, anyplace"). The asynchronous nature of the class allows students time for reflection and research and to compose their message with more thought. The learning experiences tends to become more student centred, resulting in students being for active participation and taking on more of the responsibility for learning. Teachers become more creative with their teaching.

STRENGTHS

- Any place
- Any time or pace
- Student cantered
- Access to resources
- Immediate feedback

WEAKNESSES

- Accessibility
- Limitations for hands-on learning
- Technical difficulties
- Distraction, anxiety & confusion

OPPORTUNITIES

- Convenience and flexibility
- User can be of any age
- Enriching experience and designing flexible programs
- Problem solving, critical thinking etc skill developed

CHALLENGES

- Encouraging collaboration
- Building a community of learner
- A knowledge and comfort in the use of technology

Note: SWOC – Strengths, Weaknesses, Opportunities & Challenges.

Figure 1: The SWOC analysis of OnlineTeaching - Learning During Such Crisis.

The Anywhere - anytime features of online learning is beneficial in the time of Covid-19 situation also. The technology provides innovative solutions at times of crisis to combat disruption and helps people to communicate and even work virtually without the need of face-to-face interaction. This leads to many system changes in organisation as they adopt new technology for interacting and working (Mark & Semaan, 2008).

Weakness

Online teaching-learning has certain weaknesses in the form that it can hamper the communication between the learner and the educator, that is, direct communication and human touch are not there. Even users can face so many technical difficulties and slow down the teaching-learning process (Favale et al., 2020). Online education is a response to the need for more accessibility to campus courses. And because of the asynchronous nature of the class it takes an independent, self-directed learner to be successful - one who will do the work without seeing the instructor at class every week. All students and learners are not the same, they vary in their capabilities and confidence level also. Some do not feel comfortable while learning online leading to increased frustration, anxiety and confusion.

Opportunities

Online teaching-learning, remote working and e-collaborations exploded during the outbreak of coronavirus crisis (Favale et al., 2020). This crisis will be a new phase for online teaching-learning process and will allow people to look at the fruitful side of e-learning (ICT) technologies. Teachers can practise technology and can design various flexible programmes for students better understanding. It will enhance problem-solving skills, critical thinking abilities among the students. In this critical situation, even users of any age can access the online tools and get benefit from it. It is beneficial for both teachers as well as students.

Challenges

Online teaching-learning process may faced many challenges. It is a challenge for institutions to engage students and make them participate in the teaching-learning. It is a challenge for teachers to move from offline mode to online mode, changing their teaching methodologies and managing their times. It is challenging to develop content which not only covers the curriculum but also engage the students (Kebritchi et al., 2017). And whenever some technical issues emerge, they find it difficult to solve the problem in such a scenario. They face difficulties with live classes, usage of appropriate icons, communication-related apps and websites, browsing study material etc. A step-by-step guide can be prepared by academic institutions that can guide the teachers and students on how to assess and use various e-learning tools and how to cover major curriculum content via these ICT technologies thereby reducing digital illiteracy. It is beneficial of educators complement their lectures with video chats, virtual meetings, and so on to get immediate feedback and maintain a personal connection with the students in a teaching-learning process.

One should not merely focus on the pros attached to the adoption of online teacher-learning process during COVID-19 but should also take account of developing and enhancing the quality of virtual courses delivered in such emergencies (Affounch et al., 2020).

Online Teaching-Learning for Teachers

Advantages

- Allows innovative methods of teaching with the help of technology and online tools.

- Allows reaching out to a large number of students across geographies.
- Especially useful for distance learning.

Disadvantages

- Online teaching takes time and practice.
- There is little consensus on how students can be evaluated in a fair manner.
- Inability to have a face-to-face connect with students and facilitate free conversations, discussions, and mentoring.
- Inability to reach all students because of technological limitations.

ONLINE TEACHING LEARNING FOR STUDENTS

Advantages

- The ability to learn using different online tools and methods.
- No disruption in learning because of the pandemic.
- Listening to recorded and live conversations and working at their own speed.

Disadvantages

- Lack of free flowing conversations, debates, and discussions.
- Technological difficulties related to weak devices or access to the internet.
- Getting used to learning and being evaluated online.
- Studying while living at home, with family and other distractions.

Conclusion and Suggestions

In short Information and Communication Technology (ICT) have profoundly influenced today's life in every walk. After the emergence of changing role of ICT practices in teaching-learning process, the whole world has become a global village where all activities related to human and material resources are utilised for optimum result. ICT facilitates self-pacing with increased capacities to deal with individual learning styles as students can work at the pace and intensity suitable to their needs.

As per the World Economic Forum, the Covid-19 pandemic also changed the way how several people receive and impart education. To find new solutions for our problems, we might bring in some much–needed innovations and change. It will be beneficial for the education section and could bring a lot of surprising innovations. We cannot ignore and forget the students who do not have access to all online (ICT) technology due to financial resources restrictions; therefore, they may lose out when classes occur online.They may lost out because of the heavy cost associated with digital devices and internet data plans. This pandemic has also taught us that students must possess certain skills such as skills of problem-solving, critical thinking and most importantly adaptability to survive the crisis.

Students can be in constant touch with their faculties with the help of online classes conducted through Skype, Zoom, Google Hangouts, Google classroom etc.. All these online applications making a lot of news because of its viable features. It allows conducting live online classes, web-conferencing, webinars, video chats and lives meetings. As most of the schools, colleges, universities, and companies are closed due to lockdown/ curfew and most of the people are working from home, these applications helped in keeping people connected via video conferencing. These applications is trending on Google play store amidst the ongoing crisis at present situation.

Disasters will continue to occur and technologies will likely help us cope with them (Meyer & Wilson, 2011). Reliability and sufficient availability of Information and Communication Technology (ICT) infrastructure, learning tools, digital learning resources in the form of Massive Open Online Courses (MOOC), e-books, e-notes and so on are of almost importance in such a situation (Huang et al., 2020). Instruction, content, motivation, relationships, and mental health are the five important things that an educator must keep in mind while imparting online education (Martin, 2020).

This will also reduce the stress, fear and anxiety levels of people. For this proper technique and learning support should be provided to teachers and students and Government support is also crucial at such stage. Online methods of teaching support and facilitate teaching-learning activities, but there is a direct need to weigh the pros and cons of technology (ICT) and harness its potentials.

ICT will also requires a modification of the role of the teacher, who in addition to classroom teaching, will have other skills and responsibilities. Some will become specialists in the use of distributed learning techniques, the design and development of shared working spaces and resources, and virtual guides for students who use electronic media. Ultimately, the use of ICT will enhance learning experiences for children, helping them to think and communicate creatively, and work collaboratively. It will also prepare our children for successful lives and careers in an increasingly technological world.

This is the time of learning and educating others and at the same time compating Covid-19 as well said by Michael Allen, "There are no refunds; learners cannot get their time back if waste it." Let's beat COVID -19 not learning.

References

- Affouneh, S., Salha, S., N., & Khlaif, Z. (2020). "Designing quality e-learning environments for emergency remote teaching in coronavirus crisis". *Interdisciplinary Journal of Virtual Learning in Medical Sciences, 11(2), 1-3.*
- Basilaia, G., Dgebuadze, M., Kantaria, M., & Chokhonelidze, G. (2020). "Replacing the classic learning form at universities as an immediate response to the COVID-19 virus infection in Georgia". *International Journal for Research in Applied Science & Engineering Technology, 8(III).*
- Baishakhi Bhattacharjee and Kamal Deb 2016. "Role of ICT in 21st Century's Teacher Education." *International Journal of Education and Information Studies* ISSN 2277_316Vol B, No. 1(2016), pp. 1-6.
- Brain A. Jacob 2016. "The opportunities and challenges of digital learning." Available at http://www.brookings.edu/research/the-oppertunities-and-challenges-of-digital-learning. Assessed on 29 August 2020.
- Carey, K. (2020). Is everybody ready for the big migration to online college? Actually, no. *The New York Times. https://www.nytimes.com*
- Clark, R., Mayer, R. E. (2011). *E-learning and the science of instruction* [electronicresource]: *proven guidelines for consumers and designers multimedia learning / Ruth Colvin Clark, Richard E. Mayer*. San Francisco, Calif. : Pfeiffer, 2011. Hall, B. (2013, May 17). Smartphones have bridged the digital divide [Web blog]. Retrieved from http://readwrite.com/2013/05/17/smartphones-have-bridged-the-digital-divide#feed=/author/brain-s-hall&awesm=~o9sE3cAylgBANm
- Cojocariu, V.-M., Lazar, I., Nedeff, V., & Lazar, G. (2014). "SWOT analysis of e-learning educational services from the perspective of their beneficiaries." *Procedia-Social and Behavioral Sciences, 116,* 1999–2003.
- Deepali Kasrekar & Gayatri Wadhavam-Tapaswi 2020. "Impact of Covid-19 on education system in India." Available at : http://www.latestlaws.com/articles/impactof-Covid-19-on-education-system-inIndia/. Assessed on 29 August 2020.
- Embide 2020. "Online Learning Challenges & Solutions." Available at : http://www.embide.com/exams/online_learning_challenges_and_solution/ .
- Favale, T., Soro, F., Trevisan, M., Drago, I., & Mellia, M. (2020). "Campus traffic and e- Learning during COVID-19 pandemic". *Computer Networks, 176, 107290.*

- Kebritchi, M., Lipschuetz, A., & Santiague, L. (2017). "Issues and challenges for teaching successful online courses in higher education". *Journal of Educational Technology Systems, 46(1),* 4–29.
- Keeton, M. T. (2004). "Best online instructional practices: Report of phase I of an ongoing study". *Journal of Asynchronous Learning Networks, 8(2),* 75–100.
- Khusboo Kuddus 2013. "Challenges Roles of Teachers with ICT in Teaching and Learning of English Language." Available at : http://www.eltweekly.com/2013/05/changing-roles-of-teachers-with-ict-in-teaching-and-learning-of-english-as-second-and-foreign-language-by-khushboo-Kuddus/ . Assessed on 28 August 2020.
- Kim, K.-J., & Bonk, C. J. (2006). "The future of online teaching and learning in higher education: The survey says". *Educause Quarterly, 4,* 22–30.
- Li, C., & Irby, B. (2008). "An overview of online education: Attractiveness, benefits, challenges, concerns and recommendations". *College Student Journal, 42(2),* pp. 449-458. Retrieved from http://proxy1.ncu.edu/login?url=http://search.ebscohost.com/login.aspx?direct=true&db=s3h&AN=32544879&site=eds-live
- Martin, A. (2020). How to optimize online learning in the age of coronavirus (COVID-19): A 5-point guide for educators. https://www.researchgate.net/publication/339944395_How_to_Optimize_Online_Learning_in_the_Age_of_Coronavirus_COVID-19_A_5-Point_Guide_for_Educators.
- Mark, G., & Semaan, B. (2008). "Resilience in collaboration: Technology as a resource for new patterns of action". In B. Begole & D. W. McDonald (Eds.), *Proceedings of the 2008 ACM Conference on Computer Supported Cooperative Work* (pp. 127–136). *Association for Computing Machinery. https://doi.org/10.1145/1460563.1460585*
- Meyer, K. A., & Wilson, J. L. (2011). *Online journal of distance learning administration* (vol. IV, no. I). University of West Georgia, Distance Education Center.
- Parkes, M., Stein, S., & Reading, C. (2014). Student preparedness for university e-learning environments. *The Internet and Higher Education, 25, 1–10. https://doi.org/10. 1016/j.iheduc.2014.10.002.*
- Pelgrum, W. J., Law, N. (2003). "ICT in Education around the World: Trends, Problems and Prospects UNESCO-International Institute for Educational Planning". Retrieved from www.worldcatlibraries.org/wcpa/ow/02d077080fcf3210a19afeb4da09e526.html.
- Preeti Kanwar 2020. "Role of ICT during Covid-19 outbreak." Available at: http://www.digianalysys.com/role-of-it-during-covid-19-outbreak/ . Assessed on 26 August 2020.
- Rieley, J. B. (2020). Corona Virus and its impact on higher education. Research Gate. Save the Children. (2014). No child left behind, Education in crisis in the Asia-Pacific.
- Sarah Farooqui 2020. "Education in the time of Covid-19: How institutions and students are Coping." Available at: http:/www.business-standard.com/article/education/education-in-the-time-of-Covid-19-how-institutions-and-students-are-coping-120043001575-/html.

- Saxena, K. (2020). Coronavirus accelerates pace of digital education in India. EDII Institutional Repository.
- Singh, V., & Thurman, A. (2019). "How many ways can we define online learning? A systematic literature review of definitions of online learning (1988-2018)". *American Journal of Distance Education, 33(4),* 289–306.
- Song, L., Singleton, E. S., Hill, J. R., & Koh, M. H. (2004). "Improving online learning: Student perceptions of useful and challenging characteristics", *The Internet and Higher Education, 7(1),* 59–70.
- Steve Wheeler 2001. "Information and Communication Technology and the Changing Role of the Teacher". *Journal of Education Media,* Vol. 26, No. 1, 2001."
- Tinio, V.L. (2002). ICT in education: UN Development Programme. http.www.eprmers.org
- UNESCO (2002) "Information and Communication Technology in Education– A Curriculum for Schools and Programme for Teacher Development. Paris: UNESCO. UNESCO, (2002), 'Open and Distance Learning Trends, Policy and Strategy Considerations',14 UNESCO.
- Voogt. J. (2003). "Consequences of ICT for aims, contents, processes, and environment of learning". In *J. van den Akker.* W. Kuiper & U. Hameyer (Eds.). *Curriculum landscapes and trends.* Dordrecht: Kluwer Academic Publishers.
- Yusuf, M.O. (2005). "Information and communication education: Analyzing the Nigerian national policy for information technology". *International Education Journal* Vol. 6 No. (3), 316-321. http://academic.son.wiseedu/wistree/archive/onlinelearning/Strengths.htm.

20

COVID-19-A Pedagogical Development

Amanpreet Kaur

The present outbreak of Covid-19 constitutes a public health emergency. Corona virus is a huge congregation of various types of viruses. Some of them are the reason behind the common cold in humans, while some cause infectious diseases in animals like bats and cattle. Coronavirus disease 2019 or COVID-19 is a disease that occurs due to severe acute respiratory syndrome (SARS).World Health Organisation got its first report on December 31, 2019.WHO declared the COVID-19 outbreak a global health emergency on January 30, 2020.On March 11, 2020 it was designated as a global pandemic by WHO. Earlier than this, H1N1 influenza was declared a pandemic in 2009.

International centers for disease are monitoring this infectious disease. In this disease, one gets infected when we come in contact with the saliva of infected patients. The COVID-19 is a transmitted disease through oral fluids as droplets and aerosol. The transmission of disease is caused with the droplets that fall during human respiratory activities as sneezing, coughing and talking. Aerosols are generated during the clinical procedures. Covid-19 effects the respiratory system in the lower and upper track and enter in the body through oral cavity (Zhou, 2020). COVID-19 other pathway is from mouth as an oral cavity specific exudates that contains local proteins (Silva, 2013). And next pathway of this infectious disease is major and minor salivary glands (Liu, 2011).

The mortality rate of this virus is into its initial stage was considered to be 2 percent but actual WHO estimated it to be 3-4 percent (Worldmeter, 2020) and in some countries like Indonesia its 8 percent (Crawfoed, 2020). In comparison with other viruses like SARS and MERS that has mortality rate of 10 percent and 34 percent, COVID-19 has 3-4 percent till the date (Worldmeter, 2020). But COVID-19 is a new type of virus. At present humans are not immune to it and moreover no vaccine exists that could be used to prevent its infection. Antibiotics cannot be used as a treatment because it is a viral infection.

This health emergency leads to most governments around the world for closure of the educational institutions. Its predicted that with that if the schools/colleges/Universities will get closed then the effect of COVID-19 will be 2-4 percent lesser than it could as till date it's more important to break the chain with the help of preventive measure of social distancing (Worldmeter, 2020). But this pandemic is impacting around 91 percent of the students in the world. It is stated that it affected 1,576,021,818 learners, 91.3 percent of total enrolled learners and 188 country-wide closures of these institutions. So keeping in mind the great loss, student's alternative learning has become priority of the education ministry globally. UNESCO, a global body is providing support to the countries to alleviate the impact with new pedagogical developments using remote learning (UNESCO, 2020) as depicted in Table 1.There are list of technological resources that can help the students, teachers and administrators in this time of crisis. The university around the countries has switched on to the concept of remote site learning concepts.

Table 1: Technological Resources

Digital Learning Technologies		Video conferencing Platforms	
Century Tech	Micro lessons for math's, science and English.	Dingtalk	It also manages attendance track, calendar and instant messaging
classDojo	Connects teachers and students	Lark	Cloud Storage in Japanese, Korean, Italian and English
Edmoda	Manage classroom and engage students	Teams	Integrated with Microsoft Office software
Edraak	Arabic language course	Zoom	Cloud Platform for conferencing
EKstep	Open learning Platform	Hangouts Meet	Integrated with Google G-Suite tools
Google classroom	Connect classes and communicate with teachers and students	Skype	Videoand other collaboration and audio calls
Moodle	Open learning platform to create your own site	MOOC (Massive Open Online Course)Platform	
Nafham	Arabic language online learning platforms	Alison	Available in English, French, Spanish, Pertuguese Language
Paper Airplanes	Video conferencing platforms.	Canvas	Course Catalogue free for teachers
Schoology	Learning, Grading, collaboration and assessment tool.	Coursera	Taught by instructors from recognized universities and Companies.

(Contd...)

Seesaw	Digital learning Resources	EdX	For educational institutions
Skooler	Tools to turn Microsoft Office software into an education platform.	Future Learn	To build professional skills with help of experts
Tools For Teachers to Generate E-content		External repositories	
Thinglink	Tools to create interactive multimedia resources	Brookings	Digital content
Buncee	Supports the Creation and sharing visual contents	Common wealth of Learning	List of resources to learn during closure
EdPuzzle	Video lesson creation software	Education Nation	Learning solutions
Kaltura	Video management and creations	Global Business Coalition For Education	List of e-learning Platforms
Nearpod	Software to create lessons	Keep learning Going	Free tools for teaching online
Squigl	It transforms speech or text into animated videos	EdSurge	Distance learning resources till secondary
Learning content			
Byzu's	Application with huge repositories of e-content	Khan Academy	Free online lessons, also used to track student progress
Mind spark	Online tutors to learn mathematics	You tube	Repository of educational video's
British Council	Application for learning English language	Code.Org	Coding resources available
Code it	Application to learn basic Programming	Polyup	Learning content for mathematics

Methodology of the Study

This paper adopts a desktop analysis and considers all the information from the high quality of research papers, newspaper and websites. The data of countries are gathered from of research papers and other government sources. The motive of author is to provide transparent information. We tried to discuss the criteria followed by both the developed and under developed countries and their universities. We tried to focus on the country it got originated and followed by the countries with high cases of COVID-19 epidemic.

How UNESCO Responded?

UNESCO is working along with the education ministry to support students through other means of learning. UNESCO for this global education coalition supported the distance learning by defining technical assistance up to anyway. For inclusive education webinars are organised to share the information. UNESCO supported the students, teachers and parents by helping them in selecting technological resources available.

Obstacles in Digital learning?

UNESCO report stated that 25 percent of student population is not able to access computer. 45 percent of teachers reported that they are naïve to ICT resources, as they never used it earlier. So before taking these points into consideration mentoring is required (UNESCO, 2020). Online courses available should be multilingual and have open access. Countries like India, Brazil and many more are facing with the problem of poor internet connectivity. No such mechanism is opted for the slow learners in remote learning. The digital learning is not as effective as face-to-face learning that has feedback and follows up mechanism for slow learners. There is no surety whether the students are actually studying or spending time on the systems.

How the students are responding to it and its affects?

- First and foremost, the students are not used to online studies. So they find it difficult to carry on while some of them don't take it seriously.
- Online study is complex issues than blackboard concept.
- The economic condition of some families is such that they can't afford the required gadgets and internet access. The students and parents have to struggle with the limited resources that they have.
- Another hurdle is the speed of internet due to network's congestion, so the continuity of learning process receives a setback.
- There are frequent power cuts due to the harvesting season's the disturbed power supply becomes a hindrance in the success of online education.
- The students don't get the learning environment at home. So the assimilation of the content remains incomplete.
- It is hard to cover the entire material and moreover some of the students are not able to comprehend it to the full because the assimilation capacity varies from person to person.
- The students are not able to stick to their daily routines thereby making the success of online education doubtful.

- Moreover the students remain devoid of the benefits of practical studies because only the theoretical work could become possible in this scenario.

Few Other Issues

1. As many students depend on the meal provided to students at school which lead to poor nutrition level in the students.
2. It also leads to high economic cost on online learning that will affect the dropout rates of the children.
3. The social isolation faced by the students during this time will have adverse effect on their health as more cases of depression could be aroused.
4 It increases the pressure on parents with lesser education and least knowledge of computer and it can distract the student mind.

How countries responded?

Crawford *et al.* has detailed about countries and higher education scenario during this pandemic. In Australia when the students were reported with the positive test of COVID-19, some universities started sanitising activities and majority moved up with the online learning or alternative forms of learning. It included face-to-face classes not beyond the gathering of 500 people, than changed to 100 people as the government changed the banned norms in the country. These classes were conducted in the form of groups on alternative days. Some of the universities in country adopted the online medium but those who didn't have significant effects.

German as one of the developed country is also among the most affected countries from these pandemics. The university of Passau (Bavaria) suspended the face-to-face teaching ,written examination was conducted in the mean time but oral examination got suspended. They did not relied upon Skype, face time and other technologies as has no legal basis. The universities like Lower Saxony's suspended the teaching but with virtual environment carried out committee meetings.

America's first case was suspected in the month of February but the higher education does not respond till late March so the infection rate increased rapidly and cases surpassed than China. Harvard University announced on 10 March. Yale, Princeton, Stanford, and the University of California also moved with online delivery of courses. Southern Oregon University announced on 19 March to deliver for remote education. Whilst some websites by mid-March were reporting only 5 percent of the higher education institutions had decided to move to online classes.

Italy reported positive with the first case of COVID-19 on 31 January. The cases in the north of Italy increased by 22 February and later the government imposed the quarantine in the numbers of related cities but citizens did not followed it and continued to travel. The Italian Minister of University announced the closure of schools/Colleges and followed the online lessons conducted using Skype. The universities of Bologna, Turin, and Milan and even the polytechnics institute set up remote learning and teaching with examinations especially via Webex. The Turin University with diverse 155 courses have more than 2500 conferencing session and 3500 academician with their recorded material. The University of Catania, Sicily has carried the concept of e-learning. The government planned the mobility programmes for the students conducted under project Erasmus.

China was the first country with positive cases of COVID-19, so it had very little time to prepare with higher education sector during this time slot. New York University Shanghai started online classes from 17 January, Zhejiang University and Duke Kunshan University from 24 February and Shanghai Jiao Tong University reported their first online class on 1 March.

United Kingdom level of risk is high in England as the first UK case of virus detected in the Chinese student of University of York. The British government declared a nationwide closure on public gatherings. The employees and employers followed the social distancing and isolation. Later on 25 March, the Prime Minister declared national emergence and isolated public at their own homes for 3 weeks, during that time universities-Scotland's University, University of Hull and Exeter shifted to online learning and delivery of content. Admission to the university got affected by this epidemic and even exams got postponed. In the meantime students created their volunteers group to support the fellow students and other communities.

Egypt has also declared closure of educational institutes in the country and opted with the technological resources to upgrade the students using Moodle, Microsoft team software and class notes. For face-to-face interaction they used the technology of Zoom and Blackboard in the British university of Cairo.

Jordan is among the one of the country that got strongly affected with this epidemic. The country has closed all its borders to prevent the virus to spread. Jordan imposed curfew and moved with the concept of online delivery of the content. The teaching got digitised from the chalk board towards web based repository. During this crisis the lectures were broadcasted using skype, face book, Google class room and moodle, Jordan universities are required to provide the Ministry of Higher Education and Research with the number of courses converted to online media and the number of students who log on to a university's online learning platforms.

Hong Kong, as this city is very close to the originated country of COVID-19 and has 1048 numbers of confirmed cases (Worldmeter, 2020) that is relatively lower than China, Italy and America. As the action taken by the government is on time from 27 January with closure to schools/ colleges and even other gatherings got suspended. The government announced the conduct of online classes. Consequently, the universities of Hong Kong provided the students with the online training to the staff and students by creating videos and teaching guides by conducting online workshops to facilitate the staff and students to use online resources.

Indonesia government cancelled the national exams that were to be scheduled on 30 March. The University of Indonesia in Depok and Gajah Mada University in Yogyakarta have closed their campuses and staff are delivering training online. Whilst the University of Indonesia has published a prevention protocol. The high ranked university of country Universitas Indonesia also recommended for online learning from 16 March.

Brazil has reported 5812 cases despite of taking precaution in which passengers are checked at the port and also asked to sign the declaration form. Further the health minister has also declared the 8 years of prison on violations of the quarantine. As a preventive measure in Latin America all the mass events got cancelled. The University of São Paulo (USP) in Brazil announced a committee to monitor COVID-19. At present, USP remains open and the Institute of Tropical Medicine team is investigating the genomic diversity of the virus that infected two patients in Brazil. The Laboratory of Immunology at Incor (Heart Institute) at the Medical School of USP is developing a vaccine against COVID-19.

India has taken a protective measure by implementing lockdown nationwide, as it has large population and poor health system. So the spread of COVID -19 has forced educational institutions for campus closure and move to the technological resources like Coursera and provided the student with online learning resources (New Indian Express, 2020). The educational ministry and university grants commission has provided the faculty and students with the SWAYAM PRABHA, Information and library network (INFLIBNET) and Consortium for educational communication (CEC) educational portals in digital platform (India today, 2020) as listed in Table 2. Despite of all these pedagogy Ministry of Human Resource Development has generated E-content like NPTEL, Virtual Labs, Talk to teacher, Spoken tutorials, E-Yantra, Quantum and Nano computing, ERP mission, ISLERS, Oscar++, Fossee, E-kalpa, Pedagogy project and SOS tools with the aim that education should not stop (MHRD, 2020). State governments are also putting their efforts to engage the students at home with the programme as "Mo Prativa", "Ambassador of hope". These initiatives were taken by the government of Odissa, Punjab and even other states are following it too. These online programmes used the ICT as medium to engage the students. It is an online cultural event for the students to explore their talent and to engage the students in their free time (India Today, 2020).

Table 2: Educational Platforms

Educational portals	*Platforms used*
Swayam Online Course	Provides teaching learning resources
MOOCs	Learning Material for Undergraduate and post graduate
e-PG Pathshala	e-content containing 23000 modules
e-content courseware in UG subjects	Modules of e-content on CEC site
Swayamprabha	A group of 32 DTH Channel
CEC-UGC youTube channel	A free educational curriculum
National Digital Library	A digital repository.
Sholdhganga	A digital repository of theses and dissertation for Ph.D students
e-Shodh Sindhu	Access to peer reviewed journals
Vidhwan	A database of experts

Conclusion

This paper highlighted the COVID-19 responses by UNESCO and some of the developed countries and developing countries that lead towards the technological resources in this time of quarantine. Universities in countries moved from face-to-face teaching to digitised world a pedagogical development in the education system. But it's very hard to follow this digitized education as it has number of hurdles to be faced by students, teachers and parents.

References

- Crawford, J., Butler-Henderson, K., Rudolph, J., & Glowatz, M. 2020. "COVID-19: 20 Countries' Higher Education Intra-Period Digital Pedagogy Responses". *Journal of Applied Teaching and Learning*, Vol. 3, No. 1.
- Liu, L., Wei, Q., Alvarez, X., Wang, H., Du, Y., Zhu, H., ... & Lackner, A. 2011. "Epithelial cells lining salivary gland ducts are early target cells of severe acute

respiratory syndrome coronavirus infection in the upper respiratory tracts of rhesus macaques". *Journal of virology*,Vol. 85, No. 8, pp. 4025-4030.

- Silva-Boghossian, C. M., Colombo, A. P. V., Tanaka, M., Rayo, C., Xiao, Y., & Siqueira, W. L. 2013. "Quantitative proteomic analysis of gingival crevicular fluid in different periodontal conditions". *PloS one*, Vol. 8, No. 10.
- Viner, R. M., Russell, S. J., Croker, H., Packer, J., Ward, J., Stansfield, C & Booy, R. (2020). "School closure and management practices during coronavirus outbreaks including COVID-19: a rapid systematic review". *The Lancet Child & Adolescent Health.*
- Wang, D., Hu, B., Hu, C., Zhu, F., Liu, X., Zhang, J., ... & Zhao, Y. 2020. "Clinical characteristics of 138 hospitalised patients with 2019 novel coronavirus–infected pneumonia in Wuhan, China". *Jama*, Vol. 323, No. 11, pp. 1061-1069.
- Zhou, P., Yang, X. L., Wang, X. G., Hu, B., Zhang, L., Zhang, W., ... & Chen, H. D. 2020. "A pneumonia outbreak associated with a new coronavirus of probable bat origin". *Nature*, Vol. 579, No. 7798, pp. 270-273.
- Zhu, N., Zhang, D., Wang, W., Li, X., Yang, B., Song, J., & Niu, P. 2020. "China Novel Coronavirus Investigating and Research Team. A novel coronavirus from patients with pneumonia in China, 2019". *N Engl J Med,* Vol. 382, No. 8, pp. 727-733.
- Corona virus Outbreak. Available at: https://www.worldometers.info/coronavirus/ . Accessed 12 May 2020.
- India Today coronavirus update. Available at https://www.indiatoday.in/education-today/news/story/coronavirus-outbreak-top-5-education-highlights-of-the-day-1662875-2020-04-03. Assessed on 25April 2020.
- India Today Education System. Available at https://www.indiatoday.in/education-today/featurephilia/story/ugc-students-teachers-utilise-time-online-learning-1660021-2020-03-26. Assessed on 25April 2020.
- Ministry of Human Resources and Development. Available at https://mhrd.gov.in/e-contents. Assessed on 25April 2020.
- New India Express education during COVID-19.Available at https://www.newindianexpress.com/cities/delhi/2020/mar/21/education-in-the-times-of-covid-19-and-how-to-keep-up-with-studies-2119688.html. Assessed on 24 April 2020.
- UNESCO. Available at https://en.unesco.org/covid19/educationresponse . Assessed on 23 April 2020.

21

Impact of COVID -19 on Psychology of Students and Their Experience in Lockdown

Sharnjeet Kaur

The outbreak of COVID-19 in Wuhan, China, at the end of 2019, was a significant general wellbeing crisis that had the quickest spread, and the most difficult to prevent. WHO declared Novel Coronavirus Disease (COVID-19) outbreak as an epidemic and repeat the call for nations to take immediate steps and minimize the communication to save human's lives. According to the report of WHO, there has been now 1.3 million people have been infected, and almost 80,000 people have lost their lives till April 29, 2020. On 30 January, India announced its first instance of COVID-19 that was found in Kerala, which rose to three cases by 3 February; all were students who had come back from Wuhan, China. No huge ascent in cases was found in the remainder of February. On 4 March, 22 new cases became visible, including those of an Italian vacationer bunch with 14 contaminated members. After that transmission of COVID-19 raised during March, after a few cases were accounted for everywhere throughout the nation, the vast majority of which were connected to individuals with a movement history to influenced nations. On 12 March, a 76-year-elderly person who had come back from Saudi Arabia turned into the main casualty of the infection in the country. In India, according to the Ministry of Health & Family Welfare (MoHFW), a total number of 31332 cases of COVID-19 have been reported till April 29, 2020. To reduce the spread of the infection, several schools and higher educational institutions have been closed down. According to the UNESCO report, there are more than 157 crore students across 191 countries all over the world which are affected by COVID-19 outbreak. In India, more than 32 crore students have been affected by nationwide lockdown, which was announced by Prime Minister Narendra Modi on 25 March. In India, to reduce the transmission of Covid-19, schools and colleges have been closed for over a month now. All educational institutions in the country will remain shutting down till 3 May, after Prime Minister extended the nationwide lockdown by 19 days. Nationwide Lockdown has affected academic activities at many levels, including the postponement of board exams, college exams and even entrance exams such as the Joint Entrance Examination (JEE) for engineering and National Eligibility and Entrance Test (NEET) for medical, among others. During this period, online classes of students are being held at home. To continue learning of students, the Union Ministry of Human Resource Development has made numerous online learning opportunities, including online portals and academic channels through Direct to Home TV so that students can access from homes. To keep the brain of understudies ticking during the lockdown, online platforms that used are, The SWAYAM Moocs courses are online multi-media courses structured particularly for students in the advanced education segment, E-PG Pathshala is another stage on which digital books upto PG level can be gotten to, Digital Infrastructure for Knowledge Sharing (DIKSHA), CBSE PODCAST, National Digital Library of India, IIT Pal, Vidwan, Shodh Sindhu, E-Classes on Swayam Prabha, DTH Channels, UMANG versatile application etc. By making good use of these online platforms, they can enhance their skills also. During this period, online teaching is only one of the ways. In India, the computerised move is moderately new. In India, however in Asia too. The main Asian Massive Open Online Course (MOOC) was created by the Hong Kong University of Science and Technology in the year 2012 in particular. Indian Colleges will set aside some effort to deal with the change and be available to the new strategies as the methodology of the teaching framework here is a lecture-based approach to teaching. Digital teaching is increasingly understandable in schools and the school students/teachers/parents are progressively OK with this methodology when compared with advanced education system in India. Due to the outbreak of COVID-19, web based teaching has become a need, for schools, Colleges and Universities in India as well as globally to search for creative activities in a brief timeframe. Although there are numerous online portals to benefit the students by Union Ministry of Human Resource, but online learning reflects some problems and also effect on mental status of students. For example, students mostly face self-discipline, lack of direct interaction with teacher, lack of company from other students; feel overburden as compared to traditional education.This study, therefore, aims to determine mental status about online learning among undergraduate students.

Survey and Data Collection

The study was online survey in which the students of Guru Nanak College for Girls, Sri Muktsar Sahib were participated and was led from April 23, 2020 to April 25, 2020. The target students were all students of B.Sc. Non-Medical and B.Sc. Medical studying in the college. The student's age was in between 17 to 21.The study was conducted by using a simplified, structured, self-administered questionnaire. A questionnaire was constructed according to the aim of study. The questionnaires were built by using Google Forms on Google Docs. Total no. of questions which asked to the students were 12 related to their classroom study loss, experiences of online study for the first time in this critical pandemic situation and their future plans in the post-COVID period. Questions were sent through a link on Whatsapp groups of B.Sc. I, II, III Non-Medical and Medical students. For each question, there were potential choices. All the questions were required; they were able to submit the form only by giving the answers of all the questions. Prior to sending the inquiries, a short clarification of the study was given to the students. Students were told not to talk about the inquiries with their classmates and present the structure based on yourself. Time taken to collect the data was 3 days and complete data were collected on April 25, 2020 through Google Docs. Average time to fill the form by students ranged from 5-10 minutes. Analysis of collected data was done by using pie and bar charts in the spreadsheets of Google Docs.

Data Analysis

Out of 80 students, only 75 students completed the questionnaire (response rate of 94 percent).

Figure 1 shows the response of students regarding the question which learning method is more effective to gain the knowledge? Classroom learning is progressively useful because of a persistent interconnection among students and teacher, as it encourages students to dispose of their fears in regards to tests, which can once in a while occur with online learning. Out of 75 students, 65 students (86.7 percent) were keen on Classroom learning and just 10 (13.3 percent) students gave the alternative web based learning.

Figure 2 shows number of students faces challenges during online learning. There were five options of this question (Technical Problems, Poor Concentration, Computer Literacy, Time Management, and Self-Motivation). Time management and poor concentration are difficult task for students, as online learning requires a lot of time and intensive work. Out of 75 students , 24 (32 percent) students mostly has lack of concentration

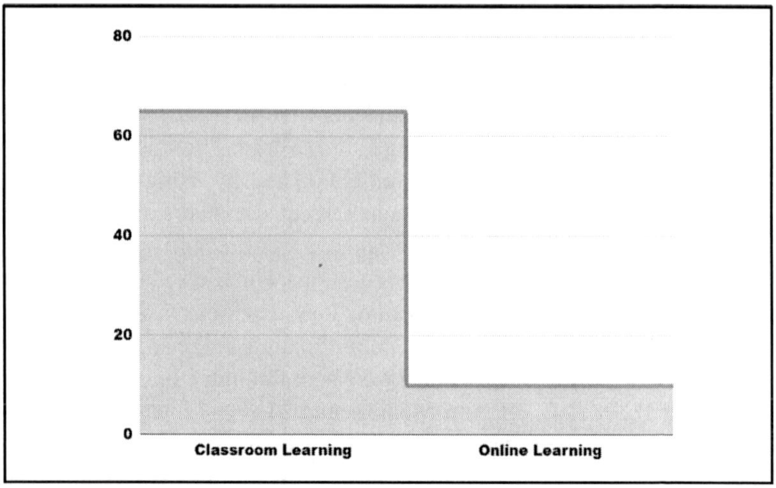

Figure 1: Count of students which learning is more effective to gain the Knowledge.

at home, 22 (29 percent) students find problem of time management to complete their assignments as given by their teachers, 15 (20 percent) students are not provided with the strong internet connection that online learning require, and thus fail to continue their classes especially in rural areas. Their learning experience becomes challenging, 13 (17.3 percent) students concurred that self-inspiration is a basic prerequisite, just 1 (1.3 percent) face the issue PC proficiency.

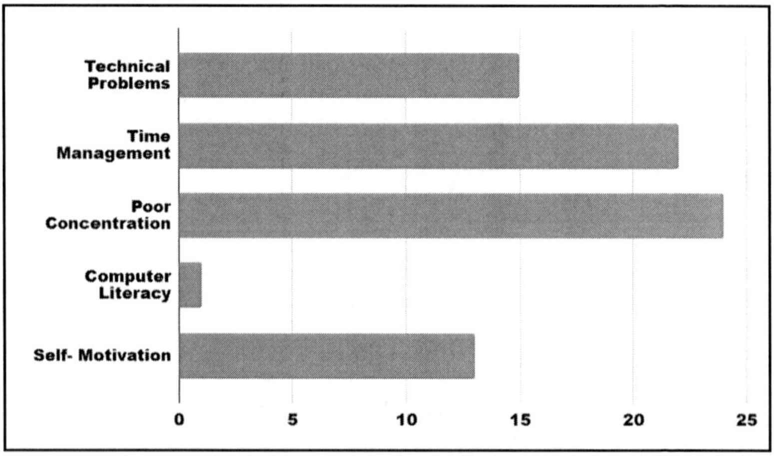

Figure 2: Count of students who face the challenges during online classes.

Figure 3 shows number of students who fulfil with online classes. Students needed to answer Yes or No. 40 (53.3 percent) students accepted that online classes are bad wellspring of data and were not happy with online classes, in any case, 35 (46.7 percent) students were with online classes.

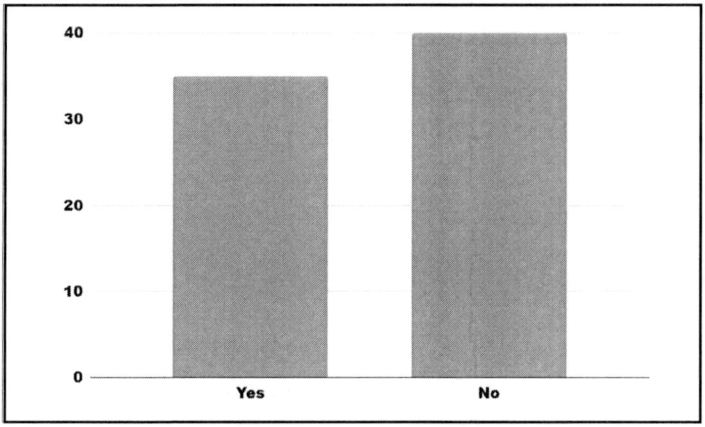

Figure 3: No. of students satisfy with online classes.

Figure 4 shows number of students who make their own perusing plan during Lockdown circumstance. There were two choices (Yes or No) given to students. 62 (82.7 percent) students concurred that they made their own perusing plan during Lockdown to score good marks in final exams and 13 (17.3 percent) students said that they didn't.

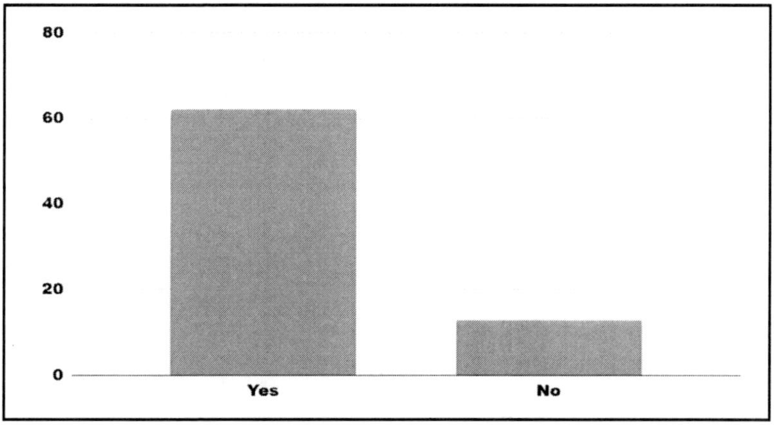

Figure 4: Count of Students Who Make Their Own Reading Schedule during Lockdown.

Figure 5 shows number of students who are missing the things about classroom study. Five options were given to the students (Classroom with teacher and classmates, Thought Provoking Discussions, One on One teacher and student Relationship, Motivation from teachers, study material). During the lockdown, out of 75, 32 (42.7 percent) students were missing classroom with teacher and classmates about their classroom learning the most, while others 15 (20 percent), 13 (17.3 percent), 13 (17.3 percent), 2 (2.7 percent) students were missing Thought Provoking Discussions in classroom, One on One teacher and student Relationship and motivation power and study material of class respectively.

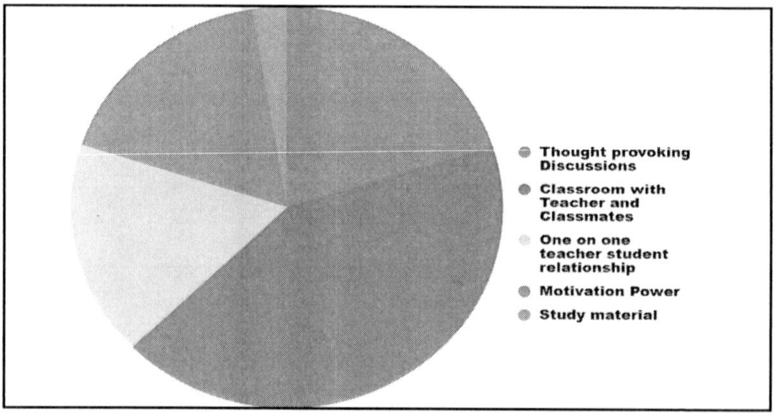

Figure 5: Number of Students Who Are Missing the Thing about Their Classroom Learning.

Figure 6 shows number of students whose day by day schedule is influenced by online classes. 31 (41.3 percent) students accepted that their every day schedule was influenced by online classes. At times they have a ton of assignments which are submitted around the same time, to finish the assignments they need to sit for 4 to 5 hours and some of the time they are absolutely free, nonetheless, 8 (10.7 percent) students said that their every day schedule were not influenced by it and 36 (48 percent) student's day by day schedule didn't know about it.

Figure 7 shows counts of students who feel overwhelm about their study during the Lockdown. Out of 75, 32 (42.7 percent) students felt overburden of every day homework, 26 (34.7 percent) students didn't know whereas 17 (22.7 percent) students report that they did not feel any burden of their study.

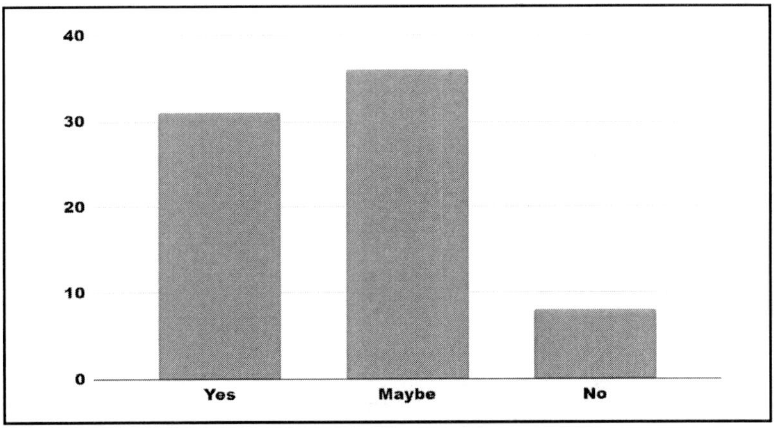

Figure 6: Number of Students who's Daily Routine Were Effected by Online Classes.

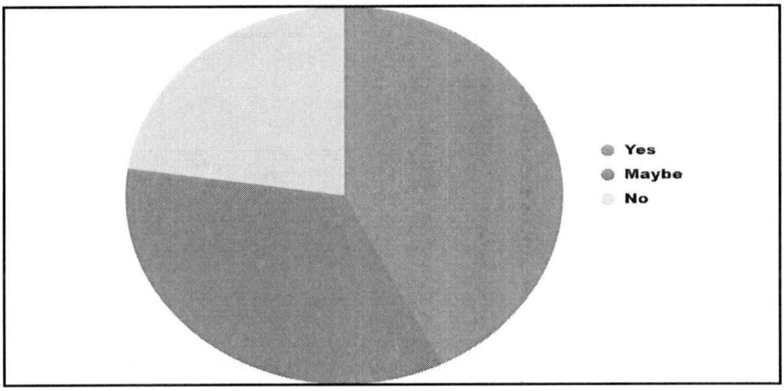

Figure 7: Number of students who feel overwhelm about their study during the Lockdown.

Figure 8 shows the number of students who feel their classroom study loss really affect their study. 61 (81.3 percent) students said that their study was truly influenced because of conclusion of colleges and universities, 9 (12 percent) students didn't know and 5 (6.7 percent) student's study has not influenced by it.

Figure 9 shows number of students who truly eager to return to college after lockdown. Out of 75, practically every one of the 74 (98.3 percent) students' needs to return to college very soon. They all are trusting that lockdown will end and will proceed with their ordinary timetable at college.

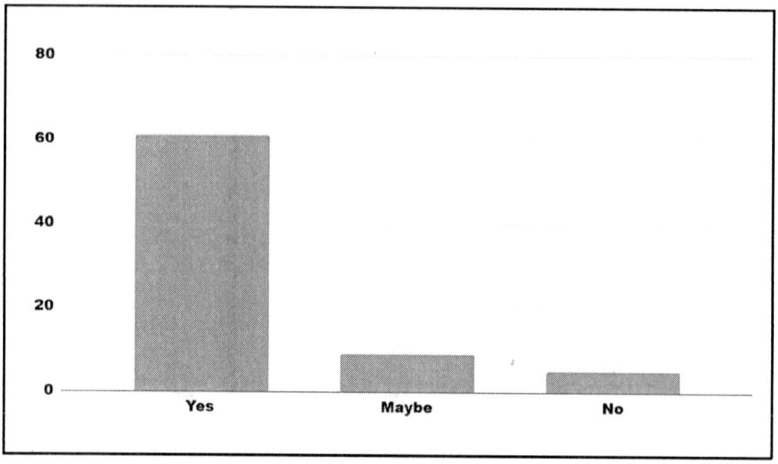

Figure 8: Number of Students Who Think That Loss of Their Classroom Study Really Effect on the Study.

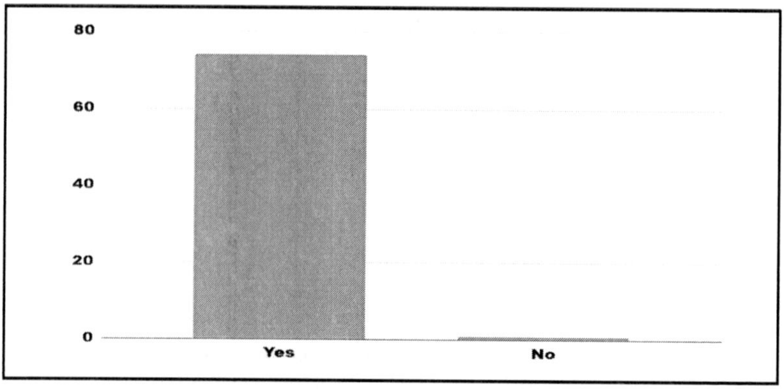

Figure 9: Count of Students Who Really Excited To Get Back To College.

Figure 10 shows the number of students who think that preparation of final exam is obviously superior to prior final exams. Out of 75, 52 (69.3 percent) students said that preparation of exams were not as good as earlier exams without classroom learning and support of teachers, while others 14 (18.7 percent) student's exam preparation were good, 9 (12 percent) were in question about it.

Figure 11 shows the number of student's first experience about online learning during the lockdown. There were four options given to the students (Good, very good, bad, very bad). The vast majority of the students 58 (77.3 percent) reports that they have great experience of web based learning and 6 (8 percent) students have excellent experience, though others 10 (13.3 percent) reports the awful experience. Just a single student said that she has extremely terrible experience of it.

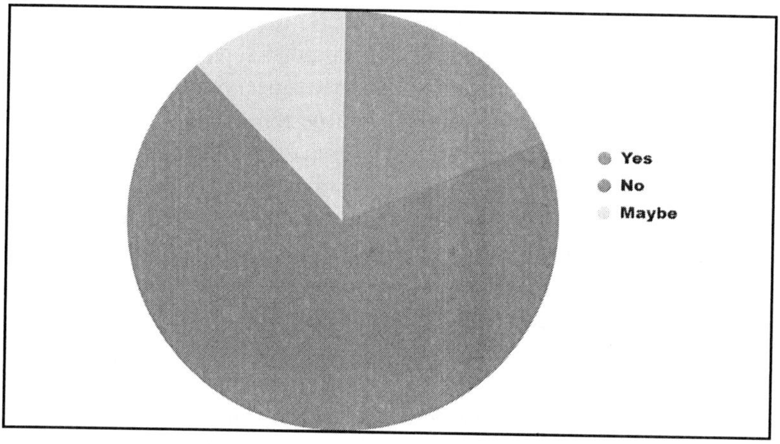

Figure 10: Number of Students Who Think That Preparation of Final Exam is Much Better Than Earlier Final Exams.

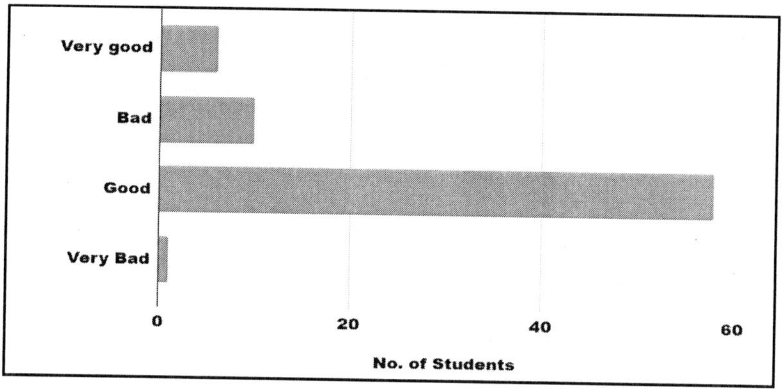

Figure 11: Count of Students about Their First Online Experience of Online Learning.

Discussions

This survey enrolled 75 respondents and revealed a high prevalence of mental status among students about their online classes during lockdown. Ever since the Government announced a 21-day national lockdown to prevent the spread of COVID-19 on 22 March, 2020, many colleges have started taking online lectures using different apps like Zoom, Google Classrooms, You Tube channels and so on. The classroom is the real and touchable place to teach and to learn. It is the place where teachers value the students from the whole class and develop the conclusions and thoughts raised by students. The students and teachers are physically present in the classroom. The classroom learning also promotes socialisation among the teachers and the students through team projects, peer evaluation, and group discussions. These communications can't be repeated in online classes. Teacher-to-student interactions, along with student-to-teacher and student-to-student interactions, are all part of the learning experience. Unconstrained and arbitrary associations through inquiries or expressed feelings are important in introducing a full extent of the subject being educated. In the virtual classroom, the teacher is generally ready to associate with just a single student at once and it is from behind a PC screen. Bringing up issues and tuning in to other students conclusions regularly happens through gathering message loads up, instead of continuous, eye to eye communication. In spite of numerous advantages of online learning such as time flexibility, study at any time but the finding tells that during the lockdown 86.7 percent students found online learning difficult during the lockdown (Figure 1). Online teaching is only the way to continue the learning of students during the lockdown but mostly students found many problems during the online classes. Analysis of Survey tells that it is comfortable to attend the college from home, but many students said that they find it difficult to sit through the lectures. It gets boring and dull at many times, poor concentration, time management and internet connectivity all factors are responsible for it (Figure 2). The most challenging part of learning is that mostly students get easily diverted when they try to learn at home. It is hard to work at home since there is no distinct separation of school vs. home. At Colleges and Schools, there is a work environment and students communicate face-to-face with those around them. Also students found lack of motivation to finish tasks. There are some remote areas where internet access and Wi Fi are hard to get and, as a result, students were not only anxious about college but also find it difficult to join and maintain access to online classes and assignments. The lab periods, which are necessary for science students and also give hands on experience to the students that can't happen over Zoom or You Tube channels. In spite of many benefits, for example, they can work at your own pace, at anywhere and anytime and has less stressed environment with deadlines. But more than a half percentage students were not satisfy with online classes according to the analysis of Survey (Figure 3). For the preparation of final examination and the revision of the syllabus, mostly students (82.7 percent) have made their own schedule during the lockdown (Figure 4). Instead of learning through lecturing, students learn from each other in the classroom. One on one communication is a really essential part of education at Schools and Colleges. Mostly students missed a classroom with teacher and classmates (Figure 5). College is not only a place for learning, but a place where students prepare themselves for future life that is helpful to live in complicated society and interpersonal relationship. Online education cannot replace academic institutes thoroughly in this aspect. Colleges also taught the students many things e.g. responsibility. Students had a schedule when going to classes and when to wake up and go to bed. Now during the lockdown, they have no reason to have a schedule; they have been going to bed and waking up much later than used to (Figure 6). Workload of assignments and class test also affect the daily routine of students (Figure 7). Distressing for students has become more difficult because they felt like college is there with them the whole day. In the near future, the students are really excited to get back to college (Figure 9) since they are not receiving the best education at home. Students found that loss of classroom study really effect on their study (Figure 8). It was hard whenever they didn't understand topics and instead of being able to ask teachers and get an immediate response, they message to the teacher and wait for reply that effect on their study. That's why the preparation of Exams is not better than earlier final exams (Figure 10). But some students have believed that they enjoy getting to work at their own pace, set their own schedule and be free from the stressful environment of College. Although, others recounted the challenges of distance learning, from struggling to understand assignments and getting easily unfocused to not having reliable internet connection. Online teaching also reflects some problems. For example, in online teaching, some teachers copy classroom teaching content to online teaching courses, ignoring subjective guidance and lacking teacher-student interaction. At the same time, some students also face lack of self-control and self-learning ability, lacked face-to-face teacher or even parental supervision. So all these factors are responsible for the disturbance in the mental behaviour of students.

Future Plans of Students after the Lockdown

During the survey, one question was asked to the students about their future plans after the lockdown. The students had shared the following future plans in the post COVID-19:

Practically all the students state that they are truly eager to return to college soon and will give more opportunity to points that they find hard to master during lockdown and truly need to return to day by day schedule with the goal that will more focus on their study and accomplish better the work. They will proceed with the examination and begin finishing the schedule amendment whose significance really acknowledges during the lockdown time frame. They would be glad to meet their friends and teachers since it's very nearly a month they haven't met. They would be extremely eager to be in classroom and study as they used to concentrate before. Being planning for last, most important test and score preferred stamps over the previous tests. They need to go to additional classes to clear questions in classroom conversations. It turned out to be anything but difficult to contemplate when they have the teacher with them. The most of students state that they need to conceal their syllabus once more. Students likewise need to do their Practical after the Lockdown especially.

Effect of COVID-19 on Future of Students

Due to the postponed in board exams, university exams, college exams, the entrance tests, it will be a big challenge for students to complete their syllabus without motivation and guidance of teacher. So, the scholastic year of the students that will be effected due to the shutdown of schools and colleges. A considerable lot of them face vulnerability regarding their future that their subsequent stages of further admission to college and universities or career/job opportunity are depend upon clearing of their school or college leaving exams. Some students think that, it is not confronting a troublesome issue, but others think that may face a level of vulnerability concerning future. Due to the disturbance in the education process, mental status of students are also effected, however they additionally face a major test of proving themselves for their next excursion. Without hard scholarly pointers, for example, evaluations and marks, a significant number of these students wind up in a circumstance where they can't separate themselves and come up short on a strong organisation to prepare themselves for the jobs and education happenings they face in next session. As of now examined, because of the Coronavirus outbreak JEE Main which is the pass to building training in India has just been deferred and will prompt the postponement in the beginning of academic sessions for most of the engineering colleges and most of the other colleges will observer a postponement too. Not simply that it is evaluated that students seeking to take admissions in 2020 are presently confused concerning how and where they ought to apply to college or universities from here on. Country like China that rehearses largely more incorporated training framework, a change to computerised learning will be simpler. Though even in a nation like the USA, there are some low-pay students who don't approach broad bands and workstations, advanced learning probably won't be the ideal solution. The equivalent is the situation with India where the backbone for online learning was not ready and the curriculum was not designed for such a format. Only one out of every odd student here is well informed or approaches the rapid web and will thus be endure. At the point when classes really begin on the web, numerous students will endure due to their inability to manage the expense. Except if India makes web accessible to all, there are chances that the gap in education quality may broaden. China propelled a Rain Classroom Teaching Platform in 2016 - one of the most exceptional web based presentation stage which has in excess of 19 million clients. So the regular attention has been on offline centers of education, we accept a blend of on the web and offline is the thing that will work in the coming months, which can ideally be changed over to a perpetual section. COVID-19 will indirectly affect the students in India, however what it has encouraged us is to manufacture flexibility to face such dangers later on. The outbreak of Coronavirus has advised us that change is inevitable. Students need to benefit as much as possible from the vulnerability that wins and utilise this opportunity to get ready for tests or take up online courses, that may help them in their future.

Limitation

In spite of the valuable contribution of this study in exploring the mental status of College students toward COVID-19 during the lockdown, there is a problem considering the generalisation of the findings of the study to the students of all colleges which is restricted to students of one college. Also, because the COVID-19 infection is a newly emerging disease, there is a lack of references on similar studies conducted on this topic. So there is no place for comparing the results of our study with other studies.

Conclusion

Despite the fact that this investigation has a few impediments, it is viewed as a significant expansion in the endeavours to know the psychological status of students about their study during lockdown as it features the generally students are not content with their online classes and need to do their further classes just at college. It will at that point impact on their self-motivation to accomplish work and furthermore on mental status of students.

References

1. Russell, M Viner, Chris Bonell, Claire Stansfield, Helen Croker, Jessica Packer, Joseph Ward, Oliver Mytton, Robert Booy, Simon J Russell 2020. "School closure and management practices during coronavirus outbreaks including COVID-19: a rapid systematic review". *Lancet Child Adolesc Health.* Vol. 4 April. pp. 397–404.
2. April 9, 2020. "WHO Director-General's opening remarks at the Mission briefing on COVID-19". Available at: https://www.who.int/dg/speeches/ detail/who-director-general-s-opening-remarks-at-the-missionbriefing-on-covid-19. Assessed on April 29, 2020.
3. January30, 2020. "India-confirms-first-case-of-the-coronavirus." Available at https://www.cnbc.com/2020/01/30/india-confirms-first-case-of-the-coronavirus. Assessed on April 29, 2020.
4. February14, 2020. "Kerala defeats coronavirus India's three Covid-19 patients successfully." Available at https://weather.com/en-IN/india/news/news/2020-02-14-kerala-defeats-coronavirus-indias-three-covid-19-patients-successfully. Assessed on April 29, 2020.
5. March 12, 2020. "6-members of Delhi patients family test positive for coronavirus." Available at https://www.thehindu.com/news/cities/Delhi/covid-19-6-members-of-delhi-patients-family-test-positive-for-coronavirus. Assessed on April 29, 2020.
6. March 12, 2020. "First coronavirus death in Karnataka." Available at https://www.hindustantimes.com/india-news/india-s-first-coronavirus-death-in-karnataka. Assessed on April 29, 2020.
7. April 29, 2020. "WHO, India- Ministry of Health & Family Welfare (MoHFW)-India situation report on COVID- 19." Available at: https://www.who.int/india/emergencies/novel-coronavirus-2019. Assessed on April 29, 2020.
8. "United Nations Educational, Scientific and Cultural Organisation- COVID-19 educational disruption and response, 2020". Available at https://en.unesco.org/covid19/educationresponse. Assessed on April 29, 2020.
9. March 19, 2020. "United Nations Educational, Scientific and Cultural Organisation. Global Education Coalition 2020". Available at https://en.unesco.org/themes/educationemergencies/coronavirus-schoolclosures. Assessed on April 29, 2020.
10. April 07, 2020. "How is the Covid-19 pandemic affecting education all over the world?" Available at https://www.indiatoday.in/education-today/featurephilia/story/how-is-the-covid-19-pandemic-affecting-education-all-over-the-world. Assessed on April 29, 2020.
11. March 23, 2020. "Impact on higher education in India." Available at https://www.collegedekho.com/articles/covid-19-impact-higher-education-india. Assessed on April 29, 2020.

Economic Effects COVID-19

22

COVID-19 and Its Impact on Global Economy

Shamika Kumar

The COVID-19 outbreak (previously 2019-nCoV) was caused by the SARS-CoV-2 virus. This outbreak was triggered in December 2019 in Wuhan city in Hubei province of China. COVID-19 continues to spread across the world. Initially the epicenter of the outbreak was China with reported cases either in China or being travellers from China. At the time of writing this paper, at least four further epicentres have been identified: Iran, Italy, Japan and South Korea. Even though the cases reported from China are expected to have peaked and are now falling (WHO, 2020), cases reported from countries previously thought to be resilient to the outbreak, due to stronger medical standards and practices, have recently increased. While some countries have been able to effectively treat reported cases, it is uncertain where and when new cases will emerge. Amidst the significant public health risk COVID-19 poses to the world, the World Health Organisation (WHO) has declared a public health emergency of international concern to coordinate international responses to the disease. It is, however, currently debated whether COVID-19 could potentially escalate to a global pandemic.

Companies across the world, irrespective of size, dependent upon inputs from China have started experiencing contractions in production. Transport being limited and even restricted among countries has further slowed down global economic activities. Most importantly, some panic among consumers and firms has distorted usual consumption patterns and created market anomalies. Global financial markets have also been responsive to the changes and global stock indices have plunged. The spread of the coronavirus bring the global economy to its knees? The answer lies in two methods by which coronavirus stifled economic activities. First, the spread of the virus encouraged social distancing which led to the shutdown of financial markets, corporate offices, businesses and events. Second, the exponential rate at which the virus was spreading, and the heightened uncertainty about how bad the situation could get, led to flight to safety in consumption and investment among consumers, investors and international trade partners. We focus on the period from the start of 2020 through March when the coronavirus began spreading into other countries and markets.

The Coronavirus has become a major humanitarian challenge and requires a lot of sacrifices to combat the disease. It has been declared a global pandemic by the World Health Organisation (WHO) and the virus continues to spread rapidly around the world through myriad active centers of transmission. The disease is highly transmissible and disproportionately affects those with underlying conditions. It has led to a global breakdown and affected almost all major countries of the world bringing a slowdown and recession in the economy due to consistent lockdowns by the nations. The Coronavirus has greatly impacted the Indian Economy. The research is being carried out by different organisations and researchers to predict the financial and economic health of the nation in the near future but it is still at an early and rampant stage. The health as well as wealth is both important pillars for the economy to survive and grow and hence, steps are being taken to improve the health conditions and financial conditions by launching support schemes and booster plans for various sectors of the economy. Looking on a global front, the growth in confirmed cases across the globe has accelerated rapidly. The following graph depicts the current situation as follow on considering the above situation, India is taking the situation very seriously and is striving to achieve virus free country by complete lockdowns and proper implementation of social distancing norms in areas of essential services. The lockdown in India has led to closure of all areas which involve public gatherings like colleges, schools and educational institutions, places of worship, marriage and party halls, event organising places, sports grounds, businesses and corporate offices dealing with non-essential items etc. In consideration to this, the situation of India having COVID-19 infections is not that great. In this paper, we show how the coronavirus outbreak led to spillovers into major sectors of the global economy, and how fast policy response by several governments both triggered and prolonged the recession while trying to save the lives of citizens.

Spillover to the Hospitality Industry

Restaurant businesses have been affected during the pandemic mainly through the government announced 'stay-at-home policy' and 'social distancing' movement restriction imposed by the government in many countries. This led to rapid shutdowns in cities and states to control the spread of the coronavirus, which threw many restaurants and hotels across the country into sudden shock. Hotels across the world witnessed booking cancellations worth billions of dollars, and the hotel industry sought a $150 bn bailout. 11 Restaurant executives laid off staff as they shut down their businesses temporarily. Many customers stayed at home, preferring to eat cooked meals at home. Some restaurant executives criticised the government for imposing the stay-at-home and social distancing policy which destroyed many small restaurants and pub businesses in small cities.

Spillover to the Sports Industry

The sports industry was severely affected during the coronavirus outbreak. In the football segment, major European football leagues in England and Scotland announced the immediate suspension of football matches for 6 weeks until 30th April. The Turkish super league was the last major European league to suspend its matches. In Formula One, the Monaco Grand Prix was cancelled. The Tokyo Summer Olympic and Paralympic games were also postponed. In the hockey segment, the 2020 hockey games in England was postponed. England's FIH Pro League games scheduled for 2nd to 3rd and 16th to 17th May were postponed. In rugby games, the Pro14 final scheduled for 20th June at the Cardiff City Stadium was cancelled. The major league rugby (MLR) was cancelled for the remainder of the 2020 season.

Spillover to Oil-Dependent Countries

The oil price war: A contributing factor Early in 2020, the price of oil fell due to the oil price war between Russia and Saudi Arabia. The coronavirus pandemic worsened the situation through the reduction in the demand for oil. The imposed travel restrictions during the pandemic, which led to a reduction in the movement of people and goods, resulted in a fall in demand for aviation fuel, coal and other energy products, which subsequently led to a fall in oil price due to low demand. The coronavirus crisis also affected a wide range of energy markets such as the coal, gas and renewable energy markets, but its impact on oil markets was more severe because it stopped the movement of people and goods, which led to a drastic decline in the demand for transport fuels. When Saudi Arabia later supplied excess oil to the world, the market was flooded with too much oil, exceeding demand during the COVID-19 pandemic, and subsequently leading to a fall in oil price.

Loss of oil revenue to oil-dependent countries: The effect of the pandemic on oil-dependent countries was severe. The global decline in oil price combined with the low demand for oil products in the international market led to a significant shortfall in oil revenue to oil-dependent countries, which increased current account deficits and worsened the balance of payment position of many oil-dependent countries such as Venezuela, Angola and Nigeria. These countries also faced increasing pressure on their foreign exchange reserves, which subsequently led to the devaluation of local currencies against the dollar. Countries like Kenya, Nigeria and South Africa experienced a reduction in the price of petrol in the local gas stations. National budgets were also affected.

Spillover to the Financial Sector

The macroeconomic slowdown led to a rise in nonperforming loans in the banking sector by 250 basis points. Private sector banks had the highest exposure to credit risk during the outbreak. Nonperforming loans arose from loans issued to small and medium scale enterprises (SMEs), airlines, hotels, tour operators, restaurants, retail, construction and real estate businesses. During the pandemic, there was a general decline in the volume of bank transactions, a decline in card payments and a fall in the use of ATM cash machines worldwide. This led to fewer fees collected by banks which negatively affected banks' profit. FinTech businesses were also affected. Some FinTech businesses witnessed very low patronage by consumers leading to loss of revenue and profits, which negatively affected the equity investment of venture capitalists that funded existing and new FinTech firms. This made many venture capitalists begin to hoard new equity which led to the drying up of financing for some FinTech businesses. On the other hand, the lockdowns due to the coronavirus outbreak resulted in higher demand for some sorts of online services such as online shopping.

Spillover to the Event Industry

Prior to 2020, the event sector contributed significantly to the economy. In 2018, for instance, business events hosted more than 1.5 billion participants across more than 180 countries (Oxford Economics). The events industry generated more than \$1.07 trillion of direct spending, representing spending to plan business events, produce business events, business events-related travel, and direct spending by exhibitors. The industry also created 10.3 million direct jobs globally and generated \$621.4 billion of direct GDP. During the coronavirus outbreak, the events industry was hit financially by a large number of cancellations exhibitions, live music shows, conference, weddings parties, corporate events, brand launches, trade shows and more. Several big events were cancelled, for instance, the E3 and SXSW tech events were cancelled which led to direct losses beyond $1 billion. Informal delayed or cancelled events worth £400 m over coronavirus pandemic. The 2020 Met Gala was postponed indefinitely. In the US, many big event management companies that were hit financially by the coronavirus outbreak appealed for federal aid from the US government. The event ticketing segment of the industry was also affected.

Spillover to the Entertainment Industry

The global film industry incurred a $5 billion loss during the coronavirus outbreak. Several Hollywood movie productions were postponed indefinitely which meant goodbye to theatre and cinema. The International Alliance of Theatrical Stage Employees (IATSE) reported that an estimated 120,000 below-the-line entertainment industry jobs were lost due to the coronavirus pandemic, most of which were theatrical stage employees. The pandemic shutdown resulted in the loss of 120,000 jobs held by its 150,000 members, and the IATSE advocated that the entertainment industry should be included in the planned federal stimulus (or bailout) package. In Italy, the COVID-19 outbreak severely affected the entertainment industry which incurred losses estimated to run into the millions of euros per week: from February 23 to March 1, 2020. There were estimated losses of 7.3 million euros in the film screening sector, 7.2 million euros in the theater segment, 4.1 million euros in the live music segment, 2.5 million euros in the dance activities segment and 1.8 million euros in the exhibition segment. In the UK, an estimated 50,000 industry freelancers were expected to lose their jobs as a result of the COVID-19 pandemic according to BECTU (Broadcasting, Entertainment, Communications and Theatre Union).

Collectively, unemployment levels in the entertainment industry rose to unprecedented highs, and yet there were doubts as to whether the entertainment industry would receive part of the planned federal stimulus package as many lawmakers argued that the entertainment industry was not a main driver of the economy, and some argued that the entertainment industry does not contribute much to economic activities compared to the financial and manufacturing sectors.

Spillover to the Education Sector

The coronavirus disrupted the $600 billion higher education industry. Educators and students around the world felt the ripple effect of the coronavirus as colleges and universities were instructed to shut down after the coronavirus was declared a public health emergency in many countries. There were school closures of some kind in 44 countries on four continents, including Africa, with hundreds of millions of students around the world facing disruptions. The outbreak had a more severe consequence on schools that did not have an online learning platform. Moody's, a credit rating agency, downgraded the US higher education outlook from 'stable' to 'negative', because 30 percent of the colleges and universities in the US already had a weak operating performance, and it was difficult for these colleges and universities to adapt with the financial and academic changes required to cope with the coronavirus outbreak. Also, UNESCO reported that the COVID-19 outbreak disrupted the education of at least 290.5 million students worldwide. Public schools in the US were closed, Australia shut down some schools, while countries like Israel, Nigeria, Egypt, Italy, France, and Spain shut down all schools, and this created some form of unemployment for teachers. Northern Ireland's government suspended all examinations in its colleges and universities. Multiple US based universities that ran a study abroad programme overseas instructed students to return home from Italy, France and Spain as the coronavirus outbreak became severe in those countries. On the positive side, there were suggestions that the coronavirus outbreak increased the importance of online education and distance learning, but the reality was that only a small percentage of the world's education is taught online.

Ozili and Arun (2020), the US alone, about 2.4 million undergraduates which is equivalent to 15 percent of the total undergraduate students in the US studied entirely online in the fall of 2019, according to Eduventures. This showed that, even before the outbreak, the use of online education was already low for some reasons, and it was unlikely that the outbreak would lead to a radical shift from classroom education to online education. Only few schools had the capacity to arrange a distance learning programme for their students. Finally, countries like Canada, UK and US combined lost billions in education revenue as foreign students either quit their studies or had to return home, while other foreign students looked elsewhere for quick education when the travel restrictions prevented them from studying in Canada, UK and US during the outbreak.

Conclusion

The world is battling COVID-19 and economies across the globe have declared a lockdown. Work from home (WFH) has become the norm, especially for service organisations. Following government instructions, even the academic institutions had to shut down temporarily. While the lockdown strategy is an essential step to curb the exponential rise of COVID-19 cases, but the spread of the coronavirus bring the global economy to its knees. First, the spread of the virus encouraged social distancing which led to the shutdown of financial markets, corporate offices, businesses and events. Second, the exponential rate at which the virus was spreading, and the heightened uncertainty about how bad the situation could get, led to flight to safety in consumption and investment among consumers, investors and international trade partners.

The coronavirus outbreak led the governments of many countries to impose restrictions on nonessential travel to countries affected by COVID-19, indefinitely suspending tourism travel, work visas and immigrant visas. Restaurant businesses have been affected during the pandemic mainly through the government announced 'stay-at-home policy' and 'social distancing' movement restriction imposed by the government in many countries. This led to rapid shutdowns in cities and states to control the spread of the coronavirus, which threw many restaurants and hotels across the country into sudden shock. Policy makers in many countries were under pressure to respond to the coronavirus outbreak. As a result, many governments made fast policy decisions that had far-reaching positive and negative effects on their respective economy many countries plunged into a recession. Social distancing policies and lockdown restrictions were imposed in many countries, and there have been arguments that such social policies can trigger a recession. Lawmakers in many countries supported an extended social distancing policy, damning the consequences of social distancing on the economy. The recession that followed, which many countries experienced, was a reflection of the difficult choice that policy-makers had to make in choosing whether to save the economy before saving the people or to save the people before saving the economy; many countries chose the latter. There were criticisms that the policies were too fast, premature or insufficient, and that the policies contradicted one another in some areas, for instance, the accommodative monetary policy encouraged economic agents to engage in economic activities while the lockdowns and social-distancing (stay-at-home) policy prevented economic activities from taking place. On the bright side, the coronavirus-induced public health crisis created an opportunity for many governments to make lasting reforms in the public health sector. Countries like the UK and Spain repaired their public healthcare system, and fixed other shortcomings in public infrastructure such as the transition to online education, transportation systems and the disease detection systems in public hospitals.

References

- Atkeson, A. (2020). *What will be the economic impact of covid-19 in the US? rough estimates of disease scenarios* (No. w26867). National Bureau of Economic Research.
- Baldwin, R., & Tomiura, E. (2020). "Thinking ahead about the trade impact of COVID-19". *Economics in the Time of COVID-19, 59.*
- Baker, S. R., Bloom, N., Davis, S. J., Kost, K. J., Sammon, M. C., & Viratyosin, T. (2020). *The unprecedented stock market impact of COVID-19* (No. w26945). National Bureau of Economic Research.
- Chakraborty, I., & Maity, P. (2020). "COVID-19 outbreak: Migration, effects on society, global environment and prevention". *Science of the Total Environment*, 138882.
- Fernandes, N. (2020). "Economic effects of coronavirus outbreak (COVID-19) on the world economy". *Available at SSRN 3557504.*
- Gössling, S., Scott, D., & Hall, C. M. (2020). "Pandemics, tourism and global change: a rapid assessment of COVID-19". *Journal of Sustainable Tourism*, 1-20.
- Gupta, M., Abdelmaksoud, A., Jafferany, M., Lotti, T., Sadoughifar, R., & Goldust, M. (2020). "COVID-19 and economy". *Dermatologic therapy.*
- McKibbin, W. J., & Fernando, R. (2020). The global macroeconomic impacts of COVID-19: Seven scenarios.
- Muhammad, S., Long, X., & Salman, M. (2020). "COVID-19 pandemic and environmental pollution: a blessing in disguise?" *Science of The Total Environment*, 138820.
- Nicola, M., Alsafi, Z., Sohrabi, C., Kerwan, A., Al-Jabir, A., Iosifidis, C., ... & Agha, R. (2020). "The socio-economic implications of the coronavirus pandemic (COVID-19): A review". *International journal of surgery* (London, England), *78*, 185.
- Oldekop, J. A., Horner, R., Hulme, D., Adhikari, R., Agarwal, B., Alford, M. & Bebbington, A. J. (2020). "COVID-19 and the case for global development". *World Development*, *134*, 105044.
- Ozili, P. K., & Arun, T. (2020). "Spillover of COVID-19: impact on the Global Economy". Available at *SSRN 3562570.*

23

Impact of COVID-19 on Indian Economy

Navneet Kaur

COVID-19 is the infectious disease caused by the most recently discovered coronavirus. This new virus and disease were unknown before the outbreak began in Wuhan, China, in December 2019. COVID-19 is now an epidemic affecting many countries globally. Quite 1.9 million coronavirus infections have been reported and over 119,483 people have died worldwide as on April 14, 2020. Governments across the world are struggling to regulate the spread of COVID-19 virus that originated from Wuhan in China in December 2019. The main concern of governments all over the world is to avoid new coronavirus hot spots and flare-ups of infections.

The epicentre of COVID-19 has moved from China to the United States which now has the highest death toll at 23,568. New infections appear to have levelled off in much of Asia and Europe, including Italy, France, Spain and Germany. In India, the Central Govt on April 14 extended the lockdown for two more weeks as its caseload crossed 10,000.

Table 1: Cases by Continents over the World

Situation in numbers (by WHO Region) Total (new cases in last 24 hours)		
Globally	21 294 845 cases (267 291)	761 779 deaths (5 985)
Africa	945 165 cases (9 103)	18 476 deaths (190)
Americas	11 420 860 cases (149 645)	414 326 deaths (3 843)
Eastern Mediterranean	1 723 673 cases (13 401)	45 704 deaths (343)
Europe	3 754 649 cases (19 888)	214 092 deaths (410)
South-East Asia	3 040 168 cases (69 064)	59 875 deaths (1 031)
Western Pacific	409 589 cases (6 190)	9 293 deaths (168)

Source: World Health Organisation (WHO).

The Covid-19 epidemic is the first and foremost human disaster in 2020. More than 200 countries and territories have confirmed effective medical cases, caused by coronavirus declared an epidemic by the WHO.

India is a developing economy, it is stated as an economy passing through demand depression and high unemployment, with 21-day lockdown announced by Prime Minister Narendra Modi on March 23, 2020, it might slowdown the supply-side, accelerating the slowdown further and jeopardising the economic wellbeing of millions.

Table 2: Top 10 Countries with Highest Cases of Covid-19

#	Country, Other	Total Cases	New Cases	Total Deaths	Total Recovered	Active Cases	Total Tests	Population
	World	23,397,619	+26,433	808,942	15,918,353	6,670,324		
1	USA	5,841,428		180,174	3,148,080	2,513,174	75,475,175	331,282,824
2	Brazil	3,582,698		114,277	2,709,638	758,783	14,144,344	212,776,644
3	India	3,049,855	+6,419	56,875	2,281,982	710,998	35,292,220	1,381,937,641
4	Russia	956,749	+4,852	16,383	770,639	169,727	33,814,105	145,943,650
5	South Africa	607,045		12,987	504,127	89,931	3,535,067	59,414,253
6	Peru	585,236		27,453	391,144	166,639	2,950,589	33,036,403
7	Mexico	556,216	+6,482	60,254	380,492	115,470	1,253,432	129,125,341
8	Colombia	533,103		16,968	359,792	156,343	2,450,441	50,959,957
9	Spain	407,879		28,838	N/A	N/A	7,955,615	46,757,437
10	Chile	395,708		10,792	369,730	15,186	2,172,028	19,139,679

Source: World Meters statistics.

The labour sector under the MGNREGA, 2005 are worst impacted as they're not provided jobs thanks to lockdown, most of the labour sectors are related to the construction companies and daily wage earners. Travel restrictions and quarantines affecting many people have left Indian factories in need of labour and parts, just-in-time supply chains and triggering sales warnings across technology, automotive, commodity, pharmaceutical and other industries.

The economic impact of COVID-19 is extremely disturbing. No one has been spared of its ill effects. Economies of about 100 plus countries have been destroyed out of which few of them have asked for financial help from IMF. Businesses across the globe namely, hospitality, entertainment, aviation etc have seen a serious negative impact. Various sports events like IPL, world cup and Olympics have been postponed. Schools and colleges have been temporary closed. The virus has also disrupted the functioning of varied online giants such as zomato, flipkart. amazon etc. Countries such as India, USA, Italy and Spain are suffering the foremost since their death toll is very high.

There is an enormous shift in the world economic market and therefore the share market has witnessed crashes day by day. Factories, Restaurants, Pubs, Markets, Flights, Super Markets, Malls, and Colleges etc. were shut down. Fear of corona virus has limited the movement of the individuals.

Developing countries like India has more fragile economic and social fabric and the present situation will create more suffering for the unorganised sectors and migrant labour. Borrowing the words of former RBI governor C Rangarajan, "Government of India must provide lifelines to businesses - extend loans and tax waivers to small businesses and the self-employed to retain staff give direct support to severely affected industries and supply more funds to states, tax waivers to households etc."

India has recorded the third highest number of coronavirus cases globally, behind only the United States and Brazil, with over 1.8 million confirmed infections and more than 38,000 deaths, according to a Reuters tally. That has forced state and central governments to impose strict lockdown measures to curb the spread of the virus, keeping people at home and businesses closed, stifling demand and cementing fears of a deep recession.

At this juncture, the war against COVID-19 is most intense, and the world is bracing up for a second wave as it cautiously opens up. The pandemic poses a challenge of epic proportions, but our collective efforts, intrepid choices, innovations and true grit will eventually take us to victory. As Mahatma Gandhi had said, "Patience and perseverance, if we have them, overcome mountains of difficulties"[2]. The challenges of today will only strengthen our resilience and self-belief. We shall remain alert and watchful and collectively do whatever is necessary to revive the economy and preserve financial stability. Courage and conviction will conquer Covid-19.

Need of Study

This study will help the individuals, companies and organisation as how to accommodate and to formulate strategies in this Covid-19 prevailing environment. This study aims to bring the impact of Covid-19 on Indian economy and the possible solutions, so that this will help all the sections and individuals of society to know about the current economic conditions which influences their daily buying and selling decisions, so that they will be better prepared for their future.

This study is based upon various macroeconomic indicators like inflation, industrial activity, and Future conditions of market, GDP and factors impacting its growth. Thus, this research is very beneficial to companies currently struggling to find their strategy in this sluggish conditions of market.

This study also covers all aspects of industrial growth, which in turn help organisations and companies to know about the manufacturing and services industry conditions, hence this study is beneficial to all sections of society.

Research Methodology

This study examines how this Covid-19 pandemic impacted and will impact the Indian economy. The research is secondary research and data is driven from several sources mostly pertaining to Government of India and Reserve Bank of India. This study is considering the Impact on India's Economy (GDP) due to Monetary policy (Inflation rate), Purchasing Manager Index (PMI), Fiscal Deficit, Industrial activity (by IIP index) and Balance of Trade (EXIM).

Conceptual Model

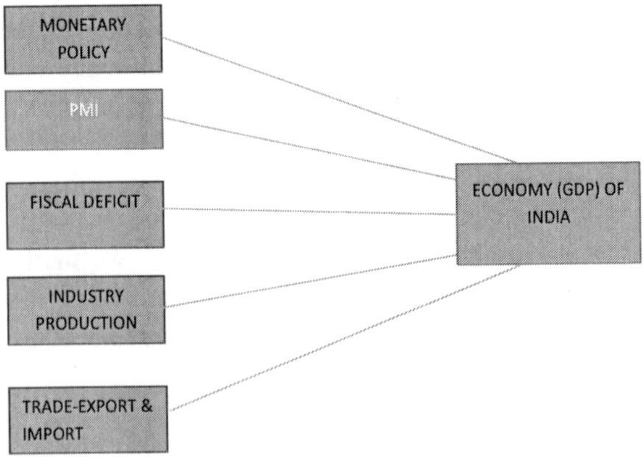

Objective of the Paper

- To know about the impacts of Covid-19 Pandemic on Indian economy.
- Future of Indian Economy and potential Solutions in order to revive the economy.

Data Collection and Instruments

Data is collected only from secondary resources mostly from following sources:

- Ministry of Statistics and Programme Implementation
- Ministry of Commerce and Industry
- Reserve Bank of India
- Various national newspapers
- World Health Organisation
- World Bank and IMF

Limitation of the Study

- The forecasting of macroeconomic conditions depends upon various assumptions, which if unmet will produce different results.
- There is always some discrepancy between actual results and results from statistical surveys.

DATA ANALYSIS AND INTERPRETATION

Global Economy

Global economic activity has remained fragile and in retrenchment in several geographies. While the uneasy and differently-paced withdrawal of COVID-19 lockdown restrictions in some countries enabled a sequential improvement in high frequency indicators during May-July, a renewed surge in possess weakened these early signs of revival. Contractions in economic activity have been more severe COVID-19 infections in major economies and threats of a second wave of infections appear to in Q2:2020 than in Q1, and the near-term outlook points to a slow, uneven and hesitant recovery pushed into the last half of the year, with risks steeply slanted to the downside. Among advanced economies (AEs), output in the US and the Euro area underwent a deeper contraction in Q2:2020 than in the preceding quarter. Emerging market economies (EMEs) are expected to shrink in Q2 as reflected in high frequency indicators.

Global financial markets have rebounded since end-March 2020 with intermittent pauses, shrugging off the volatility and sharp correction recorded in Q1:2020. Portfolio flows returned to EMEs in Q2 after a huge reversal, though there was moderation in July from the previous month's level. EME currencies have also appreciated in close co-movement, tracking weakening of the US dollar. Petroleum prices have remained supported on supply cuts by oil producing countries (OPEC plus) and improved demand prospects on the gradual easing of lockdown restrictions since May. Gold prices have rallied to an all-time high on August 5 on the back of safe haven demand. In AEs, benign fuel prices and soft aggregate demand have kept inflation subdued. In many EMEs, however, cost-push pressures arising from supply disruptions and demand revival have shown up in consumer prices in June 2020. Global food prices are elevated across the board.

Domestic Economy

On the domestic front, economic activity had started to recover from the lows of April-May following the uneven re-opening of some parts of the country in June; however, surges of fresh infections have forced re-clamping of lockdowns in several cities and states. Consequently, several high frequency indicators have levelled off.

The agricultural sector has emerged as a bright spot. Its prospects have strengthened on the back of good spatial and temporal progress of the south-west monsoon. The cumulative monsoon rainfall was 1 percent below the long-period average (LPA) up to August 5, 2020. Spurred by the expanding precipitation, the entire area sown under *kharif* crops on July 31 was 5.9 percent greater than the traditional area measured by the average over the period 2014-15 to 2018-19. As on July 30, 2020, the live storage in major reservoirs was 41 percent of the complete reservoir level (FRL), which bodes well for the *Rabi* season. These developments have had a salutary effect on rural demand as reflected in fertiliser production and sales of tractors, motorcycles and fast-moving commodity.

The pace of contraction of commercial production, measured by the index of industrial production (IIP), moderated to (-) 34.7 percent in May from (-) 57.6 percent a month ago, with the easing of lockdowns in several parts of the country. All manufacturing sub-sectors, except pharmaceuticals, remained in negative territory. The output of core industries in June contracted for the fourth successive month though with a considerable moderation. The Reserve Bank's business assessment index (BAI) for Q1:2020-21 hit its lowest mark in the survey's history.

The services PMI continued in contractionary zone in July to 34.2, although the downturn eased relative to the May and June readings. The manufacturing PMI remained in contraction, shrinking further to 46.0 in July from 47.2 in the preceding month.

Table 3: Manufacturing PMI-Country-wise

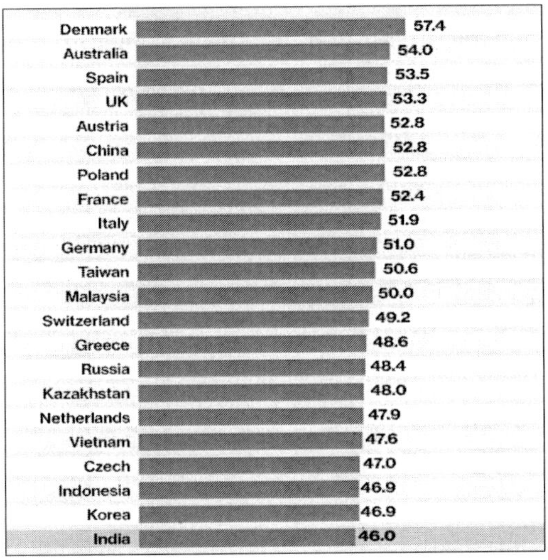

Source: Business Today.

High frequency indicators of services sector activity for May-June indicate signs of a modest resumption of economic activity, especially in rural areas, although at levels lower than a year ago. Notably, the decline in passenger vehicle sales moderated to (-) 49.6 percent in June from (-) 85.3 percent in May, indicative of tentative urban demand, and faster recovery of sales in rural areas. On the other hand, domestic air passenger traffic and cargo traffic continued to post sharp contraction. Construction activity remained tepid – cement production fell and finished steel consumption moderated sharply in June. Imports of capital goods – a key indicator of investment activity – declined further in June.

The National Statistical Office (NSO) released data on headline CPI for the month of June 2020 on July 13, 2020, along with imputed back prints of the index for April and May 2020. This resulted in a sharp upward revision of food inflation for the month of April and May. During Q1:2020-21 food inflation moderated from 10.5 percent in April to 7.3 percent in June 2020. Meanwhile, fuel inflation edged up as international kerosene and LPG prices firmed up. Inflation excluding food and fuel was at 5.4 percent in June, reflecting a spike in prices across most sub-groups. Inflation in transport and communication, personal care and effects, pan-tobacco and education registered significant increases in June. Headline CPI inflation, which was at 5.8 percent in March 2020 was placed at 6.1 percent in the provisional estimates for June 2020.

Table 4: Consumer Price Index (Inflation)

Item	*2019*		*2020*		*Percentage Variation of Current Month*		
	Jun.	*Jul.*	*Jan.*	*Jul.*	*Over Previous Month*	*Over End-March*	*Year-on-Year*
	1	2	3	4	5	6	7
1. Consumer Price Index (2012=100)	**142.9**	**144.2**	**151.8**	**154.2**	**1.6**	**3.8**	**6.9**
1.1 Rural	143.6	144.9	152.7	155.1	1.6	3.5	7.0
1.2 Urban	142.1	143.3	150.8	153.1	1.5	3.9	6.8
2. Consumer Price Index for Industrial Workers (2001=100	**316.0**	**319.0**	**332.0**	-	-	-	-
3. Wholesale Price Index (2011-12=100	**121.5**	**121.3**	**119.3**	**120.6**	**1.1**	**0.2**	**-0.6**
3.1 Primary Articles	141.0	142.8	139.3	143.7	3.2	4.6	0.6
3.2 Fuel and Power	102.2	100.6	88.3	90.7	2.7	-8.8	-9.8
3.3 Manufactured Products	118.5	118.0	118.6	118.6	0.0	0.0	0.5

Source: Ministry of Statistics and Programme Implementation.

For the second successive round, households' three months ahead expectations remained above their one year ahead expectations, indicating their anticipation of lower inflation over the longer horizon. Producers' sentiments on input prices remained muted as their salary outgoes fell. Their selling prices contracted in Q1 in the April-June round of the Reserve Bank's industrial outlook survey.

India's merchandise exports contracted for the fourth successive month in June 2020, although the pace of fall moderated on improving shipments of agriculture and pharmaceutical products. Imports fell sharply in June in a broad-based manner, reflecting weak domestic demand and low international crude oil prices. The merchandise trade balance recorded a surplus in June (US$ 0.8 billion), after a gap of over 18 years. The current account balance turned into a marginal surplus of 0.1 percent of GDP in Q4 of 2019-20 as against a deficit of 0.7 percent a year ago. On the financing side, net foreign direct investment moderated to US$ 4.4 billion in

April-May 2020 from US$ 7.2 billion a year ago. In 2020-21 (till July 31), net foreign portfolio investment (FPI) in equities at US$ 5.3 billion was higher than US$ 1.2 billion a year ago.

Table 5: Merchandising Exports and Imports

Export and Import: US $ Billion		
Provisional	**July**	**April- July**
Exports (Including re-exports)		
2019-20	26.33	107.41
2020-21	23.64	74.96
percent Growth 2020-21/2019-20	**-10.21**	**-30.21**
Import		
2019-20	39.76	166.80
2020-21	28.47	88.91
percent Growth 2020-21/2019-20	**-28.40**	**-46.70**
Trade Balance		
2019-20	-1343	-59.39
2020-21	-4.83	-13.95

Source: Ministry of Commerce and Industry

Table 6: Services Exports and Imports

Export and Import (Services): US $ Billion		
Provisional	***July***	***April- July***
Exports (Receipts)	17.00	50.21
Imports (Payments)	9.96	29.20
Trade Balance	7.04	21.01

Source: Ministry of Commerce and Industry.

In the debt segment, however, there were outflows of US$ 4.4 billion during the same period as against inflows of US$ 2.0 billion a year ago. Net investment under the voluntary retention route increased by US$ 0.9 billion during the same period. India's foreign exchange reserves have increased by US$ 56.8 billion in 2020-21 so far (up to July 31) to US$ 534.6 billion – equivalent to 13.4 months of imports.

Supply chain disruptions on account of COVID-19 persist, with implications for both food and non-food prices. A more favourable food inflation outlook may emerge as the bumper *Rabi* harvest eases prices of cereals, especially if open market sales and public distribution off take are expanded on the back of significantly higher procurement. The relatively moderate increases in minimum support prices (MSP) for the *kharif* crops and monsoon are also supportive of benign inflation prospects. Nonetheless, upside risks to food prices remain. The abatement of price pressure in key vegetables is delayed and remains contingent upon normalisation of supplies. Protein based food items could also emerge as a pressure point, given the tight demand-supply balance in the case of pulses. The inflation outlook of non-food categories is, however, fraught with uncertainty. Higher domestic taxes on petroleum products have resulted in elevated domestic pump prices and will impart broad-based cost-push pressures going forward. Volatility in financial markets and rising asset prices also pose upside risks to the outlook. Taking into consideration all these factors, headline inflation may remain elevated in Q2:2020-21, but may moderate in H2:2020-21 aided by large favourable base effects.

Turning to the growth outlook, the recovery in the rural economy is expected to be robust, buoyed by the progress in *kharif* sowing. Manufacturing firms responding to the Reserve Bank's industrial outlook survey expect domestic demand to recover gradually from Q2 and to sustain through Q1:2021-22. On the other hand, consumer confidence turned more pessimistic in July relative to the preceding round of the Reserve Bank's survey. External demand is expected to remain anemic under the weight of the global recession and contraction in global trade. Taking into consideration the above factors, real GDP growth in Q2-Q4 is expected to evolve along the lines noted in the May resolution. For the year 2020-21, as a whole, real GDP growth is expected to be negative. An early containment of the COVID-19 pandemic may impart an upside to the outlook. A more protracted spread of the pandemic, deviations from the forecast of a normal monsoon and global financial market volatility are the key downside risks.

India's federal fiscal deficit in the first two months through May stood at Rs 4.66 trillion ($61.67 billion), or 58.6 percent of the budgeted target for the current fiscal year, government data showed on Tuesday. Net tax receipts during April-May period were Rs 33,850 cr ($4.48 billion), while total expenditure was Rs 5.12 trillion, the data showed, indicating the

Table 7: Government Revenues and Expenditures

Indicator	*2019-20 (BK)*	*2019-20 (RE)*	*2020-21 (BE)*
1. Revenue Receipts	9.3	9.1	9.0
a. Tax Revenue (Net)	7.8	7.4	7.3
b. Non-Tax Revenue	1.5	1.7	1.7
2. Non-Debt Capital Receipts	0.6	0.4	1.0
3. Revenue Expenditure	11.6	11.5	11.7
4. Capital Expenditure	1.6	1.7	1.8
5. Total Expenditure	3.2	13.2	13.5
6. Gross Fiscal Deficit	3.3	3.8	3.5
7. Revenue Deficit	2.3	2.4	2.7
8. Primary Deficit	0.2	0.7	0.4

Source: Union Budget 2020-21.

government was front-loading its budgeted spending to combat the impact of pandemic. India's federal fiscal deficit touched 4.6 percent of GDP in 2019/20 fiscal year ending March, from initial estimates of 3.3 percent.

The latest figures for India's fiscal deficit come at a time when the Centre is said to be seriously considering direct monetisation of the fiscal deficit by RBI having sidestepped the idea for the first half (H1) of 2020-21 (FY21). Business Standard has learnt that it is being seriously considered for the second half of FY21.

"It is a high possibility," said a top government official, when asked if the Centre was considering direct deficit monetisation. "In the latter half of the year, we will have a clearer picture of the economic damage the Covid-19 pandemic has unleashed, and may require further resources to provide support to the economy," the official added.

The final decision may be taken before the borrowing calendar for October 2020-March 2021 is announced in late September. Earlier, the Chief Economic Advisor to the Government of India, Krishnamurthy Subramanian had told Business Standard that the Centre's fiscal deficit in 2020-21, could be 1.7-1.8 percentage points higher than the 3.5 percent of gross domestic product, which was targeted in the Budget.

Impact on GDP

If the Indian economy were a person, her income in 2020-21 and 2021-22 would be less than what it was in 2019-20. At least, this is what the latest World Bank forecasts tell us. There is enormous, perhaps unprecedented, economic pain ahead. Both policy and politics will have to play an important role to alleviate this. Bad policy can delay, even derail economic revival. Good politics can ensure that the suffering of the masses is minimized.

World Bank on Monday sharply scaled down its projections for India's economy, forecasting 3.2 percent contraction in the fiscal year 2020-21 because of the Covid-induced lockdown. It had earlier predicted 1.5-2.8 percent growth.

The country's economy grew 4.2 percent in 2019-20, the slowest in 11 years. "Stringent measures to restrict the spread of the virus, which heavily curtail short-term activity, will contribute to the contraction," World Bank said in its latest edition of the Global Economic Prospect.

It, however, stressed India's economy should bounce back in 2021-22 and pegged growth at 3.1 percent. Still, it is lower than 4-5 percent growth projected by the bank earlier. India could lose the tag of the fastest-growing large economy to China for two years. China is projected to grow at 1 percent in CY2020, and 6.9 percent for CY2021.

The bank also sharply cut its 2020 forecast for the world economy 5.2 percent contraction, as against 2.5 percent growth projected in January. If this comes true, the contraction will be the deepest global recession in eight decades, despite unprecedented policy support.

Following the report, World Bank has joined scores of international agencies that forecast contraction in the Indian economy as the aftermath of the lockdown. The worst has been predicted by US-based brokerage firm Bernstein, which sees India's economy contracting 7 percent in FY21.

Table 8: GDP Growth Forecast (2020-21) by Rating Agencies

Bernstein	**-7.0**	India Rating	**-2.1 to1**
SBI Research	**-6.8**	CII	**-0.9 to 1**
Godman Sachs	**-5.0**	Moody's Investors Services	**-4.0**
Nomura (for 2020)	**-5.0**	World Bank	**-3.2**
Fitch Rating	**-5.0**	IMF	**1.9**
ICRA	**-5.0**	Asian Development Bank	**4.0**

Source: Respective Agencies Most agencies have pegged it to shrink 5 percent.

Now, the International Monetary Fund (IMF) remains one of the few institutions which still foresee India's economy growing. It pegged growth at 1.9 percent in 2020-21. It is also slated to come out with revised projections later this month and is likely to see a contraction in the economy.

Earlier, former chief economic advisor Arvind Subramanian had termed World Bank's and the IMF's projections as "optimistic". The Washington-based multilateral lender said the Covid-19 pandemic and the multi-phased lockdown imposed to curb its spread dealt a devastating blow to the Indian economy.

World Bank said spillovers from weaker global growth and balance-sheet stress in the financial sector will also weigh on activity, despite some support from the fiscal stimulus and continued monetary policy easing. According to the report, the central bank has been purchasing government bonds to further ease the financial conditions.

The Indian government has also increased its spending on healthcare to bolster the Covid-19 response, wage support, in-kind and cash transfers to lower-income households, and deferral of tax payments, as well as loan and liquidity support for small businesses and financial institutions.

SECTORAL IMPACT

E-Learning Programmes

- E-learning has shown a 25 percent uptick since March 2020
- Zoom's market capitalisation has reached $48.8 billion on May 15, 2020
- 30 million minutes of watch time by students on Un academy every single day
- Coursera provided free access to its Course Catalog for Campus until July 31, 2020
- Digital initiatives taken by the government include, DIKSHA portal serves as National Digital Infrastructure for Teachers e-Pathshala hosts educational web resources for students, parents, researchers and educators in rural areas.

Online Educators and the New Normal

- 98 percent of educators think that interactive video will be essential in the future
- 93 percent of educators believe predictive analytics will change education
- 89 percent of educators are interested in immersive technologies.

Future of E-Learning

- The market for e-Learning will reach a $300 billion market value by 2025
- Use of Artificial Intelligence in education to grow by 48 percent by 2022
- Mobile internet users in India to reach 85 percent of households by 2024.

Pharmaceutical Industry in India

The pharmaceutical firms are set to see growth in the near term.

- India's Nifty Pharma Index has risen 18 percent this year
- From March to May 2020, healthcare products are being sold on a large scale
- Around 4-5 million N95 masks by HLL Lifecare
- 2 million pairs of Nitrile gloves
- 1 million protective goggles

- 2 billion three ply surgical masks
- 2 million 500 ml bottles of hand sanitisers
- Respiratory therapy drugs witnessed the highest sales and a growth of 23 percent in April 2020
- Prices of vitamins and penicillin saw a surge of 50 percent in April 2020.

Tourism Industry in India

The World Travel and Tourism Council India Initiative (WTTCII), Federation of Associations in Indian Tourism and Hospitality and Confederation of Indian Industry (CII) predict that in the months of April, May and June 2020:

- 70 percent of the workforce in the tourism sector will be jobless
- Hotel occupancy to be dropped by 45 percent
- Airlines to fly at 25-30 percent of current capacity
- The industry will take up to 10 months to recover
- Occupancy in the branded hotels is estimated to decline by 16.7 percent to 20.5 percent
- Revenue per available room will witness a significant decline of 31 percent to 36.2 percent.

Risks to Economy

The main downside risk to India's growth forecast is the continued spread of the COVID-19 pandemic as the health crisis has not yet been contained, a top IMF official said on Tuesday, noting that the country's near-term growth outlook continues to be clouded by the global and domestic slowdown and uncertainties relating to the coronavirus.

"Concerns about the virus could also dampen consumer confidence and delay the economic recovery," Chang Yong Rhee, who is director of IMF's Asia and Pacific Department, told PTI in an interview.

The economic impact of COVID-19 has been substantial and broad-based. High frequency indicators point to a sharp decline in economic activity, as reflected in industrial production, business sentiment (e.g., in the Purchasing Managers Indices), vehicle sales, and trade, he said.

Exchange Rate

The exchange rate of the Indian rupee vis-à-vis the US dollar has moved in both directions in recent months. Renewed bouts of global financial market volatility caused by the uncertainty of macroeconomic impact of the COVID-19, as in February-March 2020, could exert pressure on the Indian rupee. Should the INR depreciate by 5 percent from the baseline, inflation could edge up by around 20 bps while GDP growth could be higher by around 15 bps through increased net exports. In contrast, should COVID-19 normalise quickly, strong capital flows could revive. An appreciation of the INR by 5 percent could moderate inflation by around 20 bps and GDP growth by around 15 bps vis-à-vis the baseline.

International Crude Oil Prices

Global crude oil prices have declined sharply from their October 2019 levels mainly due to weakening of global demand following the outbreak of COVID-19, and Saudi Arabia's decision to cut prices. However, the short and medium-term outlook of oil remains highly uncertain. A V-shaped global recovery due to an early containment of the COVID-19 or renewed geopolitical tensions or an agreement on production cuts could lead to a sharp reversal in international crude oil prices. Should the Indian basket of crude oil prices increase by 10 percent above the baseline assumption, inflation could be higher by 20 bps and growth could be weaker by around 15 bps. If COVID-19 were to persist longer, global economic activity and demand for crude oil could fall further in an environment of sustained oversupply due to Saudi Arabia's decision to enhance production. Should the Indian basket crude price fall by 10 percent vis-à-vis the baseline, inflation could ease by up to 20 bps and growth higher by up to 15 bps, depending upon the extent of pass-through to domestic product price.

Conclusion

COVID-19, the accompanying lockdowns and the expected contraction in global output in 2020 weigh heavily on the growth outlook. The actual outturn would depend upon the speed with which the outbreak is contained and economic activity returns to normalcy. Significant monetary and liquidity measures taken by the Reserve Bank and fiscal measures by the government would mitigate the adverse impact on domestic demand and help spur economic activity once normalcy is restored. Risks around the inflation projections appear balanced at this juncture and the tentative outlook is benign relative to recent history. But COVID-19 hangs over the future, like a spectre. The deterioration in aggregate demand conditions in 2019-20, was exacerbated by contraction (1.3 percent) in gross fixed capital formation, and moderation in government expenditure in H2. Although private consumption held up in sequential terms, it was slower in H2:2019-20 on a y-o-y basis. Overall, the drag on GDP growth in H2:2019-20 can be decoded to unfavourable base effects, since momentum – measured by the q-o-q seasonally adjusted annualised growth rate (SAAR) - accelerated in H2. With COVID-19 having taken a grievous toll in February and particularly in March, it is unlikely that this momentum was sustained as the year closed. Accordingly, the NSO's estimate of real GDP growth for the year as a whole at 5 percent in 2019-20, which itself was down from 6.1 per cent in 2018-19, may be at risk.

References

- The Economic Times 2020. "Impact of Covid-19 on the Indian Economy". Available at:https://bfsi.economictimes.indiatimes.com/blog/impact-of-covid-19-on-the-indian-economy/4241. Assessed on 21 August, 2020.
- Financial Express 2020. "COVID-19 crisis: Continued spread of Coronavirus pandemic poses risk to Indian economy, says IMF official" .Available at: https://www.financialexpress.com/economy/covid-19-crisis-continued-spread-of-coronavirus-pandemic-poses-risk-to-indian-economy-says-imf-official/2009181/. Assessed on 21 August, 2020.
- Business Standard 2020. "Covid-19 impact: India's economy to shrink by 3.2 percent in FY21, says World Bank". Available at: https://www.business-standard.com/article/economy-policy/covid-19-impact-world-bank-sees-india-s-economy-shrinking-by-3-2-in-fy21-120060801688_1.html. Assessed on 22 august, 2020.
- Economic Times 2020. "Opinion: Impact of Covid-19 on the Indian Economy". Available at: https://government.economictimes.indiatimes.com/news/economy/opinion-impact-of-covid-19-on-the-indian-economy/75021731. Assessed on 22 August, 2020.
- Hindustan Times 2020. "Economic impact of Covid-19 pandemic to vary in sectors" Available at: https://www.hindustantimes.com/india-news/economic-impact-of-covid-19-pandemic-to-vary-in-sectors/story-DIWjwnBZoON7ZUvgSMSFOL.html. Assessed on 22 August, 2020.
- Indian Institute of Management Udaipur. "Impact of COVID-19 on The Indian Economy". Available at: https://www.iimu.ac.in/blog/impact-of-covid-19-on-the-indian-economy/. Assessed on 22 August 2020.
- Reuters Trust 2020. "India's services activity contracted for fifth straight month in Jun-PMI". Available at: https://in.reuters.com/article/india-economy-pmi/indias-services-activity-contracted-for-fifth-straight-month-in-july-pmi-idINKCN2510FD. Assessed on 22 August, 2020.
- India Central Government Budget 2020. "Compare budget by country". Available at: https://tradingeconomics.com/india/government-budget. Assessed on 23 August, 2020.
- Ministry of Commerce & Industry Department of Commerce 2020. "India's foreign trade: July 2020" Available at: https://commerce.gov.in/writereaddata/UploadedFile/NTESCL_637330240112020361_Press_Release_July_2020.pdf. Assessed on 23 August, 2020.

- Ministry of Statistics and Programme Implementation 2020. "press release". Available at: http://www.mospi.gov.in/press-release. Assessed on 23 august, 2020.
- The World Bank 2020. "GDP growth (annual percent) – India". Available at: https://data.worldbank.org/indicator/NY.GDP.MKTP.KD.ZG?end=2019&locations=IN&start=1961&view=chart. Assessed on 23 August, 2020.
- Bloomburg Quint 2020. " India's Fiscal Deficit In April-June Reaches 83 percent of Budget Target". Available at: https://www.bloombergquint.com/economy-finance/indias-fiscal-deficit-in-april-june-touches-83-of-budget-target. Assessed on 24 August, 2020.
- The Hindu 2020. "Fiscal deficit touches 83 percent of full-year target". Available at: https://www.businesstoday.in/current/economy-politics/india-weak-manufacturing-pmi-for-july-one-of-the-worst-globally/story/412002.html. Assessed on 24 August 2020.
- Reserve Bank of India. "Covid-19 related measures". Available at: https://www.rbi.org.in. Assessed 25 August, 2020.

24

COVID-19 Pandemic: A Tough Break to Indian Trade and Industry

Monika Garg

An unprecedented outbreak of corona virus now called as COVID-19 was first reported in Wuhan city, in China on 31st December 2019. A new virus called the severe acute respiratory syndrome corona virus 2(SARS-COV-2) has been identified as the cause of the disease. This virus primarily disseminate through the droplets of saliva or discharge from the nose of an infected person when he/she sneezes or coughs. People could also catch it by touching contaminated surfaces or objects and then touching their eyes, nose and mouth.(Venkateswaran, D., 2020) The world health organisation named the disease caused by virus as COVID-19 and declared it as pandemic. The first case of Covid-19 in India was recorded in the state of Kerala on 30th January, 2020. As it is transmitting via social contact and human touch, so our honourable Prime Minister Mr. Narendra Modi announced a nationwide complete lockdown from March 25, 2020 to curb the spread of this pandemic. Only essential goods and services such as agriculture, mining, financial and IT services were allowed to operate. Constantly evolving Covid-19 pandemic has mess up people's life and casted a long shadow on the global economy. The substantial breakdown that shut majority of factories and industries, bans on travels, suspended flights, stopped trains, closure of borders, restricted movement of vehicles and people has interrupted the economic activities around the nation. All this lead to prolonged disruption of all types of business, trade and industry be it a wholesale or retail business, travel industry, food industry, apparel manufacturing, entertainment and many more. Lockdown of crowded places like educational institutions viz, schools, colleges, universities, Malls, gyms has declined the revenue in these sectors. The sectors most severely impacted are transport, airlines, tourism, hotels, restaurants and real estate activities.

However, the extent of actual impact would depend on the severity and duration of outbreak which is still unknown.

Research Methodology and Method of Data Collection

- To conduct this study published source of data collection such as books, journals, newspapers, research articles and websites etc is used.
- The study is totally based on secondary data which is collected from different websites, news channels, e-newspaper, e-magazines, journals, Google scholar articles etc.
- The news, articles, journals, magazines up to 28th April, 2020 is taken for the study.

Objective of the Study

- To analyze the impact of Corona Virus on the different sectors of economy viz pharmaceutical industry, tourism and aviation industry, automobile industry, oil industry, textile industry, hospitality industry, entertainment and sports industry and poultry industry.
- To investigate hit and brunt of this corona pandemic on Indian business, trade and Industry.

CORONA VIRUS

A Corona virus called COVID-19 is a kind of common virus that causes an infection in respiratory tract. It can affect upper respiratory tract i.e. nose, sinuses or upper throat) or lower respiratory tract (windpipe and lungs). The Corona virus outbreak which started in China, has so far killed over 316,658 people across the globe and infected 4,801,510 (as on May 18, 2020). The virus has spread to 187 countries. In India, 90,927 confirmed cases and 2,872 deaths have been reported so far, according to official figures released by the Union Ministry of Health and Family Welfare.

Symptoms of COVID-19

The main symptoms include:

- Fever
- Coughing
- Shortness of breath
- Trouble breathing

- Fatigue
- Chills, sometimes with shaking
- Body aches
- Headache
- Sore throat
- Loss of smell or taste
- Nausea
- Diarrhea

Impact of COVID-19 on Indian Economy

COVID-19 crisis has caused an unprecedented collapse between the economic activities over the last few months. According to Dun & Bradstreet, COVID-19 no doubt disrupted human lives and global supply chain but the pandemic is a severe demand shock which has offset the green shoots of recovery of the Indian economy that was visible towards the end of 2019 and early 2020. The revised GDP estimates for India downwards by 0.2 percent points for the fiscal year 2020 to 4.8 percent and by 0.5 percent for the fiscal year 2021 to 6 percent. According to the report three major channels namely, linkages, supply chain and macroeconomic factors have impacted Indian businesses. The data of the Dun & Bradstreet shows that at least 6,606 Indian entities have legal linkages with companies in countries with a large number of confirmed COVID-19 cases. And business activity in the foreign markets is slow which implies a negative impact on the top line of these companies. Sectors that would be much affected includes logistics, auto, tourism, metals, drugs, pharmaceuticals, electronic goods, MSMEs and retail among others (Goyal, Shikha. 2020).

Pharmaceutical Industry

According to the Trade Promotion Council of India, approximately 70-75 percent of Active Pharmaceutical ingredients (APIs) are imported from China which has impacted manufacturing operations in India. The APIs are used in antibiotics, vitamins and other essential medicines, and are heavily sourced from China. These APIs are paracetamol, aspirin, azithromycin, amoxicillin, ofloxacin, metronidazole; vitamins such as B12, B1, B6, and E; female hormone progesterone; HIV drugs lopinavir and ritonavir and blood pressure-controlling drug valsartan. (The Economic Times, 2020) India's heavy reliance on China for these APIs exposes it to raw material supply disruption and price inflammability. Due to the increasing spread of this pandemic the demand for medicines and safety measures is shooting up but shortage of APIs as an ingredient to manufacture drugs leads to skyrocketing prices. The prices of vitamins and penicillin alone see a 50 percent surge. (Muthukrishnan, Manjula, 2020) China's corona virus pandemic is threatening to disrupt India's $39-billion drug production by halting and severely impacting the imports of bulk drugs (Times Economic, 2020).

Tourism Industry

India is a mosaic of multicultural experiences with a rich heritage and myriad attractions; the country is among the most popular tourist destinations in the world. The outbreak of Corona virus COVID-19 presents the tourism sector with a major and evolving challenge. Due to the suspension of Visas, flights and trains the whole tourist value chain which encompasses the hotels, restaurants, travel agents and tour operators is expected to face losses worth thousands of crores. (Muthukrishnan, Manjula, 2020). As the uncertainty has led to the cancellation of travel plans by both foreign and domestic tourist, there has been a drop in both inbound and outbound tourism of 67 percent and 52 percent since January to February 2020 as compared to same period last year. Foreign tourist arrivals (FTA) in the month of February dropped 9.3 percent month on month and 7 percent year on year according to government data. In February 2020, there were 10.15 lakh FTAs, against 10.87 lakh in February 2019 and 11.18 lakh in January 2020. (Business Line, 2020) Nearly 90 percent booking of hotels and flights stand cancelled. There has been 20 percent reduction in domestic and 70 percent reduction in international travel booking. The corona virusimpact could render 3.8 crore people jobless, which is around 70 percent of the total workforce in the tourism and hospitality sector, according to a grouping. (The Economic Times. 2020).

Aviation Industry

Aviation has turned out to be worst affected sector admist COVID-19 pandemic due to the travel restrictions and slump in the demand among the travellers. Several air carriers including Vistara, Go Air, and Spice Jet have suspended international flights as a result of dwindling demand and fares. (Punj, Vivek, 2020) 585 international flights are cancelled by private carriers on March 6, 2020. As many as 16 international airlines have cancelled 492 flights and four private Indian airlines have cancelled 93 flights during this period. (Business Line, 2020) Cash reserves of airline company are running low and many are almost at brink of bankruptcy. Employees of this sector are also facing the difficulty of job losses and pay cuts as some of the airlines have asked their employees to go on leave without pay. *Family entertainment venues and air, land and sea transport have been severely hit.* (The Economic Times. 2020)

Automobile Industry

This sector was already witnessing a sluggish demand for the last one year. The current situation has further aggravated the problem leading to acute liquidity crisis. China accounts for 27 percent of India's automotive part imports. Most of the auto part factories are located in Hubei, a province in Wuhan so the supply chain of the automotive sector has been hit significantly. There has been a delay in production and delivery of BS-IV model vehicles due to the shutting down of these factories. (Economic Times, 2020). According to a report in ET Auto, the Indian automobile sector is witnessing an estimated loss of around Rs 13000 crore to Rs 15000 crore due to this pandemic. Majority of the manufacturers like Maruti, Hyundai, Honda, Suzuki, TVS have opted for the temporary shutdown of the operations. Passenger Vehicle production in March, 2020 stood at 91,602 units as against 1,35,236 units in March units in March 2020, a fall of 32.26 percent. (Business Today, 2020). According to the report, the country's largest car maker Maruti Suzuki has decreased production by 32.05 percent in March. The company produced a total of 92,540 units in March as against 1,36,201 in the year ago.

Electronic Industry

China is the primary and big supplier both for the raw material as well as final product used in electronics industry. India's total electronic imports accounts for 45 percent of China. India's electronics industry is scared of supply disruptions, production reduction, impact on product prices due to heavy dependence on electronics component supply-directly and indirectly- and local manufacturing. The spread of this pandemic have squeezed the sales of top electronic companies and smart phone makers which have major supplies to India. All large manufacturers including LG, Voltas, Samsung, Haier and Panasonic have decided on a 3-5 percent price increase across models. This means a price hike of Rs 3,000-4,000 for premium and large capacity models. (Economic Times, 2020). India's contribution to global smart phone production has jumped to 16 percent in 2019 from 9 percent in 2016. But in 2020 again it falls back to 9 percent i.e. India's share in global smart phone product has fallen to levels seen four years back as factories have halted manufacturing activities due to lockdown and demand is likely to stay weak till June-July.

Oil Industry

The plunging demand arising due to the Corona Virus pandemic combined with a savage price war has left the fossil fuel industry broken. Petrol, diesel consumption likely to burn out on corona virus heat due to travel restrictions, lockdowns as well as a slowdown in industrial activity. One important impact of the corona virus outbreak on the downstream oil industry is that the price of crude oil has fallen significantly in a short time, taking billions off the stock prices of major oil and gas companies. The demand for fuel in India has dropped by a steep 10-11 percent in the first two weeks of March as the outbreak of corona virus (Covid-19) led to the cancellation of flights and reduction in industrial activity. "The petroleum industry is witnessing the impact of corona virus on sales of all petroleum products. The overall demand for liquid fuels has gone down by 10-11 percent in the first fortnight of March 2020," said Indian Oil Corp (IOC), the country's largest fuel retailer, in a statement. (Business Line, the Hindu) Petrol and diesel demand is down 66 percent in April, while aviation turbine fuel consumption has collapsed by 90 percent as most airlines have stopped flying, industry officials said. (Bloombergquint, 2000)

Textile Industry

India exported over Rs 1 lakh crore of garments in 2018-19, according to the Ministry of Commerce. These exports bring in 60 percent of Indian apparel marker's revenue. (Rani, Rekha, 2020) As the Chinese Textiles factories have halted the operations, Indian textile & Apparel Industry is affected mainly because of heavy reliance on China for textile raw material i.e. synthetic yarn, synthetic fibres, zippers, buttons and hangers. India also exports bulk of cotton yarn to China. (Kapur, Rohit et al, 2020) The prices of cotton yarn have come down as the traders anticipate a curtailed demand from China due to corona virus attack. (Pratheesh, J.T et al, 2020) Due to the lockdown all factories small or big, spinning, weaving, garmenting etc are temporarily closed. According to Delhi based exporter of Garments, around 70 percent orders have been postponed or cancelled.

Micro, Small and Medium Enterprise Sector

Micro, Small and Medium Enterprises play a very dominant role in the economic development of India. Small and medium scale enterprises assists the government in increasing infrastructures and manufacturing industries, reducing issues like pollution, slums, poverty, and many development acts. Apart from providing employment to crores of people, it has the added benefit of minimum capital requirements. According to Recent annual reports, Micro, Small and Medium Enterprises (MSMEs) indicate that the sector contributes to around 30 percent of India's GDP, and based on conservative estimates, employs around 50 percent of industrial workers. The current corona virus pandemic (Covid-19) lockdown will substantially disrupt the operations of these MSMEs due to their dependence on the cash-economy that is severely hit by the lockdown, the physical non-availability of workers, and restrictions in the availability of raw materials and transport infrastructure. (Hindustan Times, 2020). More than one-fourth of India's 69 million micro, small and medium enterprises (MSMEs) may shut shop if the lockdown extends beyond four to eight weeks, as a majority of them will have a cash crunch, said Ravi Venkatesan, chairman, Global Alliance for Mass Entrepreneurship (GAME). (The Economic Times, 2020). Biswajit Dhar, a professor of economics at Jawaharlal Nehru University, said the government should immediately come out with an incentive package for exporters as the current crisis will severely hit the MSME sector.

Hospitality Industry

The cascading effect of the corona virus pandemic on the India's hospitality is very disastrous. This sector is also likely to be impacted by large scale cancellations and drop in room rates. Most of the owners are struggling to recover the fixed cost as the business hotels in various metro cities are lying vacant. The impact will be more severe on the four-star and above categories since their occupants are business and foreign tourists and there is negligible demand from both. (Business Standard, 2020) Restaurants at Malls have recorded a violent drop. Indian hospitality industry is expecting to lose to the tune of Rs 620 crores.(Business Line, 2020) Pre lockdown, hotel occupancy rates of 70 percent declined to 20 percent with restaurants losing 30-35 percent of their business.

Entertainment and Sports Industry

To curb the spread of COVID-19 various crowded places like Cinema theatres, multiplexes, Shopping Malls, Gyms have been totally closed. Various promotional and sports events are also being called off. One of the major cricketing events in the country –Indian Premier League (IPL) has been deferred for the time being. Cancellation of IPL matches alone could hit the industry with the loss of approximately Rs 10000 crores. (Televisionpost, 2000) Massive impact of this pandemic is also seen on television and film industry due to the cancellation of shootings and promotional events. As the cinema, theatres and PVRs are closed, global box office has to bear the loss of millions of dollars. The International film academy awards planned to take place on 27th March was cancelled (Lawyersclub, 2020). Hollywood studios are being forced to postpone the release of various blockbuster movies and to drastically alter the production schedules around the world. (Rani, Rekha, 2020)

Poultry Industry

Untrue rumors regarding the transmission of COVID-19 through chicken, meat, eggs, fish has hardly hit the poultry industry. India is the largest producer of eggs and 5th largest producer of broilers so the poultry farmers are suffering the heavy losses. Due to the fall in demand, the sale of poultry sector come down by 80 percent losing business of approximately Rs 1500-2000 crores daily. (Economic Times, 2020) Also to prevent the stockpile up, poultry companies have been forced to sell the birds at Rs 25 per kg, a third of the raising cost, says B Soundrarajan, chairman of Poultry Company. (Rani, Rekha, 2020) Poultry farming offers direct and indirect employment to over five crores Indian citizens engaged in poultry production, trading, feed manufacturing, agriculture crops, logistics, exports and others. So the income of the persons engaged in these sectors is adversely affected.

Agriculture Industry

COVID-19 is badly disrupting activities in marketing of agriculture and supply chains due to lockdown. Its impact on agriculture is multiple and varied across diverse segments that constitutes the agricultural value chain. In India, State and district borders are closed to avoid and stop the spread of corona and the transport system is stopped. The non-availability of migrant labour is interrupting some harvesting activities, particularly in the northwest India where wheat and pulses are being harvested (Dev, S.Mahendra, 2020). Huge crisis have been seen in harvesting and marketing crops at the farm level because of the disruptions in the procurement of food grains by government agencies, collection of harvests from the farms by private traders, scarcity of workers to harvest the *rabi* crop, a shortfall of drivers in the transportation sector. All these factors led to huge crisis in the variety of crops viz wheat, grapes, watermelons, bananas, muskmelon, *chana*, cotton, chillies, turmeric, cumin, coriander, onion, and potato. According to report, Tomato growers in Maharashtra are receiving not even Rs 2 per kg and Grape growers are facing an aggregate loss of Rs 1000 crore as the demand has fallen. Wheat prices in Madhya Pradesh are reported to have fallen from Rs 2200/Q to about Rs 1600/Q by March 25, 2020. In Punjab, vegetables that were sold at Rs 15/kg are now being sold at a mere Rs 1/kg. (Kumar, R.Rama, 2020)

Education Industry

The Novel Corona virus, also known as COVID-19 will have a far-reaching impact on all schools, colleges and universities including pre-primary, primary, the secondary and higher secondary and higher education. (Hindustan Times, 2020) In order to ensure the reduction of mass gatherings and to avoid the spread of the novel corona virus disease and as a precautionary measure, almost all the state Governments across the country has ordered to shut down all schools (government, government-aided including private schools) and colleges. As per the present situation, there is an uncertainty regarding the re-opening of schools and colleges. No doubt, this is the crucial time for education sector because entrance tests of several universities and competitive examinations are held during this period. All major entrance examinations are postponed including engineering, medical, law, agriculture, fashion and designing courses, etc. (Jagran Josh, 2020). Universities may face impact in terms of a slowdown in student internships and placements, lower fee collection that can create hurdles in managing the working capital. Students are likely to confused about the eligibility for admissions to various courses because of absence or delays of entrance tests and related decisions of the government. Payment potential shall get affected due to jobs getting lost, pay cuts, layoffs, and sectors getting closed. Students and parents may be more inclined towards low-fee courses, short-term courses, or online learning for quick re-skilling options. Also parents will prefer their children staying at home and studying locally. (Majumdar, Dr Swati, 2020)

Conclusion

From the present study it is concluded that corona virus has challenged almost every sector of the Indian economy. This corona pandemic is a severe demand shock for the Indian economy and could lead to further moderation in country's GDP growth as the corona virus induced lockdown is causing significant disruption across the multiple sectors. Reduction in the consumption due to lockdown leads to decrease in demand which ultimately reduces revenue and profits of almost all the traders and industrialists. So the fall in disposable income further leads to decline in consumption as now people are focusing more on necessities which ultimately puts adverse effects on the national income, output, employment and growth rate of the economy. (Koshle, Himanshu et al., 2020) All the players in the economy such as producers, consumers, debtors, creditors, government, entrepreneurs, banks, financial institutions will bear great loss due to this pandemic. Time alone will tell the extent and severity of the loss. Due to the non-availability of vaccination till now we should avoid unnecessary travel, meetings and participation in social gatherings. Protect yourself and others from infection by washing your hands or using an alcohol based rub frequently and not touching your face. (Venkateswaran, D., 2020)

References

- Bloombergquint.2000. Petrol, Diesel Demand Slumps 66 percent in April as Demand Evaporates. Available at: https://www.bloombergquint.com/markets/petrol-diesel-demand-slumps-66-pc-in-apr-atf-down-90-pc-as-coronavirus-eviscerates-demand
- Business Line, The Hindu. 2020. India's fuel demand drops 11 percent in March as corona virus hits aviation, transport. Available at https://www.thehindubusinessline.com/economy/macro-economy/coronavirus-impact-indias-fuel-demand-drops-11-per-cent-in-march/article31109662.ece
- Business Line. 2020. Corona virus impact: Hospitality industry to suffer losses up to Rs. 620 crore. Available at https://www.thehindubusinessline.com/economy/coronavirus-impact-hospitality-industry-to-suffer-losses-to-the-tune-of-620-crore/article31106611.ece
- Business Line. 2020. Corona virus impact: Over 580 flights cancelled to and from India between February 1 and March 6. Available at https://www.thehindubusinessline.com/news/coronavirus-impact-over-580-flights-cancelled-to-and-from-india/article31051980.ece
- Business Line.2020. Travel industry among hardest hit by corona virus lockdown. Available at https://www.thehindubusinessline.com/economy/travel-industry-hit-hard-by-the-coronavirus-clampdown/article31149014.ece
- Business Today.2020. Corona Virus : Maruti Suzuki production falls 32 percent in March amid lockdown. Available at https://www.businesstoday.in/sectors/auto/coronavirus-maruti-suzuki-production-falls-32-in-march-amid-lockdown/story/400790.html
- Dev, S. Mahendra.2020. Covid-19 Pandemic and agriculture: A note. Available at https://www.mssrf.org/content/covidpercentC2percentAD-19-pandemic-and-indian-agriculture-note
- Goyal, Shikha. 2020. What is the impact of Corona virus on Indian Economy? Available at https://www.jagranjosh.com/general-knowledge/what-is-the-impact-of-coronavirus- on-indian-economy-1582870052-1
- Hindustan Times.2020. The MSME sector is critical in times of Covid-19. Available at https://r.search.yahoo.com/_ylt=AwrxhWqW075es0sA6A3nHgx.;_ylu=X3oDMTEyZnJrZm1tBGNvbG8Dc2czBHBvcwMzBHZ0aWQDQjg4NjhfMQRzZWMDc3I-/RV=2/RE=1589593111/RO=10/RU=httpspercent3apercent2fpercent2fwww.hindustantimes.compercent2fanalysispercent2fmsmes-is-critical-in-times-of-covid-19percent2fstory-6Juiu9zs4jKUdkHLobT6WJ.html/RK=2/RS=lL7yF3E5fO6gCVzyCDBYZk.Kd.o

- Hindustan Times, 2020. Schools, colleges shut down amid spread of corona virus. Available at https://r.search.yahoo.com/_ylt=AwrxgzMMC8JeVjwANAnnHgx.;_ylu= X3oDMTEyMTdhbmo0BGNvbG8Dc2czBHBvcwM4BHZ0aWQDQjg4NjhfMQRzZWMDc3I-/RV=2/RE=1589803917/RO=10/RU=httpspercent3apercent2fpercent2fwww.hindustantimes.compercent2findia-newspercent2fschools-colleges-shut-down-amid-spread-of-coronaviruspercent2fstory-5tY5gpyNsCVg4BOd7NJXZP.html/RK=2/RS=CmzpKzgvAtcqOFQq79eA1idULqM
- Jagran Josh.2020. Impact of Coronavirus on Education in India. Available at https://r.search.yahoo.com/_ylt=AwrxgzM7AsJeugYAdQPnHgx.;_ylu= X3oDMTEyZnJrZm1tBGNvbG8Dc2czBHBvcwMzBHZ0aWQDQjg4NjhfMQRzZWMDc3I-/RV=2/RE=1589801659/RO=10/RU=httpspercent3apercent2fpercent2fwww.jagranjosh.compercent2fgeneral-knowledgepercent2fimpact-of-coronavirus-on-education-in-india-1587642880-1/RK=2/RS=ncawxPkmTv33sNCRXXWMVWz6WyI-
- Kapur, Rohit et.al. 2020. Social and economic Impact of Covid-19 on India and recovery potential. Available at https://www.india-briefing.com/news/social-economic-impact-covid-19-india-recovery-potential-20202.html/
- Koshle, Himanshu et.al.2020. Breakdown of Business and Workers in India: Impact of Corona Virus. Available at SSRN:https://ssrn.com/abstract=3557544 or HYPERLINKhttps://economictimes.indiatimes.com/https://economictimes.indiatimes.com/industry/healthcare/biotech/pharmaceuticals/coronavirus-outbreak-drug-pricing-regulator-asks-companies-to-give-information-on-price-inventory/articleshow/74364592.cms?utm_source=contentofinterest&utm_medium=text&utm_campaign=cppst
- Times, Economic. 2020. Coronavirus: Chicken prices fall, poultry industry affected. Available at https://m.economictimes.com/news/economy/indicators/coronavirus-chicken-prices-fall-poultry-industry-affected/articleshow/74546189.cms
- Times, Economic. 2020. Impact of corona virus on Indian tourism could run into thousands of crores of rupee. Available at https://m.economictimes.com/industry/services/travel/impact-of-coronavirus-on-indian-tourism-could-run-into-thousands-of-crores-of-rupees/articleshow/74592482.cms
- Times, Economic. 2020.Corona virus & its impact on various sectors. Available at https://r.search.yahoo.com/_ylt=AwrxhSTCyb5e8jQAdhTnHgx.;_ylu= X3oDMTEyMXNxbXIyBGNvbG8Dc2czBHBvcwMxBHZ0aWQDQjg4NjhfMQRzZWMDc3I-/RV=2/RE=1589590594/RO=10/RU=httpspercent3apercent2fpercent2feconomictimes.indiatimes.compercent2fmarketspercent2fstockspercent2fnewspercent2fcoronavirus-its-impact-on-various-sectorspercent2fcovid-19-impactpercent2fslideshowpercent2f74490812.cms/RK=2/RS=mF0_N.yRcx3DWZqPUJPNhqTWOGs-
- Times, Economic. 2020. Electronic goods set to get expensive amid short supplies from virus hit China. Available at https://economictimes.indiatimes.com/industry/cons-products/electronics/electronic-goods-set-to-get-expensive-amid-short-supplies-from-virus-hit-china/articleshow/74327481.cms?utm_source=contentofinterest&utm_medium= text&utm_campaign=cppst

- Venkateswaran, D.2020. The impact of COVID-19 on India. Studies in Indian Place Names .Vol-40-Issue 71-March. Pp. 1581-1589.
- www.televisionpost.com.2000.Cancellation of IPL matches will cause Rs 10,000 crore loss for sports industry: FICCI. Available at https://www.televisionpost.com/cancellation-of-ipl-matches-will-cause-rs-10000-crore-loss-for-sports-industry-ficci/

25

Impact of Corona Pandemic on Banking and Financial Sector in India

Jagmeet Kaur

The Covid-19 pandemic has caused a severe blow to the global economy. Governments of all the countries of the world are working day and night towards its control and solution. India was trying to recover from the economic downturn of the previous year, when Covid-19 struck and put an end to its industrial and commercial momentum. About 125 countries of the world, including the United States (US), India, Singapore, Australia and many others are facing this deadly disease. The only effective solution is lockdown for the control of the disease. This crisis has derailed the economy of all developed and developing countries, and it is difficult for underdeveloped countries to cope up in the next few years.

Even as the Indian economy strives to recover from a slowdown, the Corona virus outbreak has further hit the possibility of revival given the negative impact on the various sectors of the economy. As the economy battles a new scare, stock markets are witnessing fresh volatility negatively impacting investors. With the cases of Corona virus getting detected in India, the sentiment is expected to further go down. World Bank and credit rating agencies have downgraded India's growth for fiscal year 2021 with the lowest figures India has seen in three decades since India's economic liberalisation in the 1990s. The former Chief Economic Advisor to the Government of India has said that India should prepare for a negative growth rate in FY-2021 and that the country would need a 720 lakh crore stimulus to overcome the contraction. However, the International Monetary Fund projection for India for the financial year 2021-22 of 1.9 percent GDP growth is the highest among G-20 nations.Within a month, unemployment rose from 6.7 percent on 15 March to 26 percent on 19 April, 2020. During the lockdown, an estimated 14 crore people lost employment. More than 45 percent of households across the nation have reported an income drop as compared to the previous year.

On 14 April 2020, the Prime Minister of India extended the lockdown to 3 May 2020. A new set of guidelines for the calibrated opening of the economy and relaxation of the lockdown were also set in place which are taking effect from 20 April, 2020. On 17 April, the RBI Governor announced more measures to counter the economic impact of the pandemic including 50,000 crore special finance to NABARD, SIDBI, and NHB. On 18 April, to protect Indian companies during the pandemic, the government changed India's foreign direct investment policy. The Department of Military Affairs has put on hold all capital acquisitions for the beginning of the financial year.

Impact on Indian Economy

As per FICCI, up to 53 percent of Indian businesses have specified a certain amount of impact of shutdowns caused due to COVID-19 on operations.Various businesses such as hotels and airlines are cutting salaries and laying off employees. By 24 April the unemployment rate had increased nearly 19 percent within a month, reaching 26 percent unemployment across India. According to the Centre for Monitoring Indian Economy, around 140,000,000 Indian lost employment in the lockdown. More than 45 percent households across the nation have reported an income drop as compared to the previous year. On 4 April, former Reserve Bank of India chief Raghuram Rajan said that the corona virus pandemic in India may just be the "greatest emergency since Independence". He further added that China has lost around 10 percent of its GDP in the first quarter and the projections for the United States and European countries say that they will end up losing a similar percentage of their GDP in the second quarter of the current year.

Impact on Banking and Financial Sector

Recently Fitch, a rating agency, has revised the operating environment score of India from BB+ to BB. This is due to the fact that Indian banks are already under-capitalised and has bad loans, having less consumer confidence, the COVID-19, will worsen the situation of Banks. Forecast from the Financial Stability Report released in December shows that the gross NPA of public sector banking group may rise to 13.5 percent from 12.7 percent and it may rise to 5.4 percent from 3.9 percent for private lenders. If lockdown is extended for more days, job losses and pay cuts will be increase. For banking, it may dent in loan growth and lead to higher default. In addition to it, due to less lending exposure of banks, the Credit Cost will also rise.

The spread of the virus has triggered panic across the world and shaken the confidence of investors. Making things worse is the crude oil war between Saudi Arabia and Russia, which has injected volatility into other assets. Earlier only the equity and debt markets were impacted by the Covid-19 scare but now the commodities and currency market are in turmoil due to the crude oil war. After a crash of this magnitude, market confidence usually does not come back soon. On 23 March 2020, stock markets in India post worst losses in history. SENSEX fell 4000 points (13.15 percent) and NSE NIFTY fell 1150 points (12.98 percent). However, on 25 March, one day after a complete 21 day lockdown was announced by the Prime Minister, SENSEX posted its biggest gains in 11 years, adding a value of 4.7 lakh crore for investors. On 8 April, following positive indication from the Wall Street that the pandemic may have reached its peak in the US, the stock markets in India rose steeply once again. By 29 April, Nifty held the 9500 mark.

Measures of RBI to Counter the Effects of Corona Pandemic

Central banks across the world are responding to the Covid-19 pandemic. In India also, the Central Bank, RBI announced its monetary policy and has paid attention to ensuring liquidity, reducing cost of loans, encouraging transmission and regulatory easing. These are elaborated as follows.

Reduction in the Repo and Reverse Repo Rates: In its seventh bi-monthly monetary policy, RBI announced reduced the repo rate by 75 basis points to 4.40 percent on March 27, 2020. Repo rate is a rate at which RBI lends to the banks. Also, the reverse repo rate has been reduced by 90 bps to 4 percent earlier than in the second round; it was further reduced by 25 basis points to 3.75 percent. Thus, it has become less attractive for banks to park their funds with the RBI. It will convince banks to lend more.

Reduction in the Cash Reserve Ratio: RBI has also announced to provide Rs 3.74 lakh crore liquidity to banks through reduction in Cash Reserve Ratio (CRR). CRR is the average daily balance that banks are required to maintain with the RBI. It will help in infusing liquidity of worth Rs 1,37,000 crore into the banking system.

Repayment Moratorium

RBI has allowed a repayment moratorium for three months on all term loans outstanding as on March 1, 2020 to the borrowers of all commercial banks which includes regional rural banks, small finance banks and local area banks along with co-operative banks, Non-Banking Finance Companies including Housing Finance Companies and Micro Finance Institutions. For the next three months, no EMI would be deducted from the account of anyone who has a loan outstanding. EMIs will resume after the moratorium period gets over. It will prove a huge relief for all EMI payers especially self-employed who have lost source of income due to lockdown. This moratorium will apply to corporate loans, home loans and car loans etc.

Ways and Means Limit

The Central Bank had already constituted an advisory committee to review the limit ways and means advance (WMA) limits for state governments and union territories. Pending its final recommendations, the RBI, through an announcement on 1 April, has raised the WMA limits for states and union territories by 30 percent to help them tide over the situation. In a second phase of RBI measures, it has now allow an increase of 60 percent in the ways and means limit of state governments with immediate effect, valid upto September 30, 2020.

Refinancing Facility to All India Financial Institutions

All India financial institutions (AIFIs) such as the National Bank for Agriculture and Rural Development (NABARD), the Small Industries Development Bank of India (SIDBI) and the National Housing Bank (NHB) play an important role in meeting the long-term funding requirements of agriculture and the rural sector, small industries, housing finance companies, NBFCs and MFIs. These All India Financial Institutions raise resources from the market through specified instruments allowed by the Reserve Bank, in addition to relying on their internal sources. In view of the tightening of financial conditions in the wake of the COVID-19 pandemic, these institutions are facing difficulties in raising resources from the market. Accordingly, it has been decided to provide special refinance facilities for a total amount of 50,000 crore to NABARD, SIDBI and NHB to enable them to meet sectoral credit needs. This will comprise 25,000 crore to NABARD for refinancing regional rural banks (RRBs), cooperative banks and micro finance institutions (MFIs); 15,000 crore to SIDBI for on-lending/ refinancing; and 10,000 crore to NHB for supporting housing finance companies (HFCs).

Relaxation in NPA Classification Norms

A relaxation in 90 days default norms before declaring them as NPAs would give relief to both the industry and the banks. The industry would continue to enjoy credit facility while the banks will not be required to make any NPA provisioning from their profits. For all accounts where lending institutions decide to grant moratorium or deferment announced by RBI on March 27, and which were standard as on March 1, 2020, the 90-day NPA norm shall exclude the moratorium period. This means that there would an asset classification standstill for all such accounts from March 1, 2020 to May 31, 2020. NBFCs, which are required to comply with Indian Accounting Standards (IndAS), may be guided by the guidelines duly approved by their boards on this front.

However, to ensure the health of the financial system is also protected while allowing for these relaxations, RBI has asked banks to set aside an additional ten percent provisioning for all accounts where they the standstill in asset classification is applied. The additional provisions can be adjusted later on against the provisioning requirements for actual slippages in such accounts.

Extension of Resolution Timeline

Under the stressed assets resolution framework of the RBI, called the June 7 circular, banks are required to set aside an additional 20 percent provision if they are unable to resolve accounts within 210 days from date of default or 180 days from turning an NPA. RBI has now decided that the period for resolution plan can be extended by 90 days.

Dividend from Banks

The Reserve Bank has said that all scheduled commercial banks will not make any dividend payout for the year ended March 2020 (financial year 2019-2020). This will be reviewed in the second quarter of FY21.

Emphasis on Digital Banking

RBI has also urged the people for more use of digital platforms such as use of debit cards, credit cards and online banking.

POST CORONA CHALLENGES FOR INDIA

Increase in the insurance claims: With increase in the number of deaths due to pandemic, the insurance sector will face lots of claims and its profitability of insurance sector be affected.

Loss of Direct and Indirect Tax collection: Due to decline in the economic activities, the tax collection will be adversely affected.

If government increases indirect taxes, it would prove increase inflation in the prices of commodities and burden on the poor which will reduce demand in the market. Further, direct taxes cannot be raised as lockdown has already hit the profits of companies and income of individuals badly.

Non-Tax revenue generation through disinvestment: In the present state of declining stock markets and negative sentiment in the markets, the disinvestment plans of the government is unlikely to be successful. For instance, presently with the airline industry being in a state of collapse, who would buy Air India? The insurance sector will face lots of claims and its profitability will be hit. The Life Insurance Corporation of India (LICI) will take big losses in the stock markets that are collapsing, while the LICI is buying stocks to support the markets. So, the sale of its equity is unlikely to take place. The sale of Bharat Petroleum Corporation Limited, pending for a while, is also unlikely to fructify since energy prices have collapsed, profitability has been hit and share prices have dropped globally. These were the three big-ticket items for raising additional non-tax revenue.

Rise in the Fiscal deficit: The fiscal deficit will rise because of above reasons. Thus, revenue will be short while expenditures to tackle the crisis will rise. But this should not be allowed to act as a constraint for increasing government expenditures to mitigate the crisis.

Number of defaulters may increase: A record numbers of consumers are trying to contact their bank with questions, concerns or to request special measures as their finances have been impacted by the fallout from the coronavirus. Many have lost their jobs due to which their incomes vanish. So, there is a fear of defaulting on loans or missing mortgage payments by such customers.

Rise in Inflation: Government has to improve supply chain so as to contain inflation in the coming times. Smoothening of Supply of food items will help in containing inflation.

Conclusion

Former governor of Reserve Bank of India Raghuram Rajan recently said that there are no real estimates as of now on how devastating impact of coronavirus will be on the global economy as well as the Indian economy. How long it will take to get it under control, how much GDP will be lost in the process, and how much can be recovered when the restrictive measures are taken off it is all unknown at the moment.

In brief, the situation is worse than that during a war, since demand has collapsed. Businesses and finance companies are likely to fail and employment severely impacted. To deal with the health and economic crisis, governments have announced emergency and set up special task forces on the economy. If a social breakdown is to be avoided the budget will have to be revamped with resources focused to mitigate the crisis confronting the marginalised sections of society. The moot question, however, is whether the crisis will bring about a fundamental change in societal thinking, with people realising that a lifestyle change is required and crucially, a well-functioning government and provision of public goods are needed at all times. After the outbreak of COVID-19 many countries like Japan and USA is looking for alternative to divert their investments outside China. All countries are looking to diversify their supply chains away from China. India can avail this opportunity and can emerge as a potential alternative choice for cost-efficient, quality products for rest of the world.

References

- https://www.epw.in/journal/2020/14/commentary/impact-covid-19-and-what-needs-be-done.html
- https://economictimes.indiatimes.com/industry/banking/finance/banking/covid-19-impact-banks-to-witness-spike-in-credit-costs-non-performing-assets-in 2020/articleshow/75004720.cms?from=mdr
- https://www.epw.in/journal/2020/15/commentary/covid-19-and-macroeconomic-uncertainty.html
- https://econsultancy.com/how-coronavirus-impacting-financial-sector-payments-banking-fintech-brand-response/
- https://economictimes.indiatimes.com/https://economictimes.indiatimes.com/industry/banking/finance/banking/coronavirus-impact-on-banks-bad-loans-may-surge-with-private-sector-banks-facing-maximum risk/articleshow/74763569.cms?utm_source=contentofinterest&utm_medium=text&utm_campaign=cppst
- https://www.cnbctv18.com/finance/here-is-the-list-of-key-relief-measures-announced-by-reserve-bank-of-india-today-5712201.htm
- https://en.wikipedia.org/wiki/Economic_impact_of_the_2019percentE2percent 80percent9320_coronavirus_pandemic_in_India.

Migrant Workers and COVID-19 Pandemic

26

Migrants and the Reverse Migration during the COVID-19 Pandemic

Rachana Sharma

Post 1990s, we are witnessing another turning point in the Indian economic history which is a result of the current pandemic, Covid-19. Much before the national lockdown was imposed, India's growth was on a slowdown which continued to be so and perhaps shrunk during the lockdown situation. The economic impacts of this pandemic have been globally disruptive and quite apparent. The social impacts of this public health crisis however have been numerous, too diverse and yet to be adequately explored. The migrant exodus in India during the pandemic became an international concern with analysts predicting the trends and implications of reverse migration and no future migration which added a fresh air to the development and marginalisation discourse. Migrants have always been ignored in the broader discourse of economic and social growth. Covid-19 public health crisis has forced us to finally acknowledge the migrants, their existence in huge numbers in our cities and villages, their role and contributions in making up our economies on one hand. While on the other hand, it has exposed some of the austere realities of inequality, marginalisation and privilege in Indian society. The article intends to look into the social impacts of Covid-19 on the migrants and the migration process in urban India. Also, it specifically looks into the vulnerabilities faced by the migrants during the lockdown situation and migration scenario in the post-lockdown. The article broadly reviews the broader discourse on the reverse migration during the current pandemic.

Migrants during Covid-19

India is witnessing the greatest exodus (since the partition of India in 1947) due to the current public health crisis and the national lockdown

(24 March 2020) followed by it. Indian government's sudden enforcement of lockdown following a 14 hour 'Janata curfew' (Economic Times, 2020) on March 22, 2020 immediately disadvantaged the vulnerable sections of the society as it restricted people stepping out from their homes. Although this was announced as a single day event, the Indian Prime Minister indirectly signaled the public through his live address about the seriousness of the Covid-19 pandemic overnight. Followed by it the national lockdown was imposed (patterned on the experiences of the western countries) and the people were left with no choices and preparedness. Initially, the lockdown was announced to last till the 14 April, 2020 and then was extended and relaxed in a phased manner. Currently, it has reached the unlock phase 4 from September, 1, 2020. As of 20 September, 2020 India has a total of 5.4 million cases with 86,752 death cases and 4.3 million cases of recovery from the Coronavirus disease (www.coronatracker.com). Although it appears that everyone is affected by Covid-19 alike yet, public health crises are certainly not an equal opportunity event. Weaker sections are worst hit by the current pandemic as their concerns have been largely ignored in the Covid-19 Management Programmes.

Migrants have always been ignored, invisibilised, underrated and considered as a non-significant community despite the crucial role they play in the process of development. Although, the literature on migration today has grown both in volume and variety due to the unfolding intricacies of migratory patterns and processes yet there are gaps in this area which need to be explored so as to provide solutions to the complex problems of the migrant labourers. The gut-wrenching stories of migrant labour during the Covid-19 pandemic, their hardships and exploitation raised a concern to address the loopholes within the political economy of migrant misery. It is estimated that lives of nearly 45 million (Singh, 2020) migrants in India have been affected directly by the Covid-19 Pandemic. The containment measures following the Coronavirus pandemic in India brought tremendous restrictions on economic activities, social interaction and movement for trade, work and leisure. Although this was a very complex situation and its impacts cannot be rightly assessed at even this very point of time when the current pandemic is also being followed by the global political crisis and is still ongoing yet certain assessment of the pandemic can be made with the help of existing and limited coverage of this phenomenon. The scale of the impact varies from state to state, city to city but definitely some disruption was caused at various levels due to the pandemic and the subsequent lockdown. On the whole, the biggest consequence of the pandemic has been the distress migration crisis that was seen across India bringing rare attention to the otherwise invisible internal migrant workers who populate our cities and villages and work largely in the unskilled and semi-skilled jobs. During this period, there has been an unprecedented migration of workers from urban to rural India. For several decades this movement has been happening from rural to urban India with millions of workers moving from the less developed regions and villages to the cities in search of opportunities, livelihood and better living conditions. India has nearly 45 million migrants as per the rough records brought out during the pandemic of which most of the migrant workers are undereducated, work in low end jobs in unorganised sector, belong to lower caste, work on daily wages, are employed on short contracts and come from large families and rural areas of our country.

Migration has been an old and complex global phenomenon. Uneven economic development, inter-regional disparity and differences in living standards between socio-economic groups are some of the important reasons responsible for migration. Arya and Roy (2006) notes that the adoption of neo-liberal policies shattered the rural as well as urban economies by instigating the forced closure of factories and mills. The new policies adopted by the government during this period eroded the regional economies by breaking the links between workers, farming and industries forcing both men, women and children to flee to more developed places in search of livelihood. In recent times, India has witnessed significant out-migrations and internal migration to the cities from rural areas and across specific states on account of changes in demography, poverty and transformations in the economy. This trend has accelerated with globalisation and urbanisation which was at 31.16 percent as per the census 2011. The Census 2011 estimates that the total number of internal migrants in India numbers at 45.36 million which include 1,40,962,280 males and 3,12,679,675 females (The Hindu, 2016). The World Economic Forum citing the Economic Survey of India 2017 estimates that close to 9 million people migrated internally annually between 2011 and 2016. It also notes that Uttar Pradesh and Bihar are the biggest source states (Sharma, 2017). Punjab, Andhra Pradesh, Kerala, Karnataka, Delhi and Maharashtra have been popular destination states. The recent years appear to have increased mobility for economic reasons (Kundu and Mohanan, 2017). Most of the internal migrants are undereducated, work in low paid jobs in unorganised sector, belong to lower caste (are Scheduled Castes and Scheduled Tribes), work on daily wages or are employed through short contracts and come from large families and rural areas of our country. The main sectors they are employed in are construction, agriculture, textile, transportation, domestic work, brick-kilns and mines. As the lockdown was imposed, the cities and villages they raised and build turned their backs towards them.

The struggles of migrants during this pandemic reveal a deeply rooted intersectional problem of the conflict and class inequalities. As the world stood still, due to the restrictions imposed on the physical movement, the Indian migrant workers faced multiple hardships during this public health crisis. As the factories, industries and the entire production work was shut these migrants in both urban and rural areas of the country had to deal with the looming fear of loss of job, loss of income, food shortage, face starvation, suicides, exhaustion, accidents, infection, police brutality and denial of timely care. At the same time, there were several news reports on the denial of help to poor and migrant labour in various cities of India due to the fear of shortage of resources and spread of coronavirus. The labour in the villages did not face these issues much like those in the heartless cities. As all forms of transportation was suspended. The families of migrant labour, the women and the children were forced to begin their arduous journeys back to the villages after reaching the close to starvation point and left with no other option (Press Trust of India, 2020). For most of them this journey was not easy. Hazardous journeys were undertaken by the migrants which entailed walking thousands of kilometres, crossing borders of various states by paying a hefty amount to the agents, with no money and food for several days fighting the weather conditions. Heartbreaking pictures and reports of the plight of migrants, the women and their children, the pregnant, ill and the old walking, cycling, and crossing interstate borders were widely in circulation on social media (Thapliyal, 2020). These social media visuals raise several questions on the seriousness and arrangements made by the state governments for the well-being of these migrant workers in the lockdown period. While many reached their destinations by using all the possible means, some were never able to make it due to the restrictions imposed on them by the state, district and national authorities. For some, the journey towards the destination did not start at all and for the others it did not end at the destination.

During this period the migrant labour, which was once considered relevant by the host areas had to face negative reactions from the local communities in the form of casteist slur and class bias and were discredited as irrelevant and stigmatised (Bhowmick, 2020). The host and native states also showed apathetic attitude towards them as insufficient help was extended to these people. Despite the essential support provided by the state governments as well as the Non-Governmental Organisations, in lakhs the labourers chose to forcefully migrate back to their native places due to the above stated reasons and also because of the fear of death in the 'No Man's Land', the concrete jungles, the cities. Initially, no arrangements or plans were initiated by the state governments to help and rescue the stranded labour. The media attention to this humanitarian crisis not only put pressure on multiple state governments and civil society to provide safe shelter and food in a time of evolving public health crisis, but also drew global attention to India's invisible migrant workers. It was only when the migrant problem started getting more severe that the state governments decided to 'get rid of' the migrants and started arranging buses to take them back to their villages. Nonetheless, it became a more challenging task due to the huge number of migrants and overcrowding in the busses. It was on 1 May 2020 the Indian Government introduced the 'special Shramik Trains' from various districts in the country (www.theprint.com). Unfortunately, the magnitude of migrant spread in the truer sense was never realised before this pandemic. An extraordinary rush and shortage of trains caused additional miseries to the migrants ranging from registration, to endless waits at screening centres. Alongwith this, special efforts were made in certain states to aid this reverse migration and charter planes, private buses and other modes were arranged by the businessmen, factory owners and employers. Maximum trains went to Uttar Pradesh followed by Bihar and Jharkhand.

Although, the exact scale of reverse migration is not known and available till date in the public domain yet, rough estimates state that nearly 23 million migrants have returned to India's villages. Media coverage on the 'exit' through shramik trains also enlightens us on the existing 'Local v/s Migrant' contestations. Although migrants contribute to the economic growth of the host societies yet, there has always been a desire among the local populations to get rid of migrants. Migrants are always looked at as a threat and a burden by the locals, particularly by the local labourers. Also, the locals regard them as inferior in the power and status hierarchy. The exit movement of migrants in many parts of the country was followed by the 'hate politics'. News from several states came up where migrant labourers were found throwing meals from the trains, buses and badmouthing their host states out of their bad experiences during this public health crisis which was followed by a similar reaction from the host residents (Lahiri and Chandra, 2020). The 'never return' slogans were shared from both sides. Migrant workers are mistreated and denied rights as equals in the place of destination and their position was more precarious during this time and numerous misleading information circulated around the migrants and their concerns.

Nonetheless, the stigmatisation not just was faced by these migrants at their workplaces, or host locations but also back in their hometowns. The migrant reverse movement also informs us that states from where the migrants were going, passing and destination states came into disagreement over ownership status of these people as they were treated like untouchables and labeled as 'carriers of the virus' and additional burden on the resources of the state. Mandatory sanitisation and quarantine was imposed on them at their reception in the native states (Gupta, Mitra and Sud, 2020). In certain cases, arrests of the stranded and mobile migrants were also made for violating the lockdown guidelines. The overarching concern was the risk of spread of coronavirus from the urban 'hotspots', to the cities and villages of destination. As in thousands the migrants were returning home every day, the host societies and receiving societies had deficient infrastructure to provide adequate services to them for the institutional quarantine, testing and tracking. The state governments had their own apprehensions related to the explosion of COVID-19 cases causing a second wave of outbreak in the villages. On the whole it can be said that the migrants faced several problems during the imposition of lockdown. The relief to the poor migrants was pressed into actual service much after the lockdown. It is obvious that both studies and policies have not adequately addressed the poverty, lack of socio-economic infrastructures and legal support that continues to leave low and unskilled migrants highly vulnerable to tough working conditions, health, trafficking, discrimination and other related problems. The massive reverse migration from working states has formed a humanitarian and health security challenge and an exceptional logistical nightmare (Iyenger and Jain, 2020).

The Challenges and Possibilities of Reverse Migration

The reverse migration debate has largely been surrounded by certain questions like 'would reverse migration bring in changes in the current migration process? Will the migrants return to the host regions? What impact would it carry for the different sections and places?'. The reverse movement of migrants towards their native places is definitely going to have debilitating impacts on the migrants, their host and receiving places as well as society and economy at large. For both, the host regions and the native regions of the migrants handling the reverse migration is a challenging task. There are various ways to understand the current migration crisis and the future possibilities led by this situation for the migrants and the post-pandemic migration process. Firstly, let us talk about the situations at their native place. Basically, the migrants face the two situations that exist at their native places: (a) challenges of absorption that would compel the migrants for a re-migration and (b) the possibilities of growth and stay, through the rural revival and hinterland development.

Rural economies in India we know are overburdened, over reliant on agriculture, have covert underemployment and are less diverse due to which employment would remain skewed and low in the push states. Therefore, these regions would not be able to absorb and sustain this additional population in the existing situation wherein loss of economic activities are taking place as per the regulations of the central and state governments. There could be certain possibilities for the future growth and absorption in these regions though. Revival of MGNREGS was proposed as a solution in many states to retain the labour and labour unrest (Verma, 2020). However, this programme can not aid much in the diminution of the existing crisis at large due to its own set of limitations.

As we know, the current pandemic is also being followed by the global economic crisis as well as political crisis. The online face- off that China is facing at the global end has given some hopeful scenarios for furthering the development in the other countries, especially India. Due to the irresponsible conduct of China as a contributor to this world crisis, and mass antipathy towards China many of the countries and investors proposed and lifted their economic base from China to other parts of the country. States like Uttar Pradesh are trying to create more employment avenues to retain their population and develop the state. The proactive stand of UP can be seen from the initiatives of the state to woo global players (US, South Korea, Japan, Thailand and members of the European Union) who are looking to exit China (https://www.livemint.com) and also through the very recent announcement by the UP Government related to the establishment of 'Film City' in the state (Bhatnagar, 2020). Nonetheless, these developments will take much time to materialise. It is hoped that agro activities and rural-urban infrastructural development will get an impetus as of now, but it will take some time however these people who come from the underprivileged section of the society won't be able to wait and delay their re-remigration for such a long. Overall, if we see, the current situation could be a take-off stage for the native locations, as they can benefit themselves from this workforce and create economic clusters by tapping them and working on rural and hinterland development, where the actual scope of absorption lies. Also, with the global political commotion and economic realignments going on it may be that more employment generation would happen in these untapped locations which would slow down the migration process and diminish regional disparities in the long run.

The second scenario exists at the receiving places. As the production and supply chain has seen slow down (www.manufacturingtodayindia.com).

It is a very compromising situation for these receiving regions, particularly the cities who have never considered the relevance, the magnitude of their dependence, their might and the unionisation. For migrants on the other end this is an opportunity wherein they can think of establishing safety nets for themselves in these places. The urban bourgeoisie has realised now that you can establish industry but you cannot run it without these invisible and footloose labourers. As from the wider reporting of experiences of migrants of the pandemic we witnessed a lot of resentment among both the hosts and the guest working population. It appeared that the migrants neither would be welcomed back, nor would choose to be back to their workplaces. However, a part of media coverage on this homecoming also informed us that how the employers and state made arrangements for their workers by high ring private vehicles, planes and booking the trains and also gave them incentives for coming back and rejoining post relaxation and promised return facilities. This holds true, when one looks at the official data of Punjab wherein the industrialists are trying their best to lure the migrants back to the workplaces by offering bonuses, increase in salary, offering stay for living, food services and other incentives to make them stay back, and come back at their own expense. It is therefore, the data of Punjab shows that dropout rate in reverse migration has gone up because of resumption of economic activity (Khanna, 2020).

It can be envisioned that post-pandemic the receiving states will have to think of a long term social and economic rehabilitation and reintegration plan for these workforces in order to boost their economies. We can see this model of development sneaking in from the southern state of India, Kerela that was first in acknowledging it and is working in this direction. The final question now is how things will ultimately turn out? Will the migrants come back? Will this re-migration be in any way different? Will our cities continue to be centres for growth? The answers to the above stated question lie in understanding not just these two situations but also demand and examination of the migrant mindset and their astuteness. It is guesstimated that re-migration will happen albeit different from how it was happening in the past. We cannot underestimate the astuteness of migrants, they are what we can call as risk takers and calculative. Long distance migration may not happen much in recent times. Also based on the experiences during the pandemic the migrants might think of choosing newer places for their come back, i.e., maybe the bigger cities will not receive the same people and the same number of people. The sundry migrants i.e., those who go to cities to enlarge their earnings may take a little longer to return than those who are actually in the dire need of work.

Conclusions

On the basis of the above discussion, it can be said that the Covid-19 pandemic highlighted the deficiencies in social security nets for more vulnerable groups in our society. Caste, class, gender and 'vulnerability' traverse each other. The struggles of migrant workers during the pandemic reveal a deeply rooted intersectional problem of the class and regional conflict in the Indian society. The coverage of migrant issues also became more complicated because there was a discrepancy in the expectation of government and functioning of media. On one end the media blamed the government for not doing enough for the migrants and presented as if India was not prepared to handle this crisis. This brought the government into clash with the media. Certain media houses were accused of spreading the panic among people by presenting the sensuous visuals and concocted reporting.

On the other end, it also led to tussle between different states, as to who will examine these people, who will keep them in quarantines, who will bear their expenditure, how they would be looked after and allowed to cross the borders. All this increased the problems for the migrants. Similarly, reporting from bigger cities of India poured in as to how they were willing and providing food to them but maybe it was not to the taste of these people. It brought their concerns forward in some way but at the same time it resulted in further stigmatisation, misinformation and discrimination against the migrants. Those who preferred to stay back than go to their native location lamented their decision and those who chose to go back to their home faced a similar fate. Therefore, it has really been mentally, physically, financially and emotionally draining journey for migrant workers and it has been extremely tough for them to voice their sufferings as often during such public health crises the voices of the marginalised are ignored. Overall, it can be said that as the world struggles to keep up the economy, the Indian government and the state governments should now focus on strengthening the social welfare systems and a fair and effective labour migration governance system for workers within the country and their regions that is an urgent need of the hour.

Acknowledgements

I am thankful to my colleague Dr Jesna Jayachandran for her inputs on media coverage of the pandemic.

References

- Arya, Sadhna and Anupama Roy. 2006. Poverty, Gender and Migration. Sage: India.

- Bhatnagar, Amil. 2020. Available at: https://indianexpress.com/article/explained/uttar-pradesh-film-city-noida-gautam-buddh-nagar-yogi-adityanath-6603443/
- Bhowmick, Nilanjana. 2020. Available at: https://www.nationalgeographic.com/history/2020/05/they-treat-us-like-stray-dogs-migrant-workers-flee-india-cities/ Updated on 27 May 2020.
- Gupta, Swati; Esha Mitra and Vedika Sud. 2020. Available at: https://edition.cnn.com/2020/03/30/india/india-migrant-workers-sprayed-intl/index.htmlMigrant workers sprayed with disinfectant in one Indian state. Updated on 1 April 2020.
- Iyenger, Karthikeyan, P and Vijay, Kumar Jain.2020. Covid 19 and the Plights of Migrants in India. *Post Graduate Medical Journal* Retrieved from : https://pmj.bmj.com/content/early/2020/08/12/postgradmedj-2020-138454
- Khanna, Ruchika, M. 2020. Available at: https://www.tribuneindia.com/news/punjab/more-labourers-opt-to-stay-put-as-industry-resumes-operations-in-punjab-87510
- Kundu, Amitabh and P C Mohanan. 2017. Internal migration in India: A very moving story. Available at: https://economictimes.indiatimes.com/blogs/et-commentary/internal-migration-in-india-a-very-moving-story/
- Lahiri, Ishadrita and Divya Chandra. 2020. Available at: https://www.thequint.com/news/webqoof/migrant-workers-throwing-food-from-train-and-wasting-it-not-quite-fact-check. Updated on 8 May 2020.
- Mohanty, Debabrata and Dhrubo Jyoti. 2020. Available at: https://www.hindustantimes.com/india-news/pandemic-teaches-a-tragic-lesson-in-migration/story-69EIk6MB70zNDX1VsRTx0J.htmlPandemic teaches a tragic lesson in migration. Updated on: Jul 03, 2020 19:42 IST.
- Press Trust of India. 2020. Available at: https://www.ndtv.com/india-news/covid-19-after-walking-100-km-migrants-wife-delivers-baby-child-dies-2234134 After Walking 100 Km, Migrant's Wife Delivers Baby; Child Dies Updated on: May 24, 2020 2:51 am IST.
- Sharma, Krishnavatar. 2017. India has 139 million internal migrants. They must not be forgotten. *World Economic Forum.* Available at: https://www.weforum.org/agenda/2017/10/india-has-139-million-internal-migrants-we-must-not-forget-them/
- Singh, S.K; Vibhuti Patel, and Aditi Chaudhary. 2020. Reverse Migration of Labourers amidst COVID-19. *Economic and Political Weekly.* Vol. 55, Issue No. 32-33. Available at:- https://www.epw.in/journal/2020/32-33/commentary/reverse-migration-labourers-amidst-covid-19.html?0=ip_login_no_cache%3D4c1881cf231ed0fcc7166ba2e2cde175
- Thapliyal, Nisha. 2020. Available at: https://feminisminindia.com/2020/06/26/migrant-women-workers-covid-19-impact Migrant Women Workers on the Road: Largely Invisible and Already Forgotten. Updated on 26 June 2020.
- Verma, Gyan. 2020. Available at: https://www.livemint.com/news/india/up-woos-global-majors-looking-to-exit-china-11589391509910.html
- Verma, Shilpa. 2020. Available at :- https://www.downtoearth.org.in/blog/economy/can-mgnrega-be-a-tool-for-post-covid-19-rural-recovery-72201Can MGNREGA be a tool for post-COVID-19 rural recovery. Updated on 9 July 2020.

- https://theprint.in/india/171-shramik-special-trains-operated-since-1-may-ferrying-over-1-70-lakh-migrants-railways/. Updated on 7 May 2020.
- https://www.manufacturingtodayindia.com/sectors/7361-the-covid-19-lockdown-and-the-indian-manufacturing-industry-effects-and-recovery. The COVID 19 Lockdown and the Indian manufacturing industry – effects and recovery. Updated on 13 May 2020.
- https://www.coronatracker.com/country/india/ Covid-19 Alerts

Role of Political Institutions & Media during COVID-19 Pandemics

27

India- European Union Relations in Context of 15th Summit between the Two Entities Postponed Due to COVID-19

Renu Bala

The fifteen annual summit between India and European Union scheduled for 13 March in Brussels, was postponed owing to the Coronavirus pandemic. In view of the developments in the political space for both entities, the theme of the summit must include certain topics that would shape the future of the India-EU relations. In India, the abrogation of Article 370 and the subsequent imposition of a communications blackout in Jammu and Kashmir, the passage of the Citizenship Amendment Act (2019), and the institution of the National Register for Citizens (NRC) have garnered significant world attention. For the EU, the existing uncertainty in trade due to Brexit is now offset by a significant slowdown in manufacturing and a large health crisis due to the widespread cases of COVID-19 across Europe. Drawing on these partnership, it is imperative that the next EU-India summit host discussions on the several issues that will define the future of the strategic partnership. (Sawhney, 2020:01)

Historical Background

The relationship between the European Union and India goes back to the early 1960s, and India was the first country that established diplomatic relations with the EEC in 1962. India and EC signed Commercial Cooperation Agreement in 1973 (CCA), Commercial and Economic Cooperation Agreement (CECA) in 1981, and after the Treaty of Maastricht and formation of EU the two entities also signed Cooperation Agreement on Partnership and Development in (CAPD) 1994, which intended to take bilateral relations beyond merely trade and economic cooperation.

Therefore, since the Treaty of Maastricht economic and political relations between EU and India have intensified considerably. In 1993, the Joint Political Statement (JPS) of the EU and India formally launched a political dialogue with annual ministerial meetings resulting in Cooperation Agreement on Partnership and Development of 1994 that extended the bilateral relationship to broader domains in the economic and political fields. The first summit between EU and India was held in Lisbon on June 28, 2000. During, this bilateral summit the EU' acknowledged India's economic achievements, and it also supported New Delhi's aspirations for a global role in the international system during the 21st century. This summit marked a watershed in the evolution of the relationship between the two entities, and it was here that a decision was taken to hold annual summits. The strategic partnership agreement between the EU and India was launched at the fifth EU-India Summit in The Hague in 2004. At this summit the EU agreed to treat India as a global and a regional leader and hence decided to have a strategic partnership with New Delhi. Apart from India, the EU has strategic partnership with only five other countries i.e. the US, Russia, China, Japan and Canada. At the sixth summit in New Delhi in 2005 the Joint Action Plan was adopted to implement the Strategic Partnership. The Strategic Partnership and Joint Action Plan (JAP) underlined the special importance of this relationship because India is one of the few countries with which the EU has signed such an agreement. In the context of an intensified political dialogue since the first summit in 2000, annual summits, as well as regular ministerial and senior official meetings have taken place on a regular basis. The EU is today India's most important trading partner, and India is an attractive market for EU exports. As a result of annual summit between India and the EU, the trade between the two giants has continued to grow. Today India's largest export destination is the EU. (Wagnor, 2008:87-88)

The relationship between the European Union and India has been evolving over the last four decades. This relationship is characterised mainly by economic ties. As such the EU and India are indispensable pillars of a new multipolar world order. Both entities favour an international order based on well-defined rules and effective institutions. They have shared values in the context of democracy, and respect for human rights; and as such their commitment to pluralism and liberalism make them natural partners. (Kumar, 2007:50)

The EU has bilateral relationship with India covering a wide gamut of areas. These areas include development cooperation, economic interlinkages, and also a very strong trade and investment partnership because the EU is India's largest trading and investment partner. However, the cornerstone of EU's link with India lies in its trade and investment relationship. In the context of development cooperation, India is also a great beneficiary of EU aid fund that helps the developing Asian countries. EU's development aid to India touches upon a large number of diverse areas such as financial and technical cooperation, food aid, emergency aid, trade promotion and industrial cooperation. Moreover, the EU-India development cooperation under which EU development assistance to India is provided, has its main objective the eradication of poverty and illiteracy in this context for sustainable development. (Gatto, 2007: 165-166)

The essence of India-EU economic relations is the interaction of a developing country with a group of developed countries. Most of the member countries of the EU are the erstwhile colonizers, and India had experienced colonial subjugation for nearly two centuries. As such, while on the one hand the Indian economy has been constantly plagued by the acute shortages, on the other hand the members of the EU are in a position to redress these shortcomings. The relationship between the EU and India dates back to 1960s, but it was only after the entry of United Kingdom (UK) into the EC in 1973, that the economic relations between the EC and India were formalised by the commercial cooperation agreement in 1973. Prior to this, India had enjoyed the preferential treatment in UK market due to the system of British Commonwealth trade preferences. However, these preferences were terminated due to the alignment of UK tariffs with common external tariffs of the EC. India's economic relations with the EC became much wider with signing of the commercial and economic cooperation agreement between the EU and India in 1981. After the signing of the Treaty of Maastricht in 1993 which led to the formation of the EU and the agreement between the India and the EU on cooperation and development partnership, was signed in Brussels on July 18, 1994. Hence the Indo-EU relations were transformed on a very large scale with regards to cooperation and development partnership.(Brar,1996:02)

The European Union and India bilateral relationship is one of great significance to both parties. This is because the trade flow between the two entities is substantial and growing. The EU is India's largest trading partner, and it is also New Delhi's main source of foreign inward investment. As such the trade between India and EU has doubled over the last ten years or so, but these two entities are not just trading partners even as a strong commercial relationship exists between them. The relationship between the EU and India is much more than just trade or investment opportunities. This is because the EU may have started out as a trading entity, but it has grown into a union of values to which India also conforms. For example both India and the EU stand for democracy, rule of law, stable institutions, human rights and free press. Thus, much common ground exists between India and the EU to act as strategic partners. (Gatto, 2007:166)

Both EU and India recognize each other's economic potential and democratic credentials. This paves the way for a consensus between the two entities on issues as such terrorism, nuclear issue and human rights. As a result, the trade between the two giants has continued to grow and today India's largest export destination is the EU. However, the vast diversity in matters of economy, polity, language and culture is seen both in India as well as in the European Union as source of strength and as such it makes the analysis of Indo-EU relations much interesting as well as difficult. However, the dialogue process at highest level initiated and followed in successive Indo-EU summits and also the Joint Action Plan, has introduced a close cooperation in this relationship. (Sharma, 2007: 335)

The 14th annual Summit between India and the European Union (EU) was held in New Delhi on 6 October 2017. The Republic of India was represented by Prime Minister Shri Narendra Modi. The EU was represented by Mr. Donald Tusk, President of the European Council, and Mr. Jean Claude Juncker, President of the European Commission. The leaders reviewed the wide-ranging cooperation under the India-EU Strategic Partnership. Recognising that India and the EU are natural partners, the leaders reaffirmed their commitment to further deepen and strengthen the India-EU Strategic Partnership based on shared principles and values of democracy, freedom, rule of law and respect for human rights and territorial integrity of States. The leaders expressed satisfaction at the progress made towards implementing the India-EU Agenda for Action 2020 - the roadmap for bilateral cooperation endorsed during the 13th India-EU Summit. The leaders committed to work in a result-oriented and mutually beneficial manner to further strengthen the India-EU Strategic Partnership by deepening their trade cooperation, enhancing investment flows in both directions and broadening dialogue and engagement on global and regional issues, including climate change, as well as migration and the refugee crisis, and resolved to further strengthen their bilateral and multilateral cooperation in these areas. The leaders commended the strong engagement of the European Investment Bank in India in a wide range of key sectors, in particular in the field of climate action and renewable energy. The leaders underlined the importance of regular high level contacts to enhance India-EU co-operation and mutual understanding. The EU closely follows Prime Minister Modi's economic reforms, including the historic introduction of the Goods and Services Tax (GST), which can facilitate ease of doing business and promotes market integration in India by realising a simple, efficient and nation-wide indirect tax system. Prime Minister Modi appreciated the ongoing participation by EU companies in the flagship initiatives and called for their deeper engagement in India's developmental priority (Hindu, 2014).

Summary

The first India-EU summit which was held in Lisbon in 2000 marked a watershed in the evolution of this relationship. Since then, there have been regular summit-level interactions. In 2004, India became a member of the EU's strategic partners. Since 2005, the Joint Action Plan has been helping India to realise the full potential of this partnership in key areas of interest for both India and the EU. India's trade with the EU has also witnessed a remarkable expansion as the EU has emerged as the principal trading partner of India. The trade between the EU and India grew due to the institutionalisation of the relations between the two India's economic relations with the EU have been widened and intensified, and have passed through certain phases from merely diplomatic relations to trade, and then trade cum economic cooperation, and now to development partnership. India is also a great beneficiary of EU aid fund which is meant for the developing Asian Countries. EU Development aid to India also touches upon a large number of diverse areas such as financial and technical co-operation, food aid, emergency aid, trade promotion and industrial cooperation. Moreover, the EU development cooperation under which EU development assistance to India is provided, for the eradication of poverty and illiteracy in the context of sustainable development.

India and the EU countries an example of democracies in the world. They share common values and beliefs that make them natural partners as well as factors of stability in the present world order. These entities share a commitment to democracy pluralism, human rights and the rule of law, an independent judiciary and free media. India and EU also have much to contribute towards fostering a rule-based international order through the United Nations. These two entities hold a common belief in the fundamental importance of multilateralism in accordance with the UN Charter, and in the recognition of the essential role of the UN for maintenance of international peace and security, promotion of the economic and social advancement of all peoples, and meeting of the global threats and challenges.

India and the EU are indispensable pillars of a new multipolar world order. These entities favour an international order based on well-defined rules and effective institutions. The yearly summits between India and the EU have improved understanding between them. These have improved trade relations between them, and this process has also made EU in a better way understand the requirements of India as a growing economy. Therefore, India and the EU as representatives of democracies in the world have reiterated that their partnership is based on the sound foundations of shared values and beliefs. They have asserted that their common commitment to democracy, pluralism and rule of law and to multilateralism in international relations is an important factor for global stability and pea Prime Minister Narendra Modi on held a telephonic conversation with Charles Michel, President of the European Council and the two leaders discussed situation created by Covid-19 and responses to the challenge. The two leaders discussed the situation of and responses to the Covid-19 pandemic in India and the European Union. They appreciated mutual cooperation extended in the face of the pandemic, including for ensuring supplies of essential pharmaceutical products. The leaders also agreed to remain in touch on the evolving dimensions of the crisis as well as the post-COVID context.

References

- (January 2010). "ABCD of India's Diplomacy", *Civil Service Chronicle*, Vol. XX, No. 5.
- (November 2008). "European Union: Unlimited Potential and Prospects", *Civil Services Times*, Year, XIV, Issue No. 11.
- Brar, Jaswinder Singh, (1996). "*India and the European Union: Issues in Economic Relations*", New Delhi: Vision & Venture.
- Bajpai, Dr. Arunoday. "India–EU summit; new areas of cooperation in pratiyogita darpan, year 3, issue 31, January 2009, p. 1189.
- Curtis, Michael, (2006). "The European Union" in Michael Curtis (ed.), (2006), *Introduction to the comparative Government*, New York: Pearson Education, Inc.
- Karns Margaret P. and Mingst Karen A., (2005). "*International Organisations: The Politics and Processes of Global Governance",* New Delhi: Viva Books Pvt. Ltd.
- Kumar, Anand, (February 2007). "India and the EU: Economy Still Dominates Strategic Partnership", *South Asia Politics*, Vol. 5, No. 2. *, Stefano, Gatto, EU –India business relations in R.K. Jain (et.al) The European Union in transition: Economy politics and society (New Delhi; Radiant publishers, 2007. Sawhney, Abhimanini," India –EU summit 2020-Defining the future of the strategic partnership, observer research foundation.* *Sharma, Dr. O.P, India "The European Union and the world trade organisation. A critical appraisal in world focus. Vol. 28, No. 9 Sep 2007, p. 335.
- Wagner, Christian, "The EU and India: A Deepening Partnership" in Giovanni Grevi (et.al), ed, (2008), *Partnership for Effective Multilateralism:*

EU Relations with Brazil, China, India and Russia, France: The EU Institute for security studies.

- http://eeas.europa.e
- The Hindu, 25 Sep, 2014.

28

Analytical Study of E-Governance Services during COVID-19 Pandemics: A Case Study of Punjab State

Sunil Kumar

With the development of information technology, the concept of E-Governance come into existence two decades ago, which is concerned to the services provided by the government through the electronic media. In the present scenario, we can call it as next age of government where citizen can take the benefit of the government service on single click by arriving the facilitation Centre of government or even at their own doorstep (Satyabrata Dasha, Subhendu Kumar Panib, 2016). National Informatics Centre known as NIC has recommendable task for the digitisation of government services. As concern to the state of Punjab, they had constituted the Punjab State E-Governance Society, which is managing the Sewa Kendra, Pawan (Punjab Wide Area Network), E-office like various e-services to provide the quick access to the citizens at their nearest possible space or at their home (S. B. Dash, H. Saini, T. C. Panda, A. Mishra 2014). Even in the present age of mobile services, government is providing the m-sewa app which provide the accurate information about the nearest school, college, hospital and police station with various online services (T. V. Prasad 2003)].

E-Governance is not only the medium to provide the e-services to citizens at their doorstep but it can fill the gap between the policy designer and implementation. If the government want, they can set the complete vigil on the activities of citizens and citizens have also the capability to present their views on the policies of government (S B. Dash, H. Saini, T C. Panda, A. Mishra, 2013). Today, whole world is facing the problem of Covid-19 pandemic, which has hit the whole society at large extent, everyone is worried about life of human species specially. At this stage, governments of every country are doing their best to manage this situation. In the time of Covid-19 pandemics, when the social distancing is root mantar for the prevention of this disease, E-Governance services can play as vital role for administration in the present scenario. In the Today's World most of people has access to technology, so the management of the pandemic can be done with the use of technology as the Chinese Government has done. As we know the first outbreak of this virus was in Wuhan city of China and now, they have controlled this virus at large extent (Kathy Leung, Joseph T Wu, Di Liu, Gabriel M Leung, 2020). Covid-19 named as due to its shape like crown and this form of corona virus found in 2019. On 30th Jan, 2020, WHO declare it as Health Emergency. Within 6 weeks the cases increased by 24 times even Health Emergency has been declared [19]. It became pandemic due to its high rate of infection in human. So, Important part to manage this virus are prevention from the virus.

Prevention Measures in Covid-19

In the present time, we know that Covid-19 have not any medicine or vaccine to cure from it as stated by the WHO, so the prevention is best strategy to keep safe us and our family from this disease. The symptom of Covid-19 is normally are dry cough, tiredness and fever but it can vary as per the immunity of the patient. Some cases come into light, who have not any of the symptoms. So, the Prevention is the best medicine in this disease. Prevention steps are (Corburn, J., Vlahov, D., Mberu, B. et al., 2020):

- Stay Home until you have acute emergency.
- Maintain Social distancing when you go outside for any emergency work.
- Wash your hands with any type of soap or use the sanitizer with interval of few hours or when you come to home from outside.
- If you feel sneeze or cough then cover your face with any tissue or your elbow to stop it from spread in the environment.
- Consult to Doctor if you feel fever and self-quarantine to yourself from your family members.

E-Governance Services before Covid-19 Pandemic

The Department of Governance Reform of Punjab has constituted a society named, Punjab State e-Governance Society (PSEGS) to design and manage the e-Governance projects for the ease of citizens of their state (Department of Governance Reforms & Public Grievances, 2020). The Aim of this society to design the e-Governance projects under the able guidance of National e-Governance Projects to improve the service delivery to their general public. The main aim of e-Governance services is reducing the cost and increase the transparency in services with improvement in administration (Dennis Linders, Calvin Zhou-Peng Liao, Cheng-Ming Wang, 2015). The society is providing various types services to the citizens, few very important services are such as (Singh, Vikram & Chander, Subhash, 2012; Hans Solisaether, 2010).

Sewa Kanderas

The Punjab Government is running 515 Sewa Kanderas to deliver approx. 166 services like Driving licence, Birth Certificate, Arm licence etc. under the Right to Service in time bound manner.

Punjab Wide Area Network

Government has established a complete fiber network to form the proper connectivity between State, District and Block level connectivity to provide fast access to the citizens regarding the services. Government of India has also established National Knowledge Network of 908 institute of India to boost up the research work at ground level, 22 Institute of Punjab has become the part of this network. Government of Punjab has also setup their own Data Centre at Mohali for hosting of Government information.

E-Office

The Government of Punjab has launched e-office in Nov 2019 to enhance the transparency and accountability of government official regarding the services providing by them to the citizens. With the help of E-office, citizens can access the status of their file which they have submit in the office use the platform of E-Procurement, which got the tender from different supplier and purchase the item District office for any type of service (Smitha, K.K, Dr. Tony Thomas, Chitaranjan, K, 2012).

Election Related Services

As per the direction of Central Government every state has designed an e-services related to creation of Voter Card, Modification of Card even the supply of human resources during the election to Chief Electoral Office of Punjab.

E-Procurement: The Punjab Government for the transparency in the purchase of equipment in the government with the lowest tender. This service is implemented by the National agency NIC.

Integrated Financial Management System: This is the E-Governance service which is used by the state for the planning and expenditure control.

Human Resource Management System: This service is used by the state, which is complete HRM software which has all features like creation of employee database to salary management and pension management of employees of Punjab Government.

Objective of the Study

This paper is completely focused on analysis of e-Governance Service during the Covid-19 pandemics. During this pandemic e-Governance services can play a vital role to recover the society from this critical situation. This paper has made a deep vigil on the e-service provided by Punjab Government during this situation and provided an analytical view regarding their activities in term of citizens satisfaction. Some suggestion are also given as concluding words at the end of this article on the basis of analytical study of e-governance steps taken by state.

Research Methodology

According to Yin (R. K. Yin, 2010), the case study method is preferred in examining contemporary events, especially when the focus is on a contemporary phenomenon within some real-life context. The case study's unique strength is its ability to deal with full variety of evidence. In this paper we are measuring the performance of State of Punjab in management of Covid-19 pandemics in context to e-Governance. For this purpose, sample set has been chosen from the whole Punjab by distributing the Punjab in three regions: Malwa, Majha, Doaba to lead the heterogenous approach for the investigation purpose. A questionnaire has been designed with the help of google form which has 25 questions to access the performance of state regarding e-governance during Covid-19 phase. This questionnaire has been disseminated through the WhatsApp Group and email to respondents of sample set. According to Gerring (Geering John, 2007), in the field of information research interpretive study work as a vital element to achieve the accurate results. According to Orilkowski (Orlikowski, W J and J J Baroudi, 1991), an interpretive understanding is imminent when citizens attach to the social phenomena under study. In this paper, complete interpretive study has been done to achieve the real-life figures regarding the study.

E-Governance Services during the Covid-19

Coronavirus is an infectious disease which is enveloped RNA viruses.

It can cause to respiratory illnesses, which may vary its severity from the common cold to fatal pneumonia. First type of coronavirus was firstly discovered in 1930 in animals but only 7 coronaviruses causes the disease in human being. Covid-19 is SARS-Cov2 is a novel coronavirus, which found in Wuhan, China in late 2019 catch the whole world because it spread at fast speed from human to human. Till date no medicine has been discovered to cure from it that's why prevention is best policy in today's scenario. This virus has badly collapsed the economies of whole world. This section is concerned to E-Governance steps are taken by the Punjab Government to manage this crucial situation.

First case of Coronavirus in India was found on January 30, 2020 in Kerala and in Punjab first case was found on 9th March 2020 in Hoshiarpur. To prevent the citizen from this infectious diseases Punjab Government announced the Curfew from 23rd March, 2020 to combat coronavirus. To combat with this Covid-19, social distancing is root mantra, so responsibility e-Governance boost at large extent. In this context government has taken various steps with the help of e-Services such as (Government of Punjab, 2020).

WhatsApp BOT and Chat Box on Facebook to Update: In a unique initiative to make people aware of detailed information related to COVID-19, the Information and Public Relations Department Punjab has launched WhatsApp bot and chat bot on Facebook in association with Facebook. people would have to save the COVID helpline no. 7380173801 in their mobile phones and send a message 'Hi' on this number. Afterwards, read all the options displayed on the mobile screen.

Cova-App: Cova-App (Corona Virus Alert): Government has launched an App to provide continuous update about the Corona patients in the Punjab State with detail of suspected cases in every district of Punjab, this app is enable with the feature which define nearest Covid-19 patient on the basis of location of mobile and Punjab Government later on integrated the feature of curfew pass in case of emergency. Citizens can also use this app to demand the essential products and online OPD Services.

E-Sanjeevani: It is Online OPD (Doctor to Patient), integrated telemedicine solution developed by C-DAC Mohali. It extends the reach of specialised healthcare services to the masses in both rural areas and any isolated community pockets. It provides a platform for citizens to connect with a network of Specialist doctors over video conferencing and obtain medical treatment and advice for common health related concerns while sitting at home through website https://esanjeevani.com/. This facility is also integrated with the Cova App of the state.

E- Passes: After the implementation of curfew to protect the citizen from Covid-19, the Punjab Government provided online link for E-Passes for persons who are in emergency duty like health services, delivery of essential goods and medical emergency, so that citizen can stay healthy at their homes.

Toll Free Numbers: Being the first step, government launched toll free number for the medical emergency, any health emergency or any other query regarding anxiety during curfew.

Surveillance through CCTVs and Drones: With the implementation of curfew, the major challenge to Punjab Government is to assure that citizens are following the rules of curfew, to maintain the strict surveillance Government has deployed the Punjab Police with CCTV Cameras and also provided the Drones to maintain the surveillance. If they found any person moving outside without work, they are stuck to temporary Jail for at least 24 Hrs, so that they feel punished and stay at Home.

Online Education through Online Platforms: When the curfew prevailed by the government that was mid of semester, so it was great challenge for government that study of students should not be suffered. Government ordered to teacher of schools and higher education they will continue their study with the help of online Platforms like google classroom, zoom etc.

Media Bulletin: To aware the citizens of state, government is continuous giving the media bulletin on every evening from state control board, which can be accessed by Facebook or can be accessed from the official website of state.

Tie-up with Zomato, Swiggy: To maintain the supply of essential good to citizens government has made the tie-up with Zomato and Swiggy. Government has taken the benefit from their supply chain and designed platform so that citizens can easily get their essential goods without going outside and stay safe at home.

Analytical Experience as Concern to the State of Punjab

In this pandemic phase, every state government is trying their best to tackle this situation. But Punjab Government has major challenge because this virus was coming from the foreign countries and Punjab Government has major set of population, who are living in foreign countries and as per the statistics approximately 70,000 foreigner has come from different countries during January to February, this is not only challenge another is State level function being held on 10th of March at Anandpur Sahib. As per sample set chosen by us, most of the person said the government has done good in the usage of e-Services like Cova app and supply of essential to citizen but they are not satisfied by the e-Services provided by the health department especially very few persons are knowing about it. As we know that our state has some set, who are not techy they are not aware about these tools and few are not sincere about this pandemic due to our low literacy rate. As concern to surveillance through drone is very negligible, Punjab police has installed 34 drones in 10 districts to trace the persons violating the rules of curfew and black marketing and people indulge in business of intoxication even they got success to trace this type of establishments.

After that government has taken decision to take back approximately 4000 pilgrims and students who are stuck in Hazoor Sahib and Kota city due to lockdown. This has also become the great challenge for the government. In this context, government has made mistake regarding not to quarantine them at the boarder of Punjab. Due to their negligence, Positive cases of Punjab boost to nearest 2000 within week. Punjab Government and opposite parties was blaming each other instead to deploy any online tracking system such as in China, they have taken preventive measure and successfully recover their Citizens and Economy from this pandemic. Instead of these there are few elements who causes as major hurdle in the implementation of e-Governance such as:

- **Poverty:** E-Services are concerned with access to Internet but there are various people who are fighting for their livelihood. As per survey of The Tribune approximately 30 percent people doesn't have Internet access in the Punjab (The Tribune, 2019). During this period government's major manpower is involved in providing the Food packets to poor families even lot of NGOs done fabulous job in the context but one of the major failures of government is that few people take over haled benefits due to dirty politics of leaders and few families far away from these benefits.
- **Technical Illiteracy:** In the state there is a large set which is technical illiterate or not interested to adopt this technology due to they are not aware about the benefits of this technology. With the increase in the use of smartphone in the urban population technical literacy rate has increased but there is dire need to work on the rural population because major chunk of Punjab is residing in the villages. Such as State Government has given WhatsApp BOT and Chat Box on Facebook for continuous update about corona, most of people have no knowledge what is this and how to get the benefit from this technology.

- **Language Dominance:** Punjab is the state where most of people are interested to work in Punjabi and E-Services are mostly in English even Government is working in the field of Unicode especially Punjabi University, Patiala has done lot of work in this field. But in the case of India, 70 percent of the population does not speak English. Due to such overwhelming dominance of English over these communication channels, computers and the internet are quite useless in Indian villages. Punjab Government Designed the App with named Cova but it is available only in English even it should be in multilingual.
- **Infrastructure:** Lack of infrastructure has become the major hurdle in the implementation of programme even with the involvement of Jio Company in market of Internet facility, it has increased the Infrastructure at large scale but there is still need of improvement to give the right services to citizens at right time.
- **Lack of Awareness:** Due to the low literacy rate in Punjab as compared to other states like Kerala, Punjab citizens are not aware about the e-services provided by the government. Most of the people who live in the rural areas and slum areas of Punjab they are not aware about the e-governance. Few people are aware about the Cova App developed by Punjab Government even who knows and downloaded the app they are dissatisfied from the updating feature of App means government statistics about state are not matched with their own Media bulletin.
- **Inhibitions for the Re-Engineering Process:** E-Governance projects required lot of restructuring in the administrative process, which is not approved by all the government official, who are non-technical and it can cause to non-implementation of projects or delay in the projects (Kiran Yadav and Sanatan Tiwari, 2014). To overcome this problem Government should deploy an IT cell with Collaboration of government official, which can maintain continuous vigil and provide the suggestion to overcome from this problem on the basis of data analytics.
- **Security:** E-Services are provided through Internet so the prime concern is Security of the services provided by the government. Peoples afraid from the hacking activities so they involve to less activities on Internet (S. B. Dash, H. Saini, T. C. Panda, A. Mishra 2014). So, government should assure the security of their services, such as one of the hackers has raised voice about vulnerability

in the ArgoyaSetu App of Central Government. Government has taken the preventive measure to make it secure (Gadget 360 NDTV, 2020).

Even, these are the hurdle in implementation of E-Governance projects but in the present age, the technology can play a role as vital element for the complete vigil on the people as the government is moving towards the upliftment of Lockdown, which is basically required to manage the economy of our state/country. There is dire need to design an centralised control system with the help of new technologies like machine learning, Artificial Intelligence and Data Analytics, as the Central Government has distributed the complete country into three zone in Red, Green and Orange as per number of cases in that District but Central Government should give the complete access rights to the states to change movement rules as per the need of region so that spread of this virus can be controlled and economy of country also be managed by giving the rights to the region where cases of virus are controlled or no cases are there.

Conclusion

In this crucial moment, every state/country is trying to assure that their citizen should not affected by pandemic. But due to our population density and low quality of health services as compared to other developed countries like Italy, it is great challenge for Punjab as well as India. But with earlier lockdown and curfew government has tried to control this pandemic at large extent. In the age of Artificial Intelligence, with use of Hi-Tech technologies China has recovered their citizens from this pandemic and moving towards to become world power again. As concern to e-governance Punjab state government has tried its best but there is dire need to deploy special IT cadre for effective implementation of e-governance Programmes and emergence of new technologies in every field. As today's competitive environment government should lead toward the Proactive E-Governance by taking data driven steps for the benefits to society with emergence of today technologies such as machine learning and Artificial Intelligence in the age of data intensive society.

References

- Dennis Linders, Calvin Zhou-Peng Liao, Cheng-Ming Wang. 2015. "Proactive e-Governance: Flipping the Service delivery model from pull to push in Taiwan", Government Information Quarterly, pp. 1-10.
- T. V. Prasad 2003. "e-Governance and Standardisation", IEEE TENCON, pp. 1-5.

- Corburn, J., Vlahov, D., Mberu, B. et al. 2020. "Slum Health: Arresting COVID-19 and Improving Well-Being in Urban Informal Settlements", *Journal of Urban Health,* pp. 1-15.
- Department of Governance Reforms & Public Grievances, 2020. "Punjab State e-Governance Society". Available at: https://dgrpg.punjab.gov.in/psegs// >Assessed on 22nd April 2020.
- Singh, Vikram & Chander, Subhash. 2012. "E-Governance in Punjab-A SWOT Analysis" *International Journal of Management, IT and Engineering,* pp. 20-25.
- Hans Soli saether 2010. "An Analytical Framework for e-Government Interoperability" eChallenges e-2010 Conference Proceedings, pp. 1-9.
- R. K. Yin 2010. "Case Study Research: Design and Methods" 3rd ed. Thousand Oaks, CA: Sage Publications, Inc.
- Geering, John 2007. "Case Study Research: Principles and Practices", New York Cambridge University Press.
- Orlikowski, W J and J J Baroudi 1991. "Studying Information Technology in Organisations: Research Approaches and Assumptions", Information Systems Research, Vol. 2, No. 1, pp. 1–28.
- Government of Punjab 2020. "Key Initiatives". Available at http://punjab.gov.in/web/guest/key-initiative, Assessed on 29 April 2020.
- Satyabrata Dasha, Subhendu Kumar Panib 2016. "E-Governance Paradigm Using Cloud Infrastructure: Benefits and Challenges", *Procedian Computer Science* 85, pp. 843–855.
- S. B. Dash, H. Saini, T. C. Panda, A. Mishra 2014. "Service Level Agreement Assurance in Cloud Computing: A Trust Issue", *International Journal of Computer Science and Information Technologies,* Vol. 5, No. 3, pp. 2899-2906.
- S B. Dash, H. Saini, T C. Panda, A. Mishra 2013. "Prediction of Trustworthiness in the Cloud Computing Environment using Predator-Prey Model" *International Journal of Cloud Computing and Services Science,* Vol. 2, No. 5, pp. 336-344.
- S. B. Dash, H. Saini, T. C. Panda, A. Mishra 2014. "A Theoretical Aspect of Cloud Computing Service Models and Its Security Issues: A Paradigm", *Journal of Engineering Research and Applications,* Vol. 4, No. 6, pp. 248-254.
- Smitha.K.K, Dr.Tony Thomas, Chitaranjan K 2012. "Cloud based E-governance System: A Survey", ICMOC-2012, *Proceedia Engineering* Vol. 38, pp. 3816-3823.
- The Tribune 2019. "In Punjab, over 70 percent people access internet on phone" Available at:https://www.tribuneindia.com/news/archive/business/in-punjab-over-70-people-access-internet-on-phone-766809. Assessed on 29th April 2020.
- Kiran Yadav and Sanatan Tiwari 2014. "E-Governance in India: Opportunities and Challenges" Advance in Electronic and Electric Engineering, Vol. 4, No. 6, Pp: 675-680.
- Kathy Leung, Joseph T Wu, Di Liu, Gabriel M Leung 2020. "First-wave COVID-19 transmissibility and severity in China outside Hubei after control measures,

and second-wave scenario planning: a modelling impact assessment" The Lancet Journals, Vol. 395, pp. 1382-1395.

- Gadgets 360 NDTV 2020. "French Hacker Claims Aarogya Setu Flaw Reveals Unwell People in PMO, Army HQ, After IT Minister's Assurance of Security" Available at: https://gadgets.ndtv.com/apps/news/aarogya-setu-security-flaw-elliot-alderson-response-it-minister-ravi-shankar-prasad-2224403, Assessed on 6th May, 2020.

29

Role of Media and Communication during COVID-19 Pandemic

Meenu Sharma

A novel coronavirus is a virus that causes the disease COVID-19 (SARS-CoV-2, previously known as 2019-nCoV), which causes an acute respiratory illness has started in China in December 2019 and spread throughout the world. On 30 January 2020, following the recommendations of the emergency committee, the WHO Director-General declared that the outbreak constitutes a Public Health Emergency of International Concern (PHEIC). Due to outbreak of COVID-19 Disease more than half of the world is practicing lockdown, which made a deep impact on our daily life routine, unlike we used to practice before. But as we know that to lower the spread of virus we require social distancing. We're more dependent on internet, mobile and laptop, with which we could work from home or study from home. Online content are made available by many educational institution for free in order to help the student and teacher across the world. Here media plays a vital role in our life. Media is the mirror of society, as it reflects the society. These days massive effect of media is seen in the rouse of global pandemic COVID-19, in India, social media activity experiences a bounce of 50X. It has also been witnessed that there is a huge jump in the intensity of the social media when Prime Minister Mr. Narendra Modi addresses the nation related to lockdown. Here we can see the strength of media as they provide emotional support to the community. They are never back behind in order to entertain us, each day we came to see different level of creativity, as I can think of many funny memes, to deal with lockdown.

Positive outlook of sudden increase in social media can be due to various awareness campaign shown on social media, with which people across the nation knew about the essentials as well as the precautionary measures that should be taken during lockdown. It also shows the state, like the number of people being affected by virus at a particular area; it educates us of safety tips as well as the symptoms of COVID-19. There is an increase in number of I'd on social media. Social media has become one of the best tact to spread news nowadays, even if we are alerting people about something serious, in posthaste. As social media platform such as Face book, WhatsApp, Instagram, twitter, etc. gives a bundle of information each day, has led to increase in fake news and misinformation, which causes panic among people. People who read or see that misinformation interpret it as true fact. In order to distinguish between facts and false narrative, we need to crosscheck the information that we get from social media with at least two different credible sources. We can break the chain of false narrative by doing a little research before forwarding it next.

Electronic media has also made a special effect on the public. Media is something that could create panic as well as provide relief from panic. As most of the part of India is in rural area so dependency on electronic media increases, because it is easily accessible. Even illiterate people of villages and town, could understand the presentation that is given on television screen. Nobody could ignore to repeated items of information and news by the speaker of television set. There is open discussion about what people hear or watch. Media around the nation reaches our heart and brain at the same time. With news, documentaries and telefilms close to social issue increases awareness in youth and children also make them responsible towards society.

During this crucial time, electronic media such as television and radio could bring a change in attitude and belief of people by sharing the positivity, as it is most impactful on elders as well as youngsters. Print media is most badly affected. Due to lockdown, distribution of newspapers and magazine are adversely affected. Many people were posting on social sites about not getting newspaper, while others asked vendors to not circulate the newspaper. Due to fear of spreading disease, many people refused to take the newspaper and many vendors refused to circulate it. People are turning to online edition rather than risk their life to buy newspaper. Think of the consequences for the print that was already facing end in the era of digital media.

Nowadays, everyone have a lot of time therefore, they can take in a lot of material. Also a number of old shows are re-telecasted and also getting lot of engagement. Ramayana is bringing the same craze in viewers like it was before 33 years back. Small screen is not focusing on bringing new episode rather entertaining people, with old content only. Those youngsters who have only listened to the name of shows, too, could now watch them. Film industry has been brutally impacted due to lockdown. Many shooting plans for film, web series, film releases were postponed. There were many daily wages workers, spot boy, who are waiting for film industry to reopen. The trouble with lockdown is people don't want to risk their life to watch the fresh telecast; instead they are happy watching old content. 183 billion film industries is facing this crisis phase because of lockdown caused due to COVID-19. Many films were forced to remove from theatres; other film's release date was postponed. Many of them have seen a few losses in its second week. The loss that film industry is facing is still being evaluated.

Role of Media

Media is known as one the most important means of communication, in this era. During this crisis situation, mass media informs and aware the people. Media has the power to calm the people as well as encourage people for positive action, and vice versa, terrorise people and make chaos. Here we aim to analyze the role of media in making people aware of the crisis. With increasing reach and influencing of media in today's time, they became a most important part of society in crisis. Media helps to access the situations by bringing information to managers, policymakers and citizens, and speed is increased with the help of which information are collected, accumulated and supplied. However, Media could be portrayed as evil of society, but anyways they have to increase the scope of positivity. In crisis situation, public opinion is badly affected; here media could control the emotions of public and their opinion with positivity. Media worker should collect information only from credible sources in order to stop the confusing or contradicting facts. Indian media is one of the biggest media in the world.

DIFFERENT CATEGORY OF MEDIA

Electronic Media

Media states different means of communication just like communication device is use communicate and interact between people. Electromechanical device is the medium through which content of electronic media can be accessed. Nowadays most of the people are getting information through this medium only, as it makes the communication easier and get relevant data. In this crisis situation electronic media has found their place, as other medium are in tragic situation and not easily accessible. As a number of social media platform can be shown, a number of channels are shown on television, a number of radio station are in air at present time. So the reach of electronic media is growing day by day and lockdown gave a boost to its usage.

Social Media

Social media has changed the way transmission and consumption of information. For the organisations it can be boon for marketing their ideology, as it allows the direct contact between consumer and organisation. It can also be curse to many organisations, as it could damage the reputation in seconds. The viral hashtag says everything. Even after so many restrictions people are posting and spreading fake news. While you're an active user of social media you should react with open eyes and ears to every post. In this challenging time, social media have played a massive role. Lockdown has made a new time of compulsive isolation and also probably increase on mental strain. This time is scary and fearsome, but positive thing is people are coming out to help each other. We've always been alleged that we're selfish and self-centered, but the way people came out for offering help was incredible. While being online every time we should be careful of information that is overloaded on social media. In comparison to amount of information available, rumours and propaganda are in greater amount. It's the duty of author to give credible and authentic information with fact to their followers. They should not focus on gaining profit by sacrificing their ethical rules; rather create the positivity in their write-ups.

The shared information by any platform should be verified truthful content. They should more focus on positive news and ignoring negative, after fact checking. They should be presenting the information in a way that is easily accessible by the audience, like adding info graphics from the government official updates.

Social behaviours are directly encouraged by Facebook information centre that could save our lives. While sharing photos and videos owner of page should share the content that is motivating and inspirational, so that someone could start their day with positivity. Even in this scary time, the humour should go on, and people with smiling faces should be shown everywhere.

Use of the Internet and Other Social Media Applications to Seek Health-Related Information

About 71 percent of the world's Internet users are youth aged between 15–24. In India, there were 197 million active social media users (14 percent of the total population). According to the 2014 Digital Health Literacy Survey among European Citizens, 59 percent of Europeans used the Internet to check for health information. 55 percent requested general information, 54 percent requested information about a particular illness, 23 percent sought detailed information on a diagnosis, and 10 percent used the net to get a second opinion after consulting their physician. Approximately 82 percent and 87 percent of people looking for health-related information used search engines for their queries. The second source of information (47 percent – 48 percent people) was relevant and dedicated websites such as health blogs and forums, while between 33 percent and 38 percent were looking for information from official health websites, such as the Ministry of Health or the WHO.

Corona Virus: How Panic Spreads Through Social Media

Social media has also set new and special challenges, including phenomena of Cyber-bullying, exploiting public opinion, and other forms of crime. The pandemic of CoV is affecting global health and now become a Public Health Emergency of International Concern (PHEIC) as declared by the WHO.

- To constitute a public health risk to other States through the international spread of disease.
- To potentially require a coordinated international response. This definition implies a situation that: is serious, unusual or unexpected; carries implications for public health beyond the affected State's national border; and may require immediate international action. While the Internet is seen as an effective source for obtaining health information, it can be used as a means of disseminating misinformation· As standard research methods include methodology and peer review, this analysis also includes a framework for inspections which balances to minimize the risk of inaccurate or inappropriate content dissemination; social media platforms will often encourage open membership, and in large part unrestricted exchange of ideas under 'protecting and allowing free' principles expression – sadly because of short legal consequences, there is little or no accountability for what is said or communicated.

Impact of Social Media on Education

Positive Effect of Social Media on Education: The access of web-based social networking gives the chance to instructors to show great computerised citizenship and the utilisation of Internet for profitability.

Negative Effect of Social Media on Education

- Reduced learning and research capabilities
- Reduction in real human contact

IMPACT OF SOCIAL MEDIA ON SOCIETY

Positive Effect of Social Media on Society

Connectivity – The first and foremost benefit of the social media is connectivity. People rom anywhere can connect with anyone. Regardless of the location and religion. The Prettiness of social media is that you can attach with anyone to learn and share your thoughts.

Education – Social networking provide various benefits to the students and teachers. It is very easy to educate from others who are experts and professionals via the social media. One can follow anyone to learn from him/her and enhance his knowledge about any field. Regardless of our location and education background we can educate ourself, without paying for it.

Negative Effect of Social Media on Society

- Cyber Harassing
- Hacking
- Addiction

IMPACT OF SOCIAL MEDIA ON HEALTH

Positive Effects of Social Media on Health

- Sharing of Doctors prescriptions to friends, relatives and colleagues.
- Consulting Doctors online anywhere and anytime.
- Sharing Suggestions among friends, relatives and colleagues about various diseases and its symptoms.
- Access to information in developing regions.
- Support and mutual accountability on online health Forums.
- Support for health-related causes.
- Helping health services to prioritise critical cases.
- Increased accountability to consumers.
- More data available to health researchers.

Negative Effects of Social Media on Health

- Incorrect self-diagnosis
- Potential breach of privacy

Television and Radio

As per cases of Covid-19 is increasing day by day, the load of media to entertain people is also increasing. Here the role of Television and radio is very crucial, as most of the medium is not accessible. They are loaded with dual responsibility is not only entertaining the audience but also providing with relevant and genuine data. Television has a very crucial role in building any society. It has changed the world a lot that we can't lay aside its presence. In this pandemic time, television can be used as the source of information as media plays a valuable role in everyone's life. The initial role of media in this time or anytime is to educate, inform and entertain. And here the credibility arrives, things should be told with facts to avoid further conflict or confusion. It works as breeze between government and general public.

Television is becoming the voice of those whose voice had been graved. There are two aspects for everything in this world and i.e., positive and negative. In this situation there are some positive as well as negative effects of media on society. Biased form of media could be most dangerous kind of media. When lockdown was suddenly announced, people were barely given 4 hours of advance notice, which took turn in panic, in which migrants were mostly affected. With no money and no work left, they were forced to go back to their respective places on foot. However, a few media houses shown the unpleasant condition of migrants but other media coverage shown them as the evil for their irresponsible behaviour during lockdown. Well some of media were forced to cover this issue as it made the news.

In order to continue learning process in lockdown among the students living in remote villages with poor internet connections. On doordarshan the lectures are scheduled for two hours in morning and evening every day for interested students. At the same time audio lectures are also broadcasted on radio. For visually challenged students efforts are made to get similar content on radio so that students can listen to the lectures and continue their learning. As of now, classes from 1st to 9th will be assigned on doordarshan, later it will be extended to 12th.

Print Media

Most affected medium due to lockdown is print media, the distribution of print media's like newspaper and magazines have gone down. Many people fear and don't want to risk any possible transmission of virus through newspaper. For just a minute, remember how newspapers are made and distributed. In factory it is printed by machines and then sent to different location in the dark morning then the vendors collect it from different spots and then give it to subscribers of that particular. Now what people fear is transmission, as it is transferred through different peoples and different places. As it was officially announced that no transmission is possible through newspaper, but most of the people seems not satisfied by it. Most of the people are still taking the subscriptions. Honorable Prime Minister has also said that newspaper is having tremendous credibility, and play a critical role in creating awareness about the Covid-19 outbreak at national and local level. This loss is not only confined to newspaper organisations but also vendors who supply newspaper door to door. They are going through heavy losses as only few newspaper copies are purchased. They buy the newspaper from depot, but no one is buying. In fact many people called them and said to not to deliver newspaper at their home. Their business were suffering very much losses as printing and distribution was stopped. Coronavirus pandemic has deepened the crisis for newspaper industry. As it was already suffering a lot in the era of digital media, was this loss acceptable? Due to lockdown, distribution of newspapers and magazine are adversely affected. Many people were posting on social sites about not getting newspaper, while others asked vendors to not circulate the newspaper. Due to fear of spreading disease, many people refused to take the newspaper and many vendors refused to circulate it. People are turning to online edition rather than risk their life to buy newspaper.

Major Challenges

Media should show the impact of social distancing by creating general awareness among people. A crucial role is being played by media in spreading information to the people across the nation. Media should let the people know about the lockdown that states has ordered and about what is necessary, beside highlight data of other countries should be included with the impact of epidemic and journals by scientist of other countries. In case people show any symptoms, in any case they should be told protocols to be followed. To inform the people about medical facilities and isolation protocols. Many channels and journalists have been criticised for spreading fake news. Our society has been seriously affected by "fake news", which led to increase in hatred and violence, and horrific incident of lynching". As per credibility, over 80 percent of people in metro have turned to radio. People are not finding the credible source in television or internet. Narratives are shown as facts and this causes the rise in fake news. Many important information are not given privilege, instead rumours and narratives are shown for whole time. The current situation of media is out of order, and in this case it's too rigorous to expose lurking data out of haze of government. Thus, other than inquiring government's action freely, media is limited to only exhibit to the news which has ability to influence the importance placed on the topic of public agenda proposed by them. In this time when everywhere else in the world, all the prisoners are being released from the jail, here 25 to 30 arrested since the lockdown was announced, this incident is not getting any media privilege. News executives are impelled to show or promote influencing and constructive narrative done by the government. Misleading of information has been done throughout. There is a crisis of credibility in Indian media, in the race of the TRP and rating, sensation are put above sense. On private news channels debates have been condemn for being shrill and strident. In India, we have world's most vibrant and competitive media environment. Now it's high time to organise a reality check and have a look at what is wrong with it? The media should never be anti or pro government, rather it should what actually is going in the society. In this crisis news channel should more focus on entertaining the viewers with letting them know about the medical facilities available in country, what equipment are necessary in fighting this crisis, showing the fact based things rather than creating a hostility between two religion, caste, state or country.

Conclusion

As we know social media is spreading its steps day by day, and becoming one of the most popular online activities for entertainment, but in these days it has become most popular for getting information about the world. According to study, it is true that majority of people are using social media for information. From this study it is clear that most of the people don't feel positivity in news shown on television. As we know negatives are always sensational, which increases the viewership and TRP, so in short they show what people want to see. That doesn't mean the way news are shown is correct. Moreover, news is news, it can't be fiction. Most of the people don't trust news so they cross check it with some authentic source. Advertising is most impactful tool for conveying the message, by this study it is proved, as majority of people are being satisfied by the advertising and understood the message that was given. Media is doing a fabulous job during quarantine, media has won the battle of providing all the information to the people, and it is proved by this survey, as most of the people are satisfied by media.

References

- Gadekar, R., Krishnatray, P., & Gaur, S. 2012. "A descriptive study of Facebook use among Indian students". *Media Asia.* Vol. XXXIX, No. 3 January. pp. 140-147.
- Rajagopal, A. 2001. Politics after television: Hindu nationalism and the reshaping of the public in India. Cambridge: Cambridge University Press.
- Coronavirus. Available from: https://www.who.int/emergencies/diseases/novel-coronavirus-2019. [Last retrieved on 2020 Apr 24].
- Ministry of Health and Family Welfare. (n.d.). Available from: https://www.mohfw.gov.in/dashboard/index.php. [Last retrieved on 2020 Apr 24].
- Shabnoor, S. & Tajinder, S. 2016. "Social Media its Impact with Positive and Negative Aspects". *IJCATR*, Vol. V, No. 2, pp. 71-75.
- Gurleen, K., & Sukhmani. 2011. "A study of TV viewership patterns among youngsters in north India". *International Journal of Multidisciplinary Research.* Vol. I, No. 5 September. pp. 141-160.
- Khalid M., Hakim, A., Bhat, N. & Mehraj, R. 2014. "Impacts of Media on Society: A Sociological Perspective." *International Journal of Humanities and Social Science Invention.*
- Philo, G. 1990. Seeing and believing: The influence of television. London: Routledge.
- Huesmann, L.R. & Malamuth, N.M. 1986. "Media violence and anti social behavior'. *Journal of social issues.* Vol. XXXXII, No. 3, pp. 1-6.
- Katz, E. 1980. "Of mutual interest". *Journal of communication.* Vol. XXVIII, No. 2. pp. 133-141.

Environment and Ecological Impact of COVID-19

30

Environment/Ecological Effects of COVID-19 Pandemics

Sukhvinder Kaur

Almost whole world is now struggling to survive through Covid-19 pandemics. It has also caused widespread loss of life and health, all over the world. It has caused changes in human behaviour which has created a rare opportunity for the scientists, so that they can study how humans are interacting and influencing the environment on a global scale. We can call it a natural experiment, where a sudden change has occurred from the normal, giving us an opportunity to study, the stop and its response, by our planet earth. It is providing us an opportunity to assess which aspects are necessary for human's in today's world and what positive changes can be possible if we change our habits, on an international level.

India has seen 'silver lining in case of air quality during the recent month, it has been breathing more easily'. If we talk about Delhi, air quality index (AQI) was 93 in last month, much lower when it was 161 in March 2019, as per IQ Air reports. It seems that mother earth seems to have rejuvenated in climate conditions as smog is not there, but blue skies are there, pollution levels have dropped, animals and birds are moving more freely. According to environmental resource economist Mr. Marchal Burke from Stanfort University, two months of pollution reduction has saved the lives of 4,000 children below 5 years of age and of adult above 70 years, upto 73,000. We can see it is more than the toll of death which are occurring because of Covid-19 pandemic.

Environmental response with regard to Pandemic:- But will the environmental relief which we are getting at present, will have long term impacts in means of better conditions? Combined emissions from industrial processes, construction and manufacturing together makes up to 18.4 percent of global anthropogenic emissions. Even when financial crash occurred in 2008-09, overall decrease in emissions was only about 1.3 percent, it quickly rebounded by 2010 as the economy recovered and showed high valves. The emissions have dropped due to various reasons, like transport, which makes up 23 percent of global carbon emissions, which has now reduced. Driving and aviation are also the main contributors for emissions from transport, which contribute 72 percent and 11 percent of the transport sector's emissions from green house gases respectively. India is home to 21 of the whole worlds' 30 cities known for maximum pollutions, but now conditions are getting better according to the weather channel. Air quality can soon slip into 'good' category with reduced traffic and rise in temperature and present restrictions, due to Covid-19, according to the channel.

Data from Central Pollution Control Board has shown that, there has been 71 percent decrease in Nitrogen Dioxide levels in India, due to the decrease activity because of the pandemic. Even within one week of the lockdown, unhealthy 91 micrograms per cubic meter of pm 2.5, fell to 26 micrograms per cubic meter, considered almost safe by WHO. People's driving in India, has decreased by 83 percent upto 13 April.[1]

But it is very important to remember that this is a temporary relief and situations will again turn bad for climate, once the restrictions are over and industry and traffic returns.

Visible positive impacts, due to improved air quality are temporary, because they come when there is human distress. The pandemic will also result in an increase in the amounts of medical and hazardous waste generated. Pollution may decrease temporarily but it is not a sustainable way of cleaning up the environment. Pandemic may bring many other environmental problems that might lose for a much longer duration, and they might by harder to deal with.

Pandemic has caused reduction in human caused seismic noise, because of which earthquakes of smaller magnitudes are also being detected by the scientists with more accuracy and specificity. Seismic noise otherwise is an unwanted component of signals recorded by seismometers. In India, there has been a drastic reduction of about 75 percent in terms of human's walking and driving has decreased up to 83 percent until 13th April.

It's still too early to response in terms of Earth breathes and changes in this changed conditions. We will see the better picture in many weeks to come. Accepting the deaths of many human beings and life with vulnerable and extreme restrictions is not a good and realistic way for fighting climate change. After lockdown, countries may focus on restarting and boosting economies by funding various industrial activities and people may travel more than in past. Even if 'home quarantines' may be helping in reduction of climate change, it would not be a appropriate method for cleaning up our environment. By reducing the climate pollution, we can save lives of millions of people, when we will clean our air and water, heart and lung disease can be reduced, diabetes, osteoporosis and obesity can be controlled, by improving the nutrition and switching to healthier means of transport.

Problems Due to Medical Waste

Another type of problem due to Covid-19 is the chances of spread of infection from medicinal waste. In US some cities have halted recycling programmes as authorities worry about risk of spreading the virus by the recycling centres. Particularly in European hard hit nations, waste disposal options have been taken back. Italy has banned sorting of waste by its infected. Disposable plastics are again started being use, although environmental industry has told that single use plastics can still contain viruses and bacteria. Businesses which have been telling people to bring their own bags for shopping, has switched on single-use packaging with the fear of the pandemic spread. Medical waste increased due to the pandemic. Hospitals in Wuhan of China produced less than 50 tons of waste before outbreak and over 200 tons of such waste when outbreak was there. These are very infectious and need to be properly treated. Even sewage treatment plants in China were instructed to disinfect routines, to prevent spread of virus through sewage. Since infected individuals are able to shed the virus in their stool for up to 5 weeks, even if they have recovered from the disease, additional research is needed for confirmation that whether transmission can occur through this route. Researchers from recent water Research Foundation Webinar have stated that the 'likelihood of catching Covid-19 from faeces is low' because of its susceptibility to UV radiation and inability to live for long in waterways, but still it should be properly confirmed before ruling out.

It is highly recommended that one should use masks on face for prevention from Covid-19 viruses. These masks are usually made up of non-woven fabric like poly propylene (20-25 gms per square meter in density). They can also be made up of polystyrene, polyethylene, polycarbonate etc. they are mostly plastic base, liquid resistant products which after use, add up to the landfill or oceans.[2] Surgical masks are supposed to be worn for not more than one day, after that they must be changed. Similarly, empty hand sanitiser bottles and soiled tissue papers, are leading to adding up of clinical waste in the environment. They are having adverse effects on natural habitat of animals both in water or land. Animals, may mistake this trash for food, which can cause choking, ingestion, entanglement and death among them. Besides this, medical waste can also increase changes of infection to garbage collectors, cleaners and many more who spend more time in public places. Virus droplets present on the masks is also threat for other types of infections like meningitis, Hepatitis B etc.

According to the instructions from WHO, soiled tissues and used face masks must be thrown only in litter bins, and any medical gear used by affected patients must be burnt at high temperature in decided incinerators. These incinerators operate at 850-1100°C temperature with special gas cleaning equipment, which can burn them according to the international emission standards. Some countries are having proper corona virus specific decontamination services. India should also take suitable action in this matter more seriously.

Pandemic Effects on Other Ecosystems

There have been informal reports regarding reduced human pressure on the wild animal species. In protected areas, there has been decline in number of visitor due to park closures, or restriction in travel. All this, has caused reduction in stress on sensitive animals and is decreasing pressure on the popular species. According to some reports, wild species which venture into rural and urban areas like parks and beaches, have not done earlier due to traffic and other human activity, which has decreased now due to pandemic.[3]

Natural ecosystem and protected species are at risk during the pandemic crisis. Many countries, environmental protection workers working at national parks and land and marine conservation zones are not allowed to visit their working areas, due to which these areas are kept unmonitored. Due to this, there has been increase in illegal deforestation, wildlife poaching and fishing. The stoppage of ecotourism activity has also left natural ecosystems at risk of illegal harvesting and increase in encroachment. In addition to this, ecotourism stoppage resulting in unemployment has caused many household to honest the precious resources from fragile ecosystem, unsustainably to make their both ends meet.[4]

Role of other Ecosystems in the spread of Pandemic

The connection between wildlife, diseases and humans are not new as we have seen quite increase in diseases emergence over the last 50 years due to land use, climate change and habitat fragmentation. Many human activities like disruption of forest due to mining, logging roads, rapid urbanisation, population growth and agriculture expansion is bringing humans close contact with different animal species even some for the first time. When proximity increases between people, wildlife, pets, livestock etc. diseases are likely to emerge in both urban and natural environments. Besides this, pollution also adds to susceptibility to viral and bacterial infection. US Centres for Disease control and Prevention (CDC) estimates that three-quarters of new or emerging diseases that are spreading in humans like Ebola, Dengue, Yellow Fever, Zika, have their own origin from wildlife.[5]

When people venture into the home of animals, the forests, for finding resources, and when animals come out of their homes for attaching crops, the chances of transmission of zoonotic or animal to human diseases, increase. HIV, is an example for this, as it jumped from world primates to humans through bodily fluids which were infected. Sometimes humans enter deep into the primate habitats in search for construction material, which increases the proximity between the two. Similarly expansion of agriculture land nearby forest is also increasing the chances of transmission of diseases. Shrinking habitat of animals is forcing them and their pathogens to go out of their boundaries, including the human habitats. In some cases, scientists have found that at the top of the food chain, when animals disappear they are being replaced by bottom animals including rats and mice, to fill up the space, but they have more pathogens on them, which can spread. According to Alice Latinne at the Wildlife Conservation Society, it's not how many species we have in a ecosystem, it's about which species we have. Latinne gives an example of emergence of Nipah virus in Malaysia in the late 1990's, where deforestation caused fruit bats to leave their forest habitat and invaded the mango trees in the pig farms. Bats usually carry pathogens that don't bother to them, but when pigs came in contact with droppings and saliva of bats, they became infected. These infected pigs then continued to infect farmers. As stated by Yan Xiang, Professor of Virology at the University of Texas Health Science Centre, we are getting closer and closer to wild animals, which are bringing us in close contact with these viruses.

"Wet Markets" which sell meat and live animals act as incubator for the emergence and spread of many infectious diseases. Scientists believe that there is a strong possibility of emergence of SARS – COV – 2 in the wet market of Wuhan, China. According to Scientist, Spangenberg, there should be strict restrictions on live animal markets, as they give a "Perfect

Setting" for incubating new pathogens, as stressed, sick animals are crammed in cages there. We are part of nature – we are part of ecosystem and our health is linked to one another (Life of wildlife, livestock and health of environment) and we have to live together safely, for this we have to find a better way, according to Alice Latinne.[6]

According to a new study, by the School of Earth, Energy and Environmental Sciences of Stanford University, deforestation can lead to a rise of the occurrence of diseases like Covid-19, as stated above also. In the Amazon, a study showed that an increase in deforestation by around 4 percent increased the changes of Malaria by nearly 50 percent in mosquitoes, which causes transmission of the diseases; live in recently areas which are deforested. Major killers of human beings in the recent history – small pox, flu, TB, malaria, cholera, measles have evolved from animals crossovers but are now mostly confined to humans.[7]

Viruses which come from animals to humans, are likely to become more common in future, if humans continue to transform natural habitats into agricultural land, according to studies.

Humans have to change their eating habits and also the way they keep the animals. Today 70 billion land animals (if we exclude fish) are slaughtered every year for consumption by humans often under horrible conditions. In the last 50 years, this figure has doubled and again it will get doubled by the year 2050, if same trend continues. Two-third of these animals are usually reared by intensive methods or by concentrated animal feeding operations (CAFO's) as they are being used in the trade. Actually Covid-19 originated from a virus which is carried by bats that mutated to humans using pangolins as a species for transition and both were sold in the same market and were butchered on the site. It has occurred in the past also, when SARS virus, in 2002 (which also caused respiratory illness) which was endemic to bats in China and has thought to have transitioned to humans through civet cats. Having jumped between species, pathogens need a minimum threshold of population of humans in order to survive. According to Jared Diamond, measles are likely to die out in any population where less than half a million people are in close proximity.

Reversing the process of urbanisation and decreasing the population density can come out to be fruitful, but we have to start taking steps in the direction. Eco socialically we can say that it means putting a sustainable planet at the heart of whatever progress we do.[8]

The host environment is a big factor and affect their vulnerability to the Covid-19 in several ways. Unequal access to housing which is safe increases the exposure to outdoor air pollution and indoor pollution; damp conditions further increase the risk of respiratory and heart diseases. Not getting proper access to affordable, nutritious food and diet in proper way, increases the risk of obesity and diabetes. When we talk about transmission, a combination of density populated lining conditions and large urban centres together with global inter connectedness increases the people's likelihood of catching more viruses. Unequal access to proper sanitation and drinking water makes most vulnerable one to have reduced capacity to fight the virus attack.

Measures for preventing future outbreak of such type of viruses

As this year, we are experiencing 50th Anniversary of Earth Day, we should recess its purpose. We should realise that we cannot address this or any future emergencies of environment or health without addressing their economic, social and political determinants, our response cannot be restricted to any one area but instead we have adopted a wholesome approach. We need to consider the interconnection between systems which influence planetary health and balance between ecological well being and human, which will help in building a sustainable future. We should understand that the damage we have already done to our planet is having a direct impact towards the spread and severity of the viral disease Covid-19. However, how we are responding globally is demonstrating our ability to work together.[9]

One thing which Covid-19 has made clear is that our collective actions can ripple out to impact all of our planet's natural systems, from climate to agriculture. Proper mixing of nature protection, using natural resources sustainably and education of local communities about changes of zoonotic diseases can play a appreciable role in sustainable development with necessary co-benefits for people, biodiversity and climate. We can say that, land conservation and reduction in fragmentation of forest is our method to reduce human-wild animal interactions and so spreading of zoonotic diseases according to Tyler Mcintosh, from center for Western Priorities. To decrease the risk we should achieve zero carbon by 2030, by adopting new green energy infrastructure, massively extending public ownership; ending habitat destruction, reducing deforestation reducing pollution of all types, localising agriculture, adopting vegetarian eating habits and stopping the trade in wild animals for pets, fake medicines and for bush meat.

European Society of Cardiology has called air pollution a pandemic, which can be held responsible for shortening lives even more than malaria, war and violence, smoking and HIV if combined together. Pandemic and climate change are both global in nature, none of them bothers national borders and no human is immune from its impacts. We can effectively control a pandemic or reduced global climate pollution, only by cooperative action across cultures, geographies and government all over the globe. We will never to make medicines to decreae climate pollution, but with the help of technology we can reduce climate pollution now. If we do not initiate actions now, we have to face irreversible changes in climate and further catastrophic health consequences. After the Pandemic is over, it may boost extra stimulus packages for recovering economy. According to some reports, it may prove to be counterproductive for the climate as it may fuel up fossil fuel consumption and relax environmental controls.[10] People need accurate evidence based and scientifically sound information for understanding the action which they and their communities can take for protecting their health from such types of pandemics in future. There is a need of strong public health systems for prevention and health protection. With changing temperature and rainfall profiles due to changing climate, there are chances that new diseases will emerge in future. It can occur especially when it is coupled with stress of wild animals, which are already facing shrinked, it can transmit diseases to humans, as they are in more contact with humans.

If we really want some long-term solutions, when we have to look for cleaner energy, forest conservation and effective waste management systems. According to R. Rammurthy (an environmental activist) Covid-19 has proven to be eye opener. It has shown how earth can bounce back to life if humans don't interfere it.

Coronavirus has demonstrated the fragility of our system and has shown how there is an urgent need for building strong safety nets for our disadvented groups. If the pandemic continues then the people will show low consumers demand for some time due to decrease in wages. It has also caused lower emissions but no body wanted cleaner air in this way, as Covid-19 has taken toll on lives, health services, jobs and mental health of human beings. Any positive impact with regard to this pandemic, in terms of environment will be our changing habits regarding production and consumption towards cleaner and greener earth. So, when we will boost our production after the crisis, should do so with green packages and investments of renewable energy, with smart buildings and green and eco-friendly transport options. There should be green growth aftermath, because health of human beings and health of earth are one and the same and both can live together with equal measures.[11] The climate health emergency may not be as urgent as now, like Covid-19, but need for further action in this regard is just as urgent. There are some wide areas which are to be paid attention of, for minimising the losses in the future like:

1. **Citizen-centered policy in the cities:** Narrow sidewalks and crowded public spaces should be taken care of. Steps should be taken to widen them, so that people can maintain distance between each other.
2. **Better Public Transportation:** Fare free public transport system should be boosted. It will help in improving environmental conditions, reducing vehicles miles, helping lower income communities to use transit, also help in pandemic times as it will help in keeping social distancing between driver and passengers. Cycling can be promoted to help in solving both the problems.
3. **Better natural surrounding:** More parks and small gardens should be encouraged near the houses or residential area to provide fresh air and provide exercise areas (maintaining social distancing) during the lockdown periods, if such pandemic occur in the future.
4. **Building Infrastructure:** As during pandemic mostly people are being encouraged for work from home, so need for more capacity building has decreased. High capacity buildings can be discouraged in future, putting loss burden on environment and on owners.[12]

Although we can say pandemic has caused reduction in Carbon emissions, but the figures are so high that it will take lot of efforts afterwards to bring actual better environmental conditions. The pandemic has also caused animals to have more space, which we should think of providing them, after the Covid-19 is over. Economy has suffered a lot, before boosting it up and stressing production, we should think of sustainable way of improving economy and returning back to normalcy after the pandemic. We should have improved city infrastructure and have habit of personal hygiene, for the benefit of mankind.

References

1. 7 April 2020. Covid-19 lockdown didn't make earth shake less, but improved quake detection Scientists say, available at https://m. Economictimes.com
2. 20 March 2020. Covid-19: Unmasking the Environmental impact. Available at https://. Earth.org.
3. 8 April 2020. Impacts of the Corona virus pandemic on biodiversity conservation. Available at 10.1016/j.biocon.2020.108571.PMCID:PMC7139249.
4. 20 April 2020. Environmental impacts of Corona virus crisis, challenges ahead by Robert Hamway. Available at http://unctad.org

5. 5 April 2020. What is the link between Covid-19 and the ecological and climate emergencies? Available at http://blogs.iadb.org
6. 14 April 2020. Corona virus pandemic linked to destruction of wildlife and world's ecosystems. Available at www.ecowatch.com.
7. 15 April 2020. Forest loss could make disease like Covid-19 more likely. Available at http://www.weforum.org
8. 6 April 2020. Covid-19: The ecological dimension. Available at http://www.europe-solidaire.org.
9. 22 April 2020. Covid-19 is showing us the link between human and planetary health. Available at http://www.weforum.org.
10. 11 April 2020. Covid-19 and climate change: what can we learn about saving lines? Available at https://www.thehill.com
11. 5 April 2020. First person: Covid-19 is not a silver lining for the climate says UN Environment chief UN News. Climate change
12. 8 April 2020. Covid-19 provides lessons on climate adaptation for cities by Amy Turner. News from Earth Institute.

Index

C

D

E

F

I

M

T

U

V

W